ENVIRONMENTAL CONSERVATION

FIFTH EDITION

Raymond F. Dasmann

Environmental Studies Board
University of California
Santa Cruz, California

D0165164

JOHN WILEY & SONS

New York   Chichester   Brisbane   Toronto   Singapore

BOOKS BY R. F. DASMANN

Environmental Conservation
Wildlife Biology
The Last Horizon
The Destruction of California
African Game Ranching
The Pacific Coastal Wildlife Region
A Different Kind of Country
No Further Retreat
The Conservation Alternative
Ecological Principles for Economic Development
California's Changing Environment
Planet in Peril

Production supervised by Linda Indig
Text designed by Rafael Hernandez
Cover Photos: Front: (top) David Muench/The Image Bank
                        (bottom) Charlie Ott © 1977/Photo Researchers
                  Back: Jacana/The Image Bank
Background: Fern Logan
Photo researched by Kathy Bendo
Illustrations by John Balbalis with the assistance of the Wiley Illustration Department
Manuscript edited by Eugene Patti

Library of Congress Cataloging in Publication Data:

Dasmann, Raymond Frederic, 1919–
  Environmental conservation.

  Includes index.
  1. Conservation of natural resources.   2. Ecology.
3. Human ecology.   4. Conservation of natural
resources—United States.   5. Ecology—United States.
6. Human ecology—United States.   I. Title.
S938.D37   1984   333.7'2   83-21767
ISBN 0-471-89141-X

Printed in the United States of America

10 9 8 7 6 5 4 3 2 1

PREFACE

In 1958 when I was putting the finishing touches on the first edition of *Environmental Conservation,* I had no thought that 25 years later I would be writing the preface to the fifth edition. Conservation was then a subject in the college's natural resource management program, predominantly of interest to those who sought to be professionals in one of the resource management fields. There was no environmental movement. Outside of a few long-established conservation organizations—the Sierra Club, National Audubon Society, and the like—there was no great public interest.

Things have changed, and not in the way I had hoped they would. A tidal wave of humanity has flooded the earth, more than two billion more people. Places that seemed wild, remote, secure during the 1950s are no longer so. No remote places remain. Nothing is secure. It would be easy to write a bitter chronicle of destructive change.

But while there were few allies in the 1950s, there are millions today—everywhere. The growth of the environmental movement has been heartening to watch. Whether this new willingness to undertake the task of restoring the environment will grow faster than the accelerated destruction of life on this planet is a question I cannot answer. There is hope, but there are bad times ahead.

I hope this edition has more *answers* than previous editions. It will explore ways to achieve a better balance between human demands and ecological necessities for long-term survival. Any way of life we pursue must be or be able to become ecologically sustainable. There is no time or space for the continuance of ways that deplete or damage the life-support systems of the planet. A change must take place in the attitudes of people toward nature and themselves. It can come voluntarily, or it will be forced by painful circumstances. But it will come.

This book is intended for the beginning university student and the interested public. It provides a text for a course concerned with environmental problems and natural resource management. The emphasis is on the United States, since this country has been a leader in conservation and must continue in this role. But the problems are planetary and cannot be solved by one nation, and in 1983 the United States no longer can claim any position of leadership. This is my effort toward helping us regain it.

To acknowledge my indebtedness to others for the inspiration and ideas that resulted in the various editions of this book is almost impossible. As a student at Berkeley, I was exposed to the ideas of Starker Leopold and, through him, his father Aldo. Later I encountered Carl Sauer, whose teaching had a great impact on my thinking. When I first started teaching conservation at Minnesota and Humboldt, I was aided by the appearance of the most impressive collection of environmental knowledge then available: *Man's Role in Changing the Face of the Earth,* edited by W. L. Thomas. Here I started absorbing Lewis Mumford's words, which I followed in his many books and finally in various meetings with him. My work in Africa brought me in touch with Frank Fraser Darling, who later became my friend and colleague at the Conservation Foundation. I owe him an important karmic debt.

The turmoil in America during the Vietnam War years taught me that government is not a benign force acting in the public interest. I do not know why it took me so long to learn. My wife and co-worker, Elizabeth, through her pursuit of knowledge concerning psychology, anthropology, and the women's movement, helped shatter my original male chauvinism. In this she was aided by Sandra, Marlene, and Lauren. More than that, she introduced me to Carl Jung and later, R. D. Laing, Maslow, and others. But this was a time of turmoil, with rebellion in the air, and new ideas bubbling over. I was influenced by Roszak, Commoner, Schumacher, and Kohr, and later more directly and personally by my friends Jimoh Omo-Fadaka, Gary Snyder, and Peter Berg. This list could go on.

Through it all my working colleagues at Humboldt State, the Conservation Foundation, UNESCO, the International Union for the Conservation of Nature, and now U.C. Santa Cruz have done their bit, and my employers have been tolerant. Here it is, another try. Thank you.

R. F. DASMANN
Santa Cruz
September, 1983

CONTENTS

ONE

INTRODUCTION

CHAPTER

1

CONSERVATION—
THE
SURVIVAL
OPTION

INTRODUCTION

The future of life on earth was once entirely beyond human control. We lived for most of our time on this planet as one species among many, depending on natural processes that functioned without our intervention. Today the future of life on earth depends on human action. At no time during the last hundred thousand years has the survival of the human species along with most other species been so imperiled. We have reached this state through an overwhelming increase in human numbers, made possible through our growing command of energy resources that we have used to modify the surface of the earth. With the dawn of the nuclear age we have achieved access to the power that binds matter together, a power so immense that it exists primarily not as an aid to human endeavor, but as a threat to survival of life. During this process of growth and change we have failed to develop either the self-knowledge or the social institutions needed to accommodate the abundance of people or to control their use of power. We lack understanding of ourselves, of others, and of the environment on which we depend. Most particularly we lack appreciation of the total interdependence that exists among all living creatures and the physical environment that we all inhabit.

During the past several centuries and most markedly in the past 40 years, there has been a severely unbalanced development of human knowledge. In the physical sciences and in the technology derived from them, a sophistication has been gained that permits us to shatter atoms and to send rockets beyond Neptune. In biology, through searching for the factors controlling the growth, development, and reproduction of organisms, we have gained sufficient ability to create new forms of life, not seen before on earth. But there has been no similar growth in the knowledge of how living creatures interact. There has been even less gain in understanding of the factors influencing our social interactions, or the forces affecting the behavior of individuals. We are consequently able to apply great skill and power to physical achievements without necessarily knowing why we are doing so, much less what the full consequences of our actions will be. To go on in that way now holds too much risk. At no time since the earliest beginnings of humanity have the dangers of human extinction been so severe. At no time in the story of the earth has the survival of all life been so linked to the behavior of one species. We do not just stand on the edge of an abyss, we stand, to use Herman Kahn's imagery, on a slippery slope leading to an abyss, where a false step may be irrevocable (Schell, 1982, p. 207).

We are increasingly overwhelmed by ecological crises, each of which seems to demand our attention and action. None of them need to have happened; all seem to grow worse. The list is long—accumulation of toxic substances, destruction of tropical forests, desertification, loss of soil, loss of species, depletion of vital resources. But to those who have looked carefully at our world situation, the threat of a nuclear holocaust appears the most immediate and the most fearful. Through miscalculation, electronic error, desperation, or madness, a relatively few people could, within less than hours, destroy all of civilization, eliminate most if not all wildlife and land vegetation, possibly exterminate the human species, possibly destroy all life on earth. If there is any cause worth dying for, as individuals, the prevention of nuclear war and the elimination of nuclear armaments is that cause, for if we do not win this one, it will not matter much if we achieve all lesser goals. The threat of human extinction is the ultimate threat. The words of Jonathan Schell in *The Fate of the Earth* (1982) bear repeating here: *As long as politics fails to take up the nuclear issue in a determined way, it lives closer than any other activity to the lie that we have all come to live—the pretense that life lived on top of a nuclear stockpile can last. Meanwhile, we are encouraged not to tackle our predicament but to inure ourselves to it: to develop a special, enfeebled vision, which is capable of overlooking the hugely obvious; a special, sluggish nervous system, which is conditioned not to react even to the most extreme and urgent peril; and a special, constricted mode of political thinking, which is permitted to creep around the edges of the mortal crisis in the life of our species but never to meet it head on. In this timid, crippled thinking, "realism" is the title given to beliefs whose most notable characteristic is their failure to recognize the chief reality of the age, the pit into which our species threatens to jump; "utopian" is the term of scorn for any plan that shows serious promise of enabling the species to keep from killing itself (if it is "utopian" to want to survive, then it must be realistic to be dead); and the political arrangements that keep us on the edge of annihilation are deemed "moderate," and are found to be "respectable," whereas new arrangements, which might enable us to draw a few steps back from the brink, are called "extreme" or "radical." With such fear-filled, thought-stopping epithets as these, the upholders of the status quo defend the anachronistic structure of their thinking, and seek to block the revolution in thought and in action which is necessary if mankind is to go on living.*

It is not enough for us to dismantle our nuclear armaments—they could be assembled again. We must understand the conditions of our minds and souls that have permitted these nuclear arsenals to be built up. How have we become so shut off from ecological reality and empathy for life on earth that we could use atomic weapons and plan for the use of hydrogen bombs? If a person refuses to face reality and lives in a make-believe world, she or he is considered insane. But for decades most of our government leaders, aided and abetted by the voting public, have lived in a make-believe computer world of statistics and symbols, playing a monstrous military game of threat and counterthreat, unable to comprehend that on our fragile planet, the very possession of such weapons of annihilation is insane.

Unfortunately, the same mental attitudes that have permitted this military madness have directed our actions toward use of our planet, all of its resources, all of its life. Playing political and economic games that confuse symbols with reality, we have sacrificed major elements of the life support systems of the earth, and of life itself, in return for transitory monetary wealth or political power. So today we face ecological crises, second only to the nuclear threat in the peril they hold for life on earth.

When a volcano erupts or there is a major shift along a fault line, we all realize our vulnerability and know that the future cannot be guaranteed. We live in an uncertain universe where suns can explode and comets or asteroids go astray. We can, however, cease to be our own greatest danger. We can enhance the means for continuing life on earth. We can keep from destroying our own environment and with it ourselves. We can create a conserving society that is ecologically sustainable.

We are at a turning point in human history. Astrologists point out that, like it or not, we are entering the Age of Aquarius. More prosaic and perhaps less optimistic folk note only that we are reaching the end of a millennium, the second since the Christian calendar began. We have fewer than 20 years before the beginning of the twenty-first century. During most of that time the human race will face rough going. For reasons to be examined in this book, civilization must change its course, and it will not be easy to do so. For those who relax in the hope that things will go on as they have during the past few decades, there is no basis for that hope. Life will not go on as it has been. There are various options to choose from, but there is no option that allows present trends to continue.

During the history of humanity, people have made many mistakes in their relationship to the world and to one another. Our ancestors, however, were usually able to postpone the day of reckoning. They were able to seek present profit without too much concern for its future effects. There were many who said "let posterity worry about it!" Today, you are the posterity they were talking about. You have no way of postponing the reckoning. Either the major problems that face the world will be solved or alleviated in the lifetime of those already born, or there will be no further posterity. *You* have to change the ways in which human societies operate or none of you will survive.

THE MEANING OF CONSERVATION

The word *conservation* has been derived from the verb "to conserve," defined in *Webster's Dictionary* as "to keep in a safe or sound state." Conservation itself is in the same place defined as "a careful preservation and protection of something; especially planned management of a natural resource to prevent exploitation, destruction, or neglect.'' I see conservation as a way of looking at the world and a way of action based upon that point of view. Conservation includes the recognition of limits, since we would have no interest in conserving something that was in unlimited supply. But on planet Earth nothing can any longer be considered to be in unlimited supply. To be meaningful a conservation viewpoint leads one to behavior as a responsible citizen of the planet, living in a particular environment, and being involved with its protection. From modifying one's own actions, conservation leads to efforts to influence the behavior of others, so that all shall seek to maintain a suitable environment in which life can exist and living beings can thrive. This results in setting up standards of behavior for human communities for the benefit of all members of those communities. Conservation action in the United States leads from research, to determine the facts about the environment; to education, to spread knowledge of those facts; and where necessary, to regulation, legislation, administration, and other action for protection of environmental values. In an ideal world only the first two steps would be necessary; when knowledge was available, all would act in accordance with it. But this is no ideal world.

Conservation can be given both narrow and broad meanings. Oil conservation is an activity aimed at safeguarding petroleum supplies—an important, if narrow, concern. I would define environmental conservation as the use of the environment to sustain the greatest possible diversity of life while insuring for humanity the physical basis for continued well-being. It represents the broadest concern for the total human environment. It is based on a recognition that in any environment all things are tied together, and actions that change one part of that environment will have effects on all parts. Through maintaining the greatest possible diversity and variety of life, we can achieve not only a better chance for human survival, but also the opportunity for living in a world of richness and abundance where the full range of human hopes and dreams can be pursued.

CONSERVATION IN THE UNITED STATES

Conservation, as an influence on human activities, has a history reaching far into the past. As a publicly defined movement, however, sponsored and supported by government, conservation had its origins in the United States. It has since had its greatest support and following in those countries most exposed to the impact of European immigrants—people who drew on the power and resources of a civilization that was building a sophisticated industrial technology. These immigrants were capable of doing great environmental damage and of changing the landscapes and life that they encountered. At the same time they had memories of the ''old country,'' of a long-settled continent where change had not come suddenly or with such dramatic consequences, and where people were not so obviously at odds with nature. They could see the difference between what had been there in the new land when they first arrived, and what they had done to it. Thus, among those who were sensitive, a concern for the environment appeared.

It is difficult to say where or when the American conservation movement started. Wildlife conservation began in the early British colonies as some wild species began to disappear before the onslaught of the colonists. Worry about the future of forests may have been next as those in the East were cut or burned. Erosion of soils and loss of productivity on farmlands newly established but poorly cared for was a problem of interest to Thomas Jefferson. Concern for the overgrazing of rangelands and with it the creation of new deserts came later, when the West was colonized. One of the last interests to appear was a concern with pollution and poisoning of the land, air, and water along with the urban condition in general. But all of this new involvement with conservation took place in a land where the original inhabitants, then being pushed back and in places exterminated, had long been careful stewards of land and wildlife.

In the 1830s, George Catlin, an artist and naturalist, expressed his feeling about the future of the buffalo and the Plains Indians that depended on it. He proposed a vast "national park" extending throughout the Great Plains where Indians and wildlife would be left alone. Nobody paid much attention, and when national parks were created there was no place left in them for the Indians who had lived there (Nash, 1968). In the 1850s, Henry David Thoreau, writing in *Walden* and other journals, expressed his concern for the future of all wild nature and saw in wildness the hope for the preservation of the world. He had the foresight to realize that people have a relationship with and obligation to nature, to ecological reality, that overrides the rules of society. He called attention to the "more sacred laws" of nature, which take precedence over the regulations enacted by human institutions. But few were listening (Thoreau, 1860).

The 1860s brought the first overall statement of conservation issues when George Perkins Marsh (1864) put together his observations in the old homelands of civilization with those in the New World in his book *Man and Nature; or Physical Geography as Modified by Human Action.* In the same decade John Muir was pleading for the protection of nature, and along with Frederick Olmstead and others, helped protect the Yosemite Valley as a state park. In 1872 Congress established the first official national park in Yellowstone. In the 1880s forest reserves were being set aside and other national parks proclaimed. It was not, however, until 1908 that President Theodore Roosevelt provided the name "conservation" to describe all of these activities. With the aid of his chief forester, Gifford Pinchot, he was able to give a new organization and strength to the federal role in conservation (Udall, 1963).

After Roosevelt's time the conservation movement grew by fits and starts. It received new emphasis during the presidency of Franklin Roosevelt in the 1930s. By then the federal and state roles in promoting conservation were generally accepted. As a popular movement, however, conservation had relatively few active followers. In the 1960s this began to change. Sparked by the student revolt against war and social injustice, a spreading activism was directed against all of the ills brought on by the established society and by too-active pursuit of the "American way of life." There was an increasing awareness of the dangers resulting from pollution, increasing populations, and the general destruction of nature in favor of economic profit. Conservation, under the new name of the "environmental movement" or the "ecology movement," developed enough clout to depose congressmen or governors, and to influence presidents who, unlike Roosevelt, had little inherent interest in the subject. Since then those whose main concern is the exploitation of nature wait anxiously for the environmental movement to collapse and look for hopeful signs in each election to show that environmentalists are losing their influence.

THE ROLE OF ECOLOGY

Recognition that people exist as a part of nature, inseparable from their environment, that Thoreau had foreseen, was to follow the development of the science of ecology. The pursuit of ecological knowledge was to verify those "yet more sacred laws" that must take precedence over mere human regulations. Yet ecologists, as scientists, are often remote from any direct involvement with the conservation of the species and natural processes that they study. Writing in the early 1970s, Theodore Roszak (1972) pointed to this contradiction: *Ecology already hovers on the threshold of heresy. Will it be brave enough to step across and, in so doing, revolutionize the sciences as a whole? . . . It is the one science that seems capable of assimilating moral principle and visionary experience, and so of becoming a science of the whole person. But there is no guarantee ecology will reach out to embrace these other dimensions of the mind. It could finish—at least in its professionally respectable version—as no more than a sophisticated systems approach to the conservation of natural resources. The question remains open: which will ecology be, the last of the old sciences or the first of the new?*

Ecology remains more than a systems approach to the conservation of natural resources. Indeed, as a science it is not that involved with conservation, although individual ecologists may be. But Roszak is perhaps too demanding of ecologists, most of whom work for government or university and must take interest in their professional respectability, unless they wish to assume the role of dropout, saint, or martyr. The same demand could be made of physicists, whose new vision of the universe calls into question many traditional human activities, beliefs, and customs (Kapra, 1982).

Regardless of the penchant of individual ecologists, ecology forces recognition on those who study it that individuals are coexistent with their environment, cannot be separated from it, and are continually changing and being changed by it. Thus ecology, albeit unwillingly, has come to a certain coincidence with the old nature religions of humankind and with the transcendental philosophies of Asia. Writing from the viewpoint of Zen Buddhism, Alan Watts (1965) had stated, "The hostile attitude of conquering nature ignores the basic interdependence of all things and events—that the world beyond the skin is actually an extension of our own bodies—and will end in destroying the very environment from which we emerge and upon which our whole life depends."

CONSERVATION ACTION

To anyone who accepts the importance and necessity of environmental conservation it is apparent that conservationists must call into question the activities of governments, groups, and individuals. They must ask questions about the behavior and motives of people, and about ways of life and institutions. Since many who are in positions of power prefer no such questions to be asked, conservationists will encounter strong opposition. A conservation viewpoint, however, must challenge the right of nations, human institutions, and individuals to engage in activities that impair the long-term well-being of other humans, other species, or the environments on which they all depend.

The words of conservationists, no matter how well spoken, have shaken no empires thus far. Yet in their full implications they must appear revolutionary to those who believe in the sacredness of continued economic growth at the expense of the environment. Nevertheless, conservation as a movement has never fitted well into a political structure of left versus right, capitalist versus socialist, or conservative versus liberal. Conservationists seem to come from all parts of the political spectrum. In action conservation is moved by shifting groups and coalitions of people, joined together temporarily for a specific cause—to save a wilderness, protect an endangered species, oppose a nuclear plant, or pass an environmental protective act. There are always more issues than any one person can follow, so that conservationists tend to split into separate interest groups that may not necessarily agree on all issues. Yet it is the interrelatedness of all of these issues that is important to comprehend, and this will be an emphasis of this book.

SOME DEFINITIONS

Before going further it is worthwhile to consider some basic definitions. The term **environment,** as used in this book, refers to the biosphere, the ecosystems of which it is composed, and the modifications of these brought about by human action. The **biosphere** is now defined as the thin layer of soil, rock, water, and air that surrounds the planet Earth along with the living organisms for which it provides support, and which in turn modify it in directions that either enhance or lessen its life-supporting capacity (UNESCO, 1970). Some prefer the term *ecosphere*, for this concept and restrict biosphere to life itself, but this involves separating the inseparable. We are all part of the biosphere and are supported by it, yet we are seldom aware of its presence and much of it is beyond the reach of our senses. In this lies some of the difficulty in making people aware of the reality of an environmental crisis. Relative to the size of the earth, the biosphere is like the skin of an apple—a shallow layer not more than 15 miles deep from the bottom of the ocean to the highest point in the atmosphere where life can exist without protective devices.

Ecosystems are subdivisions of the biosphere. They consist of communities of plants, animals, and microorganisms along with the air, water, soil, or other substrate that supports them. They may be large or small—the term is flexible. Some talk about "balanced ecosystems" contained in an aquarium; others use the term to describe the tropical forests of South America. Ecosystems may be very simple, such as those supporting a community of lichens growing on a rock in the high Arctic; or very complex, such as a tropical rain forest or a coral reef in tropical seas. All ecosystems are powered by energy derived directly or indirectly from the sun.

Natural resources is a vague term. At one time it referred to the things, or sources of energy, in the environment that were used by humanity—coal, iron, timber, rivers for hydropower, and the like. As our knowledge of the environment and our use of the planet have expanded, however, virtually everything on earth along with the sunlight impinging on earth has come to be considered a natural resource. Some resources, such as the Antarctic ice cap, are only potential resources, since we are not using them, but there are some who would haul Antarctic icebergs northward to modify climates and provide urban water supplies.

In earlier conservation books a nice distinction was made between renewable resources and nonrenewable resources. The former were the living things and their derivatives, the latter, the minerals and nonliving mineral resources. This was convenient but too simple. Soils are a mixture of living and nonliving. They are renewable if properly handled, meaning that through the presence of life on them and within them they can be rebuilt and repaired. They are nonrenewable if handled in such a way that their fertility is exhausted or they are washed or blown away. Water is nonliving, and yet it is an inexhaustible resource—since all of the uses we make of it simply move it from one place or state to another. Fresh water in a particular place may be a nonrenewable resource. For example, many underground reservoirs represent the accumulations of thousands of years. If we pump from them at a rapid rate, they become exhausted. Despite all of these overlapping boundaries, it is worthwhile to define certain categories of resources.

Inexhaustible resources are those such as sunlight, which will continue to pour onto the earth for as long as humanity will be around, whether we use it in certain ways or not. Water in the global sense and air also come into this category, as do those resources for which our foreseeable rate of use is relatively minute in relation to the supply—table salt from the ocean, for example. Nonrenewable resources are not regenerated or reformed in nature at rates equivalent to the rate at which we use them. Petroleum is an example. Given some millions of years, new petroleum reserves could be formed by natural processes. Considering our rate of use of oil, however, petroleum is nonrenewable and will not be available for much longer. A special category of nonrenewable resources is called recyclable resources. These are resources such as many metals, which are not lost or worn out by the way we use them and can be reprocessed and used again and again. Renewable resources include all living things that have the capacity for reproduction and growth. As long as the rate of use is less than their rate of regeneration, and as long as their environments are kept suitable, they will go on replacing themselves. They can, therefore, be used forever without exhausting them as long as they are protected and managed. Products formed at a relatively rapid rate by living organisms are in a similar category—for example, the alcohols produced by fermentation bacteria or the methane generated by the decay of dead organic matter. However, living species are not necessarily renewable if the way in which we use them is destructive. No living species can survive if we crop it at a rate more rapid than it can reproduce, or if we destroy the habitat on which it depends. Both of these processes are at work over much of the world today, and the living resources that could last forever are being "mined" out of existence.

Ecology is the science concerned with the interrelationships among living things and their nonliving environment. It is not a new science. The word was first used by Ernst Haeckel in 1869 (Odum, 1971), but ecological studies have been carried out since antiquity, and many indigenous people are first-rate practicing ecologists although they know nothing of modern science.

THE NATURE OF ENVIRONMENTAL STUDIES

The study of the human environment is of necessity an interdisciplinary field. It involves consideration of the physical and biological functioning of the living systems on the planet, and in addition the ways in which these have been modified, are being affected, and can be changed in the future. The study of human environment is of necessity goal directed since it examines ways of life that people seek to pursue in the light of the criterion of sustainability, with a view to defining environmental

a

NATURAL RESOURCES

Natural resources are those forms of matter or energy considered useful or essential by human societies. They may be considered under several categories.

Inexhaustible resources. Energy from the sun **(a)** has, until recently, powered all living systems on earth. For the foreseeable future it will always be available as an energy resource; we cannot use it up. The same can be said, in a general way, for hydropower **(b)** which is derived from solar energy. For so long as the sun shines, rain will fall and water will flow downhill. Using it as a power source does not exhaust it.

c

Renewable resources. Forests (c) and all living things are renewable resources, meaning that if we balance our rate of use against their rate of growth or reproduction they can continue to renew themselves and will always be available. **Nonrenewable resources.** Coal (d) and petroleum (e) are present on earth in limited quantities. When we use these resources they are destroyed. The rate at which new reserves can be formed is too slow to compensate for our rate of use. Hence, they are nonrenewable.

d

Recyclable resources. Many metals are not destroyed by use. The objects made from them, (f) and (g) can be melted down and the metals used again for other purposes.

e

f

g 15

limits within which human beings must confine their activities if they, as a species, and the other species on which they depend are to survive. In other words, we do not study the environment only for the intellectual satisfaction gained from doing so—although this may be a motivating force. We study it to seek ways for restoring conditions deemed desirable, maintaining such conditions, or shaping new arrangements that may be considered more desirable.

One can look at the environment from a number of different points of view—those of the economist looking at flows of goods and services, of the chemist concerned with nutrient flow or the physicist interested in energy flow. We can take the anthropological view and look at various human cultures in their relationships with their environments, or we can look from the viewpoint of the political scientist at institutions, policies, and pressures affecting environmental change. Yet to talk of environmental studies as being interdisciplinary suggests that if we just get the proper mix of disciplinarians we can address all environmental concerns. For this to be even close to the truth, each disciplinarian, whether an economist or a biochemist, must see his or her discipline in its relationship to the total living system, the totality of the environment. Students of the environment must be systems oriented since they are dealing with ecosystems in which actions in one place, affecting one species, have reactions in other places and sometimes impact on all species.

Those who work with environmental problems, whether in urban areas or the wilderness, are most frequently trained as interdisciplinary professionals—city planners, foresters, architects, wildlife managers—rather than experts in particular natural or social sciences. Consequently, any effort to break environmental studies down into some combination of natural and social sciences falls short. It falls short also because there is a strong element of the humanities involved—in history and philosophy, values and ethics, esthetics, all of the ideas and feelings people have had about the kind of world in which they live or want to live. The contribution of fiction to environmental studies is perhaps as important as that of any science, since in the free range of creative expression, writers may give better definition to human aspirations and environmental constraints than the most careful social investigator could achieve.

If one parent discipline for environmental studies had to be stated, it would be the science of ecology. But to state that would be evading the issue, since ecology in the full scope of its science is an interdisciplinary activity, and no one ecologist would have a sufficient grasp of human environmental concerns to pretend to a general environmental expertise.

Nevertheless, one must start somewhere. This book starts from the viewpoint of an ecologist looking at environmental conservation. It attempts to draw, however, from the widest range of knowledge as presented in books and other publications. It is of necessity eclectic, and this is hazardous, since one may present what appears to be a generally accepted paradigm in some area of knowledge just at the point when that paradigm is being discarded by the experts in that area. The risk is worth taking.

SOURCES

Kapra, Fritjof, 1982. *The turning point. Science, society and the rising culture.* Simon and Schuster, New York.

Marsh, George Perkins, 1864. *Man and nature; or physical geography as modified by human action.* Scribner's, New York.

Nash, Roderick, 1968. *The American environment.* Addison-Wesley, Reading, Mass.

Odum, Eugene P., 1971. *Fundamentals of ecology,* 3rd edition. W. B. Saunders, Philadelphia.

Roszak, Theodore, 1972. *Where the wasteland ends: politics and transcendence in post-industrial society.* Doubleday, New York.

Schell, Jonathan, 1982. *The fate of the earth.* Alfred Knopf, New York.

Thoreau, Henry David, 1960 edition. *Walden, or life in the woods. On the duty of civil disobedience.* New American Library, New York.

Udall, Stewart, 1963. *The quiet crisis.* Holt, Rinehart and Winston, New York.

UNESCO, 1970. *Use and conservation of the biosphere.* Natural Resources Research, X, UNESCO, Paris.

Watts, Alan, 1965. *The book on the taboo against knowing who you are.* Abacus, Sphere Books, London, 1973 edition.

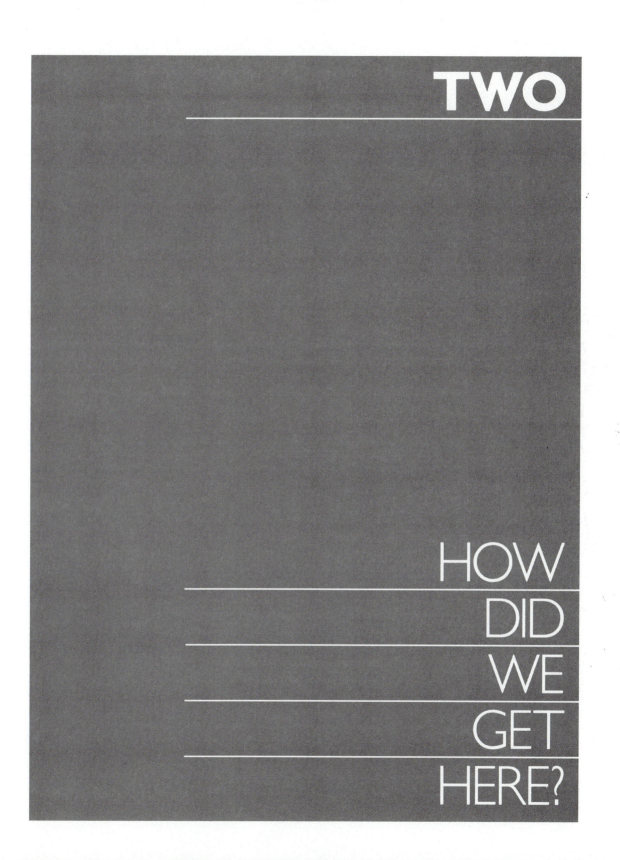

TWO

HOW
DID
WE
GET
HERE?

CHAPTER
2

THE
OLDEST
WAYS

PART I
THE PRIMEVAL ENVIRONMENT

INTRODUCTION

It is difficult to determine the sequence of events in human history even with written documents and artifacts of various kinds available to the historian. It is far more difficult to reconstruct the geological history of our planet from a record of twisted rock, deposits of silt, or volcanic debris. It is not surprising that some of the early theories have been proven wrong. It will not be strange if our present knowledge proves to be inaccurate.

Not long ago it was generally accepted by geologists that the continents occupied the same general space on the earth's surface during the entire history of life. Biogeographers engaged in ingenious theories to account for the odd patterns of distribution of plant and animal life in the absence of any connection between what are now widely separated continents. Why, for example, did the Antarctic beeches (*Nothofagus*) have a distribution in southern South America, Australia, and New Zealand, but not in northern continents? Why were the main centers of marsupial mammal distribution also in these southern continents, but not the northern? Why did certain species occur only in eastern Brazil and western Africa? How did they cross the Atlantic? As early as the 1920s Alfred Wegener had postulated a theory of continental drift that accounted for these patterns of distribution, but required that the continents move from earlier connected positions to their present separation. Thus he pointed out that it was no coincidence that the horn of Brazil seemed to fit so neatly into the Gulf of Guinea in West Africa. They were once connected and had drifted apart. But Wegener's theory was considered amusing at best by most geologists. In the words of three of the leading ecologists of the 1930s: "Wegener's hypothesis of continental drift is not in accord with many geological observations and not only is not needed to explain zoogeographical distribution but actually creates more difficulties than it adjusts" (Hesse, Allee, and Schmidt, 1937).

Research on the earth's magnetism and the geology of the deep ocean floor led to a change in opinion. Now it is accepted that the earth's crust is not stable. Continents rest on plates of crustal material that shift around on top of a more fluid layer of rock beneath. The continents were once connected in one large southern hemisphere block. They have since moved and are still moving. The implications of this for plant and animal distribution have yet to be fully explored. The relationship to the human story on earth is still uncertain.

It does appear that the history of *Homo sapiens,* as a distinct species, is encompassed by the Pleistocene epoch, an unusual time in the history of the earth. It is a time marked by crustal unrest, mountain building, and most strikingly by glaciation. We have lived and still live in a glacial age, characterized by polar ice caps and mountain glaciers on the higher ranges. These are periods of climatic change and stress. Humanity has not existed, so far as we know, in one of the more tranquil periods of earth history, when continents were mostly low-lying and climates were mild and uniform (Brooks, 1949). Perhaps we never will. We seem to be a stormy species that has thrived on instability. In a nuclear age that could be a very frightening thought.

THE OLD STONE AGE

For most of the human story on earth we have little knowledge. There are a few fossils and artifacts here and there, separated in space and often separated in time by thousands of years. What we call civilization, highly developed and differentiated cultures that built cities and left remains in stone and brickwork, goes back about 6000 years. We find signs of animal and plant domestication, the rise of agriculture and pastoralism, somewhat earlier, over 10,000 years ago. Written accounts, the historical record, go back only a few thousand years and the earlier accounts are only fragments. So we are guessing when we try to reconstruct the human story. Furthermore, there are those who have different ideas—from strict interpretation of the Bible, to beliefs in lost continents, Atlantis and Lemuria, with high civilizations now sunk beneath the sea, to those who see the origins of civilization in extraterrestrial intervention by astronauts from other planets. It may be fun to fantasize about such things; here, however, I will try to stay with the facts and with generally accepted scientific explanations, while recognizing that these also could be mistaken.

The longest period in the story of humanity is included in the Paleolithic or Old Stone Age, characterized by relatively crude stone implements that have been found in many parts of the world. During most of this period people were probably restricted in their distribution to the tropics and subtropics of Asia and Africa. In the latter part of the Paleolithic, however, they spread widely over the Earth. Human cultures at this time were based on food-gathering, the collecting of edible plant parts supplemented by some hunting and fishing. Dependence on wild plants and animals was complete, and the distribution of people depended on the abundance of wild species. Late in the Paleolithic, however, efficient hunting cultures developed that could make use of the then abundant herds of big game. These were the people who made the famous cave paintings of southern Europe. Gary Snyder (1980) has written of these Magdalenian people: *Our self, biophysically, as an animal of great complexity, was already well formed and shaped by the experience of bands of people living in relatively small populations in a world in which there was lots of company: other life forms, such as whales, birds, animals. We can judge from the paintings, from the beauty and accuracy of the drawings, and also from the little Magdalenian stone carvings, the existence of a tremendous interest, exchange, and sympathy between people and animals. The most accurate animal drawings that have been done until modern scientific animal drawings are these cave drawings: right perspective, right attention.*

One sees similar qualities in the much more recent, but pre-European invasion, cave paintings of the African Bushfolk (San) preserved in the Matapos caves of Zimbabwe. These too were hunter-gatherers who knew the spirit and form of the animals on which they depended.

FIRE AND SAVANNA

So far as we know the world that was the home of the early hunter-gatherers was similar to the natural world that still exists, albeit in remnant form, today. In the humid tropics of southern Asia, central Africa, and Latin America, the most complex of all natural ecosystems, the humid tropical forests, dominated. Outside the area where rain falls throughout the year were the seasonally dry forests, the raingreen or monsoon forests of the tropics, less diverse in plant species and less luxuriant in plant growth. At the drier tropical margins these in turn gave way to tropical dry forests, the thorn forests and scrub. In the more arid areas these were replaced by steppe—short grass and scrub—and these finally by desert in the driest regions.

Although it is somewhat speculative, it appears that people were originally confined to the drier tropics of Africa and Asia, areas represented in part by the climate and habitat found at Olduvai Gorge in East Africa. Much of this area is now dominated by savanna, vegetation derived from dry forest but with a grassy layer separating the scattered trees or forest groves. Since there appears to be a direct relationship between the use of fire as a means for opening up vegetation and the existence of tropical savanna, it would appear that human activity could have been an important element in the creation of the savannas that are now widespread. It has been argued that savanna is the natural habitat of people since they are not adapted to either dense forest or open grassland. It is also pointed out that fire is a useful means for providing a greater supply of the plants and animals that people can use for food. Even where not used deliberately to change vegetation, in dry climates fire often escapes from human control. If these arguments are valid, it would seem that the major environmental modification brought about by pre-agricultural people was the spread of savanna vegetation. It may be significant that this vegetation provides the habitat for the great variety of large mammals characteristic of tropical Africa and Asia. By creating more savanna people would increase the numbers of animals available as a food supply (Sauer, 1950; Bartlett, 1956).

EXTINCTION OF LARGE MAMMALS

It has been stated that people were a major factor causing the extinction of the large mammals characteristic of the late Pleistocene in North America and Eurasia (Martin, 1973). The presence of efficient hunting cultures using spear throwers and with fire as an aid to hunting is associated with the disappearance of mammoth, mastodon, giant ground sloth, and many other large animals. Although the presence of these hunting peoples in North America coincides with large mammal extinctions, there is still no certain cause and effect relationship. The areas with the longest history of human occupancy in tropical Asia and Africa are places in which the greatest variety of large mammals has survived. Clearly the evidence for an early human role in species extinction is not all in, although since the appearance of civilization the disappearance of wildlife has accompanied the spread of humanity (Baumhoff and Heizer, 1965).

> ### Writing of the Cree Nation in Seventeenth Century Canada
>
> *Moreover, if it is a great blessing to be free from a great evil, our Savages are happy; for the two tyrants who provide hell and torture for many of our Europeans, do not reign in their great forests,—I mean ambition and avarice . . . as they are contented with a mere living, not one of them gives himself to the Devil to acquire wealth.*
>
> Paul LeJeune (1897), quoted in Marshall Sahlins,
> *Stone Age Economics* (1972), p. 14

ECOSYSTEM PEOPLE

It is difficult to know at what time people spread from the tropical regions of Asia and Africa into more temperate and even arctic areas. People have been in Europe and northern Asia through more than one of the glacial advances and retreats of the Pleistocene epoch. It is widely accepted that the Americas and Australia were the last continents to be occupied by humans, but even in these places the human story may go back 30,000 years or more. In all areas there has been a long period of time available for humankind to learn to live with the environments that prevailed. Virtually every kind of environment was eventually occupied, from the dense tropical rainforests of the Congo basin to the tundras and barrens of the far Arctic. In each locality some group of people learned the pattern of the seasons, the comings and goings of rain or snow, the location of plant species, and the travels and ways of animals. In each area, through this knowledge, people developed the understanding of their environment necessary for their own survival, over the long term. Through necessity they became conservationists in their overall behavior. This does not imply that each individual, or even any one individual, understood the concepts of conservation, but rather that the behavior of the social group, the clan, triblet, or the tribe was shaped over the centuries in a conserving direction. People who destroyed their food supply could not survive. People who overhunted or overfished were left with no meat in the following year. Each tribe became fine-tuned to its environment and collectively behaved in such a way as to guarantee its long-term survival. Each was adapted to a particular ecosystem—Great Plains grasslands, California woodland or chaparral, eastern hardwood forest, Arctic tundra. Each depended totally on the continued flow of energy and chemical nutrients through that ecosystem. The survival of the people depended on the continued productivity of the ecosystem; they had, for the most part, no outside sources to draw on if their own food supply failed. Potentially, of course, they could move on to somewhere else if they overharvested or damaged the resources of one area. But this could not easily occur once an entire region was occupied, since those living in one area would be expected to resist movement of strangers into their territory (Klee, 1980).

> Generally speaking, the natives live well; in some districts there may be at particular seasons of the year a deficiency of food, but if such is the case, these tracts are, at those times, deserted. It is, however, utterly impossible for a traveller or even for a strange native to judge whether a district affords an abundance of food, or the contrary. . . . But in his own district a native is very differently situated; he knows exactly what it produces, the proper time at which the several articles are in season, and the readiest means of procuring them. According to these circumstances he regulates his visits to different portions of his hunting ground; and I can only say that I have always found the greatest abundance in their huts.
>
> Sir George Gray (1841), quoted in Marshall Sahlins,
> Stone Age Economics (1972), pp. 7–8

The hunting-gathering way of life did not disappear with the development of agriculture or even with the coming of civilization. Agricultural peoples were limited in their distribution. Agricultural ideas were not necessarily accepted by hunter-gatherers, particularly where game and wild foods were abundant. Even when agriculture was adopted, it was often used only as a supplement to a basic hunting-fishing-collecting way of life, a situation characteristic of many American Indian peoples, who have been referred to as hunter-gardeners.

Hunter-gatherers have the longest history on earth and represent a way of life basic to humanity. Where not too much disturbed by outside pressures, they still live lives of leisure in most years. Contrary to earlier concepts, their lives are not a desperate struggle for survival from which people gladly turn to agriculture. Rather it is a way of life preferred by its practitioners, and if we judge from the hunter-gatherer survivors, it is a way of living they do not willingly abandon. Rather, they must be forced unwillingly into accepting different ways of life (Sahlins, 1972).

EXOTICS AND NATIVES

It is worthwhile to distinguish two different roles that people have played at different times in different places. One is the role of an *exotic,* an invading species newly arrived in an area. Judging from what we have learned from wild and domestic animal introductions into new areas, exotic species either fail to become established, which is most usual, or they become established with disruptive effects on the existing ecosystem. Thus the introduction of exotic birds and mosquitoes associated with them to Hawaii brought avian malaria, which decimated native birds. The introduction of the house sparrow and starling to North America initially led to the displacement of many native birds. In time, however, an exotic species fits in, finds usually a narrower niche within the ecosystem than that occupied initially, and becomes an established member of the community in dynamic balance with other species (Elton, 1959).

People have similar effects. The Polynesians who reached New Zealand around 1300 A.D. were the first people to inhabit those large islands. The full extent of their impact on the island ecosystem is not known; however, the extermination of the large flightless birds, the moas, is attributed to their hunting, since those birds had not before known any predators and presumably had no defenses. Similar impacts are believed to have occurred when people first reached the island of Madagascar. The effects of European colonists on the new lands they occupied have almost invariably been destructive to the more vulnerable species or to those feared and considered to be dangerous.

By contrast, in the role of a *native,* people adjust to the ecological realities of their new environment and, if they are to survive, become members of the ecosystems that they inhabit. In preindustrial times hunter-gatherers, hunter-gardeners, pastoralists, and others received their energy and nutrients from the ecosystems where they lived and formed parts of the food chains and webs that characterized the systems. Like all other species, their waste products and, upon death, their bodies returned to the system to provide food for other species, which in turn recycled the materials through the ecosystem to become available at some later time for human use again. The human species becomes adapted as ecosystem people, belonging to a particular ecosystem (or group of ecosystems) and in turn contributing to it (Dasmann, 1974).

Any major technological change, however, particularly if introduced suddenly, can change a native back to the role of an exotic once again. This sort of change was affecting the Plains Indians, who acquired the horse and the rifle from Europeans shortly before the major encounter with European colonists was to take place. The horse-riding, rifle-shooting culture was having different effects on the bison and other species of the plains than existed before this technological change took place. No doubt a new balance was being reached, but this was disrupted by the European invasion. Throughout the world today many people who had occupied their lands in relative harmony over centuries, who were truly native or ecosystem people, have been converted into the role of exotic invaders of their own lands by new technologies brought in from the industrialized countries of the world. The disruptive effects that such people are having threaten natural communities and the basic productivity of many of the world's ecosystems.

During the time when European cultures spread over and colonized most of the world, there were few land areas on Earth that had not long been occupied by others. The so-called empty wilderness that the Europeans took over was in fact not empty, but the home of hunter-gatherers who cared for the lands, maintaining them in what Europeans were to call their natural or primeval condition. Europeans could not understand the space requirements or the ways of life of these people, so they assumed the lands to be free for their taking. Only where agriculture clearly existed could they recognize land occupancy—not that this stopped them from taking over.

It is a characteristic of hunter-gatherers that much space is required to supply their needs through the natural reproduction of wild species. One of the most densely populated areas of Indian America was what was to be the state of California, a place where nearly all of the Indians depended on food gathering, fishing, and hunting (Heizer and Elsasser, 1980). The original Indian population has been variously estimated at from 250,000 to 750,000. Taking the median figure of 500,000 means that the population density was roughly 3 per square mile. Considering the large area of desert, high mountain, and other relatively nonproductive land, this was a high density. It can be accounted for in part by the high productivity of the coastal marine ecosystems, which provided an abundance of seafood for the coastal dwellers, and it was near the coast that most of the population was found. Today, 23 million people live in the same area, but these draw on the resources of the entire planet.

Hunter-gatherers, along with those who were partially dependent on a shifting agriculture, have been and in some places still are custodians and stewards of the wild places of the world. With the spread of industrial civilization, however, they have also been targets of attack. Deliberate policies of genocide, aimed at exterminating whole peoples, have been employed against them when they proved unwilling to give up their land or their old ways. More destructive, however, has been the spread of introduced diseases, which killed tens of millions in the Americas alone. More permanent has been the destruction of the environment on which they have traditionally depended. Today the original hunter-gatherers and shifting forest farmers are endangered peoples, certainly deserving as much recognition as any endangered species. Apart from ethical and moral considerations, which should be paramount, these peoples are the last who have any detailed understanding of the wild plants and animals on which they have always depended. Civilization has already benefited enormously from their knowledge of the medicinal values of wild plants. They have much they could teach us, if we would take time to learn. It is ironic that many who seek to conserve wild nature have themselves been destructive in their attitudes toward the original people who have guarded the wild places of the Earth and have been only too willing to move them out of their homelands in order to protect the nonhuman species that live there.

> *Furthermore, entire cultures, not just their particular elements that seem desirable for our own immediate needs, should be nourished and protected, not disrupted or permanently changed. Our planet has millions of different plants and animals, yet there are only a few thousand human cultures. For the former, public awareness of environmental problems has been heightened by the Endangered Species List, which is a protection device under the Endangered Species Act. What we need is a kind of "Endangered Cultures List" that identifies specific cultures that are at the point of being the next victim of careless industrialization.*
>
> Gary A Klee, *World Systems of Traditional Resource Management* (1980), p. 284

SOURCES

Bartlett, H. H., 1956. Fire, primitive agriculture and grazing in the tropics. Thomas, W. L., Jr., ed. *Man's role in changing the face of the earth.* University of Chicago Press, pp. 692–720.

Baumhoff, M. A. and R. F. Heizer, 1965. *Post-glacial climate and archaeology in the Desert West.* Quaternary of the United States. Princeton University Press, New Jersey, pp. 697–703.

Brooks, C. E. P., 1949. *Climate through the ages.* Ernest Benn, London.

Dasmann, R. F., 1974. Difficult marginal environments and the traditional societies which exploit them: ecosystems. Symposium on the future of traditional "primitive" societies. Cambridge, U.K. *Survival International News* 11:11–15.

Elton, Charles S., 1958. *The ecology of invasions by animals and plants*. Chapman and Hall, London.

Heizer, R. F. and A. B. Elsasser, 1980. *The natural world of the California Indians*. University of California Press, Berkeley, California.

Hesse, R., W. C. Allee, and K. P. Schmidt, 1937. *Ecological animal geography*. John Wiley, New York, p. 111.

Klee, Gary A., 1980. *World systems of traditional resource management*. V. H. Winston, Halsted Press, New York.

Martin, Paul S., 1973. *The discovery of America*. Science 179:969–974.

Sahlins, Marshall, 1972. *Stone age economics*. Aldine, Chicago.

Sauer, Carl O., 1950. Grassland climax, fire, and man. *Journal of Range Management* 3:16–21.

Snyder, Gary, 1980. *The real work*. New Directions, New York.

Thomas, W. L., Jr., editor, 1956. *Man's role in changing the face of the earth*. University of Chicago Press, Chicago.

Wegener, A., 1924. *The origin of continents and oceans*. Methuen, London. Original German edition, 1915.

PART 2
THE MANAGED ENVIRONMENT

AGRICULTURAL ORIGINS

At some time during past millennia people began to pay particular attention to certain wild food plants that were both good to eat and reliable in their production. These included annual grasses, later to become our cereal grains, the seeds of which could be collected and transported. They included certain roots and tubers that could be carried along as rations, but then put into the ground when they had sprouted. There was probably no single group of people who "discovered" agriculture, but more likely a multiplicity of origins with different peoples in different places. It should be no great step for people who cared for wild plants to discover that they could be domesticated.

One way of looking at agricultural origins was developed by the geographer Carl Sauer, who postulated that the cultivation of wild plants began with tropical people and originally emphasized perennial plants, those that grow year after year from the same root stock. He considered two centers of origin, one in the tropics of southeast Asia, the other in Central and northern South America (Fig. 2.1). In both areas root crops such as taro and cassava, yams and sweet potatoes were dominant as carbohydrate sources, along with various tree crops, sago, coconut, breadfruit, and others. This root crop-tree-shrub culture persists in the humid tropics today. Outside the edges of the humid tropics where such root crops would not grow, cultivation of cereal grains took over: millets and later wheat, barley, and rye in western Asia, northern Africa, and Europe; rice along the river bottoms of eastern Asia; corn in tropical America. Along with the grains, various protein-rich and nitrogen-fixing legumes, the great variety of peas and beans, were cultivated (Sauer, 1952).

Others seek agricultural origins in the river basins of northern Africa and western Asia, where civilization also had its start, along the Indus, the Nile, and the Tigris and Euphrates rivers. Seed beds were provided each year by the silt left behind when the annual floods of the river retreated. Grain crops could be planted by scattering the seed, without preparation of the ground. In time water could be channeled into irri- **31**

FIG. 2.1
Relationship of areas glaciated
during the Ice Ages to places
in which agriculture and
civilization had their
beginnings. (Data from Flint,
1947, Sauer, 1952, and
Wissman et al., 1956.)

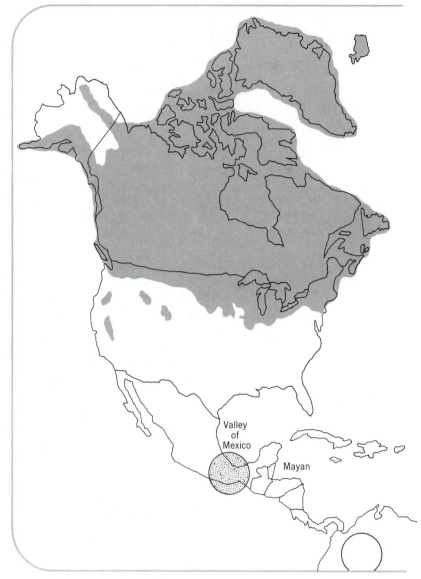

gation systems to provide for longer periods of growth and higher production.

Others believe one should seek the areas with the greatest numbers
of wild relatives of existing domestic crops to find where agriculture had
its beginnings. The Ethiopian region in the horn of Africa is such an area.
Most agree that agricultural knowledge developed separately in the Old
and the New Worlds, although some seek early connections through the
voyages of seafaring peoples.

Whatever its origins, agriculture, along with the collecting of wild
plants, was most likely the business of women and not men. Men were
later to take specific roles, plowers of the fields for example, or to take

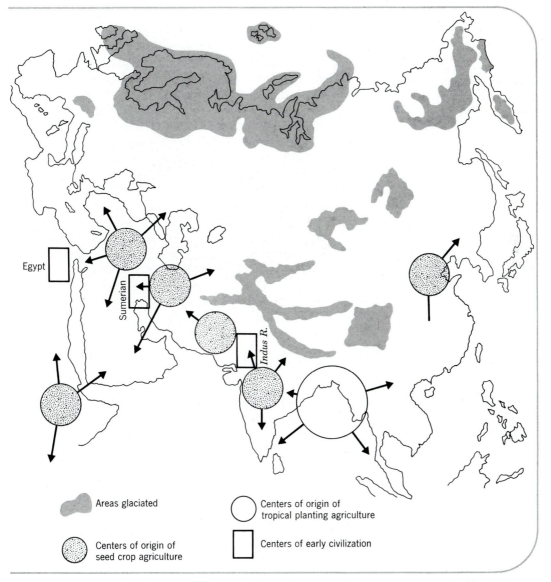

Egypt

Sumerian

Indus R.

Areas glaciated

Centers of origin of
seed crop agriculture

Centers of origin of
tropical planting agriculture

Centers of early civilization

over the care of certain crops. In most areas of the world, however, agriculture has persisted as primarily a women's activity. Even with the increasingly mechanized farming of Europe, which became men's work, the kitchen garden, which yielded most of the table vegetables, remained women's domain.

It was pointed out earlier that agricultural practices did not necessarily spread among hunter-gatherers and were rejected by some of them. Among tropical forest people some combination of hunting-gathering with agriculture usually developed, commonly with sex-role segregation, the hunting being done by men. Relationship with the natural world did not change greatly with this combination of practices. In tropical forests some clearing was required before garden beds could be prepared and planted. Since tropical forest soils are usually low in nutrients and unable to sustain productivity in the absence of natural plant cover, shifting agriculture, various known as slash-and-burn, *milpa* (Mexico), *ladang* (Malaysia), *chitemene* (Central Africa), or *swidden* (Europe) became the rule. One plot would be planted to root crops for as long as its yields held up, usually a few years. Another would then be cleared and planted, while the first would continue to yield bananas, palm fruits, or other tree crops for a longer period of time. Still another would then be cleared and planted so that within the area of cultivation a whole series of plots in various stages of recovery to forest would be found, each of them yielding some kind of product. Eventually, after 30 to 40 years, the original plot would be returned to and cleared again, with its productivity restored by forest growth. The relative size of the entire area brought under cultivation need not have been great, so long as human populations did not increase to high levels. There were enough cultural controls, along with natural checks (diseases for example) on human population growth to prevent a high degree of pressure on the forest environment.

The need to care for crops, even in shifting agriculture, led to a sedentarization of people greater than would be convenient for hunter-

By the Sweat of Their Brows?

There is no doubt at all that the Kuikuru could produce a surplus of food over the full productive cycle. At the present time a man spends only about 3½ hours a day on subsistence—2 hours on horticulture, and 1½ hours on fishing. Of the remaining 10 or 12 waking hours of the day the Kuikuru men spend a great deal of it dancing, wrestling, in some form of informal recreation, and in loafing. A good deal more of this time could easily be devoted to gardening. Even an extra half hour a day spent on agriculture would enable a man to produce a substantial surplus of manioc. However, as conditions stand now there is no reason for the Kuikuru to produce such a surplus, nor is there any indication that they will.

Robert L. Carneiro, quoted in Marshall Sahlins, *Stone Age Economics* (1972), p. 68

Since the Kapauku have a conception of balance in life, only every other day is supposed to be a working day. Such a day is followed by a day of rest in order to "regain the lost power and health." This monotonous fluctuation of leisure and work is made more appealing to the Kapauku by inserting into their schedule periods of more prolonged holidays (spent in dancing, fishing, visiting or hunting . . .).

Leopold Pospisil, quoted in Marshall Sahlins, *Stone Age Economics* (1972), p. 57

gatherers. Village life therefore replaced the life of the shifting camp, although with shifting forest agriculture, villages might move with the clearing of new areas. A much greater tendency toward permanent human settlements took place in the river basins, particularly where their soils were derived from nutrient-rich upland sources. In Southeast Asia and in the region from the Nile to the Indus, the major river-basin soils were highly productive. This was maintained by the annual deposition of fresh silt carried from the highlands. Crops planted in such areas gave high yields, and surpluses of food could be accumulated and carried over for future use. Greater numbers of people could be supported in larger settlements. With more people came the possibility of greater water management, making water available to grow crops for longer periods of the year. Irrigation agriculture thus took the place of rain-fed, or flood-fed crop production. This in time was to support cities, kingdoms, and empires.

ENVIRONMENTAL EFFECTS

Agriculture was to follow two different main streams from its early origins. One was the field planting of cereal grains and other, mostly annual, crops; the other the perennial-plant based gardening pattern of the humid tropics. The two were to mix to various degrees in some areas as in the rice-growing river basins of tropical Asia. The annual plant–cereal grain pattern was likely to become destructive to the environment. The tropical perennial system was less destructive and until recently has been environmentally benign (Sauer, 1952).

In the homelands of cereal grain agriculture in North Africa and Southwest Asia we find most evidence of land use failure, with deserts spreading in areas once considered "granaries" of the old empires (Lowdermilk, 1953). This is associated with the vulnerability of cleared, plowed, and cultivated fields to soil erosion. Blowing winds and rainfall runoff on lands from which the original plant cover has been removed cause soil loss, unless a replacement cover is sufficient to protect the soil. Cereal grains and row crops usually do not provide such a cover where these crops are grown in monocultural fields—fields planted to a single species. By contrast, the American Indian system of planting corn, beans, and squash in the same plot both provides cover against erosion and helps restore soil nutrients—but this was not the system used in the areas where deserts have spread.

Deserts have also spread where once elaborate canal irrigation systems have broken down. These are most commonly a result of shortcomings in land care resulting from civilization and its attendant ills, rather than farming use alone. Where irrigation systems were simple and governed by the seasonal rise and fall of the river, as in the Valley of the Nile, cereal grain agriculture could continue without soil deterioration over thousands of years (Dale and Carter, 1955).

a

ECOSYSTEM PEOPLE

(a) Hadza hunter-gatherers in the Savanna of Tanzania. (b) Nomadic pastoralists with sheep herds—on the move in Afghanistan.

c

Traditional agriculture. (c)
Planting paddy rice in Java.
(d) The Ifugao people of the
Philippines maintain high rice
yields from their carefully
tended terraces.

d

ANIMAL DOMESTICATES

Which came first, the domestication of plants or of animals, could long be argued. There seems little doubt, however, that one domestic animal at least, the dog, has accompanied hunting-gathering people in their treks around the earth. Most others came later and appear associated with a more settled village life—although some would argue that hunters took delight in taming dangerous wild animals long before they took an interest in crop farming. Pigs, chickens, and other domestic fowl are linked with the garden agriculture of the humid tropics. Cows, goats, sheep, donkeys, camels, and horses appear tied in with the cereal grain agriculture of the West. These are the herding animals, and their care and culture gave rise to a way of life separate from agriculture, that of the so-called nomadic pastoralist. The term *nomadic* applied to these people is unfortunate, since nomadism suggests a wandering without necessary return to any one place. Pastoralists tend to be migratory rather than nomadic.

Transhumance, the seasonal movement of animals from plain to mountain following the retreat of the snow and the greening of grass in the spring, is a frequent travel pattern of pastoralists. Other seasonal travels are away from permanent water in the wet season, with return to it in the dry. Pastoralists, although requiring more space than farmers, tend to be strongly attached to the lands they know, with movements that are predictable. Through their domestic animals they were able to use areas that were nonproductive for farming, to make use of plants that could not be directly consumed by people, and thus to produce surpluses of meat, milk, cheese, and other animal products that they could exchange with village-based farmers in return for grain.

Unfortunately they were also capable of exerting excessive grazing pressure on lands with limited capacity to support domestic animals. Where this occurred, plant cover was destroyed and erosion followed. Many highland areas, used over the years by pastoral peoples, have lost their soil and productivity.

THE NEOLITHIC WAY

With the aid of domesticates, animal and plant, people during the Neolithic or New Stone Age, starting roughly 10,000 years ago, were able to create for the first time a managed environment, shaped and in part controlled by human action. Energy flows from solar radiation were channeled in chosen directions rather than following their natural channels through wild species. Minerals from soil, air, and water were directed in their cycles through crop plants and animals. The human landscape of field and woodland, lane and village was not at odds, however, with normal ecosystem processes. Materials were cycled through new food chains, but were returned in time to the soil. Solar energy flows were used locally, and not exported to centers of population away from the land. Human communities were for the most part stable and peaceful, tuned to their environment, celebrating its seasons.

This way of life did not vanish with the appearance of civilization. Instead it has persisted, providing a background of stability, a source of food, despite the comings and goings of kings and empires. The peasant agriculture of Europe and Asia, at least until very recent times, has been more sophisticated than its Neolithic predecessor, but not basically different. Even the old earth religions have persisted, as an undercurrent to Christianity, causing priests and ministers to have dark dreams of witchcraft.

But while many who work the land today feel a certain nostalgia for the older Neolithic ways of peasant agriculture, not all feel that agriculture has come as a blessing to humanity. Nigel Calder (1967), in a book he may wish he had not written, has this to say: *If men were intended to work the soil they would have longer arms. In truth, we evolved as hunters and we remain the most efficient predatory animals of all, shrewd of brain, infinitely adaptable of body, and with hands to make and wield weapons. Yet since the invention of agriculture some 10,000 years ago, most men have been obliged to bend their straight backs to cultivate the land. We have grown mightily in numbers, and have constructed remarkable civilizations on the basis of agriculture. But we have made it a distinctly boring world for most people; only in sport and in war can we recapture something of the excitement of the chase, which was the everyday occupation of the first of our species.*

By contrast Wendell Berry (1978) has this to say: "But the care of the earth is our most ancient and most worthy and, after all, our most pleasing responsibility. To cherish what remains of it, and to foster its renewal, is our only legitimate hope."

SOURCES

Berry, Wendell, 1978. *The unsettling of America.* Avon, New York.

Calder, Nigel, 1967. *Eden was no garden.* Holt, Rinehart and Winston, New York.

Dale, Tom and V. C. Carter, 1955. *Topsoil and civilization.* University of Oklahoma Press, Norman, Oklahoma.

Lowdermilk, W. C., 1953. *Conquest of the land through 7000 years.* U.S. Department of Agriculture, Washington, D.C.

Sahlins, Marshall, 1972. *Stone age economics.* Aldine, Chicago.

Sauer, Carl O., 1952. *Agricultural origins and dispersal.* American Geographical Society, New York.

Thomas, W. L., Jr., editor, 1956. *Man's role in changing the face of the earth.* University of Chicago Press, Chicago.

CHAPTER
3

THE
NEWER
WAYS

PART I
THE CIVILIZED ENVIRONMENT

BEGINNINGS OF CIVILIZATION

The meaning of the word *civilization* is in some dispute. Kenneth Clark, author of the BBC television series and the book derived from it entitled *Civilisation* has this to say: "What is civilisation? I don't know. I can't define it in abstract terms—yet. But I think I can recognise it when I see it." The dispute derives from the preemption of the word by the industrial-urban cultures, particularly those from Europe, and has developed connotations that imply that all those outside these civilized cultures are savages, barbarians, primitives, or in other inferior categories. To avoid such pejorative connotations it seems best to define the word as meaning city-based cultures associated with the use of writing and written records. Civilisation is thus associated with cities, and we seek its beginnings where the first cities, now usually in ruins, can be found. In this sense, civilisation reached its first development in the river basins of the Tigris and Euphrates rivers in present-day Iraq and Iran, in the Nile basin in Egypt, and in the Indus basin of present-day Pakistan. It had apparently separate and later origins in China, in the basin of the Hwang Ho or Yellow River, and in the Mayan and Incan lands of the Americas. To what extent each of these centers influenced the others cannot be known for certain. The oldest records appear to come from the lands of Sumeria, Chaldea, and Elam in the lower reaches of the Tigris and Euphrates rivers, in cities known as Ur, Uruk, Nippur, and others. Sumerian civilization had its origins where irrigation agriculture was to provide the food base for an expanding urban population, and in time an elaborate system of canals was to channel water from the rivers to the farm lands.

We don't know why people gave up the peaceful, stable village-centered agricultural life styles of the Neolithic to move into urban centers. Mumford (1961) believes that the first cities took shape in what were sacred places where people came to seek spiritual guidance: "The first germ of the city, then, is in the ceremonial meeting place that serves as the goal for pilgrimage: a site to which family or clan groups are drawn back, at seasonal intervals, because it concentrates, in addition to any natural advantages it may have, certain 'spiritual' or supernatural powers, powers of higher potency and greater duration, of wider cosmic significance, than the ordinary processes of life."

Civilization

The beginnings of early urban civilization often coincide with the building of large-scale irrigation works and the resulting creation of an agricultural surplus. The rise of male work forces with male bosses spells out the virtual end of anything approaching matriarchy; no longer can women hold sway over small, home-based plots for rainfall farming. Early urban civilization also spells out the end of egalitarianism. . . . .

It may be said that with the coming of legalism the true state arises. At this point, for the first time, economics, politics, religion and so on are organized into separate institutions, and leaders rule by hereditary right rather than by charisma. Social heirarchies evolve. Status becomes a factor in human existence. Slavery takes its place among the other formal institutions. Priests begin to replace shamans. Art separates out from daily life. Full-time specialists emerge. Markets spring up and with them the beginnings of true money. Villages become cities, which serve not only as administrative centers but as redistribution points for the goods which pour in as tribute and taxes. Territory becomes power. Territorial war is born. . . . .

The process of formalization, bureaucratization, alienation, fragmentation—call it what you will—has gone through many states of wax and wane, development and intensification, over the past five thousand years. But the ultimate direction is now clear. We of Civilization are the direct heirs of the first man who was moved to think of another human being as a component. We are the heirs of that component himself.

George B. Leonard, *The Transformation* (1972), pp. 52–53.

This is perhaps a better explanation for the tendency of people to return and rebuild, century after century, in the same place when the original city has been destroyed. Perhaps the first permanent inhabitants of the places to become cities were the shamans or priestesses of the old earth religions, the people who were to become the followers of the Great Goddess.

Merlin Stone (1976) has made a strong argument for the belief that the first cities were formed around centers of worship for the Great Goddess, and that the first civilizations were matrilineal and matriarchal, with a queen and not a king in a position of leadership. In her view these early matriarchies were relatively benign and peaceful, drawing from the woman-oriented agricultural villages of the Neolithic. They were to be overrun and taken over by patriarchal, war-oriented nomads, who believed in a male god—a story told in all of its gory detail in the Biblical account of the movement of the Jews into the settled civilizations of the land of Canaan—the "promised land" for the followers of Jehovah.

Lewis Mumford postulates that it was the hunter class in Neolithic society who moved from being providers and guardians of the agricultural villages to become the organizers and rulers of the cities that were to be their centers of power and influence.

Robert Carneiro (1970) in reviewing the origin of the state has made a convincing biological case that states arose through motives that were basically coercive and aggressive. Cities and empires did not come into existence as voluntary or chance associations of peoples but through fear and the exercise of coercive power.

Regardless of the nature of the first cities, civilization in its first flowering exhibited all of the evils that have continued to plague it to this day. The cities brought heirarchies of power and prestige, as compared to the egalitarian ways of the farming village. Cities brought for the first time organized slavery. They brought for the first time armies and organized warfare. They brought taxation and with it the need for census taking. George Leonard (1972) has been particularly critical of those forms early civilization was to take and maintain to the present time. Distinguishing Civilization (with a capital C, from other forms of high culture) as "that mode of social organization marked in general by political states, markets, legal sanctions and social heirarchies, . . ." he writes, "We of Civilization are the direct heirs of the first man who was moved to think of another human being as a component. We are the heirs of that component himself."

Why then did people accept this form of social organization? Obviously it provided wealth and leisure for those who were at the top, since they were able to channel the efforts of others for their own benefit. For the ordinary citizen who had been a farmer, herder, or hunter it may have provided in the short run greater security in a physical sense, perhaps an improvement in the level of physical comforts and possessions. It would certainly provide more excitement with its marching guards, processions, its temples and palaces—all the panoply of power that still attracts the public to Buckingham Palace or the White House. For those who preferred specialized endeavors—arts, crafts, technics—to the more generalized work of the village, it provided contact with other like-minded people and a ready market for what was produced. Nevertheless we do not know very much about the origins of civilization. There are no written accounts to tell us the whys, wheres, or hows, nor could the people of those days have told the story since they lacked any real knowledge of the world as a whole, of its peoples, or of ecosystems different from their own. It is impossible to put oneself into the mind-set of those who built the first cities. For most people at that time a journey outside their own territory was more a venture into the unknown than our recent travels to the moon or the depths of the ocean.

We do know that towns and cities are not now and never have been self-sufficient. They have always been tied to flows of energy, materials, and for the longest time also human beings from the countryside. Without highly productive farm land yielding surpluses of milk and honey, grain, grapes, and meat, and lakes, streams, and estuaries yielding fish and other seafood, there could not develop an urban population dedicated

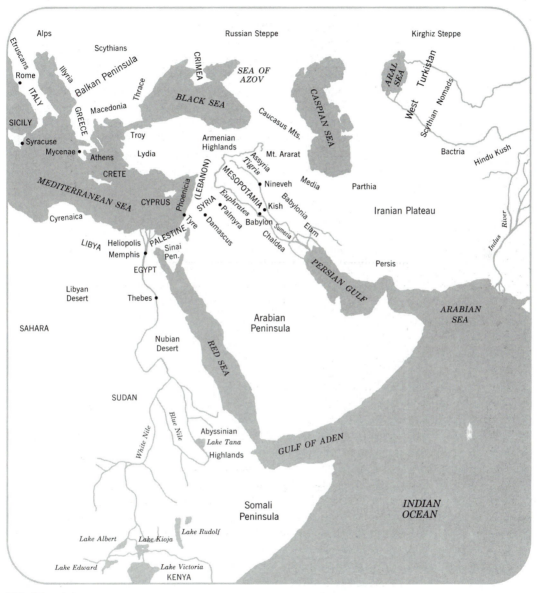

FIG. 3.1
Location of ancient civilizations in the Mediterranean and western Asian regions.

to nonagricultural pursuits. It is ironic then that the earliest dated ruins of towns of large size are in places such as Jericho in Jordan, Jarmo in Iraq, Catal Huyuk in Turkey—areas where until recently deserts have spread, and erosion has exposed the bare bones of mountainsides. It is ironic also that the old cities of Sumeria, Babylonia, and Assyria were discovered in the midst of ruined landscapes. Civilization appeared to carry with it the means for its own destruction (Fig. 3.1).

It is easy to think of cities as parasitic upon the countryside—drawing food and energy, but returning little. Initially, however, this was probably not true. Lewis Mumford has pointed out that as centers of concentration for people and animals, cities initially were centers for the production of manure, which was often returned to the farm lands to enrich them. Cities provided for greater storage of seeds, for improvements in methods of farm production, for collection and distribution of water for irrigation. They made possible more massive agricultural enterprises with greater production than would have been possible without them. In time, as cities grew in size and return of wastes to the countryside was disrupted by the construction of sewers, cities became an increasing drain on their surrounding ecosystems.

EGYPT AND MESOPOTAMIA

The Nile River and the Tigris-Euphrates system provide a contrast that throws light on the question of land deterioration in the region where western civilization began (Dale and Carter, 1955). The farming lands of Egypt, irrigated by the floodwaters of the Nile, have been farmed for at least 6000 years and yet remain productive. Egypt is still a densely populated country, supported primarily by the Nile bottomlands. By comparison the lands of Mesopotamia have until recently supported only a fraction of the population that thrived there in the days of Sumeria, Babylonia, and Assyria. Desertification and salinization of once productive lands is widespread. A look at the headwaters of the two river systems provides part of the answer to the differences between these regions. The headwaters of the White Nile lie in the swamps of Uganda and the great lakes of East Africa; for the Blue Nile the headwaters are in the highlands of Ethiopia. In its passage through the Sudan the White Nile traverses the swamps of the Sudd, which regulate its flow. Until recent times these headwaters were sparsely populated and spared from the devastating influences of mass movements of people and their livestock. The Nile has had its annual flood throughout history, fed by the monsoon rains from the Indian Ocean. It has carried a load of silt and humus, which, when deposited each year on the farm lands of Egypt, has maintained or added to their fertility. Until recent times the silt load of the Nile has been relatively light and manageable, not choking the fields.

The headwaters of the Tigris and Euphrates lie in the highlands of Armenia, in areas that in the past have supported numerous people and greater numbers of domestic livestock. More than that these headwaters have been in the path of invaders from Europe and Asia, with their horses, cattle, sheep, and goats. They have been subjected, therefore, to all of the pressures hillside farming and overgrazing by livestock can bring to bear. They have been deforested to provide timbers for the growing cities or to provide new grazing lands for flocks and herds. The erosion that has resulted has caused an ever-increasing silt load to be carried by the Tigris and Euphrates. In Sumerian times the indications are that the silt load was manageable by the downstream farmers and irrigators. Subsequent empires had an increasingly difficult task in keeping it controlled. Armies of laborers and slaves have been fully occupied keeping the irrigation canals free of silt. Silt has filled in the Persian Gulf to a distance of 180 miles out from where the rivers emptied in Sumerian times (Davis, 1956). As long as strong empires centered in the lands between the two rivers, the canals were kept open. But the region was plagued by invaders who disrupted the existing system. The final breakdown is said to result from the Mongol and Tartar invasions in the thirteenth and fourteenth centuries A.D. These armies of horsemen were interested in crushing forever the Arab states then based in Mesopotamia. They destroyed the irrigation canals and killed or carried off the inhabitants of the cities. Until recent years the task of coping with silt, rebuilding the canal system, and desalinating soils that had suffered from too little drainage proved too much for the peoples who remained in the area. The silt-laden flood waters carried soil from the highlands to the sea (Dale and Carter, 1955).

It is easy to see today how quickly a watershed can be destroyed by too many grazing animals, particularly in dry areas. In a decade more damage can be done than a century of rest can repair. It is also easy to see the effects of deforestation on mountain slopes, particularly where forest regrowth is prevented by the presence of too many goats or sheep. Both of these processes seem to have been at work not only along the hillslopes that fed water to the Tigris and Euphrates, but also in the mountains of Lebanon. Here the Phoenicians had their empire and built the greatest navy of their day from the timber that grew on their mountains. The famous cedars of Lebanon helped to shape the cities of Egypt and were used in the temple of Solomon. Cutting them started the trouble, overgrazing by goats and sheep prevented recovery. Only in a few protected spots did cedars remain and forests of any kind are no longer extensive. Many formerly forested slopes are now incredibly barren and almost devoid of soil. From their appearance one would believe that the climate is now too dry to support forests. Yet where soil remains, in the vicinity of the few ancient groves, the cedars continue to reproduce and grow (Lowdermilk, 1953).

CIVILIZATION AND ENVIRONMENTAL COLLAPSE

It is tempting to relate the downfall of early civilizations everywhere to environmental collapse resulting from too much pressure upon the living resources of vegetation and soil. Yet in the old homelands of civilization the record is obscured by repeated wars and invasions. The causes for the invasions are themselves the subject of speculation. Considering what

> *The significance of pastoralism is not that it actually destroys forests but that it makes permanent what destruction goes before. While goats are often observed to climb trees and browse on foliage and bark, a mature forest is relatively immune to their depredations. Even the shrubby* maquis *will withstand all but the most severe overgrazing, and, as may be seen today in Mediterranean countries where economic advance has brought a halt to free-range grazing, the forest communities have a remarkable capacity for recovery. But where woodcutters or a forest fire have stripped a hillside, goats will eagerly consume the seedlings and young trees that start up, effectively preventing forest regeneration.*
>
> ** * * * **
>
> *The cycle of deforestation and erosion, once begun, tends to reinforce itself. The high forest gives way to* maquis, *a dense evergreen thicket, and this in turn to* garigue, *a sparse growth of spiny and often aromatic low shrubs that can support itself on the dry, denuded slopes. Further destruction can produce landscapes as bare as any steppe, a condition seen on countless Mediterranean hillsides today. Recovery and reforestation occur only over an extended time scale, and then only if there are surviving seed sources and all destructive impacts—especially fire and grazing—are kept out.*
>
> J. Donald Hughes and J. V. Thirgood, *Journal of Forest History* (1982)

appears to be the normal tendency of human groups—to stake out a territory and stay there (a tendency shared by most other land animals)—what was it that sent wave after wave of Indo-European, Turkish, and other central Asian peoples out of their homelands and into the old centers of civilization? Climatic changes have been advanced as a cause. Too great an increase in populations of humans and their livestock combined with environmental deterioration resulting from their pressure is another possibility. The normal tendency of some people to wander, to find new things, explore new lands could account for some of it. Whatever the cause, the effects of the movement of Medes, Persians, and other Aryan tribes, of Hittites, Hyksos, Huns, Turks, Tartars has frequently been so disruptive to settled cultures that some have given up the effort.

We need no environmental explanation to account for the fall of the Incan and Aztec civilizations. Invaders did the work, and not many invaders in either case. Discontent of subject populations, asked to produce too much for the benefit of palace and temple, contributed. Yet the footprints of civilization are marked by ruins, and environmental failures can often be deduced. The original homelands of the Mayans were abandoned, their cities covered with jungle, when first discovered by the outside world. A failure in agriculture has been advanced as a likely cause (Deevey et al., 1979; Turner, 1982) The ancient civilization of tropical Sri Lanka, dependent on carefully maintained reservoirs and irrigation canals, is said to have been destroyed by floods and silt washed from deforested mountains (Lowdermilk, 1953).

All of the early civilizations were regionally based, drawing their sustenance from the productivity of relatively few ecosystems. Although trade with other countries, including those overseas, dates back to Sumerian times, it did not provide the basis for support of the cities. Too much pressure upon local ecosystems, causing a breakdown in their productive cycles, could lead in time to the failure of the civilization. Some cultures, mostly of seafaring peoples, could continue to thrive even when their homelands ceased to be productive. Both the Phoenicians and the Greeks were in this category: they colonized remote areas and had regular seaborne trade channels bringing food and fiber to the capitals. These along with the Romans, with an empire stretching from Great Britain and Germany almost to the borders of India, were forerunners of the global civilizations that were to follow when northern and western Europe became organized along the ways of colonialism and imperialism, finally capturing the whole world in their network of raiding and trading. With this final development, civilization was no longer a threat only to local ecosystems, its passing not to be noticed elsewhere in the world, but a potential threat to the entire biosphere, to all life on earth.

SOURCES

Clark, Kenneth, 1971. *Civilisation. A personal view*. BBC and J. Murray, London.

Carneiro, Robert, 1970. A theory of the origin of the state. *Science* 169:733–738

Deevey, E. S. et al. 1979. Mayan urbanism: impact on a tropical karst environment. *Science* 206:298–305

Dale, Tom and V. C. Carter, 1955. Topsoil and civilization. University of Oklahoma Press, Norman, Oklahoma.

Davis, John H., 1956. The influence of man on coast lines. *Man's role in changing the face of the earth*. University of Chicago Press, pp 504–521.

Hughes, J. Donald and J. V. Thirgood, 1982. Deforestation, erosion, and forest management in ancient Greece and Rome. *Journal of Forest History* 26 (2):60–75.

Leonard, George B., 1972. *The transformation*. Delacorte Press, New York.

Lowdermilk, W. C., 1953. *Conquest of the land through 7000 years*. U.S. Department of Agriculture, Washington, D.C.

Mumford, Lewis, 1961. *The city in history*. Harcourt, Brace & World, New York.

Stone, Merlin, 1976. *When god was a woman*. Harcourt, Brace, Jovanovich, New York.

Turner, B. L. II, 1982. Pre-Columbian agriculture. Review of *Maya Subsistence* (Academic Press, New York). *Science* 217:345–346.

a

CIVILIZATION AND LAND-USE FAILURE

(a) Rain forest took over the old Mayan city of Tikal, Guatemala. (b) Old terraces that held the soil on Andean mountain slopes are now in ruin at Machu Picchu, Peru. (c) Deserts surround the ruins of Uruk in Iraq. (d) The ancient Persian capital of Persepolis; in the background deserts prevail.

b

c

d 51

PART 2
THE
GLOBAL
EMPIRE

COLONIES AND CORPORATIONS

Up to the time of World War II, nations attempted to secure their wealth and power by acquiring colonies and by the conquest of other peoples, who became subject and tributary. The Japanese push during World War II was to acquire a "co-prosperity sphere" of countries that would accept their exports and provide them with low-cost energy supplies and raw materials. The Germans took over most of Europe to achieve a similar goal. Japan and Germany lost the war. By some strange economic transmutation, however, Japan and Germany have become far more rich and prosperous than the wildest dreams of their World War leaders.

Following World War II the drive in all of the old colonies of Europe was toward political independence. People by the hundreds of thousands died as these independence movements struggled—in Algeria and Zaire, in India, and most recently in Indo-China and southern Africa. Independence has been achieved—or has it? Again, because of an economic transmutation, the new nations find themselves tied even more strongly to their former colonial masters, or to their new replacements from Germany, Japan, and America. Politically they are free; economically they remain colonies. They have become part of a global economic empire, not controlled necessarily by powerful nations, but rather by powerful economic organization. The new global corporations control more wealth than most governments and are capable of making or breaking nations, not by military force, but by economic manipulation. To counter them some former colonies have created their own economic groupings—OPEC (the Organization of Petroleum Exporting Countries) for example. By controlling the flow and price of petroleum, the energy source that has become all-important to the global empire, they can potentially bring even the giant corporations to heel (Barnet and Muller, 1974).

How we moved from the conditions that prevailed in the civilizations of antiquity to the global empire of today cannot be told in any detail, nor do authorities necessarily agree on what caused what effect. Here two points seem important to stress: The European invasion of the world and the technological revolution. The first had an impact on cultures, environments, and natural resources of overwhelming importance; the second is having its greatest effect on today's and tomorrow's environment.

THE EUROPEAN INVASION

The history of European expansion to the Americas, Asia, the Pacific, and Africa has been written mostly by Europeans to be read by those who identify with the European role. It is therefore rather like the history of the plague written by bacteria. The "great events" in world history look quite different when viewed from the other side. The appearance of Columbus in the West Indies in 1492 was the beginning of an unmitigated disaster for tens of millions of native Americans and for the wildlife of two continents. Similarly, the arrival of Captain Cook in Tahiti, of the First Fleet in Botany Bay, or the Dutch in the Cape of Good Hope marked the beginning of death and cultural disintegration for the original peoples of those lands. Some would brush aside these events as the unfortunate and mostly unintended consequences of actions aimed at other objectives and point to the materials benefits that have flowed from the new order of industrial civilization. From the other side, however, whatever benefits have been gained seem worth far less than the cost.

We cannot undo the past, but we could endeavor to stop perpetuating its worst aspects. It would seem worthwhile to strive for a world where those with wealth and power—whether the United States, the USSR, China, or Japan—can no longer impose their views and ways on others. We must remember that national egocentricity, feelings of ethnic superiority, racism, sexism, genocidal behavior are not only European traits. Had the Aztecs developed the greater power first, and "discovered" and colonized Europe, the world would not necessarily be a better place today.

The environmental consequences of European colonization have been marked by destruction of forests, overgrazing of rangelands, exploitative agriculture leading to soil depletion and erosion, mismanagement of watersheds leading to aggravated patterns of flooding and drought, extermination of many species of wild animals and decimation of most forms of wildlife, and eventually to widespread pollution of land, air, and water. Such destructive consequences did not occur everywhere, and to balance them stable, productive, and diversified environments were shaped in some areas, and the means for establishing them elsewhere were discovered. Conservation action was forced to take shape by the very magnitude of the environmental disruption.

THE TECHNOLOGICAL REVOLUTION

The technological revolution that began in Europe was fueled in part by the wealth that began to pour in from the newly colonized lands and in part by the organization of trade and commerce that grew up to handle it. It was not in its beginnings just an outbreak of inventiveness on the part of Europeans, since many of the inventions had been known since Ancient times—only the people of those times did not think they were worth bothering with. Neither was it brought about by the sudden availability of new sources of energy; coal, petroleum, and natural gas were also known to the people of old and distant civilizations, they just did not consider them to be important. Just what combination of circumstances touched off the technological explosion that began in western Europe and principally in the eighteenth century may never be fully understood. Jacques Ellul (1964), however, has analyzed the conditions and has come up with the following factors:

1. The fruition of long technical experience, meaning the accumulation of numerous new and old techniques and inventions that when put together form in Lewis Mumford's words a new "technical complex."

2. The population expansion that occurred in Europe at that time, which not only created a demand, but provided a source of labor.

3. An economic environment that was stable and at the same time flexible, so that investors could count on a return for any investment, but also count on a market for any new products.

4. The flexibility of the social environment that involved both the disappearance of social taboos and restrictions and also the disappearance of the social groups that had maintained the previously stable society.

This last is particularly noteworthy in that the social environment in England and France during the eighteenth century was favorable not only to the dethronement of royalty but to a displacement of the established church. Beyond that there was an attack on all established groups and communities, including not only trade guilds, which had been conservative, but also the family itself, so that many individuals were available to work within a new kind of social organization as lone individuals without social connections. In Ellul's words: *To uproot men from their surroundings, from the rural districts and from their family and friends; to squeeze thousands into unfit lodgings and unhealthy places of work; to create a whole new environment within the framework of a new human condition . . . all this was possible only when the individual was completely isolated. It was conceivable only when he literally had no environment, no family, and was not part of a group able to resist economic pressure; when he had almost no way of life left.*

We see a similar phenomenon today.

5. The appearance of a clear technical intention. This could be a clearly stated purpose of the state to achieve military objectives, such as was

true of France in the time of Napoleon, but more general and more pervasive was the realization of those who had some money that their wealth could be increased by following a technological direction, orienting capital, land, and labor for the purpose of producing greater profit.

New machines, printing presses, steam engines, spinning and weaving devices, and the like were essential. New sources of energy from coal to petroleum fueled the process. But the social, political, and economic organization of society permitted these machines and energy sources to be employed in ways they had not been before.

What was derived was a new technological orientation of society, based on a belief that production of whatever the system happened to produce was of paramount importance, whether this be steam engines, buggy whips, pins, or Cadillacs. Furthermore, efficiency was to be the criteria against which all techniques were tested, and the ultimate measure of efficiency was profit—how little did it cost, how much did it sell for? Such measures were to be weighed against all other considerations, such as the welfare of the workers, the social importance of the product, or the environmental consequences of the total activity (Mumford, 1966, 1970).

BIOSPHERE PEOPLE

The new technological society has now become a global phenomenon, blotting out formerly self-reliant cultures and essentially assigning to all people a role in the new economic order. This is accomplished not in the old way through conquest and killing but much more subtly and indirectly. People who wish to have a transistor radio become a part, willingly, or unwillingly, of the technological order that produces transistor radios, and these are hardly the product of the village smithy or cottage industry. As a result, a new type of people, biosphere people, have come into existence. These are the opposite of ecosystem people. The new biosphere culture draws on the resources of all ecosystems and is at the same time dependent on none. Destruction of resources in one area does not cause collapse of the culture since the global economy can shift to a different ecosystem and draw on its resources. It becomes possible therefore to carry out much more complete destruction of living resources than could have been achieved by the most profligate ecosystem people.

The new global technology is engaged at the present time in what amounts to war against the tropical forests of the world, and predictions are that if present trends continue (which of course they will not) most large blocks of torpical rainforest, and with them their constituent species, will have vanished within the next few decades. At the other climatic extreme, in the tropics and subtropics deserts are spreading and formerly productive dry land ecosystems are being made lifeless. The high mountains, islands, wetlands, and coastal marine ecosystems of the world are also under continuing attack with soil and vegetation loss at one extreme and siltation plus pollution at the other.

A QUESTION OF ATTITUDES

The purposes of this historical survey are not only to review the impact of humanity on the environment but to consider attitudes that have an important impact on our efforts toward achieving an ecologically sustainable way of life. We who are involved with conservation commonly hear such clichés as "you can't stop progress" or "you can't change human nature," usually spoken to end discussion and to extricate the speaker from any feelings of responsibility. But the attitudes toward economic growth and change, which go by the name of progress today, are recent attitudes brought on by the new technological order and still not accepted by most of the world's people. Economic stability and peace have been the goals of most people for the longest time. Human nature, whatever is meant by that, could best be examined by a study of hunter-gatherers since that is the state in which people have existed for the longest period of time.

What economist E. Mishan (1967) has called "growthmania," the belief that more and bigger is somehow better, is a recent concept associated with accepting the dictates of the new technological order. Economies of scale, meaning that the cost per unit declines as the number of units produced per unit of time increases, is an economic rule that applies to only certain manufacturing processes and even there has upper limits. By contrast the concept that "small is beautiful," discussed in the book by that name by E. F. Schumacher, has much more widespread validity even where one is primarily concerned with efficiency of production, and certainly where one is concerned with quality of life.

The concept of private ownership in land, which has caused so much difficulty in the dealings between European invaders and the native populations of the Americas, Africa, and the Pacific, is associated with Western patriarchal social organization and was until recently, with the rise of the industrial-technological society, largely restricted to the ruling aristocracy. Elsewhere and for the longest period of time, land was either owned communally or the concept that land could be owned at all was totally rejected.

In connection with questions of ownership and responsibility Garret Hardin (1968) has developed the concept of "the tragedy of the commons." In his important paper he has shown that land or resources that theoretically belong to everyone, but are under no one's direct control, tend to be overexploited. Each individual seeks to increase his own personal benefit by using the common resources to an excessive degree.

This concept does explain the overuse of marine resources, the over-grazing of the public domain in the United States, and other recent phenomena. Yet it is based on a belief in innate human competitiveness that does not necessarily hold up when we take a longer look at the history of humanity or study cultures other than our own. Cooperation has been as much a human tradition as has competition. In many native cultures the individual would not seek personal gain at the expense of others, or would do so only in ways that do not effect the welfare of the group. He may seek the glory of being the greatest hunter, but would distribute the meat to all. For most people in most times the idea of putting a few extra cows on the village commons to enrich oneself and one's immediate family would not have been conceivable, since such behavior would have brought no rewards.

The idea that big cities are somehow great cities is another recent concept that does not hold up in historical perspective. The greatest cities of antiquity, from Ur to Athens, were small towns by present American standards, as were the great cities of Renaissance Europe such as Flor-ence and Venice. Only Rome reached what we would consider to be the size of a major city, and that just preceding its decline and fall. The small cities supported the flowering of human culture in the arts, music, architecture, and all of the refinements of the physical conditions of life (Sale, 1980).

The dependence of cities on the countryside has already been men-tioned, but what is frequently ignored is the energy subsidy in terms of human beings that the countryside has provided to the cities. As Elaine Morgan has pointed out, the great energy cost of rearing a child from birth to independent adult status has been borne primarily by women of the rural areas. During these years young people are economically non-productive, or nearly so. The cities benefit from the immigration of pro-ductive young people seeking work, adventure, or whatever. The city has not had to pay the cost of child raising, and until relatively recently the urban population has not equaled the rural population in production of young. Furthermore, the city has not traditionally had to bear the cost of caring for the old or sick, since these people typically returned to the countryside or village when their working days were over. Today, how-ever, that subsidy has been removed and cities are forced to bear the cost, not only of child rearing and the education of the young, but also of the support of the old or handicapped. With this the older cities of the industrialized world are increasingly facing financial bankruptcy and at the same time losing productive workers who move from the decaying urban center to the periphery.

In tracing history from ecosystem people through the rise and ex-pansion of civilization to the biosphere people of today, we have seen a growing loss of identification with the basic support systems for hu-manity. Today's task is to restore that identification—to bring an aware-ness of where things come from and how they work, and with this a feeling of responsibility for the land, the water, the air, and all the living species that share our space on the planet. Without this sense of awareness and responsibility, which fortunately appears to be growing in America today, we all will lose.

SOURCES

Barnet, Richard J. and R. E. Muller, 1974. *Global reach*. Simon and Schuster, New York.

Ellul, Jacques, 1964. *The technological society*. Vintage Books, New York.

Hardin, Garret, 1968. The tragedy of the commons. *Science* 162:1243–1248.

Mishan, Ezra, 1967. *The costs of economic growth*. Praeger, New York.

Morgan, Elaine, 1976. *Falling apart*. Souvenir Press, London.

Mumford, Lewis, 1966. *The myth of the machine. Technics and human development*. Harcourt, Brace & World, New York.

———1970. *The myth of the machine. The pentagon of power*. Harcourt, Brace and Jovanovich, New York.

Sale, Kirkpatrick, 1980. *Human scale*. Coward, McCann & Geoghegan, New York.

Schumacher, E. F., 1973. *Small is beautiful*. Harper and Row, New York.

THREE

WHERE
ARE
WE?

CHAPTER
4

THE
NATURE
OF
THE
ENVIRONMENT

RULES OF THE GAME

The human story, from hunter-gatherer to global imperialist, has taken place in an environment governed by its own laws—laws that cannot be amended or repealed. We are familiar with them and few will complain that the law of gravity is unjust, or that the laws of thermodynamics must be revised to conform with the man-made "laws" of economic behavior. Following the law of gravity, soil will move downhill when it is exposed to the mechanical impact of raindrops and the hydraulic push of flowing water. It will do so regardless of our economic needs or political commands. Ecologists seek to understand the laws or principles that describe the behavior of ecosystems and the biosphere. But the interactions that take place are among the most complex in the known universe, and they are often exceedingly difficult to comprehend. For most ecological processes we are at the stage of hypothesis (this is the way things seem to work), or theory (all of our data support this model of how things work), rather than law (this is the way things always work).

It remains essential that we recognize the basic rules of the game that govern and affect the ways in which we interact with our environment. Admitting that we do not know all the rules, and that we are not prepared to give them all the status of *laws*, we must comprehend the observable rules if we are to stay in the game. Staying in the game means living on earth. If we want to keep living here we play by the rules.

The human environment is the biosphere and the modifications within it caused by human action. The biosphere is part of the planet on which life exists and of which it forms a part. It is the surface area of the earth, made up of the lower levels of the atmosphere, the oceans, the upper surfaces of continents and islands including soil, rocks, and fresh water, and the living things inhabiting this area. In the biosphere energy from sunlight activates life processes; chemicals from air, water, and soil are available as building blocks for living organisms (Kovda et al., 1970).

The biosphere can be considered as the sum of all the ecosystems on earth. At any one time people exist as part of a particular ecosystem, although at other times they may travel from one ecosystem to another. What happens to the biosphere and its ecosystems determines what will happen to people. It is impossible to separate individuals from the biosphere of which they form a part. The air they breathe, the water they drink, the sunlight that warms them, and the food they eat, all tie them to their immediate physical and biological environment. At any one time the human body, like that of any other animal, exists in a dynamic state of exchange with the environment—taking in or expelling gases, absorbing or giving off heat, and losing or gaining water and other chemicals.

This continuous process of exchange ceases only with death, at which time a different set of environmental interactions begins. A human apart from environment is an abstraction; in reality no such being exists.

Before people became dominant on earth, they were members of a biotic community and components of an ecosystem, without having much more effect on them thay any other animal species would have. In still-existing societies in remote areas of the earth, this condition remains. The dominant societies of today, however, have changed the face of the earth. Some areas have been subject to major modification, others less so, but it is probably impossible to find any ecosystem that has not been affected in some way. Nevertheless it remains useful to distinguish between the less modified, or *natural* community or ecosystem, and the highly modified, *anthropogenic* community or ecosystem. This does not mean people are not part of nature, but it does recognize our dominant role on the planet. Undoubtedly the areas subject to the most extreme modification are the major cities of the world, which often seem to exist apart from nature. This separation, however, is more apparent than real. It must be remembered that urban systems are intricately related to ecosystems on which they depend for their continued existence. They have been defined as supraecosystems, because of the degree to which they tie together what would otherwise be remote and separate ecosystems (Fraser Darling and Dasmann, 1969). The problems of urban systems differ in degree, but not in fundamental nature, from those of other areas less influenced by people.

ENERGY TRANSFER

For a community to exist in must have energy to supply the life processes of the organisms that compose it. The principal source of energy for any biotic community is sunlight. One group of organisms, however, the green plants, makes use of sunlight energy directly for the synthesis of foodstuffs. The presence of chlorophyll in the cells of plants makes possible photosynthesis, in which light energy is used in building a plant food (glucose) from simple compounds—carbon dioxide from the air and water from the soil. From glucose, with the addition of other simple chemical compounds obtained from the soil, plants can build more complex carbohydrates, proteins, fats, and vitamins. These materials, required by animals in their diets, must come from the plant world.

The dependence of animals on plants and of plants on sunlight brings to consideration a physical law of great importance to the understanding of any ecosystem. This, the *second law of thermodynamics*, states that in any transfer of energy from one form to another, some energy always escapes from the system, usually as heat; no transfer is 100 percent effective. Always energy goes from a concentrated form useful to a system to a dilute form, which is not. Most transfers of energy in natural ecosystems are inefficient. In some instances, of the total amount of sunlight energy potentially available to green plants, only 1 percent will be converted finally into chemical energy tied up in foods within the plants. The remaining 99 percent escapes. Similarly, when herbivores feed on green plants and convert plant starch and protein into animal energy and protein, another high percentage of energy escapes. When carnivores feed on herbivores, there is again inefficiency in energy transfer. The limits of available energy are soon reached. Thus, in some communities, of 10,000 original calories of sunlight energy striking on green plants, only 2 calories may remain tied up in chemical energy within the body of a carnivorous animal.

The operation of the second law of thermodynamics serves to explain many of the characteristics of ecosystems. In any ecosystem the amount of green plants is limited, ultimately, by the amount of sunlight energy and the efficiency of plants in converting it to a useful form. This is a theoretical upper limit, not approached in natural ecosystems, because lesser limits are always set by shortages of required chemical elements or other factors.

In a similar way the final limit on the number of animals in an area is determined by the amount of energy available in green plants and by the efficiency of animals in converting this to a form useful for maintenance, growth, and reproduction. These relationships within an ecosystem are often illustrated in diagrammatic ways, such as the biotic pyramid, food chain, and food web (Fig. 4.1). In the *biotic pyramid* the greatest numbers of organisms, the greatest mass, and the greatest amount of food energy are to be found in the lowest layer of organisms, the green plants. Partly because of the necessary inefficiency in energy transfer, numbers, mass, and energy decrease as you move up the pyramid. The pyramid is supported by the amount of sunlight energy received and the amounts of essential nutrients, minerals, water, and essential gases avail-

Fig. 4.1
Biotic pyramid showing portion of grassland food web.

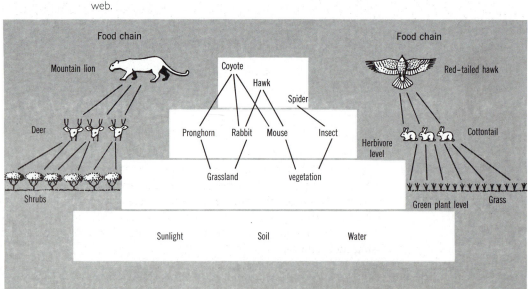

able in the soil or other supporting physical environment. In marine ecosystems the biotic-pyramid concept is less useful, since a high rate of productivity among the floating green plants (phytoplankton) compensate for a relatively low biomass at any one time. *Food chains* are simply diagrammatic representations of the food relationships within an ecosystem. A simple example is the chain that leads from bitterbrush to mule deer to mountain lion. Bitterbrush is the green plant, or *producer,* at the base of the food chain, and is said to be at the lowest *trophic level* or energy level. The deer feeding on the bitterbrush is at the herbivore, or *primary consumer* trophic level, and the mountain lion, feeding on the deer, is at the *secondary consumer,* carnivore, trophic level. Obviously there must be more bitterbrush than deer, if the deer are to be supported entirely by it, and there also must be more deer than mountain lions, if lions are to live entirely on a diet of deer meat. Although food chains like this may be artificially separated out and studied, most food relationships of species in an ecosystem are far more complicated. In natural systems, food chains are interwoven into complex *food webs.* Thus if the simple example given is expanded, it will be seen that deer feed not only on bitterbrush but on many species of shrubs, trees, grasses, and other herbs, which, in turn, support not only deer but other mammals (various mice and hares, for example), birds, great numbers of insects, and other invertebrates down to a variety of microorganisms. A deer is seldom free of a whole range of external and internal parasites that are deriving energy indirectly from the green plants the deer eats—tapeworms, roundworms, flukes, bacteria and protozoa, fleas, lice, and the like. Coyotes or wildcats in addition to mountain lions may kill and eat deer. The dead green plant, deer, or lion, in turn, provides food for a great variety of insect larvae, bacteria, protozoans, scavengers among birds such as ravens or vultures, scavenging mammals, all of the wide range of organisms that take the substance from a dead plant or animal and return it ultimately in chemical form to the soil, from whence it enters a new generation of plants and animals.

Despite the enormous complexity of food webs in nature, the number of layers in a biotic pyramid or links in a food chain is inevitably limited through the operation of the second law of thermodynamics. The loss of energy at each stage of energy transfer keeps biotic pyramids low and food chains short. Thus, there are no superpredators that feed exclusively on mountain lions. The expenditure of energy involved in the capture and consumption of these scarce creatures would certainly outweigh the energy to be gained. In aquatic ecosystems food chains are commonly longer than those on land—there may be several layers of predatory fish feeding on the herbivores; but even in these complex systems the inefficiency of energy transfer prevents the development of long food chains.

People, as carnivores, occupy the top layer of a biotic pyramid and the end link of a food chain. They can also exist as herbivores, however, and thus lower the pyramid and shorten the food chain. In those areas

a

FOOD CHAINS

At the base of any food chain are green plants, which capture the energy of sunlight **(a)**. At the next link in the chain (or trophic level) are herbivores which feed directly on plants, such as this goat herd in Lebanon **(b)** or prairie dogs in the American West **(c)**. At the top of the chain are carnivores such as the red fox **(d)**, which is shown here with a captured herbivore (cottontail rabbit).

b

c

d

of the earth where human numbers are great and productive land is limited, they cannot afford the luxury of being carnivores nor the waste of energy involved in converting plant protein to beef or mutton. In such areas they must feed on plants primarily if great numbers are to be kept alive.

Of perhaps equal importance with the limitations imposed by the second law of thermodynamics is the role played by life in conserving energy. Sunlight energy striking a bare rock or soil surface is soon lost. Much is reflected back into the air; some heats the rock or soil temporarily but is soon radiated back into the atmosphere. The earth as a whole, before life, radiated or reflected back into space an amount of energy equal to that received from the sun. In the absence of life, energy thus became degraded, that is, dispersed through space until it was no longer capable of doing work. When green plants appeared on earth, this loss of energy was slowed down. Sunlight energy was stored in organisms in concentrated form and transferred in food chains from one to another. With the development of complex biotic communities, a living system was developed that made even greater use of the incoming solar energy and stored a part of it for the future. People have been dependent upon these stored reserves of energy. When a person eats meat, he or she obtains energy that may have been stored by plants several years before. When we cut firewood for fuel, we are obtaining energy accumulated and stored by trees for perhaps a century or more. When we burn coal or petroleum, we obtain sunlight energy stored by plant life millions of years before. We are as yet unable to store significant quantities of energy without making use of the life processes of plants and animals. When living communities are destroyed and the land made bare, the energy on which life depends is again wasted and no longer is stored for future use.

CHEMICAL REQUIREMENTS

Just as each ecosystem must have a source of energy, so must it have a source of chemical building blocks or nutrients from which organisms can be constructed. In the oceans this source is seawater; on land the source is the soil. Biotic pyramids rest on an energy base of sunlight, and a chemical base of soil or seawater. Both of these sources of minerals, however, are secondary, for minerals come originally from the rocks of the earth's surface or from the atmosphere above the earth.

Rocks supply minerals to the soil slowly. Rocks break apart through weathering, the action of cold, heat, wind, and precipitation gradually cracking and shattering them into small particles. They break down more quickly through the action of organisms. Plant roots, for example, penetrate into cracks in rocks, widen them, and eventually split and separate the rock fragments. Acids released or dissolved from plant materials help the process of rock disintegration and free elements for soil formation.

Organisms also help to capture elements such as nitrogen from the atmosphere and incorporate them in the soil. Nitrogen, an essential part of protein, must be present for life to exist. The cycle by which it is transferred from atmosphere to organism, to soil, and back to the atmosphere has been well studied and is illustrated in Figure 4.2. We must recognize that the atmosphere on which life depends is in itself dependent on life for the continued existence of its life-sustaining molecules.

The Russian scientist V. I. Vernadsky has pointed out that the biosphere holds three main components. The first is *life* itself, the sum total of living matter. The second he terms *biogenic* matter. This includes all of the organic substances formed by living matter: coal, petroleum, natural gas, peat, soil humus, litter, and the like. The third, which he terms *biocosnic* matter, is represented by the minerals or chemicals formed through the interaction of life with the inorganic world. Among them, Vernadsky includes the gases of the lower layers of the atmosphere, sedimentary rocks, clay minerals, and water. Although these terms are not in general use, a gradual increasing awareness of the significance of living processes in the physics, chemistry, and geology of the earth's crust has been brought about by the work of Vernadsky, and has been emphasized by the Russian soil scientist V. Kovda (1970). The ways in which living organisms and the physical world interact to maintain the

Fig. 4.2
The nitrogen cycle.

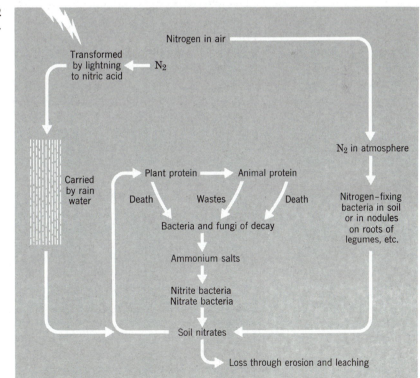

biosphere as an environment suitable to life is explored in an intriguing book by James Lovelock, *Gaia. A New Look at Life at Life on Earth.*

Roughly 99 percent of the atmosphere consists of the two gases nitrogen and oxygen, both of which are essential to life. The balance is made up of the equally essential carbon dioxide, water vapor, and various rare and inert gases. Nitrogen is a rare substance on earth, even though it is the dominant gas in the atmosphere. It is an essential component of all living matter, being involved in the chemical composition of the amino acids from which all plant and animal proteins are constructed. It is likely that all of the nitrogen in the atmosphere, through the operation of the nitrogen cycle, passes through living organisms and is returned ultimately to the atmosphere through the action of denitrifying bacteria or other processes. Even the nitrogen that escapes from the cycle to be deposited as sedimentary rock, or in the form of coal, petroleum, and the like may utlimately be returned to the atmosphere through the long reaches of geological time by movements of the rocks on the earth's crust, volcanic activity, and soil formation from sedimentary rocks. The turnover rate of atmospheric nitrogen is very slow and involves many centuries. Thus, despite the steady use of nitrogen by living organisms, there is little drain on the nitrogen supply and no fear of exhaustion of the nitrogen in the atmosphere.

It is a different story with oxygen. This is a highly reactive gas, unlike the relatively inert nitrogen. It is so reactive that most of it on the earth is tied up in chemical combination with other elements, such as iron oxides and aluminum oxides. Molecular oxygen, on which life depends, exists only in the atmosphere or dissolved in water. In both places, its presence is dependent primarily on the action of green plants. Before life appeared on earth, there was little or no oxygen in the atmosphere. The first living organisms were *anaerobic* microscopic forms able to exist without free oxygen. Only when these evolved to the stage where the first photosynthetic reaction took place was molecular oxygen released into the atmosphere. However, green plants both produce and consume oxygen. Oxygen is produced in excess in the presence of light, when photosynthesis proceeds more rapidly than respiration. In darkness, when photosynthesis cannot take place, the process of respiration burns up much of the oxygen that has been produced. During the time a plant is living, however, it is making a contribution to the atmospheric oxygen supply that exceeds its rate of use. When it ceases to live and begins to decay, various oxidative reactions take place that consume the excess oxygen the plant produced during its lifetime.

In order for oxygen to accumulate in the atmosphere, it is first necessary for green plants to produce it, and then for these plants, on dying (or for the dead bodies of the animals that consume them), to be sealed away from the processes of decay and the oxidation that accompanies them. This happens quite regularly when dead plants or animals are sealed off from the air by the accumulation of other materials on top of them. Marshes, swamps, and in particular peat bogs accumulate great amounts of such dead plant and animal material. The sediments at the bottom of ponds, lakes, seas, and the ocean also accumulate and seal off organic materials. Thus, over the long reaches of geological time enough organic material has accumulated in a reduced state to account for the amount of oxygen present in the atmosphere today. Much of this has gone into the formation of the deposits of fossil fuels, coal seams, and petroleum deposits we are now mining for energy. (Some of it exists in the litter and organic humus of the soil—some in the accumulations of peat, oil shales, oil sands, etc.) However, much of it is more widely dispersed among the sedimentary rocks of the earth's surface. If is apparent that during past geological ages the rate at which plant and animal debris accumulated to form organic sediments was much faster than it is today. During recent decades there has been no observable tendency for the oxygen level of the atmosphere to increase. In fact, the fear has been that with widespread use of fossil fuels and depletion of the earth's supply of green plant life, the amount of atmospheric oxygen would decrease. In burning coal, oil, and natural gas, one is reversing the process by which the atmospheric oxygen was formed. If all organic sediments were to be oxidized, all of the accumulation of atmospheric oxygen would theoretically be consumed. However, the total amount represented by the available deposits of fossil fuels is apparently not sufficient to bring any great change in atmospheric oxygen, and during the past 80 years, the period of heaviest burning of coal and petroleum, there has been no observable decrease in atmospheric oxygen (Broeker, 1970; Machta and Hughes, 1970).

The final atmospheric component directly related to the presence of life is carbon dioxide. Unlike oxygen, this is added to the atmosphere in considerable quantities by processes other than those directly involved with life, notably from volcanic action. The same process of photosynthesis that adds oxygen to the atmosphere removes carbon dioxide. Respiration, which removes oxygen, adds carbon dioxide. Although the total supply of carbon dioxide is relatively small, it is vital to plant growth, and increases in its relative amount will stimulate plant growth where other elements are not lacking. Carbon dioxide also plays an important role in temperature regulation of the earth, since its molecules permit the passage of the shorter waves of solar radiation through the atmosphere, but interfere with the passage of the longer waves of heat radiating from the earth's surface. Consequently, changes in the amount of carbon dioxide in the atmosphere would be expected to affect the global heat balance, to make the earth either warmer or cooler. Although human activity, in particular the consumption of fossil fuels, has not decreased the amount of oxygen in the atmosphere, it has apparently brought a noticeable increase in carbon dioxide (Wheeler, 1970). The significance of this will be discussed under the subject of air pollution in Chapter 12.

ECOSYSTEM DEVELOPMENT

To protect or manage species, biotic communities, or the ecosystems of which they form a part, it is necessary to understand the processes through which they come into existence and those through which they recover from disturbance and renew themselves. These processes of ecosystem development and recovery are known as *biotic succession*. The term *succession* reflects the ways by which biotic communities succeed and replace one another in a describable sequence known as a *sere*.

Succession is of two types, *primary* and *secondary*. The first takes place in areas that have not supported living communities—bare rock, sand dunes, newly formed lakes or ponds, alluvial deposits of silt and gravel on a riverbank, lava flows, and so on and develops over time both a mature soil and a relatively stable and complex biotic community known as a *climax community* (Fig. 4.3). The initial organisms that establish themselves on such bare areas are necessarily hardy and capable of withstanding full sunlight, fluctuating temperatures, and an excess or a deficiency of water. Lichens, consisting of a symbiotic association of algae and fungi, are typical of organisms that can invade and colonize bare rock. The annual grasses and short-lived herbs that we often term "weeds" are typical invaders of rock crevices, sand dunes, or river banks. These species establish a *pioneer community*. This is temporary by nature, but provides conditions under which less hardy species can invade, colonize, and in time replace the pioneers. Succession proceeds through various middle stages, with one set of species replacing another, until finally the climax community occupies the area. This is a community that can maintain and replace itself over time and is usually the most complex community that a particular climate and substrate can support. It will make most efficient use of sun energy and soil nutrients. Climax communities represent storehouses of energy and materials accumulated over the long years involved in biotic succession and soil formation.

Secondary succession takes place in areas where the original vegetation has been destroyed or disturbed but where the soil has not been lost. This process is generally familiar. A forest that has been cut down regenerates itself. The forest, if it has not been greatly disturbed and if

Fig. 4.3
Primary succession on coastal sand dunes in northern California. This progression of plant communities may occur on any site protected from disturbance for a long time. Disturbance will arrest succession or set it back. A zonation of communities from the pioneers of the strand, heavily disturbed by wind, sand, tide, and salt spray, to the more complex climax on the protected and less disturbed inner side of the dunes may often be observed.

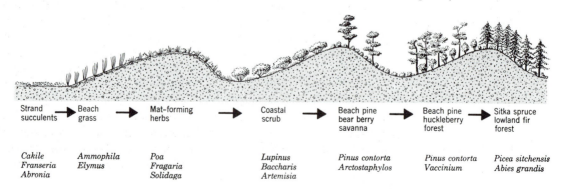

| Strand succulents | → | Beach grass | → | Mat–forming herbs | → | Coastal scrub | → | Beach pine bear berry savanna | → | Beach pine huckleberry forest | → | Sitka spruce lowland fir forest |

Cakile   *Ammophila*   *Poa*   *Lupinus*   *Pinus contorta*   *Pinus contorta*   *Picea sitchensis*
Franseria   *Elymus*   *Fragaria*   *Baccharis*   *Arctostaphylos*   *Vaccinium*   *Abies grandis*
Abronia   *Solidaga*   *Artemisia*

seed sources are available, may regenerate quickly with trees replacing trees. Usually, and particularly after a fire, there are a series of intermediate stages. A weed stage follows forest clearing. Left alone this is replaced by shrubs, then by trees and, eventually, if these have not been destroyed or the environment too greatly changed by disturbance, by the species that composed the original climax forest. The process is rapid or slow, depending upon the severity of the original disturbance. In a similar way, when a rangeland has been heavily overgrazed, the original climax grassland will go through several stages, characterized by different communities of weeds and grasses, before the climax community replaces itself. Succession tends to be an orderly and often predictable process. It is a heartening process for the conservationist, who knows that with care many of our badly abused lands will repair themselves. Unfortunately, however, this process is often forgotten by conservationists. This may result in efforts to protect a successional community by excluding all disturbance (which results in its disappearance through the normal progression toward the different vegetation of the climax), or in efforts to prevent any human use of communities that can readily withstand controlled harvesting and still regenerate themselves in a short period of time.

SUCCESSION AND LAND MANAGEMENT

The exploitation of biotic resources usually involves the removal and consumption of all or part of the elements that composed the climax communities of the earth. Successful conservation, or land management, often includes the manipulation of biotic succession in such a way that the climax replaces itself as quickly as possible. In this way a continued high yield of resources from an area is obtained.

The lumberman is interested in obtaining the greatest yield of high-quality timber from an area. In some places, such as the redwood forests of California or the subarctic spruce forests of Eurasia, the climax forest has the greatest commercial value. Successful forest management includes a study of the way plant succession proceeds after various systems of logging and the selection of the cutting system that will lead to the most rapid regeneration of the climax. Not all high-value forests are climax, however. It is likely most of the pine forests of the world represent a subclimax stage of succession, resulting from fire or other past disturbance. Left alone they would, in time, be replaced by climax species, hardwood trees or other conifers, of lower commercial value. Studies of succession indicate pine forests are often best maintained by the controlled use of fire, which removes the seedlings of the climax species and creates conditions favorable to regeneration of pine. In the longleaf pine forests of the southeastern United States, fire is now regularly employed as a management tool. In its absence, hardwood trees replace the pines.

a

BIOTIC SUCCESSION

All ecosystems develop through successional stages, starting with *pioneer* plants or animals that can invade and colonize barren areas and moving via middle stages through *subclimax* to various kinds of *climax* communities, which are relatively stable and will persist over long periods of time if not disturbed.

Pioneer stage. (a) A colony of lichens colonizes a bare rock surface. **Subclimax. (b)** An aspen woodland. Already, dark conifers, which will form the climax, are to be seen. These will overtop and replace the aspens. **Fire subclimax. (c)** This pine forest is maintained by periodic burning. Left unbdisturbed it would be replaced by a hardwood forest. **Climax. (d)** The eastern deciduous forest shown here will persist over many centuries unless disturbed by fire, storm, or human activities.

b

c

d

On rangelands where climax grasses have the greatest forage value, the range manager attempts to work out grazing systems and levels of stocking that will best perpetuate the climax. Elsewhere, successional grasses may have greater value as forage, and a different system of grazing management will be needed to suppress the climax and maintain the successional forms. In wildlife management it is found that many of the valuable species of game animals are not climax forms, and hence the wildlife manager may be interested in suppression of the climax through the use of fire, cutting, or some other technique that will maintain the necessary level of disturbance. Thus, it can be seen that in many types of wild-land management a knowledge of biotic succession is essential.

The interplay of vegetation and the disturbing factors of the environment become vital also in the management of national parks, scientific reserves, or areas set aside for the protection of endangered species. Overprotection may become as lethal as no protection when the goal is to maintain a community or species that has evolved in response to the continued presence of environmental disturbance.

LIMITING FACTORS

The human environment, whether in a natural state or in one greatly modified by human activity, is composed of complex arrangements of matter and energy and is maintained by the interactions that occur among them. Activity within it is ceaseless as energy and materials flow through food chains. Change is also ceaseless, whether it be the relatively rapid change represented by the growth and death of individuals and populations, by the processes of biotic succession, or the slow change represented by the evolution of new races and species of organisms. In some places we accelerate the pace of change, sometimes to our own detriment; but even in the absence of people change goes on.

In the environment, life is distinguished by growth, mobility, and reproduction, among other qualities. Every existing species tends to increase in numbers, to spread to new and suitable environments, to increase again there, and spread farther. Growth in individual size or in numbers of a population continues usually until some external factor of the environment causes it to cease, although in the human species and some others, self-imposed limitation on growth of populations may occur before external factors bring this limitation. A tree will cease to grow when water or an essential soil chemical ceases to be available in minimum quantity. A population of trees will cease to increase in numbers when the tree seeds encounter conditions unsuitable for their germination or for the growth of the new seedling. An animal population will cease to grow when there is no longer adequate food, water, and shelter for the sustenance of individuals, or where weather or other environmental factors result in conditions unsuitable to survival of individuals of that species. Whatever limits the growth in size of an individual or in numbers of a population is known as a *limiting factor* to that individual or population. The ecological principle of limiting factors is stated by E. P. Odum (1972) as follows: "The presence and success of an organism or a group of organisms depends upon a complex of conditions. Any condition that approaches or exceeds the limits of tolerance is said to be a limiting condition or a limiting factor." This concept is one of the oldest in ecology and traces its origin to the chemist Justus Liebig in 1840. Liebig, who studied the effect of chemical nutrients on plant growth, first stated this concept as "growth of a plant is dependent on the amount of foodstuff which is presented to it in minimum quantity"—a statement that became known as *the law of the minimum*.

The concept of limiting factors, combined with a knowledge that the earth is limited in size and in its supplies of energy and materials, leads to the obvious, but sometimes overlooked, conclusion that growth and expansion must have an end. No species, including man, can expand its population or its consumption of resources indefinitely. Any species, including man, will be better off individually if its growth is limited through its own behavior before the time when environmental limiting factors (shortages in necessities, for example) begin to take effect.

Limiting factors can be divided into two categories: physical and biological. Physical factors that limit population growth would include factors of climate and weather, the absence of water or presence of an excess of water, the availability of essential nutrients, the suitability of the terrain, and so on. Biological factors involve competition, predation, parasitism, disease, and other interactions between or within a species that are limiting to growth. In the extreme environments of the world, physical factors are generally limiting. These would include the very cold or very dry terrestrial environments or, for land organisms, the very wet environments. They also include most of the deep-water areas of the lakes and oceans of the world. Droughts, floods, unseasonable cold, extreme cold, or the absence of light or of nutrients are among the factors that limit populations in such environments. In the more optimum environments of the world (the warmer, more humid environments) biological factors more often are limiting. In such environments, complex predator–prey relationships, balances with parasites or disease organisms, and competition for light, soil minerals, or water among species with similar requirements are most frequently limiting to population growth. Thus fish populations in cold mountain lakes are most frequently limited by water temperature and the availability of chemical nutrients. Low temperatures inhibit biological activity and thus prevent the growth of plankton and of insect populations upon which the fish would feed. The low availability of chemical nutrients inhibits the growth of these organisms during the period when temperatures are suitable to growth. Fish populations are therefore small in numbers. On the other hand, in warm ponds fish populations may grow to a point of great abundance where competition among them not only prevents individuals from reaching large size but inhibits further growth of the population.

Limiting factors may further be classified into those whose operations are dependent upon the density (the number of individuals per unit of area) of the population and those that have no relation to density (Kovda et al., 1970). The *density-dependent* factors are those that increase in their intensity, that have greater effects, or that affect more individuals as the population increases in density. Thus the availability of food—grass and other herbs—may be a limiting factor to the increase in numbers of domestic cattle in a pasture. The higher the density of cattle, the less grass there is per cow and the greater number of cows suffer from food shortage. By contrast, a flood sweeping through the pasture would be a *density-independent* limiting factor. It would wipe out all the cows whether there were two or a hundred in the area.

Density-dependent factors usually hold the greatest interest to students of population because of their more general and constant operation. They are usually the factors that set absolute limits to growth, that determine the number of individuals that can be supported—the carrying capacity of the area. They are the factors that operate to decrease the individual well-being in a population that approaches the limits or carrying capacity of its environment. In crowded human populations in many parts of the world we see such density-dependent factors in operation.

SELECTIVE PROCESSES, HABITATS, AND NICHES

Over long periods of time species evolve through natural selection and develop characteristics adapted to particular kinds of environments, known as *habitats,* and to particular ways of living within those habitats that lead to their occupancy of distinctive *ecological niches.* Each species has its niche. No two species can occupy the same niche. An oak forest habitat may support a large number of insect-eating bird species, but each species will feed on particular insects in particular ways. Crevice feeders such as nuthatches and creepers will seek insects hidden in tree bark. Those deeper inside the bark will be available only to woodpeckers. Warblers, vireos, and chickadees will look for insects among the leaves and twigs, but not in the same places or not for the same kinds of insects. Thus each has not only its preferred habitat, but its particular way of feeding, nesting, and raising young. Each has its niche. These may overlap to some extent, but complete overlap would put the two species in total competition, and over time the pressure of natural selection on the two populations would favor the most efficient or best-adapted species.

Some species occupy wide niches, meaning they are generalists who can survive on a great variety of foods or tolerate a number of different habitat conditions. Others are specialist with narrow feeding habits, but great ability to exploit those food sources. Some species, the pioneers of succession, have the ability to quickly colonize new areas and to reproduce rapidly in such areas. Others, more characteristic of climax conditions, are slow to colonize and may have slow rates of population increase, but are efficient users of their particular niche and are able to maintain it against competitors.

These two types of species have been termed "r" and "K" selected species by MacArthur and Wilson (1967): *In an environment with no crowding (r selection) genotypes which harvest the most food (even if wastefully) will rear the largest families and be most fit. Evolution here favors productivity. At the other extreme, in a crowded area (K selection), genotypes which can at least replace themselves with a small family at the lowest food level will win, the food density being lowered so that large families cannot be fed. Evolution here favors efficiency of conversion of food into offspring—there must be no waste.*

The symbol r stands for the potential rate of population increase, the symbol K, for carrying capacity. Species of the r-selected group produce many seeds, lay many eggs, have large litters, breed often, mature early. K-selected species may have few young, breed less often, mature late, but can maintain stable populations when their numbers approach the carrying capacity of their environments. It follows that the r-selected group includes many we consider weeds or pests—dandelions, tar weeds, rats, mice, ground squirrels. Of the K-selected group we now find many to be endangered species—condors, rhinos, whales. The conservation and management of the two types must vary: the r-selected group can be exploited for a sustainable yield with confidence that they will reproduce and recover, but the K-selected group must be managed with care, since they have limited ability to bounce back if their numbers are depleted (Brewer, 1979).

SOURCES

Brewer, Richard, 1979. *Principles of ecology.* W. B. Saunders, Philadelphia.

Broecker, W. S., 1970. Man's oxygen reserves. *Science* 168:1537–1538.

Fraser Darling, F. and R. F. Dasmann, 1969. The ecosystem view of human society. *Impact of science on society.* Vol. 19. UNESCO, Paris, pp. 109–122.

Kovda, Viktor, et al., 1970. Contemporary scientific concepts relating to the biosphere. *Use and conservation of the biosphere.* Natural Resources Research, X, UNESCO, Paris.

Lovelock, J. E., 1982. *Gaia. A new look at life on earth.* Oxford, New York.

MacArthur, Robert H. and Edward O. Wilson, 1967. *The theory of island biogeography.* Princeton University Press, Princeton, New Jersey.

Machta, L. and E. Hughes, 1970. Atomspheric oxygen in 1967 to 1970. *Science* 168:1582–1584.

Odum, Eugene P., 1972. *Fundamentals of ecology.* W. B. Saunders, Philadelphia.

CHAPTER
5

THE
BIOTIC
REGIONS

INTRODUCTION

To understand the complex relationships between people and environment, we must know the different kinds of environments that have provided the setting for human activities. These range from ones in which conditions for human life are near optimum and in which humanity has thrived, to those that are marginal for human existence and within which, even with modern technology, the numbers of people are few. In this chapter the major biotic regions are examined. These are areas between which plant and animal life, soils, and climate vary to a marked degree. They have provided settings within which human history has taken shape. Since people first appeared on earth the same general regions have been present, from arctic tundra to tropical forest. Although the boundaries of these regions have shifted as climates have changed, their general locations on earth have not changed much during human history.

In developing as a species, the human race first learned to adapt to conditions of life within the various biotic regions, avoiding those that were too rigorous. Eventually populations evolved that were able to withstand or even thrive within the more difficult biotic regions: the Eskimos of the Arctic, the Bushmen of the African deserts, the Indians of the high Andes, and the Pygmies of the Congo forests. Often these people became poorly fitted to survive elsewhere. With increasing technology and control over natural forces, people have learned to modify the biotic regions, seeking to make them more favorable to human existence. Sometimes, however, they have made them less favorable through failure to understand the natural principles under which they operate.

Over much of the earth today, new environments of agricultural or urban forms have displaced the original ecosystems. But an irrigated desert is still within a desert region, and an Arctic city must be adapted to the stringencies of Arctic life. Any major change in the environment has been, and is, accompanied by great risks, unless there is adequate understanding of ecological processes. In the past many changes were accompanied by local disasters. Today, in a heavily populated and closely knit world, we can no longer afford major failures. When we replace complex natural processes with human simplifications we must be prepared to exercise the greatest human skills in order to keep the environment healthy and productive.

There are great differences in the productivity and habitability of the various biotic regions of earth. These differences largely result from the interaction of two climatic factors, temperature and precipitation, with the geology and physiography of the earth. In the water areas of the earth, another factor, light, becomes very important. A cliff face or an active volcano will not support much life no matter how favorable the climate may be. A flat plain with an abundance of chemical nutrients will not support much life if it is too cold, too hot, or too dry. The depths of the ocean will not produce much in the way of living matter because green plants cannot grow in the absence of light.

Balances between temperature and precipitation are of significance in determining the suitability of an area for living organisms. Temperature determines the rate at which evaporation takes place, and consequently the amount of moisture that can remain in the soil available for plant growth. It also determines whether water will exist in a solid or a liquid state. The Antarctic continent and most of Greenland are relatively lifeless because they are too cold. The balance between temperature and precipitation in these places is such that both are almost completely covered by hundreds of feet of glacial ice. Although these areas have unusual scientific interest (and some potential for future use), they have as yet been little used. At the other extreme, much of the Sahara Desert is inhospitable to life because it is too hot and dry. Evaporation removes much of the rain that falls, and little falls. Only where water can be made available is it possible for such desert regions to support human populations.

In between the areas of extreme climatic or extreme physiography are a great variety of natural areas, a remarkable diversity of climates, geological formations, and biological materials. These constitute our original heritage, the diversified Earth on which we evolved. Despite our accelerated dissipation of these riches, this diversity of environments remains part of the legacy that we enjoy today and can pass on to future generations. This includes the major ecosystems or biotic regions of the earth (Figs. 5.1 to 5.5).

The climax, end product of biotic succession, and the later successional stages are strongly influenced by the climate, soils, and other physical characteristics of a region. As environments vary, so does vegetation and animal life. Hence, if the major natural climax communities of the earth are mapped, the climate and soil regions and thus the major ecosystems are also mapped. A desert in Africa is characterized by vegetation, soils, and climate that more closely resemble those of a desert in South America than they do those of an equatorial forest in Africa. Tropical rain forests, too, are relatively similar between Africa, Latin America, and Asia, although the species that compose them may differ. Grasslands in North America present opportunities for human exploitation, difficulties for human occupancy, and penalties for unwise land use similar to those of grasslands in Asia.

CLASSIFICATION OF COMMUNITIES AND ECOSYSTEMS

The great variety of life on earth does not lend itself to easy categorization. Sometimes the differences between natural communities are sharp

Fig. 5.1
Major biomes of Australia.

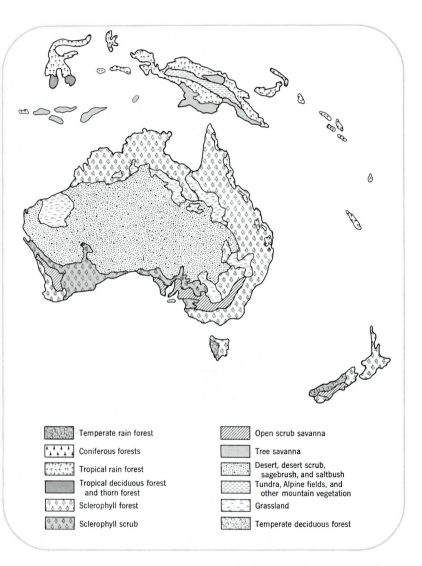

Temperate rain forest

Coniferous forests

Tropical rain forest

Tropical deciduous forest
and thorn forest

Sclerophyll forest

Sclerophyll scrub

Open scrub savanna

Tree savanna

Desert, desert scrub,
sagebrush, and saltbush

Tundra, Alpine fields, and
other mountain vegetation

Grassland

Temperate deciduous forest

and obvious, as when you leave the edge of a forest and enter a meadow. More often the differences are blurred, one type of forest grading into another through gradual loss of some species and the gain of others. How best to classify these communities is a question that cannot be answered except with reference to the purpose of the classification.

Ecosystems are usually named in accordance with their biotic communities—the exceptions being those such as cliff faces or barren deserts, which support little life. Biotic communities on land are usually named from their dominant vegetation—particular kinds of forest, grassland, or shrub. On sea, where animals are attached to the substrate, and many of the plants float around, communities are named from their dominant animals—coral reefs, mussel beds.

It is important to learn the difference between vegetation and flora. Vegetation refers to the appearance or life form of the plants that dominate a particular area. Vegetation classifications are most familiar: forests, woodlands, savannas, grasslands. The flora of an area is a list of the species that occur in the area, regardless of their appearance or life form or which species may dominate the scene. Some classifications of communities are based on the structure (life form, density, coverage) of the vegetation. Others are based on the dominant flora (a spruce–hemlock association, an oak–pine community). Most classifications are to some extent hybrids (pine–oak forest, sedge–rush marsh, chamise chaparral).

The most commonly used broad system of community classification for identifying the major climax communities of the world is the biome system, developed originally by Clements and Shelford (1939). This is particularly useful in that it relates the prevailing dominant climax vegetation (e.g., spruce–fir forest), the regional climate that permits the development of that kind of forest (subarctic, continental), and the characteristic soil type (podzol) that has developed under the influence of

Fig. 5.2
Major biomes of Asia.

Fig. 5.3
Major biomes of North America.

Legend:
- Temperate rain forest
- Coniferous forests
- Tropical rain forest
- Tropical deciduous forest and thorn forest
- Sclerophyll forest
- Sclerophyll scrub
- Open scrub savanna
- Tree savanna
- Desert, desert scrub, sagebrush, and saltbush
- Tundra, Alpine fields, and other mountain vegetation
- Grassland
- Temperate deciduous forest

that climate and vegetation. Associated with the vegetation are certain widespread forms of animal life (e.g., spruce–moose biome). The following descriptions are of the principal biomes of the world:

WORLD BIOMES

TUNDRA   In the far north of America and Eurasia is one of the more formidable biotic regions. This area, known as the tundra, is one of long winters and short summers. Winters are extremely cold. Summers have moderate to warm temperatures. Precipitation comes mostly as snow and is sufficiently low for the area to be characterized as an Arctic desert. It is preserved from desertlike qualities by the low temperatures and consequent low evaporation rates. Thus, despite the low precipitation, in summer the soils are waterlogged in surface layers. Below the surface of the ground the tundra has a layer of permanently frozen ground, the permafrost. Summers are not long enough for complete thawing to take place.

In such an environment organisms have difficulties. Plants are low growing and thus are protected from extreme cold by the winter mantle of snow. Woody plants are dwarfed or prostrate. Most of the vegetation is grass, sedge, or lichen. All of the plants are adapted to completing their life processes in the short summers: leaves must grow quickly; flowers, fruit, and seed must be produced before the winter cold returns. Summer is a time of great activity.

Animal life is of two kinds: those active or present only in summer and those active through the year. Among the summer forms are vast numbers of migratory birds, including a high percentage of the world's waterfowl. Present also are swarms of insects, which pass the winter in egg or larval state and emerge to grow, feed, and reproduce during the period of plant growth. Many mammals also emerge from hibernation or push northward in migration from the edge of the forest to join the mass of animal life feeding on the burgeoning summer vegetation. The hardy permanent residents—musk ox, caribou, Arctic fox, wolf, polar

Fig. 5.4
Major biomes of South America.

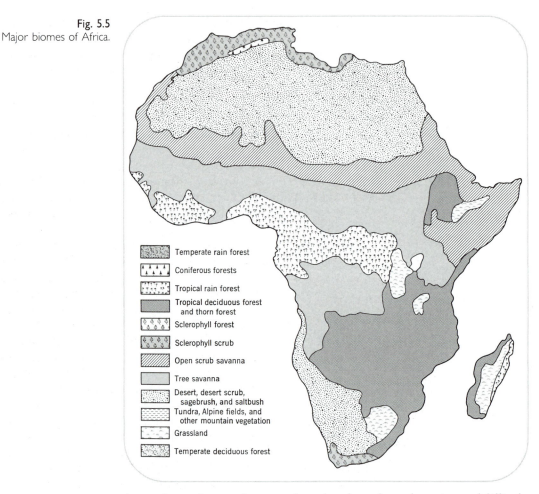

Fig. 5.5
Major biomes of Africa.

Temperate rain forest
Coniferous forests
Tropical rain forest
Tropical deciduous forest
  and thorn forest
Sclerophyll forest
Sclerophyll scrub
Open scrub savanna
Tree savanna
Desert, desert scrub,
  sagebrush, and saltbush
Tundra, Alpine fields, and
  other mountain vegetation
Grassland
Temperate deciduous forest

bear—lay on layers of summer fat to last them through a winter of difficult foraging.

Only a few peoples in the past have been able to adapt themselves to the tundra. In America, the Eskimo tribes developed the cultural skills necessary for survival. Before western culture affected them they were divided into two main ecological groups: the caribou hunters, who depended on the vast herds of caribou for food and clothing, and the coastal dwellers, who relied on the ever-present marine life of the Arctic seas. Both groups adapted to the climate, concentrating their activities in the summer months and resisting the winter storms in weatherproof dwellings. In northern Europe, the Lapps, with their domesticated reindeer herds, also learned how to live in a tundra environment. Compared with most other biotic regions, the tundra is today less exploited and modified, although the effects of civilization are now being felt on both animal life and vegetation. Since this is a highly fragile ecosystem, it is susceptible to serious damage from even minor human modifications.

The tundra ecosystem forms a circumpolar belt across North America, Europe, and Asia and reaches southward in modified form along the higher mountain ranges. It is less developed in the Southern hemisphere, where large land masses do not occur within the appropriate latitudes.

BOREAL FOREST

South from the tundra lies timberline, the northern edge of a broad belt of forest extending southward in America into the northeastern United States and in Eurasia down through Scandinavia, Russia, and Siberia. This northern forest is characterized by evergreen, coniferous trees, mostly spruce and fir (p. 92). The region has a climate slightly warmer and with heavier precipitation than the tundra. In summer, the warmest months have enough heat to eliminate the permafrost. Without this ice barrier, tree roots can penetrate more deeply, and soils can be more fully developed.

Coniferous forest vegetation helps determine the character of the soil. The leaves and litter that fall from conifers decay slowly in the cold climate and upon decaying form acid products that are carried into the soil by rain or melting snow. This mildly acid solution dissolves and leaches out of the top layer of the soil minerals that are important for abundant plant growth. The remaining topsoil tends to be sandy, light gray or whitish in color, and relatively infertile. The deeper layers of soil, in which some of the leached minerals are deposited, become rich in iron and aluminum compounds and darker in color. Such a soil is called a *podzol*. It is of poor quality for general agricultural use.

The native animal life of this region, like that of the tundra, is seasonal in abundance. In summer, migratory birds move in to breed, and insects abound. In winter, only a few permanent residents, moose, woodland caribou, lynx, fisher, wolverine, snowshoe hare, and spruce grouse among them, remain to face the period of food scarcity.

Much of this region is sparsely inhabited. The fur trapper has led the way in settlement, followed by the lumberman. Only in restricted areas where local conditions have permitted more fertile soils to develop has agriculture been successful. Most of the inhabitants are dependent in whole or in part upon the forests for their livelihood. Forest fires, often man-caused, are an important factor. Recently, however, mineral exploitation and water development have had major impacts.

The boreal-forest ecosystem, like the tundra, forms a broad transcontinental belt in North America and Eurasia, with stringers extending along the high mountain ranges to the south (p. 102). Like the tundra, and for the same reasons, it is poorly developed in the continents of the Southern Hemisphere, although the forests of Tierra del Fuego and southern Chile have much in common with it.

DECIDUOUS FOREST

Farther south, in the eastern part of America, Central Europe, and eastern Asia, one encounters a third major ecosystem, the broad-leaved deciduous forest. In this area the predominant trees are the traditionally familiar oak, maple, hickory, beech, linden, and other hardwood trees (p. 92). Unlike the northern conifers, most of these trees shed their leaves in late fall and pass the winter in a bare and dormant state.

In the deciduous forest region precipitation is relatively heavy and well distributed throughout the year. The summer rainfall and warm weather provide for abundant plant growth. In general, summers are warm and humid and winters cool to cold with heavy snowfall in the northern part of the region. Southward, as the area of cold winters is left behind, the vegetation gradually changes into the broad-leaved evergreen forest typical of the subtropics.

In primitive times the hardwood forests of America were widespread between the Atlantic and the Mississippi. From early times, however, the influence of people has helped to keep portions of the forest open. Animal life was once abundant and consisted of a greater number of permanently resident species than are found further north. Characteristic of this region are the white-tailed deer, ruffed grouse, cottontail rabbit, red fox, bobwhite quail, fox squirrel, and wild turkey. All played an important role in the pioneer history of the United States.

The forest vegetation determined the soil. Temperate-zone forest litter, whether coniferous or broad-leaved, tends to form mild acids on decomposition. These acids, carried into the soil by the abundant rainfall, have a leaching effect. In the deciduous forest, however, because of the greater amounts of litter deposited and the more abundant mineral salts contained in the leaves, the results of the leaching are less severe than in the coniferous forest. There is a constant addition of organic material and basic salts to the topsoil that help to maintain its fertility. Furthermore, the soils often support an abundant fauna of insects and other invertebrates that keep nutrients in circulation and the soils well aerated. Nitrogen-fixing bacteria and other microorganisms help to keep fertility at a higher level. The luvisols or *gray-brown podsolic soils* of the northern part of the region and the acrisols or *red and yellow podsolic soils* of the southern part are often initially fertile and readily worked when they are cleared for agriculture. Without proper care, however, they do not stand up well to continued crop production.

The deciduous forest region, more than most others, has been drastically modified by human activity. Their ecosystem has seen the growth and flowering of civilization in Europe and in China. Little remains of the once extensive forests of the Far East, and in Europe they have been widely replaced by agricultural and urban lands. In the United States, considerable regrowth has taken place as marginal agricultural lands have been abandoned, but of the old forests few areas remain that have not been changed by human action.

GRASSLANDS In every continent a grassland region is to be found lying between the forest and the desert and with climates intermediate between the two. It is a region in which relatively low rainfall is normal. Summers are warm and in favorable years moist; winters are cool to cold with snow in the north and rain in the south. The rainfall, however, is erratic or cyclic. Wet cycles and dry cycles alternate. Droughts may last for several years, causing major changes in natural vegetation and even more severe changes where the land is used for grazing or agriculture.

The vegetation is dominated by grasses. Tall grasses predominate near the better watered forest border in the *prairie* community. Shorter, sodforming grasses dominate toward the drier desert side in a region known as *steppe* (p. 36). The grasses of the climax are perennial, living for several to many years. Annual grasses, which die back to seed each year, are characteristic of disturbed areas.

The climate and grassland vegetation produce grassland soils that differ markedly from forest soils. The topsoil is usually dark in color and rich in organic matter. Minerals are not leached out of the soil because of the more limited rainfall and the abundant humus. The subsoil is usually rich in lime, whereas forest soils are normally lime deficient. On the scale of pH, or acidity, grassland soils are neutral or on the alkaline side, whereas the soils of forested regions are typically acid.

Animal life of the grasslands normally includes herds of grazing animals, the bison and pronghorn of North America and the numerous antelopes of Africa and Asia being examples. Feeding on these are large carnivores, wolves and their relatives and in Africa the big cats. A variety of mice, ground-dwelling birds, and smaller predators that feed on them are to be found. The abundance of animal life reflects the richness and fertility of the soil.

Grasslands, like the deciduous forest, have long been occupied by humanity—first by hunters of the herds of big game, later by nomadic herders with flocks of sheep or cattle, and finally by farmers with their crops of cereal grains. The fertile soil has favored agriculture since the time when man developed a plow capable of turning the tough, grassland sod. There is considerable support for the idea that extensive grasslands are a result of human interaction with the climate, soil, and vegetation. Fires, caused by people, have occurred over thousands of years. These tend to favor grassland and push back the boundaries of forests.

DESERTS   The dry areas of the world vary considerably in both the amount and the dependability of the rainfall that they receive. Some authorities consider all of those regions that receive an average of 10 inches of rainfall or less per year to be deserts. This includes the extremely dry areas such as the deserts of Peru and Chile, where no vegetation grows, and places such as the northern Great Basin region of the United States, where vegetation is relatively abundant.

In the United States there are two main desert regions, the high desert or Great Basin sagebrush region, which extends between the Rocky Mountains and the Sierra Nevada, and the low deserts, Mojave, Color-adan, and Sonoran deserts, which lie to the south of the Great Basin. In

a

b

92

c

d

THE WORLDS BIOTIC REGIONS (I)

Boreal forest. (a) White spruce taiga in Alaska. **Broadleaf deciduous forest. (b)** Beech forest in Belgium. **Temperate rain forest. (c)** Sitka spruce forest, Olympic Peninsula, Washington. **Mediterranean vegetation. (d)** Chaparral in California.

the Great Basin the vegetation is characterized by sagebrush and other low-growing shrubs, which forms an open cover over the plains, and by the small conifers, junipers, and pinyon pines, which form an open woodland at higher elevations. The low-desert region is an area of desert scrub, where widely spaced creosote bushes are the most common vegetation, giving way in places to various species of cactus (p. 98).

In both desert regions the vegetation is drought resistant, with various adaptations to prevent or withstand water loss during the long, dry season. It is also adapted to complete its growth and reproduction during the periods when soil moisture is available.

Animal life, like plant life, is adapted to dryness. Animals avoid the heat and drought by being nocturnally active, using sheltered burrows, or remaining in cover in the hot, dry season in the vicinity of the few permanent streams and water holes. Desert rodents often have physiological adaptations that permit them to get along with a minimum of drinking water. Some receive all necessary water from their food and avoid water loss by excreting a highly concentrated urine.

The arid climate and sparse vegetation are reflected in the desert soils. With little leaching there is a minimum loss of soil minerals. With sparse vegetation there is little addition of organic material to the soil, and therefore it may be deficient in nitrogen. Where minerals are in a proper balance and not concentrated in toxic quantities, desert soils are potentially highly fertile when water can be made available.

Deserts have played an important role in human history. The geography of western Asia and North Africa is such that many of the most fertile lands are located on river bottoms surrounded by arid desert. Western civilization was born on the desert edge, and through history man has had important ecological effects on the desert. Through turning his flocks of livestock out to graze on the desert vegetation or on the grasslands at the desert edge, man has changed and modified the deserts and has spread desertlike conditions into former grassland areas.

Natural as opposed to man-made deserts occupy much of central and western Australia, extending in a broad band from the Sahara in Africa, through Arabia eastward to India. Smaller areas occur in southwest Africa and South America, in addition to the major North American area already described.

Abuse of the desert vegetation through overgrazing by livestock or cutting of shrubs for fuel can be extremely long lasting because the combination of high temperatures and low rainfall is unfavorable to the establishment of seedlings.

MEDITERRANEAN

On most continents there is a relatively small area with a climate similar to that found around the Mediterranean Sea. Here there are winters with moderate rainfall but little snow and summers that are warm and dry. In North America this is the climate of much of California; elsewhere it is found in Chile, south Australia, South Africa, and in the sections of Europe, Asia, and Africa adjoining the Mediterranean Sea.

The most common type of vegetation in this region, although not always climax, is the dense brushfield dominated by medium-height evergreen shrubs. This is known in California as *chaparral* and in Europe as *maquis* (p. 93). It is often interspersed with grassland, tree or shrub savanna, or in more sheltered areas with broad-leaved evergreen forest. In California and the Mediterranean region, the evergreen live oaks predominate in this forest and in shrub form in the chaparral. In Australia, *Eucalyptus* forest and scrub dominates the Mediterranean biotic region.

In latitude, the Mediterranean ecosystem lies between the desert and deciduous forest or, in the Americas and Australia, between desert and temperate rain forest. Its location in Europe has made it the setting for much of the early development of western civilization, which spread from desert river valleys to Mediterranean regions and from there to the deciduous forest.

OTHER TEMPERATE BIOMES

Several other important biotic regions exist in the temperate latitudes, occupying smaller areas than those previously described. One, which can be called *transition coniferous forest,* occupies a zone in the mountains lying between the southward extensions of the boreal forest and the warmer chaparral, grassland, or desert of lower elevations (Fig. 5.6). Pine trees of various species characterize the climax, or near climax, vegetation of this forest. Transition forest occurs latitudinally in some

Fig. 5.6
Zonation of vegetation on mountain ranges. (a) Tropical mountains. (Data from Richards, 1952. Genera are typical of Malayan-New Guinea region.) (b) Temperate-zone mountains with vegetation typical of southwestern United States.

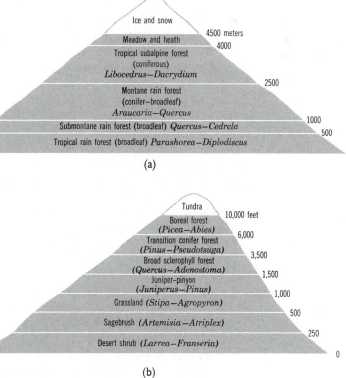

(a)

(b)

areas as a belt separating the boreal forest of spruce and fir from the deciduous forest. In the Lakes States and New England it occurs in this role.

On the northwestern coast of North America is an area of high rainfall, well distributed throughout the year, and mild temperatures—a climate of the marine west coast type. This favors the development of an unusually tall, dense, and luxuriant forest, the *temperate rain forest*. In North America, this is dominated by redwood, douglas fir, and other giant conifers (p. 93). In other continents a similar forest type is dominated by the laurel-leaved hardwood trees. Similar climates and vegetation are found in southern Chile, the South Island of New Zealand, and southeastern Australia.

TROPICAL BIOMES
The most favorable climate on earth for the development of the greatest variety of organic life is to be found in the rain forest region of the tropics, and in the tropics also is to be found one of the least favorable climates for life, exemplified by the virtually rainless deserts of Peru. Tropical rain forest climates have year-round rainfall, without periods when the soil dries out, and temperatures that are always favorable to a high level of plant and animal activity. There are essentially no climatic factors limiting to plant growth. The tropical rain forests are dominated by an unusual variety of broad-leaved evergreen trees—fig and mahogany may be familiar examples—of which dozens of different species often occur in a single acre and many acres may have to be searched to find a second specimen of a particular species of tree.

The trees in turn support a variety of plants that can survive without contact with the soil, known as epiphytes or perched plants. Orchids, bromeliads, lianas, ferns, mosses, and lichens are in this category. Dense climax forest has a compact, several-layered canopy that allows little light to penetrate to the ground. The forest floor, therefore, is often relatively free of undergrowth and usually supports little in the way of large animal life. The forest canopy, however, will provide a home for a diversity of birds, insects, arboreal mammals, and other animals that may exceed the great diversity of plant species.

Rain forests that have been opened up, either by natural causes or human activities, quickly grow into a dense, second-growth successional forest, the "impenetrable jungle" of tropical travelers. The prevalence of such dense, second-growth jungle in today's tropics indicates the extent of human disturbance. Similar jungles occur naturally on the edges of natural clearings, such as stream courses. Since most explorers in the lowland tropics traveled by boat, their accounts of the density of the vegetation were biased by what they saw at the edge of the rivers (p. 99).

Tropical rain forest soils develop under the canopy of trees and are enriched by the continual addition of rapidly decaying leaves and litter. The high rainfall and temperatures, however, favor rapid oxidation of organic matter and leaching of minerals from the soil in areas from which the forest has been cleared. Tropical soils therefore require careful treatment and protection if they are to be maintained in agricultural use. Many of them are poorly suited to agriculture.

Temperate zone writers, in describing the tropics, often overemphasize the importance of the lowland rain forests, since these are the most spectacular and in many ways the most different of the various tropical communities. However, the tropics have a greater variety of biotic communities than all other areas on earth. High on tropical mountains we encounter coniferous forests resembling those of the temperate zone, oak forests similar to those in eastern United States, as well as purely tropical vegetation such as the puña and paramo of the higher mountains, which are unlike the vegetation of temperate lands (Fig. 5.6).

In those tropical areas where a wet and dry season alternate, a different vegetation replaces the rain forest in the lowlands. This, the raingreen or monsoon forest, is deciduous, the trees shedding their leaves during the dry season. In still drier regions a thorn forest or thorn scrub will replace monsoon forest. With increasing aridity this, in turn, gives way to desert. Leslie Holdridge (1947), working from Costa Rica, has listed 37 different major biotic communities that may occur in any tropical region that displays a wide range in rainfall and altitude. Each of these communities is as distinct and recognizable as the major communities of temperate regions. Compared with the temperate zone, however, the tropics have been rarely studied. They represent a major area for future research.

Until recently, human influence on the tropics and its biota was slight. With increasing density of human populations, however, and the spread of technology, no large tropical area is any longer secure from disturbance. Without a major effort to preserve representative tropical areas, it is likely that many of the more fascinating living communities on earth will disappear before we know very much about them.

SAVANNA A glance at a vegetation map of the world (Figs. 5.1 to 5.5) will show that large areas in both tropical and temperate regions are covered by vegetation that has not thus far been described in this chapter—savanna. Savanna, sometimes known as parkland or woodland-grass in temperate countries, is vegetation consisting of scattered trees and shrubs, or groves and thickets, in an otherwise grass-covered region (p. 99). It is of natural occurrence along the boundary of forest and grassland where local differences in climate or soil favor an interspersion of vegetation. In such situations also there is normally a greater variety and abundance of animal life than is to be found in either forest or grassland.

Unlike forest or grassland there is no climate or soil that typifies savanna regions, although much savanna occurs within the region characterized by rain-green tropical forest or thorn forest. The great expanse of savanna over the surface of the earth is now believed to be caused

THE WORLD'S BIOTIC REGIONS (II)

(a) Arizona cactus desert. (b) Tropical mountain forest in Nepal. (c) Tropical savanna, Serengeti, Tanzania. (d) Lowland rain forest, Brazil.

c

d

largely by the activities of people and domestic animals. Humans seem to prefer interspersion of vegetation and create it wherever they go. Fire and grazing have been techniques used to open the forest and let the grassland enter. Grazing, irrigation, and planting are techniques for spreading woody vegetation into otherwise grassy areas.

Tropical savannas are the home of the great game herds that once roamed widely in Africa and Asia and are still to be found in areas where they have been protected. The enormous variety of wild mammals in the tropics of Africa has long attracted attention. Twenty or more species of large grazing and browsing mammals from elephants to antelope may occur in a single area, each adapted to feeding on or otherwise using different species of plants, or different kinds of vegetation. In addition to these larger creatures a variety of smaller mammals, or predators, and a profusion of species of birds and other kinds of animals will occur (Fraser Darling, 1960).

AQUATIC ECOSYSTEMS

The water surfaces of the earth occupy more than 70 percent of the total world area and support a great variety of living things. Since they are much more uniform than land areas in conditions favorable or unfavorable to life, however, they are not as amenable to classification. Classifications of aquatic environments are frequently based on major climatic differences, the amounts of dissolved chemicals, size and relative permanency of the body of water, and the depth of the water relative to the depth of light penetration. The greatest diversity of life is usually found on the edges of interfaces of land and water, the intertidal regions of seacoasts and estuaries, since here the widest range of physical environments will be encountered. By contrast, the open ocean is relatively homogeneous and shows much less diversity in forms of life (Odum, 1971).

Classification and characteristics of aquatic environments are discussed in Chapter 9. It is worth noting at this point, however, that the range in productivity of aquatic environments is as great as that encountered on land. The open oceans have sometimes been equated with the world's deserts in supporting and producing relatively little life. Cold freshwater lakes are also relatively barren. By contrast, warm ponds and estuaries teem with life and are the aquatic counterparts of warm humid forest areas on land.

ZONATION OF TERRESTRIAL ECOSYSTEMS

It is a law in physics that air temperature will decrease, in a stable air mass, as one moves upward in altitude. Measured in many places and averaged, or calculated from known physical relationships between temperature and pressure, it is found that temperature decreases approximately 3.5°F. for each 1000-foot increase in elevation. Thus a 10,000 foot mountain would, all other things being equal, be 35° cooler at its summit than at its base.

From this simple temperature rule one could expect a range of differences to exist in the vegetation on such a mountain. At the base there exist species requiring or tolerating warm conditions, while at the summit there are species requiring or tolerating cooler situations. Such differences can be generally observed (see Fig. 5.6 and p. 102).

Rainfall also varies as one moves up a mountain, however, and this complicates the situation. Mountains stand as barriers to air movement, and winds moving in off the ocean, for example, are forced to rise over coastal mountains. As air rises, it cools, and when it cools moisture condenses and rains (or other forms of precipitation) fall. On many coastal mountains, therefore, there is a range of precipitation from moderate at low elevations to a peak at medium elevations, decreasing again to the mountain peaks. On the lee side of the mountains, where air once more decends and becomes warmer, there is commonly a "rain shadow" or dry area within which little rain falls. The vegetation on mountain ranges responds as much to these differences in precipitation as to differences in temperature. The same elevation in a mountain range may, on its coastal side, support vegetation adapted to high rainfall and humidity, and on its lee side, support desertlike vegetation.

In some tropical areas it is less the prevailing wind direction than the effect of convectional currents that determines zonation of climate and vegetation. Heated air rises and as it does so, moisture condenses. Over many tropical mountains, cloud caps form and may rest much of the time throughout the year. Within the cloud region is constant high humidity and often heavy rainfall. In response to this, and to the leaching of nutrients from the soils associated with it, a "cloud forest" will develop, vegetation particularly adapted to this climatic condition.

Variations in climate and the resulting differences in soils and vegetation in mountains have long been observed and were described by Alexander von Humboldt (1849) early in the nineteenth century. Humboldt noted that changes observed as one gained altitude in the mountains resembled those observed by going northward in latitude. Still later, C. Hart Meriam, the first chief of the United States Bureau of Biological Survey, came out with his theory of life zones, which was based on the practical observation of zonation of vegetation in the mountains of the western United States (1898). His observations were accurate enough, and his life zone idea is useful, although his attempt to relate zonation to temperature is oversimplified. Merriam's altitudinal and latitudinal zones corresponded, and his highest zone in altitude and latitude is the arctic-alpine, the tundra. Below that his boreal zone, with his Canadian and Hudsonian subdivisions, corresponds with observed changes in biota both latitudinally in North America and altitudinally in western mountains. In his attempts to universalize his lower life zones, however, his system breaks down most badly, since moisture becomes far more important than temperature in determining the type of vegetation in warmer regions. One of the latest attempts at vegetation classification based on temperature characteristics is that of Leslie Holdridge (1947), working in

Zonation in Colorado Rockies showing subalpine forest and timberline with alpine tundra and bare rock at highest elevations.

the American tropics. His system, based on the relationship between temperature and precipitation, is much more closely in touch with reality than that of Merriam.

Although the broad similarities in life zones and latitudinal zones need to be emphasized, the differences must also be stressed. The Arctic, with its enormous extremes in day length, from total daylight in summer to total darkness in winter, cannot be equated with the high altitude tropics where day length is relatively constant throughout the year, and the impact of facets of solar radiation such as the total incidence of ultraviolet light is markedly different from the Arctic. The high altitude paramo, of tropical mountains, with its predominance in some areas of forms such as giant composites of genera represented at lower elevations by daisy-like herbs, is not found in polar regions.

The realities of zonation on mountains is readily observed. The explanation, however, is complex, and still not fully understood. High mountain ecosystems, like islands, are both unique and fragile. Like oceanic islands they are isolated one from the other and each becomes a center of the evolution of new species and forms not to be found in any other place. The impact of uncontrolled human use in these areas is not only destructive but often completely irremediable. We are in serious danger of losing complete ecosystems of great value before we have begun to fully describe them or have made any real progress toward understanding them.

BIOGEOGRAPHIC SYSTEMS

A knowledge of biomes and life zones will tell much about climate, soil, and the kind of vegetation one may expect to find in a particular area.

It will not tell you, necessarily, what species you can expect to find there. If you are interested in questions of species conservation, it is necessary to have a system of classification that refers to the actual distribution of species. Then you can seek to establish representative nature reserves, or other forms of protection, that will effectively protect the greatest diversity of species, as well as representative vegetation.

One of the earlier efforts to map and describe the distribution of biota was that of P. L. Sclater, who in 1858 classified the natural regions of the world on the basis of their bird faunas. His system was further developed on the basis of other animal species by Alfred Russell Wallace (1876). Wallace recognized that animal distribution was marked by marked differences between regions whose boundaries did not necessarily coincide with the boundaries of continents. Thus North America and northern Eurasia were more similar in species than were northern and southern Asia. Each of Wallace's defined regions represented a center of origin for many of the species that lived there. Similarities between regions resulted from interchange of species between them, over land bridges or other pathways, and frequently reflected the amount of continental drift that had taken place, separating lands that were once joined together. Major differences between regions reflected long periods of isolation.

Australia, cut off from the rest of the world by ocean barriers over millions of years, is the most distinctive in species. Its native animals consist mostly of marsupials (kangaroos, possums, wombats) and monotremes (echidna, platypus). The Oriental and African regions have many similarities including the presence in both of lions, leopards, elephants, rhinos, and great apes. They have been separate for long enough, however, so that each of these groups is represented by different species. The Neotropical and Nearctic regions have many differences, caused by isolation during most of the period when mammalian evolution was taking place, but also similarities resulting from the spread of species from one area into the other when the Panama land bridge emerged from the sea. Thus tapir and peccaries moved northward from Panama, whereas North American deer and mountain lion moved southward into the Neotropics. Wallace's faunal regions have been modified by Udvardy (1975), and the resultant classification is presented in table 5.1.

Following the example of Lee Dice (1943) and others in an attempt to find a system of classification useful for species conservation, I tried in 1972 and later to combine the concept of faunal and floral regions, characterized by marked taxonomic differences with the biome system. A working system of classification for the natural regions of the world was developed and further improved by Udvardy (1975) for use by UNESCO and the International Union for Conservation of Nature (IUCN). The result is a system of *biotic provinces* or *biogeographical provinces* that differ from each other in either the species of animals and plants or in their principal form of vegetation. The biotic provinces of North America (the Nearctic region) are shown in Table 5.2 and Figure 5.7. These are broad subdivisions, reflecting major biotic differences. To be more

TABLE 5.1   Biogeographic Realms

REALM	WALLACE'S TERMINOLOGY	AREA INCLUDED
Palaearctic	Palaearctic	Northern Asia, Europe and Mediterranean Africa
Nearctic	Nearctic	Northern North America (approx. to central Mexico)
Africotropical	Ethiopian	Sub-Saharan Africa
Indomalayan	Oriental	Indian subcontinent and southeast Asia through to Celebes and Sunda islands
Oceanian	—	Islands of South Pacific westward through New Guinea
Australian	Australian	Australia and Tasmania
Antarctic	—	Antarctica, sub-Antarctic islands, and New Zealand
Neotropical	Neotropical	Latin America, north approx. to central Mexico including West Indies

Source: Udvardy (1975).

useful further breakdown into biotic districts is needed, and for most provinces this work has not been done.

COMPLEXITY AND STABILITY

The terrestrial biotic regions of the earth show the effects of climatic gradients. Tropical rainforest climates support the most complex and varied plant and animal life. Moving out in the tropics along a gradient of decreasing rainfall or increasing evaporation, however, one encounters communities which are less complex and in which the numbers of species of plants and animals decrease to a low point in the tropical deserts. Similarly, moving north from the lowland rain forest climate of

TABLE 5.2   Biogeographic Provinces of Nearctic North America

1. Sitkan	12. Aleutian Islands
2. Oregonian	13. Alaskan tundra
3. Yukon taiga	14. Canadian tundra
4. Canadian taiga	15. Arctic archipelago
5. Eastern forest	16. Greenland tundra
6. Austroriparian	17. Arctic desert and icecap
7. Californian	18. Grasslands
8. Sonoran	19. Rocky Mountains
9. Chihuahuan	20. Sierra-Cascade
10. Tamaulipan	21. Madrean-Cordilleran
11. Great Basin	22. Great Lakes

Numbers refer to areas indicated on Figure 5.7.
Source: Uvardy (1975).

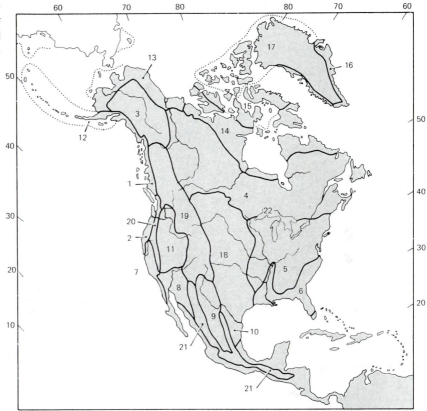

FIG. 5.7
Biogeographical provinces of the nearctic biogeographical realm (Udvardy, 1975).

the tropics along a temperature gradient, we would pass through subtropical rain forests, temperate rain forests, boreal forests, and tundra. Along this line also one passes from the most complex to the least complex biotic community, and the number of species of plants and animals would also decrease along this gradient. Thus, in the boreal forests we find the single species, white spruce, as a lone dominant in great areas of Canada and Alaska.

Within each climatic region, the climax communities will represent, usually, the most complex communities the climate and geology of the region can support; but the climaxes themselves are more simple and less varied in regions where climatic or geological factors are strongly limiting.

Complexity appears to be accompanied by stability in the sense that things do not change much from year to year. Tropical forest communities when undisturbed, are usually stable communities. They are relatively resistant to change. The numbers and arrangements of species within them vary little from month to month or year to year. By contrast, simple communities, whether of tundra or desert, are subject to regular and often violent changes in the relative abundance of species. The fluctuations of lemmings, a small Arctic rodent, are a legendary example of the instability of tundra populations. The changes in abundance of jackrabbits or mice in arid regions are well known. In the boreal forest, insect pests or diseases sometimes wipe out hundreds of square miles of trees. Locust plagues in dry regions do enormous damage. Similar outbreaks are rare in humid tropical communities, except where people have intervened.

People seek to simplify the complex so they can manage it. They depend for their livelihood on foods grown in artificially created, simplified ecosystems. Such simplification, however, can be dangerous, since it sets in motion all of the factors that contribute to instability in the normally simple communities of more rigorous natural environments. In the humid tropics, the presence of a great variety of naturally occurring species guarantees competition between species, predation of one species on another, parasitic relations between species, and other complicated interspecies relationships that keep each population under control and prevent any single species population from either increasing or decreasing greatly. When these interspecific controls are removed, as when a plantation of bananas, cacao, or oil palms is established, there is little to keep the pests or parasites feeding on these agricultural crops from becoming abundant. Similarly, in drier or colder regions, simplification of natural communities also permits the natural enemies of the introduced crop plants to flourish; however, climate offers some periodic control on the abundance of these species.

Plagues and pests have harried people through history, destroying crops and forcing them to engage in various forms of chemical or biological warfare in their own protection. Unless skillfully employed, however, such activities can make the situation worse, creating a more simple, less stable, more readily threatened system than the one that was endangered in the first place.

BIOMASS AND PRODUCTIVITY

Gradients in complexity and stability also represent gradients in the mass of living material a particular region will support (the *biomass*), and in the amount of new living material produced each year (*productivity*). Tropical rain forests support the greatest biomass or standing crop of living material per acre of square mile of any naturally occurring terrestrial community. Extremely dry or cold areas, deserts and tundra, vie for the distinction of supporting the lowest standing crop of living material per land acre.

Natural productivity varies also with the climatic and geological factors that influence complexity. The tropical rain-forest regions, with year-round growing seasons, are capable of producing more living material per acre per year than temperate forest regions where climate is seasonally limiting to plant growth. Temperate forests, however, with adequate rainfall, produce more plant material per acre than grasslands where seasonal drought restricts plant growth.

People have long had an interest in increasing productivity of plant crops and domestic animals. To some degree they have been able to improve on natural patterns through supplying nutrients, where these were in short supply, supplying water, or providing shelter against climatic factors. The highest yield of any land-based crop in biomass gain per acre per year, however, is in sugar cane grown in the humid tropics. In temperate regions, forest plantations are more productive in total biomass gain than are the grainfields that have replaced natural grasslands. In the Arctic, high crop production can take place only where soils and local climate can be modified, and in the desert only the presence of irrigation, which essentially creates a different local climate, makes possible abundant crop yields.

SOURCES

Clements, F. E. and V. Shelford, 1939. *Bioecology.* John Wiley, New York.

Dice, Lee R., 1943. *The biotic provinces of North America.* University of Michigan Press, Ann Arbor.

Fraser Darling, F., 1960. Wildlife husbandry in Africa. *Scientific American* 203:123–133.

Holdridge, L. R., 1947. Determination of world plant formations from simple climatic data. *Science* 105:367–368.

Humboldt, Alexander von, 1849. *Aspects of nature in different lands and different climates.* Lea & Blanchard, Philadelphia.

Merriam, C. Hart, 1898. *Life zones and crop zones of the United States.* U.S. Department of Agriculture, Biological Survey Bulletin 10, Washington, D.C.

Odum, Eugene P., 1971. *Fundamentals of ecology,* 3rd edition. W. B. Saunders, Philadelphia.

Sclater, P. L., 1858. On the general geographical distribution of the members of the class *Aves. Journal Proceedings of the Linnaean Society* (Zoology), 2:130–145.

Udvardy, Miklos, 1975. *A classification of the biogeographical provinces of the world.* IUCN Occasional Paper 18, Morges, Switzerland.

Wallace, Alfred Russell, 1876. *The geographical distribution of animals.* Macmillan, London.

CHAPTER 6

INCREASE AND MULTIPLY— THE POPULATION STORY

POPULATION GROWTH

In 1974 in Bucharest, Romania, representatives of most of the world's nation states met for the United Nations' conference on world population. Perhaps the most worthwhile feature of the conference is that it happened at all, since this implied some recognition that there was a phenomenon known as the "world population problem." For the most part, however, the conference provided, not a forum for rational discussion of the problem, as had been intended, but a platform from which mutual recrimination and denunciation could be launched. There are few subjects, if any, more fraught with emotion than the subject of human population growth and its possible limitation. In some quarters, mere mention of it brings out the worst in people. But the problem is real and will not go away if we pretend it is not there.

Throughout most of the world today there is an unprecedented growth in human numbers. This continuing increase not only intensifies all conservation problems, but nullifies many achievements of the past. Any type of rational management of the environment becomes more difficult as each new increment is added to the world's population. Each year during the 1980s between 75 and 90 million new people are being added to the total. With continued growth in population we face not only the loss of those values that contribute to the quality of living but ultimately the collapse of civilization in any form in which we have known it. Already it has meant the loss of many other species, and the rate of loss will increase. Any planning for conservation must take into account some method of limiting population growth, just as it must take into account means for the prevention of war between nations.

One thing is certain. Population growth of the magnitude we have seen in recent years will not continue. Either people will begin to die in greater numbers than any of us would care to contemplate, or they will learn to limit birth rates. There are no other ways. We are reaching the end of the line.

Yet this statement, which is true at a global level, obscures many realities. The question of population cannot be either addressed or solved globally. It is a local problem affecting people directly and intimately. For many of the world's ethnic groups there is indeed a population problem, but it is the reverse of the global problem. They are dying out, on the road to extinction. Some are being killed by their more powerful neighbors, some are being decimated by diseases brought from outside their own lands, some are seeing their habitat destroyed. Most of the remaining Indian nations of the Americas are under some sort of threat, and many are suffering from genocidal policies of the countries that claim sovereignty over their lands. In all the tropical world, hunter-gatherers and slash-and-burn agriculturalists are seeing their environment destroyed by forces from the industrialized world. For most of the peasant farmers of the Third World nations, and particularly for those who have drifted to the swollen urban ghettoes, the population problem is felt directly: they cannot obtain enough food or other necessities to maintain their health and well-being. For the middle and upper groups of the industrialized world, each new child added to the total population consumes from 20 to 40 times more of the world's resources than a child born to a Third World family. The demand to stop world population growth, which must be complied with one way or another, unfortunately raises the immediate question Whose growth? Who should be encouraged to have children? Who should be denied that opportunity? Who is making these decisions?

In the United States population pressure is felt in terms of pollution, physical disorganization of cities and countryside, crowding in cities and recreational areas, and except for the poorest people, in other tolerable, if unpleasant, ways. In most of the world, population pressure is felt in terms of hunger and acute human misery. We would expect, therefore, that the great demand for means for halting population growth would come from the desperately poor whereas the United States would be indifferent. Yet at the World Population Conference and other more recent intergovernmental meetings, the United States has been a principal advocate for the limitation of population growth. The poor nations, for the most part, were against it. Why?

World population problems do not exist in isolation. They are colored by the memories of European colonialism and imperialism and are affected by what many Third World people believe to be present neo-colonialism and economic imperialism. The representatives of the poor countries point out that the rich countries not only have the economic wealth, but through this are capturing most of the resources of the earth including *their* resources. They believe that first they should be given their fair share of resources, and then they will see how many people they can support. China, with a population of around one billion people, the largest on earth, is now using highly effective means for halting population growth and during the 1970s cut its growth rate by more than half. Yet Chinese leaders say economic development must come first before population problems can be addressed. India, with a population climbing toward the billion mark, has leaders who see things differently. Population growth, they believe, wipes out all gains made through economic development and demands first attention.

PAST AND FUTURE

It may not be fully realized that the population problem that faces us today is essentially new, one that has arisen in the past century without

precedent in human experience. Our historical training, which empha-
sizes city history, conveys an atmosphere of crowds and crowding. Country
history has not been written since no one was there to record it. We
need to confront a history of the vast open spaces of a little while ago,
told by tribal peoples, recording the doings of generations of buffalo and
antelope and prairie wolves. Such a history would tell us of a world that
suddenly disappeared, of a changeless land completely transformed.

It is not possible to know for sure how many people are in the world
today, since censuses are rarely exact counts and usually miss those who
do not wish to be counted. In many parts of today's world to be located
and counted for some people means to be killed; in other countries
imprisonment or deportation may accompany being located, if one belongs to the wrong minority or happens to have run afoul of the law.
Nevertheless, more than a little confidence can be given to today's estimates of population—they are more than just informed guesses. It is
more difficult to know how many people were on Earth at various times
in the past. Demographers, however, have done their detective work,
piecing together information left by census takers, tax collectors, military
commanders, and other concerned with the number of heads in their
domains. In Table 6.1 are some widely accepted estimates showing changes
in the world since 1650, when the first American colonies were beginning to thrive and Cromwell ruled in England. It took hundreds of thousands of years for the human population to reach the half-billion level
of 1650. It took less than 200 years for it to double, less than a century
for the second doubling. Now it doubles in every 35 years. If it were to
follow recent trends, there would be 22 billion people on earth by the
year 2040—less than 60 years from the time of writing this chapter. The
United Nations expects that the world population will reach 6 billion by
the year 2000, taking into account some slowing in the rate of growth.
Yet one can reasonably question such an estimate. If people are barely
surviving in much of the world today, when population levels approach
4.5 billion, by what means will 6 billion survive?

TABLE 6.1   The Growth of World Population

REGION	ESTIMATED POPULATION IN MILLIONS						
	1650	1750	1800	1850	1900	1950	2000[a]
Northern America	1	1.3	5.7	26	81	166	354
Latin America	12	11.1	18.9	33	63	162	638
Europe	100	140	187	266	401	559	880
Asia	330	479	602	749	937	1302	3458
Africa	100	95	90	95	120	198	768
Oceania	2	2	2	2	6	13	32
World total	545	728	906	1171	1608	2400	6130

[a]United Nations medium estimates (USSR included in Europe).

MALTHUS

The behavior of human populations today in relation to their means of subsistence has been such as to cause a revival of the Malthusian outlook on population. Thomas Malthus of England was one of the first to become concerned with the world population problem. In 1798 he published a book entitled *An Essay on the Principle of Population as It Affects the Future Improvement of Society*. Some basic ideas expressed were (1) that population is necessarily limited by the means of subsistence, (2) that population increases where the means of subsistence increase unless prevented by very powerful checks. Furthermore populations tend to increase at a geometric rate (1, 2, 4, 8, 16, etc.) whereas food supplies can be increased at only an arithmetic rate (1, 2, 3, 4, 5, etc.). Therefore populations tend to outstrip their means of subsistence. (3) The powerful and obvious checks to population increase, the checks that repress the superior power of population and keep its effect on a level with the means of subsistence, are all resolvable into vice, misery, and potentially perhaps, moral restraint.

When Malthus lived the population of western Europe was pressing on the limits of the then existing food supply. The overseas colonial empires were yet to be fully exploited. In the cities at least misery and vice were widespread and moral restraint at a minimum. Fortunately for mankind, but unfortunately for the reputation of Malthus, this situation changed, as the full impact of the Industrial Revolution on the new colonies was felt. For a time the means of subsistence increased much faster than population. Malthus was forgotten until populations suddenly began to catch up. Today, as in the time that Malthus wrote, his ideas bring forth severe opposition. To be called a neo-Malthusian is in some circles the same as being called an enemy of the people. A 1980 example of this controversy is provided by the words of Samir Amin, director of the African Institute for Economic Development and Planning:

"Malthusianism is a hydra whose heads need to be cut off; otherwise they grow again." Objecting to an article by American economist Lester Brown showing "direct linkage between population growth and the exhaustion of the world's nonrenewable natural resources", Amin writes: *"The origins of this crisis are to be found in the economic and social organization of the modern world; in the unequal structure of the international division of labour, confining Third World countries to import substitution based on cheap labour; in the decreasing flexibility of the economic system; in the shifts in economic balance between the United States on one side and Europe and Japan on the other with the resultant breaking up of the international monetary system."*

He goes on to question any forecast of the availability of food, energy, or mineral resources in the future, pointing to the major changes that have occurred in scientific knowledge and its technological application in the recent past. Those who agree with Lester Brown, on the other hand, might question this willingness to believe that "something will turn up" to save humanity from its dilemma. Why not get on with reducing population growth in order to reduce the obvious pressure upon existing resources?

Certainly the problem of overpopulation is not new. Many lands have known it in the thousands of years humanity has been on earth. The problem of *world* overpopulation, however, is new. Once population was an internal affair, and states whose populations outgrew their means of subsistence suffered alone or affected but a few neighbors. The collapse of the Mayan empire caused no concern in the courts of Europe. But now the world is small relative to the number of people. Communications and transportation bring awareness to everyone. Populations no longer starve in silence. Empires no longer die quietly. There were always great open spaces beyond the civilized limits where excess numbers might move. No longer are they available. There are no more land frontiers.

POPULATION GROWTH: HUMANS AND OTHERS

To understand the principles of human population growth we need, at first, only review the principles governing the growth of animal populations. Growth results when natality exceeds mortality. The rate of growth depends on two things: the *biotic potential* of the species, meaning its maximum capacity to increase under favorable conditions, and the amount of *environmental resistance,* the sum of all those factors that cause mortality or reduce natality. Influencing growth rates in local populations, but not in total species populations, is movement into a population (immigration) or out of a population (emigration). The biotic potential for the human species is relatively low compared to, for example, mice, but high in comparison with elephants. One female usually cannot produce more than one young a year, although multiple births do occur. Females can begin to reproduce, under usual conditions, no earlier than 15 years after birth and can continue usually for no more than 25 years. A significant percentage of the female population is therefore nonbreeding. The nonbreeding population is higher when there is a large percentage of males, since one male potentially can act as a sperm donor for many females. A population with fewer males, but with polygamous or promiscuous breeding habits, has a greater capacity for increase than one with more males, or one where monogamy is the usual practice. Most animal populations that press on the carrying capacity of their environment, meaning its capacity to support or provide the means of subsistence for a population, experience high mortality resulting from a higher degree of malnutrition, disease, predation, intraspecific strife, accidents, or the effects of extreme changes in the environment—droughts, severe storms, floods, and so on. Many species, and perhaps most mammals and birds, limit population growth through social behavior. One form of this is *territoriality* in which an animal is intolerant of the too close proximity of another animal of the same species, or same sex of that species. Territorial animals maintain a personal space either by aggressive action or by other means, such as mutual avoidance.

Human social behavior, including all the various means by which pregnancy is avoided, delayed, or spaced, is the only means to avoid pressure upon the carrying capacity of the environment. Carrying capacity, however, is not fixed. It can be and has been increased steadily over many centuries—through improved means of food production, more efficient means of food collecting (such as commercial fishing), elimination of diseases, improved shelter and sanitation, and the greater availability of energy resources. It is the hope that carrying capacity can continue to be increased that forms the basis for belief that populations can go on increasing.

Demographers have postulated various patterns of population growth characteristic of different types of human societies. These have been based to a large degree upon the European experience. Before the industrial revolution in Europe, populations generally pressed on carrying capacity. Birth rates were high, as much as 50 per thousand, but death rates were also high. The rate of population growth was therefore low, and for long periods relatively stable populations existed in many areas. During the plague years of the fourteenth century, the Black Death, a new and virulent form of bubonic plague, wiped out half the population of Europe, and perhaps an equal or greater percentage in other lands. A marked decrease in human populations took place, worldwide. With the Industrial Revolution, however, and with the increased availability of food and other materials from overseas colonies, carrying capacity in Europe was greatly increased. Death rates fell off rapidly. Birth rates remained high. Populations increased rapidly. A new period of stability was reached, particularly after the First World War. Birth rates declined to match death rates and stability was being reached in the 1930s; it has been achieved again today. It has therefore been assumed that populations undergoing the benefits of industrialization, with consequent rises in carrying capacity, go through a *demographic transition,* from high death and birth rates, through lowered death rates and rapid increase, to low death and birth rates. Belief in the likelihood of such a transition has caused some economists to believe that industrialization is the answer to the population problems of the Third World. Once a high level of economic production is reached, populations will level off of their own accord, without any need for public concern. This doctrine, however, could be pernicious (see Fig. 6.1 and Fig. 6.2).

In wild animal populations rapid population growth is characteristic of species introduced into a new, favorable, and relatively unlimited environment. Thus the starling or the house sparrow, when introduced

TABLE 6.2   Comparison of Population Growth in Various Nations—1981

COUNTRY	POPULATION (MILLIONS)	PERCENT ANNUAL GROWTH	NO. YEARS TO DOUBLE POPULATION	BIRTH RATE	DEATH RATE
				PER 1000 POPULATION	
West Germany	61.3	−0.2	—	10	12
East Germany	16.7	0.0	—	14	14
Sweden	8.3	0.1	1155	12	11
United Kingdom	55.9	0.1	693	13	12
United States	229.8	0.7	95	16	9
USSR	268	0.8	86	18	8
China	985	1.2	59	18	6
India	688.6	2.1	33	36	15
Libya	3.1	3.5	20	47	13
Kenya	16.5	3.9	18	53	14
World	4492	1.7	41	28	11

Source: Population Reference Bureau (1982).

into North America from Europe, exhibited a phenomenal rate of population increase, spreading quickly across the continent. In their new environment food supplies were abundant. Diseases and parasites had minimum effect because of the initial low population density and abundant resources. The overall effects of all potential mortality factors were

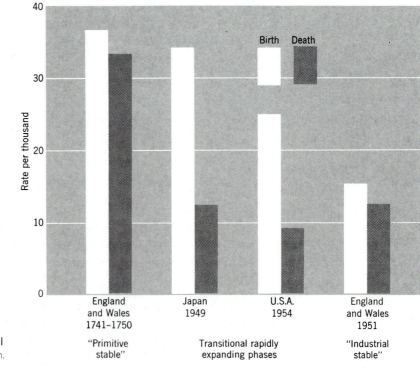

Fig. 6.1
The demographic transition.

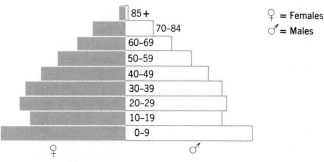

U.S.A., 1954—Slowly expanding

♀ = Females
♂ = Males

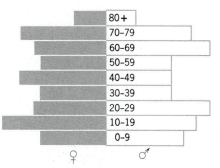

Community in Scotland, 1931—Stable

Fig. 6.2
Age pyramids for rapidly
expanding, slowly expanding,
and static populations,
showing relative proportions
of the different age groups
(*data from Political and
Economic Planning [1955], U.S.
Bureau of the Census, and F.
F. Darling [1951], American
Scientist, 39: 250*).

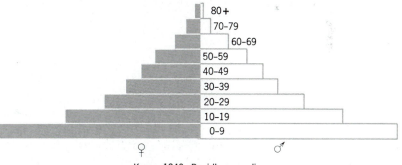

Korea, 1940—Rapidly expanding

at a minimum. Because of the abundance of resources, however, birth rates were high, and natality approached its biotic potential. A similar pattern was exhibited when European human populations invaded North America. After an initial and difficult establishment period, populations began to increase rapidly. Birth rates were high because large families not only could be supported but helped to bring in greater returns from the large amount of available land. Death rates were kept relatively low because of abundant nutrition and space. Population growth resulted.

Rapid population growth in wild animals is also characteristic of situations in which some previously limiting factor has been removed from a stable population. Thus, when moose established themselves on Isle Royale in Lake Superior, they were freed from the effects of wolf predation, a limiting factor on the mainland. Their populations grew rapidly, exceeded carrying capacity after a time, and subsequently crashed to a low level, from which another increase took place. When wolves reached Isle Royale, moose and wolf again achieved a balance that was less threatening to the moose food supply. With human populations similar effects can be observed. The population of India was relatively stable before 1850, when the effects of British transportation systems, medical care, improved sanitation, and improved food availability were felt. Rapid population growth then occurred. A still greater increase in population took place in most tropical countries when malaria, a previously limiting factor, was reduced in its effects by elimination of large populations of *Anopheles* mosquitoes through the use of DDT and when more effective drugs to treat malaria were made available.

The belief, however, that population growth inevitably slows down when economic conditions become favorable to humans, or where industrialism occurs in previously agricultural societies, is not borne out by recent events. The United States underwent an enormous "population boom" during the 1950s and 1960s, along with most European countries, and those of the Third World (see Fig. 6.3). The industrialized countries had a previous history of stability, but it required more than two decades before a similar stability was again reached. Herein lies the trap. It is not just growth rates, but the numbers in the base population to which the rate is applied, that is important. In a world with a carrying capacity for, say, 5 billion people and a population of a half billion, it does not matter too much at first if the population doubles every 20 years (which is a high rate of human increase). When the population reaches 4.5 billion, for it to double at all can bring widespread catastrophe, even if its rate of growth has been greatly decreased. We have no basis for estimating the total carrying capacity of the planet. We have reason to fear it is being approached or exceeded. We probably could not survive another population boom of the magnitude that followed after World War II. Once again, however, we must look at individual nations and groups of people. Any population growth on the island of Barbados, where over 1500 people occupy each square mile, is potentially dangerous to all of the inhabitants. By contrast, Zambia or Zaire in tropical Africa could support a relatively high rate of growth, if resources and land were equitably divided among the people.

CONTROLLING GROWTH

The question of how to control population growth is, to say the least, vexing. With domestic animals it is relatively easy. You castrate most of the males, saving a few for breeding. These are kept separate from the

Fig. 6.3
U.S. population growth.

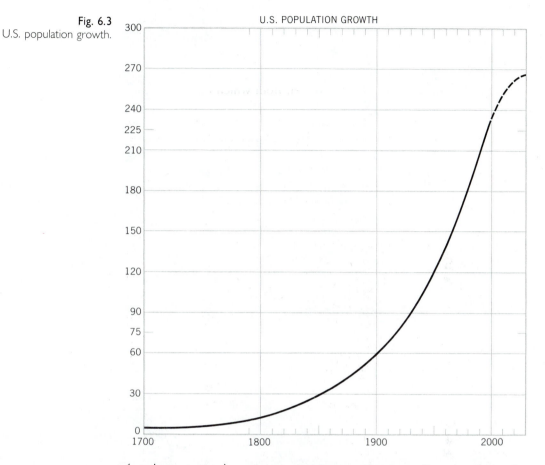

U.S. POPULATION GROWTH

females except when you want pregnancy to occur. Some tendency in this direction in early human civilizations may be surmised from the prevalence of eunuchs in some accounts. With wild animals it is not so easy. Although some success has been had with sterility-inducing drugs, or with the release of sterilized males in fruit flies or screw-worm flies, most wild animal populations are controlled, if at all, by shooting. Judging from the frequency with which wars occur, this practice is also common to human societies, but it rarely has the effect of bringing any pronounced decline in numbers. Today, neither castration nor killing is considered an acceptable means of controlling populations—although the sterilization of males through vasectomy, or of females through tying off the Fallopian tubes, has become acceptable to some.

In a human society where women had equal or greater rights and power than men, control of population would be relatively easy, since women are the ones who bear the children and bear the brunt of the problems associated with their production and care. Where women can exercise control of their own reproduction, they are unlikely to produce excessive numbers of offspring. An example is illustrative:

(a) Hong Kong—one of the world's most crowded cities—how dense can a population get? (b) The crowding of rural people into Third World cities results in *favelas* like this area in Rio de Janeiro. (c) Urban confusion in Tokyo—how do you keep urban systems operating? (d) There is still a choice—not every place is crowded, but (e) what about tomorrow?

c

d

e

121

Signe Howell, an anthropologist, has carried out studies (1981) among the Chewong, an aboriginal hill tribe in Malaysia, who live separate from the dominant Malaysian society and support themselves with swidden agriculture and with hunting, fishing, and wild-food gathering. Unlike many groups of hunter-gatherers and other original peoples, the Chewong had no idea of contraception and rather mixed up ideas about conception. Girls were married at 15 or 16, and thereafter until menopause or death conceived a child every one or two years. Infant mortality, however, was high with many of the children born not surviving. Women and men had equal status, performing different tasks often, but with no value judgment attached. Men did most of the hunting, although their wives could accompany them if not overburdened with children. Women did most of the planting and the preparation of the staple food, cassava. When the idea of contraception was introduced to the women by Ms. Howell, they accepted it enthusiastically, and soon many of the women who had born two or more children were taking birth control pills or expressed interest in doing so. Why did they not want more children? The reasons expressed were that too many children interfered with the women's work and restricted their freedom of movement, that the women wished to avoid the pain of giving birth, and furthermore, that they were grieved by the high infant mortality rate.

In most of the societies prevalent in the world today women do not have equal rights, power, or economic opportunity with men. In many of these societies men can still demand that their wives produce children, preferably male children, or suffer severe consequences. In societies where women are moving toward greater rights and opportunities, including most of the industrialized world, birth rates are falling off. In societies where women are still judged primarily by their breeding performance and their ability to care for children, birth rates remain high. It seems a reasonable first step in population control to attend to the liberation of women. but in some societies—notably fundamentalist Christian or Islamic—there is no trend in this direction.

Governments vary greatly in their approach to this problem. China has the most stringent policies and practices favoring birth control and limitation of family size. Ireland is at the other extreme, as a result of the position of the Catholic church. But it is the attitude of the people rather than the position of the government that is decisive. Ireland does not have a high growth rate (1 percent)—we will not inquire why. The socialist Eastern bloc countries, including the USSR, are strongly pronatalist, since their brand of marxism does not permit them to favor population control. Nevertheless, their birth rates have fallen off, and in some countries populations have declined. The French government, for reasons of its own, periodically launches campaigns urging the French people to have more children. The people do not respond. Yet in those countries whose people have neither the knowledge nor the means to control growth, the attitude of the government is important. Making contraceptive information available, along with the necessary chemicals or mechanical devices needed to prevent conception, can make the difference between increasing and decreasing birth rates.

POPULATION MOVEMENTS

Movement of people out of a population to new areas is not now and probably never has been an effective means of controlling population growth except for limited areas. Emigration from Ireland, initially with a small, if poverty stricken, population has helped ease growth problems. Malta in the Mediterranean along with various Caribbean and Pacific islands have essentially exported much of their population surplus. But Europe as a whole has sent great numbers of colonists all over the world without noticeably reducing the overall pressure of population at home. Today, when there are no empty lands left that are capable of supporting people, emigration cannot be looked on except as a temporary alleviation of the problems of some small nations. Immigration, however, from whatever source has been a serious problem upsetting the balance in countries that might otherwise achieve population stability. In recent years it may be contributing from 20 to 40 percent of the growth of the United States population—since many immigrants enter illegally and refuse to be counted (PRB, 1982). California, with a high level of legal and illegal immigration from Latin America and Asia, has reached its present status of the most populous state in the Union more by immigration than by births. Only in the years 1967–1974 did natural increase exceed net immigration.

Controlling immigration can be as vexing a problem as controlling birth rates for those countries that have traditionally welcomed immigrants. Autocratic governments can take more decisive action than those in which individual rights are carefully protected by law. Communities at less than the national level—states or provinces, counties, towns, and cities—can often see years of careful planning and environmental protection overwhelmed when there is a wave of immigration. There is always a danger with creating a favorable environment for people: Everyone will try to live there. Oregon, Hawaii, and California are examples of states that have tried in one way or another to limit the numbers of people moving in from other parts of the nation. None have succeeded. Local communities have tried various growth control policies: limiting new housing construction, not building new sewage facilities or reservoirs, not inviting new businesses or industries. Always they are charged with discrimination against the poor or unemployed and with attempting to maintain a sanctuary for the wealthy. Yet if there is to be any real improvement in the human condition, local people must be given a greater degree of control over the conditions under which they live; otherwise all incentive for improvement may disappear. If community facilities built or protected with great care to meet the needs of an existing population can be overrun by a wave of immigrants, there is little reason for the local population to develop such facilities. It should be the role of higher governmental authority to encourage the development of adequate facilities everywhere rather than penalize those communities that do well by insisting that they accept all comers.

Garrett Hardin, (1974) biologist and author, has proposed Draconian methods for meeting the population problem. Believing that each nation must stand on its own feet, he opposes the idea of aid and assistance to countries that have allowed too great an increase in their populations, and consequently face hunger and death. His "lifeboat" theory proposes that each nation is the equivalent of a lifeboat with enough supplies for its own passengers. Some nations have allowed their lifeboats to become overcrowded and to sink. Their people are in the water demanding to be rescued. Provident nations who have not overcrowded their boats cannot afford to rescue the drowning, lest their boats in turn capsize or run out of supplies. The alternative—let them drown. Hardin presumably would not have encouraged our accepting the "boat people" from Vietnam and Cambodia, nor would he favor sending food to save them. Although there is a certain harsh logic to his thesis, nations are not lifeboats. If they were, the hungry nations could claim that we in America built our lifeboat with their timber, and those in Vietnam and Cambodia could complain that we shot their lifeboat, adequate enough to start with, full of holes.

SUMMARY

I do not propose to provide the reader with *the answer* to the world population problem in this book. There are no panaceas. Certain needs are obvious:

1. Equal rights and opportunities for women so they can elect to drop out of the baby race if they choose

2. Freely available contraceptive information, devices, and materials, with no stigma attached to their use

3. Abortion on demand for those women who have for one reason or another failed to practice adequate contraception, or have had pregnancy forced upon them

4. Start at home, in your own community, to set an example rather than preaching to other nations

5. Make your information and materials available to those of other communities or nations if and when they request it.

The United States would probably be better off in virtually all ways, social, economic, and environmental, if there were fewer people. The humane way to achieve this goal is to produce fewer offspring. Other nations may follow our example. Some are already well ahead of us, including our European homelands where population stability has been fairly well achieved.

> *If we can put a man on the moon*
> *Why can't we put them all there?*
>
> Feminist Bumper Sticker

SOURCES

Amin, Samir, 1981. *Populi,* Vol. 8, No. 2 UNFPA

Hardin, Garret, 1974. Living on a lifeboat. *Bioscience* 24:561–568.

Howell, Signe, 1981. *Populi,* Vol. 8, No. 2 UNFPA

Malthus, Thomas, 1798. *An essay on the principle of populations as it affects the future improvement of society, with remarks on the speculations of Mr. Godwin, M. Condorcet, and other writers.* 1926 edition. Macmillan, London.

Population Reference Bureau, 1982. *World population data sheet.* Population Reference Bureau, Washington, D.C.

CHAPTER
7

ENERGY—
THE
DEVIL'S
BARGAIN

> *When the world was new the god Loki, known as a trickster, had three children. One of these was the great wolf Fenrir so savage and evil that the gods knew the world could not contain him. They asked the mountain spirits to make a magic chain to hold this monster, and this they did. The chain was woven of the sound of cat's footsteps, the breath of fish, the spittle of birds and other magic ingredients. With this the wolf was bound and held. If Fenrir breaks loose the world will fall in fire and ruin and the gods will be destroyed.*
>
> Norse mythology

HOW WE GOT HERE

During the early 1980s people in the hundreds of thousands, coming from all age-groups and ways of life, have taken to the streets in protest against the continued use of nuclear power. They have been jailed for crossing the line at Diablo Canyon, the aptly named new nuclear plant near San Luis Obispo, and for blockading the gates at the Lawrence Livermore Laboratory, the plutonium center of California, where academicians from the university join with experts from the Department of Defense in designing yet more monstrous weapons. In the East they protest against the reactivation of the Three Mile Island nuclear plant, where a variety of human, mechanical, and electronic errors were combined in the late 1970s to cause a massive breakdown and a threatened meldown that could have endangered hundreds of thousands of people.

How did we get into this predicament? Why did we choose a means of producing energy that even physicist Alvin Weinberg, (1972) who supports it, calls "a Faustian bargain." Weinberg referred to Goethe's Faust, who sold his soul to the devil to gain the love of Marguerite, but did Weinberg really want us to sell our souls, not for love, but kilowatts?

During the last part of Jimmy Carter's presidency when the possible threat of Russian intervention in Iran and the Persian Gulf was detected, the Soviet Union was warned that any move on its part into this region would be regarded as a threat against our "vital interests"—meaning we would go to any lengths including presumably the use of nuclear weapons to repel such a move. How did we get so dependent on Middle East oil that our government could contemplate such an action? Do you have vital interests in the Persian Gulf?

The answers to these questions are not simple, but it is useful to review the story of the relationship between humanity and the energy resources of the earth.

During most of the countless years that the human species has been on earth, the energy used by people came from one source only—the sun. With solar energy as their source of power they developed from the old hunting-gathering ways into agricultural and pastoral communities, from there to the first civilizations, and from these to the great achievements of high culture in Europe including the building of the cathedrals of Salisbury and Chartres, or in Asia the building of the Taj Mahal, the great palaces of Peking, the wonders of old Samarkand. With sun power alone, Europe explored and then colonized much of the world.

Initially, people received energy directly from the sun, which maintained a tolerable temperature level in the environments that they occupied. Indirectly, solar energy, at a rate of 2000 to 4000 *kilocalories* per day, was obtained from animal and plant foods. This sun energy was stored by plants through the process of *photosynthesis* and transferred from plants to animals and ultimately to humans along those ecosystem pathways known as *food chains* and *food webs*. Early in the human story, the ability to obtain materials for clothing, from animal and plant materials, and to construct shelters from the same materials, stone, or earth, made it possible to move into colder environments. Success in occupying these environments depended also on learning the use of fire, and thus liberating solar energy captured and stored by plants some decades or centuries earlier. All energy was renewable, since the sun shone every day, and plants stored energy for later use.

The domestication of animals led to greater energy use, since the calories of plant food needed to maintain a cow, horse, ass, sheep, or goat must be added to those directly consumed by people in their food supply. Following the *second law of thermodynamics,* available energy is lost when it is transformed from one state to another along a food chain. Feeding plants to animals involves a loss of at least 4 calories of previously available energy for every one that is stored in animal tissues. Thus where a vegetarian might do well on 3000 calories per day, obtained directly from plants, a person who ate meat only would require 15,000 plant calories to produce the 3000 animal calories he or she obtained from the meat consumed.

Do not jump to the conclusion, however, that meat eating is too energy expensive. Much depends on where that energy comes from. People cannot eat grass, or most broad-leaved herbs, or the twigs of shrubs. Domestic grazing animals can, and through converting these materials into a form digestible by humans, animals can make food available that otherwise would not be. It is only when we begin to feed domestic animals on food that we could eat directly, corn and other grains, or fish protein, that potential waste enters the picture.

Neolithic people may have used an average of 15,000 calories of food energy, or *biomass* energy per person per day—consumed directly or by their animals or in the form of fuels burned for heating or cooking. At the same time they benefited from the direct solar energy that kept their environment habitable. This rate of energy use did not change much with the rise of civilization. The pyramids of Egypt were built, the Colosseum at Rome was constructed, and the great buildings of Renaissance Europe went up on energy provided directly by humans with some help from domestic animal power.

Rates of energy use did increase with the smelting of metals, the forging of tools or weapons, the firing of pottery and similar enterprises. It increased with the accelerating use of animal-drawn transportation. New forms of solar energy were tapped by early civilizations. Wind energy was captured and used to move sail boats and to turn windmills, which pumped water or turned wheels. Water power was used to move boats down rivers, to turn wheels to raise water to irrigation canals, or to turn millstones which ground grain. None of this energy was "consumed" in any real sense. We have yet to drain the wind of its power, or to exhaust the force of water to move downhill.

One should not pretend, however, that there were not environmental consequences associated with the use of renewable energy resources during the flowering of civilization. Wood represents decades or centuries of accumulation of solar power. It is renewable, but only if its rate of use does not exceed its rate of growth. In Europe, China, India, and the Middle East, along with other centers of human population, forest margins were pushed back, forests then began to disappear, and wood became scarce. It was the shortage of readily available wood that led to the use of other energy resources and thus to what has been known as the "age of fossil fuels." It is hardly an "age," however, since extensive use of these fuels dates back less than three centuries.

Under the category of fossil fuels are three principle energy resources—coal, petroleum, and natural gas—along with a minor and localized resource—peat—and two resources yet to be greatly developed—shale oil and tar sands. Heavy use of these resources started with the invention of the steam engine in the eighteenth century, electricity in the nineteenth, and the internal combusion engine in the late nineteenth century.

With the increasing use of fossil fuels and the spread of industrial technology, the use of energy in the industrialized world increased steadily, from the original 15,000 kilocalories per person per day to approximately 250,000 kilocalories in the United States in the Middle 1970s. By that time most of the energy used was derived from petroleum, but during the 1960s and 1970s a growing percentage was derived from a nonsolar source, nuclear power.

It is worthwhile here to consider the question of basic energy needs as distinct from mere wants or "greeds." Every person must have food, and a means of keeping warm or cool through clothing or shelter, as well as the ability to transform unpalatable to palatable food through cooking. These are basic needs, everywhere, and were accommodated easily within the 15,000 kilocalorie per day limit. They are still the basic needs for those living close to the earth and deriving their livelihood from the land. In industrial societies, however, organized the way they

> *Mines and smelters used prodigious amounts of fuel, primarily for reducing ores to metals, but also for supports in mineshafts and for underground fires to crack resistant rocks. Reasonable estimates hold that a single major ancient metallurgical center would have required as much as a million acres of coppice forest to supply these needs.*
>
> J. Donald Hughes and J. V. Thirgood, Deforestation, erosion, and forest management in ancient Greece and Rome. *Journal of Forest History* (1982)

are today, basic needs cannot be so simply defined. The separation of home, work place, food supplies, and the sources of other essentials is so great in most urban communities that the possibility of traveling from one to the other by foot is ruled out. Even bicycles are not really useful if one lives in Queens and works in Manhattan, or must cross Los Angeles to get to the office or factory. Adequate transportation, with all of the energy use associated with it, becomes as basic as food itself, since it is the means for obtaining food. Similarly, the arrangement of urban-industrial society and the requirements for living within it establish other needs much higher than would be required for societies that were differently organized. Not that this justifies the level of energy use characteristic of American society today. This use represents a high degree of wastefulness that we are only beginning to correct.

ENERGY USE IN THE UNITED STATES

> *In the middle 1970s the industrialized nations of the world still appear determined to continue on a collision course with environmental reality. Faced with a sudden increase in the price of petroleum set by the principal oil-producing countries, and with the inevitable exhaustion of this resource in the not-distant future, little effort has been made to restrict petroleum consumption. Instead all-out efforts are being pursued to find and develop new petroleum reserves, with little concern for environmental safeguards. New impetus has been given to gouging the face of the earth with strip mining for coal, oil shale, or the development of tar sands. Great new fleets of monster supertankers, built with little concern for safety or control, are being launched to haul oil around the world's oceans. Concern for the safety of humanity and the biosphere is being set aside in a new rush to develop nuclear power as a substitute for petroleum and coal—and the problems created by nuclear wastes and the needs for safeguards are of serious magnitude. Alternative, safe sources of energy are receiving little attention, nor are people facing up to the need for revising what are basically unviable ways of life in favor of some more satisfying and enduring alternatives.*
>
> *Environmental Conservation,* 4th edition.

TABLE 7.1   Energy Consumption Per Capita
in Selected Countries

COUNTRY	ENERGY CONSUMED: KILOGRAMS OF COAL EQUIVALENTS (1974)
United States	11,485
United Kingdom	5,464
USSR	5,252
Japan	3,839
Mexico	1,269
China	632
India	201
Bangladesh	31

Note: The idea that a reduction in energy use in the United States means a return to "primitive" conditions is refuted by these facts. With a 50 percent reduction per capita we would be no worse off than England; a reduction by two-thirds would leave us at the "primitive" level of Japan.

The development and use of energy remains extremely uneven throughout the world. Some areas remain at Neolithic levels of energy consumption. Others, such as the United States, consume ever-increasing amounts. In terms of fossil fuels, hydropower and nuclear power, the United States consumes 27 to 35 percent of the world's supply to meet the needs of approximately 5 percent of the world's people. Energy consumption by the United States is ten times greater than all of Latin America, and approximately four times greater than all of non-Soviet Asia. The Soviet Union uses less than half the amount used by the United States, although its population is 40 million greater than that of the USA (Table 7.1).

For what purposes does the United States use all of this fuel? Forty-five percent went for industrial purposes with general manufacturing the largest consumer; 13 percent went for commercial and miscellaneous purposes, including agriculture; 22 percent was used for transportation, of which more than one-half went to operate private automobiles. Another 20 percent went into residential household operation, with heating

In a society that uses its 5,000-pound automobiles for half-mile round trips to the market to fetch a six-pack of beer, consumes the beer in buildings that are overcooled in summer and overheated in winter, and then throws the aluminum cans away at an energy loss equivalent to a third of a gallon per six-pack, this "primitive existence" argument strikes me as the most offensive kind of nonsense.

John Holdren, in Hugh Nash (editor), *Progress as if Survival Mattered* (1977), p. 29

being the principal area of consumption. Thus, the people of the United States use twice as much fuel for heating their houses or for running their cars as all the people of Latin America use for all purposes (Freeman et al., 1974; Lovins, 1977).

Where did the energy consumes in the United States come from? The figures in Table 7.2 are provided by Exxon:

Table 7.2

CATEGORY	PERCENTAGE OF ENERGY USED, 1980	
Imported petroleum and natural gas	22	
Domestic petrtoleum and natural gas	52	
Total oil and gas		74
Coal	19	
Total fossil fuels		93
Nuclear fission	3	
Hydropower, geothermal, and other	4	

It is interesting to note the complete absence of solar energy from this table, although in truth the solar input is far greater than all of the listed sources—since it provides most of our "space heating" and the energy contained in all of the food we consume.

Clothes Line Paradox

This refers to the fact that solar energy is never figured into the national energy use statistics; if you switch from an outdoor solar clothes line to an indoor clothes drier, the recorded energy use goes from zero to some positive figure. If you switch back to an outdoor clothes line, you suddenly drop out of the statistics once again. Statistics thus never adequately show the importance of solar energy use.

Peter van Dresser in Darrow and Pam, *Appropriate Technology Sourcebook* (1976).

Such figures are also challenged by Lovins (1981), who points out that "private wood burning in the United States has grown almost six-fold in the past 5 years with almost no subsidies, and now provides, together with industrial wood burning, about twice as much delivered energy as nuclear power" has delivered after 30 years of government subsidies for a total of about 40 billion dollars. To be fair to Exxon, however, they are dealing with energy transactions that are measurable directly in economic terms (something is bought or sold). If we could be charged for sunlight or wood from our back lot, these would enter the statistics also.

TABLE 7.3   World Petroleum Reserves

REGION	ESTIMATED PROVEN RESERVES, 1978 (BILLIONS OF BARRELS)
Middle East	366
Soviet Union	75
Africa	59
United States	30
Western Europe	27
Central and South America	26
China	20
Other Asia—Pacific	20
Mexico	14
Canada	6
Other	3
Total World	645

Although the United States is the greatest single consumer of energy, in total and on a per capita basis, it has been, and to the extent shown on the above table still is, in the fortunate position of possessing most of the conventional energy resources that it uses. By contrast, other industrialized nations in Western Europe, Japan, Australia, and South Africa have been heavily dependent on imports. Japan imports virtually all of its gas, oil, and coal, and these amount to 75 percent of its measured energy supply. Most of the industrialized world has come to depend on oil fields in the Middle East and North Africa for energy.

The decision therefore by the Organization of Petroleum Exporting Countries (OPEC) to raise oil prices from around 2 dollars a barrel in the early 1970s to a level of near 30 dollars a barrel in the early 1980s had a shattering effect on world economies, touching off inflationary pressures and probably contributing directly to the economic recession or depression of the early 1980s.

What is disturbing about the world energy picture in the 1980s is the extent to which civilization has become dependent upon fossil fuels, and particularly upon petroleum. Although the rate of increase in consumption of petroleum has slowed in recent years, there is little doubt that the supply is running out. Even Exxon, with its vested interest in petroleum, estimates that its percentage share of the world energy supply will fall from a high of 63 percent in the 1960s to a low of 5 percent in the 1990s, and of that 5 percent, more than one-third, is expected to come from oil fields that have yet to be discovered.

Table 7.4 perhaps best illustrates the distribution of the energy resources of the earth, taking into account both solar radiation as the leading source of renewable energy, and at the other extreme potential fuels for theoretical nuclear fusion reactors, which do not exist and probably will never be developed beyond an experimental level.

TABLE 7.4   Estimated Potential Energy Resources of the Earth (Figures
Expressed in 1000 Terawatt Hours)

ENERGY SOURCE	CONTINUOUSLY RENEWED YEARLY ENERGY INPUT	NONRENEWABLE ENERGY STORES
Solar energy		
Direct solar radiation	350,000	
Solar energy stored for brief periods		
Wood, waste	50	
Waterpower, potential	30	
developed	3	
Windpower	200	
Sea thermal power	100	
Tidal power	1	
Geothermal energy, readily available	10	
Fossil fuels		
Known and accessible sources		
Coal		6,000
Petroleum		1,000
Natural gas		400
Known, but not necessarily available		
Tar sands (Canada)		200
Oil shale (USA)		1,500
Nuclear fuels		
Uranium-235 for nonbreeder reactors		1,500
Uranium-thorium for breeder reactors		100,000,000
Tritium-deuterium for fusion reactors		300,000,000,000

Adapted from Kristoferson (1973) and Lovins (1973).

To interpret this table, total world energy consumption in 1970 was 50,000 terawatt hours, equal to the amount continuously supplied by wood wastes or to a fraction of one percent of the total solar energy input. These relationships have not changed greatly up to the present time.

ENERGY RESOURCES

FOSSIL FUELS   Fossil fuels are derived from solar energy captured and stored by the world's forests, or by living organisms in the shallow seas of the world during remote geological times. Since conditions favorable to the long-term preservation or fossilization of these organic materials did not occur everywhere, deposits of coal, oil, and natural gas along with other fossil fuels are unevenly distributed over the earth's surface—resulting in the economic and political problems that affect their recovery and use.

We do not know how much fossil fuel is available, but we are in a position to make some good guesses. The figures presented in Table 7.3 represent what are termed *proven reserves* of petroleum—meaning we

a

FOSSIL FUELS AND FISSION

(a) Strip-mining coal in Ohio. Coal reserves could supply energy for centuries, but mining brings environmental degradation. (b) Oil refinery, Puerto Rico. Petroleum reserves are not adequate for the future needs of industrial societies. (c) Unnecessary generation of electricity wastes energy, while electric power transmission is usually disruptive to the countryside. (d) Is nuclear the answer? The Three-Mile Island Power Plant in Pennsylvania where a partial meltdown in 1979 brought near disaster.

b

c

d

know where they are and how much is there, have the technology to extract this amount at the present time, and can make a profit from doing so. There are also *indicated* or *inferred reserves,* however, that are supplies that are believed to be or are likely to be discoverable in the future and available for use when discovered. *Resources* include both reserves and other quantities of petroleum that have been identified but cannot be extracted because of technological or economic limitations. Changes in technology or the economy can convert resources into reserves. All of these terms can result in apparent contradictions and seeming errors in energy tables.

Petroleum

The proven reserves of petroleum in 1978 were stated to be 645 billions of barrels. The best guess on total resources of petroleum that are ultimately recoverable appears to be M. King Hubbert's estimate of 2000 billion barrels (CEQ, 1980).

The greatest amount of petroleum is consumed as gasoline or diesel fuel, driving the cars, trucks, buses, and trains of the world. A large amount has been and still is used as fuel oil and is burned to provide residential heat or cooling. A significant amount is burned to produce electricity—a process in which two calories of energy are lost as heat for every one produced as electricity. This is the result of the operation of the second law of thermodynamics, the continuing nemesis of all energy users, and of course results in direct waste of energy, unless that waste heat can be captured through a process known as *cogeneration.* In some of the more modern power plants, heat lost in electrical generation is used directly for space heating or in other ways. In addition to being burned as fuel, petroleum provides the raw material for a variety of chemical processes through which a wide range of petrochemical materials—medicines, plastics, fabrics—are manufactured.

It is significant that the peak in United States petroleum production was reached in the early 1970s, shortly before OPEC began its series of price increases, since the increases depended on oil shortage in the industrial countries. Despite Alaskan oil discoveries, off-shore oil drilling, and improved technology used to increase production from existing oil fields, petroleum production in the United States will continue, in all probability, to decline. It has been variously estimated that world petroleum production will peak in the 1990s, and thereafter will decline. Oil will continue to be produced, but at increasingly higher prices, which will discontinue its use for any but the most essential purposes for the foreseeable future. Furthermore, if the major oil-producing countries behave in a manner that can be expected, oil will continue to be available in those countries, long after it becomes virtually unattainable in countries that lack petroleum resources. Thus, it is entirely likely that the Persian Gulf countries, Mexico, Indonesia, and other oil-rich nations will continue to operate a petroleum-based economy long after most of the world has had to turn to other sources of energy.

Coal

The most obvious other source of energy to which we may turn when petroleum becomes too expensive for ordinary use is coal. Compared to petroleum, coal is abundant and has for the industrialized world the advantage of being placed, for the most part, within national boundaries (see Table 7.5). Furthermore, with some energy loss and various assorted other problems, coal can be converted into liquid fuels and used for all of the purposes for which petroleum is now used. It thus has considerable appeal for those who want to see society continue along its present lines, and this appeal has led to some national effort to develop a *synfuels,* or synthetic fuels, program; deriving oil from coal, and other sources.

It would appear that the abundance of coal reserves would remove any need to seek alternative energy resources for at least another century. Coal, however, has disadvantages that were part of the reason that petroleum has taken its place on the world energy scene. It is bulky and difficult to transport. It does not burn as cleanly as oil and produces more pollutants—notably sulfur dioxide, which has already contributed to acid rainfall in many parts of the world. It is difficult and dangerous to mine—subsurface coal mining is one of the more hazardous occupations, and surface strip mining can destroy the productivity of large areas of land as well as creating a variety of serious environmental problems in the mining areas. Nevertheless, coal has the capability of bridging the energy gap between the time when petroleum is priced out of the market and other permanent sources of energy become generally available.

Natural Gas

It is more difficult to estimate the availability of natural gas, since prospecting for it has not been as far-reaching as for petroleum. It commonly

TABLE 7.5   Coal Reserves and Resources

REGION	RESERVES	BILLIONS OF SHORT TONS RECOVERABLE RESOURCES	TOTAL RESOURCES
Africa	19	53	106
Asia	130	611	1,223
Europe	192	385	770
USSR	151	3,147	6,294
North America	229	1,989	3,978
South America	7	16	32
Oceania	58	140	279
Total	786	6,341	12,682

At the 1976 rate of world coal consumption (3.7 billion short tons per year) world coal reserves could last for 212 years. However, with expected increases in coal consumption with the reduced availability of petroleum, this life span for reserves would be reduced.

Source: CEQ (1980).

occurs in association with petroleum and is the gaseous product of organic decomposition, consisting mostly of methane. It is relatively non-polluting as a fuel, but along with all other fossil or nonfossil organic substances is converted into carbon dioxide as one of the end products of combustion. Carbon dioxide (CO_2) accumulation in the atmosphere constitutes a potentially serious environmental problem, which will be discussed later. In continental areas, natural gas is most readily transported by pipeline, such as the one now under construction to bring natural gas from the Soviet Union to Western Europe. For oceanic transport, gas is converted into a liquified form (LNG) and shipped by LNG carriers. Since the potential for disastrous explosions exists with such concentrated liquid fuel, few people want an LNG terminal in their vicinity.

Based on 1976 rates of consumption, natural gas supplies could last for 50 years counting only proven reserves, and from 100 to 200 years if estimated resources were to be available (Table 7.6). Much depends, of course, upon consumption rates, and these depend in part upon the availability and cost of petroleum and other fuels.

The Net Energy Hurdle

If one reviews only the status of proven fuel reserves that have been discussed thus far, it would appear that the worst "energy crunch" that we have to fear is converting from a near total dependence on petroleum to some other mixture of fuels, including some reasonable proportion of oil. If the problem were that easily resolved, we could thank the OPEC

TABLE 7.6   Estimated Proven Natural Gas Reserves, 1982 (Trillions of Cubic Feet)

USSR	1160
Iran	484
United States	198
Algeria	131
Saudi Arabia	118
Canada	90
Mexico	75
Qatar	60
Netherlands	56
Norway	49
Venezuela	47
Nigeria	41
Kuwait	35
Indonesia	27
Iraq	27
Total of above	2598
All other countries	313
World Total	2911
Annual consumption (1976):	50
Estimated total world resources:	5,150–11,950

Source: Exxon (1981), CEQ (1980).

nations for calling our attention to it and go on our energy-independent way. Obviously it is not that easy, and one reason why is the question of net energy balance. When oil was first discovered it was oozing from the ground, coal was lying about on the surface, and natural gas was issuing from natural vents, providing "perpetual flames" of religious significance. The cost of obtaining these fuels was negligible. For virtually no energy investment, large quantities of energy were obtained. This favorable ratio between the amount of energy required to obtain the fossil fuel and the amount obtained from it remained for a long while. Most major oil fields existed originally under pressure from the included natural gas. When tapped by oil drillers, gushers resulted, spewing oil into the air until capped. Natural gas was "flared," burned at the well-head to get rid of the surplus. As oil fields are drained, however, the energy cost of obtaining the remaining oil increases. Liquids or gas must be pumped into the well under pressure to force the remaining oil out. Similarly, as mines go deeper into the earth, the energy cost of mining coal increases. For strip mining, the cost of operating the heavy machinery must be considered, as well as costs for development and transportation.

To calculate energy balances, or net energy gain from a fuel source, all energy inputs must be tallied. These involve not only the energy cost of mining or drilling, but also the cost of transporting water to the mine or well, the cost of building housing or other structures, the cost of transportation, of refining, distilling, fractionating to get the desired end product, the cost of manufacturing the machines that use the energy, and so on. The total energy input bill is often so complex as to be difficult to calculate. Fossil fuel energy is not free, however, and net energy gains are often far less than would be calculated from the caloric value of the fuel alone. This becomes a major consideration with other fossil fuels.

Energy input, or energy costs, are theoretically reflected in the money cost of the gasoline, coal or natural gas. However, because of the variety of subsidies provided by government to encourage energy exploration or exploitation, actual costs are often concealed. Only part of the price may be passed on to the customer, although ultimately the total cost is shared by the taxpayers. This becomes important when we consider the question of nuclear power.

Other Fossil Fuels

Potentially the oil derived from two sources, oil shale and tar sands, could replace the oil derived from petroleum fields. Oil shales alone are believed to contain more than 3000 billion barrels of shale oil, whereas tar sands could add almost another 1000 billion barrels to this total. This is double the estimated 2000 billion barrels of petroleum that could potentially become available. If it were recoverable to the same degree that existing proven reserves of petroleum can be pumped from the ground, there would be no need to worry about a shortage of oil until the end of the next century. Furthermore, most of the identified shale oil resources (c. 2300 billion barrels) occur in North America, and more than 700 billion barrels of the identified tar-sand resources are in Canada.

Unfortunately, shale oil (kerogen) occurs in shale rock and other sedimentary rocks. It does not pour out of this source. The oil in tar sands is semisolid or solid asphalt (bitumen), and at best is semiliquid. It also does not pour or flow. Both sources require a considerable energy input to carry out destructive distillation of oil shale and the heating and hydrogenation of tar sands. Both also require large quantities of water for processing. Oil shale occurs, however, in the dry intermountain west, where water is at a premium. Tar sands are mostly in the Athabascan fields of northern Alberta, Canada. Oil shale of the best quality will yield from 25 to 100 gallons per ton of rock. Extraction leaves great quantities of waste rock to be disposed of. The total net energy yield from either oil shale or tar sand is difficult to calculate. With some degree of government subsidy, however, it is economically feasible to extract oil. Two Canadian companies are working in the Athabascan fields. Several American companies have attempted oil shale processing, but thus far none have completed development, and the economic incentive for further work appears to be inadequate.

TERRESTRIAL ENERGY Although fossil fuels are solar energy captured long ago, the materials of the earth itself offer several forms of energy that we have now begun to use. One of these derives from the heat generated by pressures inside the earth's curst, geothermal energy; the second, tidal energy, results from the moon's pull upon the waters of the earth's oceans; the third, nuclear energy, is obtained through breaking the enormous energy bonds that hold together the ultimate constituents of matter. This will be considered first.

Nuclear Fission

When men split the nucleus of the atom, they unleashed into terrestrial nature a basic energy of the cosmos—the energy latent in mass—which had never before been active in any major way on earth. ...

President Harry Truman was speaking to this point when, in his announcement that the United States had dropped an atomic bomb on Hiroshima, he told the world that "the basic power of the universe" had been harnessed for war by the United States, and added that "the force from which the sun draws its powers had been loosed against those who brought war to the Far East." The huge—the monstrous—disproportion between "the basic power of the universe" and the merely terrestrial creatures by which and against which it was aimed in anger defined the dread predicament that the world has tried, and failed, to come to terms with ever since.

Jonathan Schell, *The Fate of the Earth* (1982).

This is *not* the way to go.

Nuclear energy was developed originally to make atomic bombs. Its development was shrouded in secrecy. The world first became aware of its possibilities when the United States without warning transformed a city of 340,000 people into an inferno. It then proceeded to repeat this performance, as though Hiroshima was not enough, by destroying much of the city of Nagasaki, in total (bringing death instantaneously or after prolonged agony to 130,000 people). The bombs used were little ones, by present standards, and would be termed "tactical weapons" in today's nuclear arsenals.

Because of these beginnings, fear and horror have dogged the footsteps of all who work with nuclear power and seek to harness the power of the atom for constructive purposes. There has been a continuing mistrust, or at least uneasiness, concerning the development of peaceful uses of nuclear energy. This has not been helped by the continuing flow of misinformation from governments about the dangers from fallout resulting from the testing of nuclear bombs. Nor has the willingness to de-emphasize costs and risks while overemphasizing potential benefits helped the advocates of nuclear energy.

The source of nuclear power at the present time is atomic fission, which takes advantage of the instability of the heaviest elements such as uranium and thorium. These elements are spontaneously radioactive, giving off atomic particles and radiation, collectively known as ionizing radiation, and changing ultimately into lighter, more stable elements. In the fission process, uranium atoms are bombarded with neutrons, one of several kinds of atomic particles. Neutrons split the nucleus of uranium atoms, releasing other neutrons and large amounts of energy. The released neutrons in turn hit the nuclei of other uranium atoms, starting a chain reaction, which can release still larger amounts of energy and radiation. The amounts of energy potentially involved are indicated by Einstein's formula:

$$E = mc^2$$

where E is the energy released, m is the mass of the particles split off in the fission process, and c^2 is the square of the velocity of light (186,000 miles per second). Even with relatively small mass, the release of energy is extremely large.

Ionizing radiation occurs in several forms: *alpha rays* are streams of particles similar to the nuclei of helium atoms. These move at high speed but have low penetrating ability and would not normally penetrate intact human skin. When taken into the body, however, in food or via the lungs, they can do great damage to soft tissues.

Beta rays are streams of high-speed electrons with considerably more penetrating power than alpha rays. Both rays can do damage to body tissue by causing ionization of the molecules that make up living protoplasm, thus disrupting the organization of body cells.

Gamma rays consist of high energy electromagnetic radiation similar to X-rays and with a similar ability to penetrate body tissues. These can penetrate skin and do damage throughout the body.

The radioactive elements occur in various isotopic forms (meaning that they have different numbers of particles in the nucleus or electron rings). Uranium-238, for example is the common isotope of uranium as it is mined from the ground. U-238, however, is not easily fissionable. To transform it into a fissionable state it is bombarded with neutrons and converted into plutonium-239. Naturally occurring uranium-235 is a fissionable element that occurs in small quantities in uranium deposits. To be useful it must be concentrated (enriched) through a process that separates U-235 from the more abundant U-238. Thorium, another naturally occurring radioactive element, is also not readily fissionable and must go through neutron bombardment to be transformed into fissionable U-233.

When ionizing radiation strikes commonly occurring elements in the biosphere, these may be transformed into radioactive isotopes. Thus carbon-14 is a naturally occurring radioisotope of normal carbon, carbon-12. It is formed in the upper atmosphere when atmospheric nitrogen is bombarded with cosmic rays, ionizing radiation from outer space. Since the chance of nitrogen being struck by cosmic rays is rather small, the concentration of carbon-14 in the atmosphere is also small and has been relatively constant in the past, since C-14 decays into normal C-12 over a period of time.

In the fission process, as when an atomic bomb is exploded, great amounts of energy are released along with large amounts of ionizing radiation. This bombards other atoms and converts some of them to radioactive isotopes. Furthermore, the breakdown products of the uranium, plutonium, or other radioactive elements include a variety of radioisotopes. All of these give off ionizing radiation potentially harmful to life. Their dangers depend on their activity, their persistence, and the extent to which they may penetrate and remain within the body.

The activity and persistence of radioisotopes is measured in terms of their *half-life,* the time required for half the atoms in any given quantity of radioactive material to disintegrate. Isotopes with a long half-life have low activity, that is, they give off less ionizing radiation per unit of time. Those with a short half-life are less persistent, but highly active.

Carbon-14 has a half life of 5568 years. Starting with one gram in that length of time it would disintegrate to half a gram of C-14 and half a gram of C-12. In another 5568 years, half of that C-14 would have disintegrated, leaving a quarter gram of C-14. The amount of carbon-14 found in dead organic matter can be used to date that material, that is, to tell how long since it died and its carbon was cut off from the normal atmospheric mix of carbon-12 and carbon-14 that had previously entered its tissues through respiration.

Among some of the more serious pollutants resulting from the use of atomic energy are plutonium, used in atom bombs, with a half-life of over 24,000 years; strontium-90 (which is readily taken up by the body as a substitute for calcium) with a half-life of 28 years, cesium-137 (which has the ability to replace sodium in the body) with a half-life of 33 years and iodine-131 with a half-life of only 8 days, but a high activity, which can be expressed if it is concentrated by the human thyroid gland.

Exposure to ionizing radiation can have the following effects on people. In large doses, as in a nuclear explosion, it can kill immediately. In lesser, but still heavy doses, from heavy atmospheric fallout, from nuclear plant accidents, and the like, it can cause radiation sickness, from which most people will die more slowly. In still smaller amounts it can cause cancer, which takes longer to kill. If it strikes egg or sperm cells, fertilized eggs, embryos, or fetuses, it can cause genetic abnormalities. No ionizing radiation is good for you. Any amount can cause some damage, but the risk of damage increases with the amount to which you are exposed.

> *One nuclear bomb can ruin your whole day.*
>
> Bumper sticker

Following World War II the United States and later the Soviet Union, Great Britain, and France, and still later China, wanted to test their new atomic weapons to see if they all really worked, and also to see how big they could make the bombs before they were completely out of control. A series of atomic tests were made, in the atmosphere and on the surface of the ground, leading from fission bombs to the more powerful fusion-based hydrogen bombs. What we would now consider reasonable precautions were not taken, since neither the scientists nor the military really knew what they were doing until after the event. It was an era of scientific *hubris,* of vainglory, egocentricity, narrow vision, seldom to be equaled, if ever, in the history of scientific experimentation. The bombs were exploded in what were characterized as "remote areas," but these were remote only from the United States. They were *home* for the people of Bikini atoll or Eniwetok in the South Pacific. They were fishing grounds for those of the Japanese boat, the *Lucky Dragon,* which unluckily was passing by when the tests took place. After the explosions people had been exposed to dangerous levels of radiation. The atolls became essentially uninhabitable for some decades to come.

All of these explosions contributed to radioactivity in the atmosphere—layers of radioactive isotopes, floating high above the ground, but ready to drift down when atmospheric conditions permitted or to be washed down by the rain. *Fallout* is the term for this leakage from atmosphere to ground. Fallout could be extremely heavy in the area near a bomb explosion, as soldiers near the Nevada testing grounds were to discover. But since radioisotopes were carried round and round the globe, fallout could occur anywhere. In 1970, however, the federal Council on Environmental Quality measured the effects of the explosions of the 1950s and 1960s. The results were at first glance, reassuring (Table 7.7):

Table 7.7

SOURCE	DOSE IN MILLIREMS (ANNUALLY)
Natural background (radiation entering the biospere from natural sources)	125.0
Medical sources (use of X-rays and radioisotopes in medicine)	55.2
Fallout—from all previous atomic explosions	1.5
Miscellaneous (TV sets, wrist watches, occupational exposure, etc.)	2.2

It would appear that fallout was of minor consequence. However, these measurements of general levels of radiation do not take into account what happens in living systems, where organisms can concentrate radioisotopes to levels far beyond what are to be found in the general environment in which these creatures live. Thus swallows flying through the stack gases of a nuclear power plant were found to have concentrations of radioactivity 75,000 times as high as those to be found in the air. (This would convert the 1.5 millirems in the table to 112,000 millirems). The phytoplankton (single-celled floating algae) in sea water concentrates radioactivity to levels 150,000 times higher than in the seawater, whereas filamentous green algae can concentrate radioactivity to levels 850,000 times that of their background environment. Because of this problem of *biological magnification,* or concentration of elements as they are passed along food chains, there is little reason to feel secure when confronted with statistics based on general atmospheric, or seawater, measurements.

> Can there be "forbidden"—or, as I prefer, "inopportune" knowledge, the possession of which, at a given time and stage of social development, would be inimical to human welfare—and even fatal to the further accumulation of knowledge?
>
> Robert L. Sinsheimer, The presumptions of science. *The Ecologist* (1981)

The question of how much is safe has never been answered satisfactorily. Essentially, no radioactivity higher than background levels is "safe," and even background levels are undesirable—that is, it does not pay to live next door to uranium deposits. Nevertheless, when it comes to different kinds of risk, most would prefer the slight risk of a medical X-ray to the assured risk of undetected cancer. Radiation protection standards issued by the National Commission on Radiological Protection and Measurement (NCRP) stated that dose limits for the general public should not exceed 500 millirems in any one year for individual, occasional exposure, but for genetic safety the average dose per individual in the population should not exceed 170 millirems—not much more than background radiation levels. Subsequent studies by the National Academy of Sciences, however, suggest that with a 170 millirem limit, there would be between 3000 and 15,000 additional deaths from cancer each year. It is agreed that the less dosage of radiation, the better off we will be (Holum, 1977).

The generation of nuclear power is one of the uses of atomic energy to which the government devoted full attention, in part to counteract the negative image that had resulted from its earlier use of atomic bombs. Large amounts of public money were devoted to this program in an effort to encourage private industry to take it over. Private industry, however, was not too anxious to get involved: the risks and costs were high and the returns doubtful. The passage of the Price-Anderson Act by Congress in 1957 removed from industry and shifted to the federal government the liability from any accident occuring in a nuclear power plant. This provided more incentive for industry to move ahead. Nevertheless, the first nuclear power plant, opened in 1957 at Shippingport, Pennsylvania, was owned by the federal Atomic Energy Agency. The first commercial venture not subsidized by the government was the Oyster Creek plant in New Jersey, which started up in 1968. Thereafter, with full encouragement from the government, it appeared that nuclear power would become a major source of energy. In 1981 there were 73 nuclear plants licensed by the federal Nuclear Regulatory Commission, 84 construction permits for new plants had been authorized, and 15 others were planned (Fig. 7.1). In all, including some government-owned plants, 176 were either in operation, being built, or planned. This in itself was a decline from 1974, when a total of 233 plants were in these categories. Subsequently, there has been a steady decline in the number of plants in operation, under construction, or planned. Some state governments have endeavored to limit or restrict further nuclear power plant development, but perhaps more important, private industry has begun to question the costs and benefits and to back away from the entire enterprise. There have been numerous accidents involving nuclear power plants. There have been even greater numbers of malfunctions. No plants have been able to stay on line, in production, full time, and all have produced less electricity than had been predicted. To top it all off, the Three Mile Island plant in Pennsylvania in 1979 suffered from a breakdown that threatened to become a "meltdown," which could have endangered hundreds of thousands of people. Although the major disaster was forestalled, enough risk and damage resulted to frighten the general public. The plant remains closed.

The nuclear power cycle is illustrated in Figure 7.2. At almost every

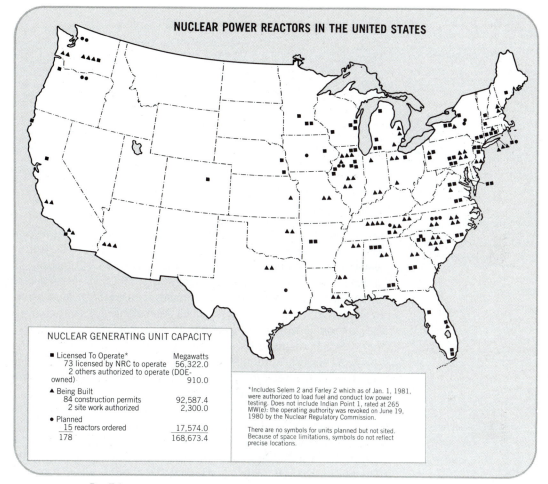

NUCLEAR POWER REACTORS IN THE UNITED STATES

NUCLEAR GENERATING UNIT CAPACITY

■ Licensed To Operate*   Megawatts
  73 licensed by NRC to operate 56,322.0
  2 others authorized to operate (DOE-
owned) 910.0
▲ Being Built
  84 construction permits 92,587.4
  2 site work authorized 2,300.0
● Planned
  15 reactors ordered 17,574.0
  178 168,673.4

*Includes Selem 2 and Farley 2 which as of Jan. 1, 1981,
were authorized to load fuel and conduct low power
testing. Does not include Indian Point 1, rated at 265
MW(e): the operating authority was revoked on June 19,
1980 by the Nuclear Regulatory Commission.

There are no symbols for units planned but not sited.
Because of space limitations, symbols do not reflect
precise locations.

Fig. 7.1
Nuclear power reactors in
the United States.

stage there is both energy input and risk. Mining uranium is a hazardous business. Miners who work underground are exposed to high radiation risks. The tailings, or residue, left after uranium ore is removed are in themselves radioactive, and serious pollution problems and health hazards have resulted when these have not been properly disposed of—for example, reburied. All of these activities take energy. Uranium ore, mostly U-238, must then be transported at a cost of energy to a mill where it is broken up and separated into uranium oxide (yellowcake). This then goes to a conversion plant where it is further processed with fluorine gas to yield uranium hexafluoride, a gas. In this gas, the U-238, being heavier, can be partially separated from U-235, which is concentrated. The enriched U-235 then is converted into solid fuel rods, in which form it is available to be transported to and used in a nuclear reactor. Within the reactor, the chain-reaction fission process takes place under controlled conditions and is used to generate heat. This heats water, which is con-

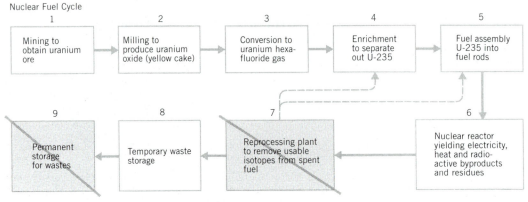

Fig. 7.2
Nuclear fuel cycle. (*Source:* Holum, 1977.)

verted into steam, which is used to turn turbines and generate electricity. Much more waste heat is generated than in fossil fuel plants, and heated water is one of potential pollutants that must be disposed of. In cold climates a heated water discharge into bays, lakes, or the ocean can be beneficial to marine life. In warm climates, heated water must be cooled, by way of cooling towers or holding ponds before it is discharged into the environment to avoid heating the receiving water bodies to levels that would be dangerous for living organisms.

Each year fuel rods must be replaced as radioactivity levels decrease. This spent fuel in theory could be taken to a reprocessing plant where the uranium would once again be reconcentrated. The reprocessing plants have yet to be built, however, and so nuclear plants must hold their spent fuel and other atomic wastes for safe disposal. Unfortunately there is as yet no safe disposal, despite investigations and attempts at deep-sea burial, which risks contamination of the marine environment, and underground burial, which risks contamination of ground water. The problem with nuclear wastes is that they remain radioactive virtually forever in human terms. Recall that plutonium has a half-life of 24,000 years. We have not figured out a safe way to lock them away for tens of thousands of years. Since the wastes continue to accumulate, we will probably end up opting for a dangerous or half-safe solution to this problem.

All of the commercial nuclear reactors in operation in the United States are of the conventional, fission reactor type using uranium as fuel. Since uranium is a nonrenewable resource and uranium ore is not abundant in the earth's crust, various predictions have been made about the time when the uranium supply will "run out." While none of these is particularly reliable, the exhaustibility of uranium fuel has caused nuclear power proponents to seek renewability of fuel supplies. This can be accomplished by building a breeder reactor. Such reactors can use the common form of uranium, U-238, or thorium as their initial fuel, with a mixture of plutonium to get the process started. During the fission process, however, U-238 is converted into plutonium, so that the end

Three Mile Island—1979

The first hint the reactor operators had that a meltdown might be possible at Three Mile Island came at 5:30 in the morning of March 28, when sensing devices detected increased numbers of neutrons apparently coming through the walls of the pressure vessel. That hint was misinterpreted by reactor operators who were trying frantically to figure out why certain pumps were vibrating. At 4:00 that morning a routine malfunction in the plumbing system had caused the reactor to shut itself down automatically. Unknown to the operators, a malfunctioning safety valve had then begun to slowly empty the pressure vessel of water. The malfunctioning of that safety valve was crucial. By 5:30 the pressure vessel was running dry. The core was no longer totally immersed in water and was in danger of melting.

Parts of the core were being cooled only by steam, which cannot cool as effectively as water. Operators thought the high neutron counts meant that there was insufficient boron (the chemical element used to stop the chain reaction in nuclear fission) in the reactor, when it actually meant there was insufficient water. . . . At 6:22, the stuck-open safety valve was finally discovered and closed, but it then became apparent that the fuel core had been damaged by heat. The fate of the reactor was hanging by a thread, and nobody knew how thin that thread was.

Howard Morland. The meltdown that didn't happen.
Environment 82/83 (1982), p. 63

Three Mile Island—1982

More than three years after the nation's worst nuclear accident, scientists late Wednesday got their first televised look inside the damaged Three Mile Island reactor and concluded that an almost complete meltdown had taken place in the center of the core. . . . the melting of the fuel suggests the level of danger at the time may have been greater than previously believed, since molten fuel could have melted through the reactor pressure vessel and re-leased great quantities of radioactive materials into the containment building.

Milton R. Benjamin, *San Jose News*, July 22 1982, pp 1A, 16A.

product is richer in plutonium than the original fuel mixture. The reactor thus "breeds" plutonium, which can be reclaimed from the fuel mixture and used elsewhere, or used to keep the reaction going within the plant. The prospect of virtually unlimited fuel has encouraged the federal government to subsidize the construction of a breeder reactor at Clinch River, Tennessee. This will be a reactor of the type known as liquid-metal fast-breeder reactor (LMFBR), using liquid sodium as a coolant and heat transfer medium. Water is used in conventional "burner" reactors to reduce temperatures and slow reaction rates. Liquid sodium flowing at 540 degrees Celsius permits the reaction to proceed at a faster rate. The sodium jacket is surrounded by a water jacket. Water, heated by the sodium, converts to steam, which turns the turbine to generate electricity. Since sodium is highly explosive when in contact with water, one trusts that no ruptures will occur in the sodium container. Previous experience with fast-breeders is not encouraging. The Fermi experimental breeder, located near Detroit, Michigan, experienced a Three Mile Island type accident in 1966. The Soviet reactor at Shevchenko experienced an accident shortly after it began operation. The French plant is operating.

Safety considerations must be even more severely enforced with breeder reactors than with burner reactors, if only because plutonium is one of the most dangerous environmental contaminants. Furthermore, the accumulation of plutonium, anywhere, is a matter of international concern, since this is the metal from which atomic bombs are most easily made.

Nuclear Fusion

The ultimate energy panacea, held forth by its proponents as the long-term answer to energy problems, is the process known as nuclear fusion. Unlike fission, fusion harnesses the processes used in the hydrogen bomb, and would yield far more energy per unit of input than the most efficient fission process. The fuels used are those sometimes called "heavy water"— deuterium (H_3O or D_2O, containing a hydrogen atom with a mass twice as great as normal hydrogen) and tritium, which contains hydrogen with three times the mass of normal hydrogen. Tritium is extremely rare in nature, but is manufactured by bombarding deuterium compounds with positive deuterium ions. It is radioactive, with a half-life of 12.5 years. It can also be made from the metal lithium, through bombarding it with neutrons.

Whereas fission involves the "splitting" of heavy atoms, fusion involves bringing together the nuclei of the lightest, hydrogen atoms, stripping the electrons from them and forcing the nuclei together. The trick then is to confine the fused nuclei or plasma. Since it has a temperature equivalent to those found within the body of the sun, no material container can hold it. Plans are to hold the plasma in a specially shaped magnetic field, or else to use laser beams to bombard it from several sides and keep it in suspension. Obviously, this is the highest level of high technology. Although many aspects of it have been tried successfully, we are a long way from a point where we can start generating electricity.

The waste products of this process, in theory, are hydrogen isotopes that could be recycled for fuel. There are supposedly no problems of pollution or storage of radioactive wastes. The only problem is that if the process did work, one would have the equivalent of a controlled hydrogen bomb to take care of. One would not want any mistakes to be made in its operation.

Whatever Happened to Kyshtym?

Soviet scientist Lev Tumerman, who emigrated to Israel in 1972, stated in an interview with United Press International in 1976 concerning a journey he took in the southern Urals in 1960, "I asked my driver why we could not stop and he told me that there had been a tremendous explosion several years before and ever since it had been like this. On either side of the road there was nothing—an empty, empty land. There were grass and trees, but where once were villages and herds and industry there was nothing. Only chimneys remained." Washington Post, 8 Dec. 1976.

The Los Alamos study speculates that this gradual environmental contamination was compounded in the late 1950s by a catastrophic release of radioactivity from yet another source. Soran and Stillman suggest that high-level radioactive wastes from the reprocessing plant were initially discharged into an open pond, which was allowed to evaporate, leaving a layer of intensely radioactive crud attached to fine, red clay particles. This material, they believe may have been whipped by high winds and scattered widely around the surrounding area, or it may have been dispersed by a series of powerful chemical explosions.

Soviet geneticist Zhores Medvedev speculated that the region was contaminated as a result of a nuclear explosion, caused by plutonium in waste material that reached critical mass.

Colin Norma, Science, (1982), p. 274. Z.A. Medvedev,
Nuclear Disaster in the Urals (1979).

On the basis of all of the available evidence, at least one major accidental release of radioactivity occurred at or near the Kyshtym site; our research defines the date of one such event to have been no later than the year 1958. Trabalka, Eyman and Auerbach, Science (1982), p. 198.

I never speculated that the disaster in the Urals was related to a "nuclear explosion, caused by plutonium in waste material which reached critical mass," as Norman writes.

The main population in rural areas between Cheliabinsk and Sverdlovsk is represented by Russian peasants and Ural cossacks (about 80 percent of the rural population of these regions). Among the rather large (and known as prosperous) villages that have diasppeared from the maps are Yugo-Koneva, Russkaya-Karbolka, Metlino, Asanovo, Belokataiski, Kuptsovykh, Te-cha-Brod, and Petrovka; these are typical names of Russian villages. Few Bashkir villages exist in Cheliabinsk region, but they have quite distinct Bashkir names.

Some cases of radioactive contamination in the area around Kyshtym were, of course, possible in the late 1940s and early 1950s. However, all available ecological information, as well as declassified documents from the Central Intelligence Agency, indicate that the large scale contamination during the winter of 1957–58 occurred as a result of a single disastrous incident.

Zhores A. Medvedev, Science (1982), p. 200.

One nuclear bomb and there goes the neighborhood.

Bumper sticker

As Amory Lovins has pointed out, we have one nuclear fusion plant in operation already: it is called the sun, and it produces all the energy we would ever need. Why try so desperately to build another?

Some would say that no nuclear source can be clean and safe; and that though nuclear power is admirable when properly sited, the source and the user should be rather widely separated—say, about 150 million km.

Amory Lovins 1973.

Pros and Cons of Nuclear Energy

The temptation to develop nuclear energy has apparently been virtually irresistible to those who run the leading industrial nations of the world, and to many in the nonindustrialized world as well. As an energy source it is virtually unlimited, if we use breeder reactors and eventually fusion reactors. We have the technological ability to harness atomic power, and it could free us from dependence on other energy sources. It is admittedly a high-risk business, but as we learn more about how to handle it, the risks can be decreased. Furthermore, although we have had many near misses, by way of serious power plant accidents, in fact we have not had massive accidental releases of radioactivity into the environment. By contrast, petroleum plants, oil storage tanks, and coal mines have exploded, and all fossil fuels give off pollutants. We can find answers to storage of radioactive wastes, and we are taking far better care of those than we are of chemical wastes that are equally toxic and dangerous to the environment. In fact, compared with other industries, it could be argued that the nuclear industry has been a model for safety precautions and environmental concern.

The other side argues that the risks, particularly from a major plant or nuclear waste storage accident, are far too high, considering that we do not now and never will need nuclear power. Nuclear waste storage is forever, and even if we use extreme care now, there is no way we can guarantee what will happen in future years. Nuclear power plants themselves, when decommissioned, must also be protected forever, since they become dangerously radioactive and we have found no way to take them apart and dispose of them.

Of particular concern is the use of nuclear power plants to generate bomb-grade plutonium and to produce atom bombs. This was a sufficiently real concern to cause the Israelis to risk further international sanctions in order to bomb the Iraqi nuclear power plant in Baghdad. India has produced its own bombs, using its power plants as a beginning source of nuclear materials. Israel and presumably South Africa have done the same. Pakistan, Brazil, and perhaps Argentina may be following this course. The more nations who have atomic bombs, the greater the risk that they will be used.

The existence of plutonium in large quantities is likely to encourage terrorists, who could use it to make bombs or simply threaten to disperse it as a deadly pollutant. Terrorists come in all varieties, poor and desperate as well as rich and powerful.

Because of the danger of theft and sabotage, the existence of nuclear plants causes a proliferation of police state mentality, greater restriction of public access and movement and of democratic freedoms.

Nuclear power is necessarily a centralizing force, since it requires for its infrastructure a centralized industrial base, and for its control a centralized authority. This brings with it necessarily a centralization of economic and political power not conducive to a democratic way of life.

None of these risks and dangers need be taken when nonpolluting, relatively risk-free solar-power sources are available that are by nature decentralized and not useful for making bombs or other weapons of mass destruction.

Geothermal Power

Geothermal power is derived from the heating differentials within the earth's crust. Heat is generated within the earth by pressure, friction, and the decay of radioactive elements. It is most manifest in volcanic activity, volcanoes, geysers, hot springs, and fumaroles. There is also a heat differential between surface rock and rock lying deeper within the earth that could be used as a basis for electrical generation. A number of geothermal power sources have already been tapped and developed. These make use of hot water and steam, which is used to turn electrical generators. In other areas, hot water from the earth is used directly for space heating. Virtually all of the space heating of homes, factories, and urban facilities in the country of Iceland is carried out by piping hot water from the earth. Geothermal power plants are also used in this country to generate electricity. New Zealand has carried out extensive development of geothermal electrical power. California, Italy, and a number of other volcanic regions are also using geothermal energy for production of electricity. The three largest geothermal plants in the world have a capacity of over 1000 megawatts. Potentially, geothermal sources could meet all of the world's energy needs (CEQ, 1980). However, it appears most likely that it will remain of significant, but local importance.

Tidal Power, Ocean Thermal Power, and Salinity Gradients

Tidal power has been developed in some local areas, but not on a large scale. Its greatest potential lies in estuaries with a large tidal range, where high tide can be used to push a flow of water through turbines. The reverse flow when the tide moves out again can also be used to turn turbines. Thus far the only major functioning plant is near St. Malo, France, where a capacity of 240 megawatts has been installed.

Ocean thermal power results from the temperature differential that builds up between surface water and deep water. It would appear to have the greatest potential in tropical regions where temperature gradients are steeper. In theory this gradient can be used to generate an electric current, but functional power plants have not yet been developed.

Salinity gradients where fresh water and salt water come together can also be used as a basis for generating electric currents. Plans exist for a salinity-based power plant to be constructed on the inland Salton Sea of California, but thus far there has been no development.

It seems unlikely that any of these three sources of energy will have more than local importance in the future. The reason is both in the continuing availability of fossil fuels and the potential for various solar power developments.

SOLAR ENERGY

Overview

Energy coming from the sun is the principal source of energy used on earth, without human intervention, and will continue to be available for as long as earth remains inhabitable for human beings. When the sun ceases to shine, humanity checks out, along with all other life on earth.

Solar energy is available in direct form for a variety of the purposes for which we want concentrated energy—direct space heating in particular, but also electricity generation, refrigeration, industrial processes, desalinization of water, and more. It is available in derived forms as hydroelectric power, wind power, and biomass energy. In all of these forms it is being used today in ever-growing amounts. To many it seems the only form of energy development worthy of major subsidy from governments and private investors. It is available everywhere, to everyone, and does not lend itself to being monopolized. The latter point may explain why it has not attracted the financial support needed for development.

Solar energy *does*, however, lend itself to centralization and private control, and to this extent it has always attracted investment. Water power can be made available wherever streams flow, but it is the massive hydroelectric power dam, generating large amounts of electricity, which is then channeled and distributed through grids of power lines covering entire regions, that has attracted and received the major development funding. Wind-generated power was traditionally used for pumping on most of America's farms. Today it is the massive "wind farm" with giant windmills producing thousands of watts that attracts attention. We are told that solar farms, covering many square miles with solar cells, could potentially generate much of our electrical demand. All of these are intended to feed current into power lines under centralized control. Meanwhile, it is the small-scale solar hot-water panels, the passive solar design, and other home-based schemes that seem to be forging ahead, with little or no government support, reducing demand for centrally generated power.

Hydroelectric Power

Water power has been used by people over thousands of years. Originally it was the direct mechanical power provided by water that was used to turn wheels, to move water into irrigation channels, or to spin the stones that ground grain. Later, with the advent of knowledge concerning electricity, it was learned that water could be channeled into jets that, directed against the blades of turbines, resulted in the spinning action that generated electricity.

The sun fueled the hydroelectric system, by evaporating water from the ocean, moving it inland in clouds carried by the wind, dropping it as rain or snow on the highest elevations of the continent. From there the stored potential energy of the uplifted water was changed to the kinetic energy of water moving downhill. The amount of energy available depended on the amount of water and the distance it had to fall. Waterfalls were indicators of water energy, and many of the first mills in the Americas were built along the "fall line" of the Appalachians, where water from the higher mountains dropped rapidly to lower elevations.

The small power dams and generators of the past, however, were to be replaced during the early decades of the twentieth century by the massive "multiple-purpose" dams that were built on every major river system of the United States. These have been criticized as "cross-purpose" dams, since the need to maintain a head of water for power generation conflicts with the need for reservoir capacity to contain floods. Nevertheless, these along with the straight power dams have contributed substantial amounts of power. According to Holum (1977) there were 1427 hydroelectric plants in operation in 1972, 22 more under construction, and 70 others were planned to be built before 1993. The existing plants contribute 15 percent of the total electrical generating capacity of the United States. Regionally they are even more important, contributing a major part of the electrical power used in the more mountainous areas.

Hydropower has a potential beyond that of the big plants tallied and catalogued in the above statistics. Small hydropwer installations can contribute all of the power needed by local communities. These need not involve the construction of dams, but only the channeling of water out of the stream and through the turbine; consequently, they can avoid the environmental consequences of major construction projects that have often served to destroy wilderness areas, wildlife, and fisheries.

Worldwide hydropower has been less developed than in the United

ENERGY ALTERNATIVES

(a) Mount St. Helens making the point that geothermal energy can be plentiful in some areas. (b) A power plant in the Imperial Valley, California transforms geothermal energy to electric power. (c) A solar furnace at Odeillo, France uses the sun's energy directly to generate high temperatures. (d) Windmills have been in use for centuries but now can be used to generate electrical power.

c

d

TABLE 7.8   Conventional Hydroelectric Resources World Totals, 1976

Developed	
Capacity (megawatts)	315,137
Average annual generation (gigawatt hours)	1,348,554
Energy content, annual (quadrillion Btus)	4.6
Undeveloped	
Capacity (megawatts)	1,911,666
Average annual generation (gigawatt hours)	8,351,720
Energy content, annual (quadrillion Btus)	28.5
Total	
Capacity (megawatts)	2,226,803
Average annual generation (gigawatt hours)	9,700,274
Energy content, annual (quadrillion Btus)	33.1

Source: CEQ (1980).

States. Table 7.8 shows the developed and undeveloped capacity (not including the small-scale potential). Although the potential is impressive at 33 quads (quadrillion Btus per year) it must be kept in mind that world energy consumption in 1976 was 250 quads. Like every energy resource we have examined, waterpower is part of the answer, but not the whole answer. In some countries it can provide for all electrical needs; in others there is no water power potential to be developed. On the other hand, each partial answer contributes to the total solution.

Like the solar power from which it is derived, waterpower is potentially inexhaustible. Its use contributes no heat and no pollutants to the environment. The only negative environmental effects are those connected with its generation, where this involves big dams and waterways, and its distribution, where it goes into extensive powerline grids.

Wind Power

When sunlight strikes the surface of the earth it provides a differential heating of the tropics and the polar regions, of continental areas and oceans. Warm air rises and cold air descends, warm air from the equator starts moving poleward to replace colder air, which flows near the surface toward the atmosphere. The spin of the earth causes this moving air to start rotating, generating the moving currents of air that are the winds of the world. Enough energy is available each year in these moving air masses to equal approximately four times the total energy that shows up in the energy use statistics for mankind (Kristoferson, 1973). For thousands of years people have used wind power to move boats across the seas or to turn windmills for pumping water or doing other useful work. When electricity became available for use, wind generators came into operation. By the 1930s not only were mechanical wind mills a standard feature on American farms, but many of these farms had their own wind-generated electricity. The advent of the Rural Electrification program, offering cheap power generated centrally in fossil-fuel fired plants, caused most of these wind energy systems to be abandoned. However, the idea of using wind power did not go away. Some countries, notably Iceland, generated most of their electricity from wind until after the end of World War II, when the lure of cheap petroleum proved irresistible.

As David Inglis (1978) has pointed out, a new surge of interest in wind power developed in America at the same time we were developing the first atomic bomb. A windmill with a generating capacity of 1.25 megawatts was installed on a mountain called Grandpa's Knob in Vermont. Mechanical failure and enthusiasm for nuclear power combined to cause this effort to be abandoned. Only with the great leap forward in the price of petroleum after 1973 did serious interest in wind power return. Since the government and private industry are still committed to fossil fuels and nuclear power, however, money for research and development has been available only in small trickles. Despite this, wind power is returning to the scene, not only in the large megawatt size commercial generators favored for central power generation, but also in small multi-kilowatt capacity machines that are once more springing up on farms and in some urban areas. Since the potential is there and the economics grow increasingly favorable, wind power will undoubtedly provide a growing share of the world's electricity. How large a share, how fast, is anybody's guess at this time.

Wind power has some disadvantages compared to water. Water can be stored in reservoirs and released when electricity is needed. No reservoir can hold the wind, which blows fast or slow, yes or no, on its own schedule. For home generators this is no great problem, since electricity can be stored in batteries. For integrated electrical grid systems it is not a great problem either as long as backup systems using some other source of power can be plugged in when the wind is not blowing. Wind energy can be used to pump water up hill, which then can be stored for hydropower. Wind-generated electricity can also be used to dissociate water molecules into hydrogen and oxygen. Hydrogen gas can potentially be used as fuel for transportation or in place of petroleum in power plants. There are no doubt other possibilities that will be developed in the future.

One of the oldest uses of wind is now also making a comeback, as more and more people are developing efficient sailing ships, including the ultimate irony, a wind-powered oil tanker. Since the nineteenth-century clipper ships could make the run from America to England almost as fast as today's diesel-powered freighters, the new ships that are beginning to appear may be the forerunners of a new "age of sail."

What Make Things Go?

In 1921, Frederick Soddy, a Nobel-prize winning chemist, presented a paper at the London School of Economics entitled "Cartesian Economics."

He asks rhetorically the question that economists are concerned with: "How do men live?" by asking what makes a railway train go. "In one sense or another the credit for the achievement may be claimed by the so-called engine-driver, the guard, the signalman, the manager, the capitalist, or the shareholder—or, again, by the scientific pioneers who discovered the nature of fire, by the inventors who harnessed it, by Labor, which built the railway and the train. The fact remains that all of them by their united efforts could not drive the train. The real engine-driver is the coal. So, in the present state of science, the answer to the question how men live, or how anything lives, or how inanimate nature lives, in the senses in which we speak of the life of a waterfall or of any other manifestation of continued liveliness, is, with few and unimportant exceptions, BY SUNSHINE."

Quoted in Hazel Henderson, *The Politics of the Solar Age* (1981), p. 225

Plant Power

Each year the vegetation of the earth captures and stores solar energy. The potential harvest from this store, on a sustainable basis, is equal to the amount of energy that the human race consumes each year from fossil fuel, nuclear power, hydropower, geothermal power, and vegetation. Thus, if we could easily make use of all the calories stored in a harvestable crop of vegetation, we could meet all of our energy needs from this source alone. There are, however, many difficulties that stand in the way. At present there are three principal ways of using the energy stored in biomass—other than the most common way of eating plants and animals. These are by direct burning of the material, and this is the most widely used approach; converting plant and animal wastes into methane gas; and the conversion of plant materials into fuel alcohols.

Firewood. Most of the people of the world still use plant materials directly as fuel—to cook food and heat their houses, as well as in blacksmithing and other manufacturing processes. Wood is the preferred fuel, but where it is scarce nonwoody plants and animal dung are used in its place. Where wood is relatively plentiful, much of it is converted into charcoal (through burning under low-oxygen conditions), in which form it can be more easily transported to towns and cities. Ironically enough, export of charcoal from the woodlands of Kenya has caused serious deforestation in that country, with most of the exports going to the countries of Arabia—the petroleum center of the world.

If wood is harvested in accordance with sustainable forestry practices, wood fuel could be available from forests, woodlands, and savannas indefinitely into the future. Unfortunately, the demand for wood or charcoal has been so high in most of the tropical countries of the world that forests have been pushed back, woodlands destroyed, and savannas changed to open grasslands. What Eric Eckholm has called "the other energy crisis" is the growing shortage of wood and the environmental consequences that follow on massive deforestation. Not only are forests destroyed, along with their associated plant and wildlife species, but along the desert margins of the world, cutting plants for fuel adds to pressures from overgrazing to cause a continuing expansion of barren deserts. The use of animal dung for fuel, in areas where woody plants have virtually ceased to exist, removes the soil restorative action of this organic material and contributes further to declining productivity.

Attempts to solve this problem have led to increasing emphasis on heat-efficient, inexpensive stoves to replace the use of open campfires, and to growing attention to the disposal of human and animal wastes, along with waste plant material in ways that lead to the production of methane, which can then be used in the same way as natural gas.

Methane. Methane is known also as marsh gas because it is produced in marshes as a product of the decomposition of plant material. The term *biogas* is today used for the same product (CH_4). Methane is produced for human use by confining animal manures and plant wastes in enclosed chambers built from plastic, metal, or cement and allowing bacterial fermentation to take place. This process generates heat, which in turn speed up the fermentation. A relatively high percentage of manure, rich in nitrogen, facilitates the process, which also demands a fairly large amount of waste matter in order to operate efficiently. Family-sized methane plants are said to require manure from at least five cows, or an equivalent amount of human and other animal wastes, as a daily contribution. More efficient production can probably be obtained from village or small community-sized plants. Many large sewage plants, where city wastes accumulate in enormous quantities, are now used for methane generation, with the fuel burned for the operation of the plant or fed into the city's gas lines.

One advantage of methane generation, as compared to direct burning of fuel, is that the end products include an organic sludge that contains all of the minerals and much of the nitrogen present in the original manure or plant waste. This can be used directly for fertilizer. The heat generated during the process has a sterilizing effect on this material, killing potential parasites and pathogens that might otherwise effect plants, animals, or human health.

Biogas plants, mostly family sized, producing two to three cubic meters of gas per day, have been developed extensively in China and India. China now has more than 7 million plants and expects to have a total of 70 million by 1985. India has more than 10,000 and expects to build 100,000 plants per year for the decade of the 1980s. Many other eastern and southeastern Asian countries are now in the process of developing biogas plants as a principle contributor to rural energy needs.

Unfortunately, where neither plant wastes nor animal manures are available in quantity, and this applies to the desert-edge countries of the world, it is difficult to produce methane in quantities likely to meet local energy needs. Nevertheless, attention to development of this energy source, wherever possible, can lead to marked reductions in demand for fossil fuel. Experience during World War II demonstrated the usefulness of methane for transportation. In Europe, as well as other parts of the world, many civilian automobiles and buses were run on methane fuel, since gasoline was rationed and used primarily by the military. The sight of taxicabs with methane gas bags on the roof was familiar in many cities.

Fuel Alcohol. It is no news that alcohol can be produced from grains, grapes, sugar cane, other fruits and plant materials, since people have been manufacturing and drinking alcoholic beverages since the beginning of civilization or earlier. Most people are also aware that in addition to drinking alcohol, it is possible to burn it as a fuel. Ethanol, or ethyl alcohol, (CH_3CH_2OH), otherwise known as grain alcohol, is obtained through the fermentation of starches or sugars and concentrated through distillation. (Pure alcohol is 200 proof or 100 percent alcohol; 100 proof whiskey is 50 percent ethyl alcohol.) Methyl alcohol, or wood alcohol, is obtained through the distillation of wood or other cellulose. This form of alcohol (CH_3OH) is toxic—a few ounces can kill you—but is useful as fuel.

Although alcohol fuels have been used for centuries, renewed interest in the possible use of alcohol as a substitute for gasoline dates from the first big boost in the cost of petroleum in 1974. Since then a considerable amount of the "surplus" grain in the United States has been used to produce ethanol, which is added to gasoline (usually in a 10 percent mixture) to produce gasohol. Countries other than the United States, and in particular Brazil, have taken the lead in fuel alcohol production. Brazil makes use of sugar cane and cassava for alcohol production and hopes eventually to drastically reduce its use of imported petroleum. Unfortunately, fuel farms are no longer food farms, and the sacrifice of food for fuel sometimes means that more people go hungry so that others can keep their automobiles running. The need for more land to grow fuel plants means more clearing of the original rain forests—which were already under too much pressure before the gasohol boom.

In discussing any form of bioconversion, the question of energy balances becomes important. If grain, or sugar cane, is grown using conventional American agricultural techniques, which are extremely wasteful of fossil fuel energy; if it is then transported some distance, at a cost of fuel, and put through a fuel-consuming industrial process, the net gain in energy in the form of alcohol may be slight, if there is any gain at all. On the other hand, if the fuel crops are grown with low-energy input organic agriculture, and the conversion to alcohol is done locally, with minimum transportation involved, a considerable energy

TABLE 7.9   Comparative Yield of Various Crops

CROP	ANNUAL YIELD IN DRY ORGANIC MATTER (METRIC TONS/ACRE)
Corn (maize), Minnesota	9.7
Water hyacinth, Mississippi	4.5–13.4
Salt marsh plants, Georgia	13
Seaweed (brown algae), Nova Scotia	13
Tree plantation, Congo	14.6
Reedswamp, Germany	18.6
Algae (sewer pond), California	20–30
Sugarcane, Hawaii	30.4
Sugarcane, Java	35.2
Napier grass, Puerto Rico	43.0

gain may be achieved. Furthermore, if the end products, which include much of the original plant material, are used as livestock feed or fertilizer, or burned directly as fuel, the gains from the process are increased.

The productivity of crops in different environments is extremely variable, and with this the potential fuel yield will vary. Particular attention should be paid, however, to sustainable yield of forms of vegetation (such as water hyacinth) that are at present unused, or even considered to be pests. Table 7.9 from Wilson Clark (1975), is illustrative.

Trash Power. An enormous amount of plant material, processed to varying degrees, ends up as waste or trash, the latter commonly picked up by garbage collectors and transported to a dump, where it is sometimes burned (thus polluting the air), or consolidated into land fill. Wood, paper, cloth, and a variety of plant and animal wastes become truly wasted in this process. More and more cities, fortunately, are now using burnable wastes in power plants, to reduce the demand for coal, fuel oil, or natural gas.

The total amount of waste generated each year in the United States is presented in Table 7.10 (from Clark, 1975):

Table 7.10

WASTE SOURCE	TOTAL ANNUAL PRODUCTION IN MILLIONS OF TONS	COLLECTIBLE WASTE IN MILLIONS OF TONS
Manure, livestock	200	26
Urban refuse	129	71
Logging residues	55	5
Farm crop and food	390	23
Industrial waste	44	5
Municipal sewage	12	2
Other organic matter	50	5
Total	880	136

Clark points out that this could have yielded the equivalent of one billion barrels of oil and 8.8 trillion cubic feet of natural gas. Even the portion deemed collectible could have yielded 170 billion barrels of oil equivalent and 1.36 trillion cubic feet of natural gas. Whether this waste is burned in power plants or to provide direct heating, used in methane generation, or in production of fuel alcohol, it can make substantial contributions to energy needs. Only the past availability of cheap petroleum and coal has permitted us to ignore this potential source of energy and other useful materials.

Direct Solar Energy

Solar energy is found everywhere on the surface of the earth, but some say it is too dispersed to be useful. Any child who has experimented with a magnifying glass to burn a hole in her jeans should know better. Anyone who parks his car in the sun on a warm day, and then tries to sit on the seat, should learn that what "some say" is not necessarily so. Solar energy is dispersed, but it can be readily concentrated.

The ways in which solar energy is employed, other than the general heating of the biosphere and production of green plants, are numerous: space heating and cooling, water heating, food drying, generation of electricity, desalinization of seawater, cooking, and high-temperature solar furnaces for industrial use are among them. Together they cover most or all of the end uses for which we employ energy today.

Perhaps the most popular solar device in use today is the solar water heater, which has appeared on the roofs of many of the homes of America during the past decade. The principle is simple: water is circulated through thin black pipes arranged in such a way as to receive the direct rays of the sun; as it is warmed it circulates to a hot-water storage tank from which it becomes available for bathing, washing, cooking. It can be hooked into a system of hot-water radiators and used for space-heating of a house. Many such devices are employed in heating water for swimming pools. The system works best in the warm days of summer, but at most times of the year it can provide at least supplemental heating, saving on fuel bills.

The circulation of warm air, rather than water, is considered to be the more economical way of house heating. "Passive-solar homes" are constructed in such a way that the sides most exposed to the sun (south-facing in the northern hemisphere) are mostly glass or plastic—usually double-layered for insulation. Sunlight coming through these windows often is directed against a "thermal mass," a blackened stone wall for example, or water tanks, to capture and store it for longer periods. Heated air circulates from the exposed area around the house, making a shell of warm air surrounding the living space. As it cools, it sinks and is recirculated below floor level through vents into the solar-heated area again. Houses designed to capture heat in this way, and to circulate the warm air, can with proper insulation remain warm throughout the year—

and at most need a wood stove for additional heat during the coldest months. A variety of designs are available, including those for houses built partly underground, where the earth serves for heat storage and insulation.

Electricity is generated from sunlight by the use of solar electric or photovoltaic cells, which make use of the special properties of silicon crystals to convert sun energy into electricity. According to Stephen Lyons (1978): "a single four-inch cell generates one peak watt at noon on a sunny day. But conditions are not always so favorable. Five cells are needed to guarantee an *average* output of one watt. A typical American household needs one kilowatt of average power, so about 5000 cells would supply all its electricity needs. An array of these cells would occupy 500 square feet, less than the roof area of most houses."

The cost of solar cells has been dropping steadily since they were first developed for use on spacecraft. They are now at least competitive with nuclear power, and it is expected that with a little boost from a major purchaser (such as the federal government) they could be reduced in price sufficiently to be available for general household use. Today many people are using them, in combination with batteries. Great improvements in solar cell technology may be expected in the next decade, even without government support (Lyons, 1978).

Sunlight energy can be concentrated to generate enormous amounts of heat for a variety of industrial purposes. One of the first uses of concentrated solar energy is attributed to Archimedes, who is said to have used solar reflecting mirrors to set fire to a Roman fleet that was besieging Syracuse in 212 B.C. His feat was not duplicated until 626 A.D., when a similar array of solar mirrors was said to have been used to drive off a Roman fleet besieging Constantinople. During the eighteenth century the French scientist Georges Buffon used solar mirrors to melt lead and silver and to set fire to a woodpile located 200 feet away. In the same century the Swiss scientist Nicholas de Saussure built a solar oven, a black box covered with glass that could generate temperatures of 320°F. Somewhat later Antoine Lavoisier used a magnifying lens to concentrate solar energy sufficiently to melt platinum at 3190°F. The French have continued to lead the way in developing high-tempeature solar furnaces, and now have a solar furnace at Mont Louis in the Pyrenees Mountains that can generate temperatures of 6000°F and produce 1000 kilowatts of electric power. Obviously we don't need further pilot projects—the technology is available for future development (Clark, 1975).

Solar energy could have replaced many of the uses of fossil fuels and all of the uses of nuclear power had the government backed its development with any of the enthusiasm it has poured into the expansion of the nuclear-power industry and into attempts to build a synthetic fuels industry, wringing oil out of shale, or gaining it from coal conversion. One can only assume that the government is responsive to the demands of the energy companies rather than to the real needs of the people.

OUTER LIMITS

There are no magic ingredients in fossil fuels that make them more wicked than other fuels. Everything contained in them is "organic," produced by living plants, animals, or microorganisms. With heat, pressure, and anaerobic conditions over millions of years, the concentration of various compounds or elements changes from what would be found in wood or grass, but they are derived originally from carbon dioxide and water, plus minerals from the soil, just as we are. If we burn coal, petroleum, or natural gas completely, the end products will be mostly carbon dioxide and water, plus the same minerals from the soil that originally went into plant tissues. It is incomplete combustion that leads to all the miscellaneous hydrocarbons, sulfur and nitrogen oxides, carbon monoxide, and other health-endangering pollutants being poured out car exhausts or factory chimneys. When we burn wood, usually with incomplete combustion, we turn loose most of the same pollutants—less concentrated probably, but not much better for the health. Whenever we burn anything, whether it is nuclear fuel, fossil fuel, wood, methane, or fuel alcohol, we release heat to the atmosphere. If heat accumulates in the biosphere faster than it is dissipated into outer space, the surface of the earth warms up. This could have serious effects for humanity if it continues, because it could lead to melting of glaciers and polar ice caps. The sea level would rise, flooding coastal cities. Since these are the places where most fuel is burned, the problem could be solved—but we would not like the solution. At present we do not detect a major warming trend in the atmosphere, but we do have "heat domes" over our major industrial cities—domes of warm air creating a different climate in city compared to countryside.

When we burn any organic fuel, fossil or otherwise, we release carbon dioxide to the atmosphere. The heavy use of organic fuels over the decades of the twentieth century has caused a measurable increase in the carbon dioxide content of the atmosphere. This produces what is called the "greenhouse effect," meaning that catbon dioxide interferes with heat loss from the atmosphere. It blocks passage of infrared and longer wavelengths, while allowing the shorter wave lengths of visible light to pass through. By continuing to burn organic fuels we not only add heat to the atmosphere, therefore, but through adding carbon dioxide, prevent the heat from escaping. The likelihood of significant temperature increase, and melting of the ice caps, thus increases (see Fig. 7.3).

To add to the problem we are removing the living green cover of the earth, the plants that capture and fix carbon dioxide and release oxygen. The more we roll back the boundaries of the tropical rainforests, and the more deserts we create in drier lands, and the more we pollute and kill off the green plankton of the oceans, the less able is the biosphere to dispose of the excess carbon dioxide load that we are feeding into it.

Fig. 7.3

Trend in CO_2 concentration in the atmosphere, parts per million by volume. (*Source:* NOAA Manuna Loa Baseline Station. From Global 2000 Report.)

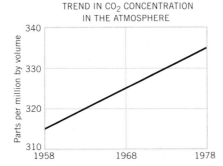

TREND IN CO_2 CONCENTRATION
IN THE ATMOSPHERE

When do we reach the danger point? At what stage does the process become irreversible (in terms of human lifetimes)? We don't know.

Meanwhile, we have forms of energy—direct solar, wind, hydro-power, some geothermal, ocean thermal, tidal power—that do not add carbon dioxide to the atmosphere and do not increase the heat burden. Why aren't we going "all out" to develop them?

ENERGY CONSERVATION

The high per capita consumption of energy in the United States compared to other countries does not mean that we are doing more than other people, despite our so-called work ethic. We are not more productive, rather less so than countries that use much less energy. Neither does it mean that we have an abundance of energy and feel we can afford to be casual about its use. It does mean that we are without rival in waste-fulness—perhaps because we developed the habit of wasting energy at a time when it seemed to be abundant and cheap. Certainly the adver-tising of the 1950s and 1960s encouraged waste—from the all-electric kitchen to the oversized, gas-gulping automobile.

Energy waste occurs at all levels from mine to mill to factory to consumer. Power plants automatically waste energy when they convert fossil fuel to electricity, and even more waste occurs if the fuel is nuclear. To the extent that we need electricity, that waste is somewhat justifiable (although the heat need not be wasted), but we have been encouraged to use electricity for tasks that are better done with less expensive fuels. We waste energy in hauling manufactured products from one side of the country to the other, often to compete with the same kind of product that is locally produced. Our planning of cities and transportation routes; the location of factories, relative to workers and consumers; our single-purpose suburbs, with homes located far from work place or shopping place; all reflect a belief that the energy bonanza would go on forever, and that food and goods would pour forever from an inexhaustible horn-of-plenty.

One of the more spectacular wasters of energy has been the driver of the private automobile. Its internal combustion engine is inefficient in its design and in the way it is used. American motor cars have featured greater inefficiency in their size and rate of fuel consumption. Despite the competition from Japanese and European rivals, the American auto industry has seemed unable to build small, fuel-efficient vehicles—although it is making considerable progress in that direction in the 1980s. Gerald Leach has noted that road transport in America—buses, trucks, and automobiles—uses 43.5 percent of all oil consumed. The comparable figures in Western Europe are 17.6 percent. Air transport, employing jet planes, is less efficient than road transport. Rail transport is relatively efficient, but could be made much more so. Table 7.11 is illustrative (Entwistle, 1973):

Table 7.11

	BTU USE PER PASSENGER MILE	BTU USE PER TON-MILE OF FREIGHT
Jet plane	7150	63,000
Private automobile	5400	—
Railroad train	2620	750
Passenger bus	1700	—
Highway truck	—	2,400
Ship	—	500
Bicycle	310	—

Despite the relative inefficiency of road transportation, the U.S. government has subsidized it to a degree that seems out of proportion to its worth—$40 billion for the interstate highway system as compared to only $900 million assistance to railroads during the same period.

Space heating—residential, commercial, and industrial—and along with it space cooling, represents one of the most serious wastes of energy. This is because of the usual reliance on fossil fuel to accomplish what solar heating could do better, and because of the lack of proper building design and insulation. Great savings in energy are accomplished through proper insulation alone. Still greater savings can be gained through proper building design—using solar heating and cooling principles. American agriculture, and those industries associated with it, is well ahead in energy wastage. To deliver food to consumers—including the cost of growing it, processing it, transporting it—may cost 10, 20, or more calories of energy for every food calorie put on the table. This does not reflect only the energy inefficiency of the farming practices employed, but also the fact that we now do in the factory much of the work that was once done on the farm and that in much of the world is still done there. This problem will be examined more closely in the following chapter.

These are only examples of the many ways in which energy is wasted and could be conserved. Amory Lovins has pointed out that if per capita energy use in the United States were reduced to the same level as in France (where living standards are equivalent), the energy saved would be enough to give everyone else on earth one-fourth more energy than they now have. He states: (1973) *In the USA, for example, a politically acceptable strategy could be devised and implemented within two years of an orderly reduction of the energy growth rate by perhaps 0.3–0.5 percentage points a year, reaching zero within about a decade despite continuing population growth. The author believes that without prohibitive cost or disruption, the level of US energy consumption could then be smoothly reduced, at a rate of perhaps 1–2%/yr, by a factor of at least two over the ensuing two or three decades—again despite continuing population growth.*

In other words, through energy conservation and some redeployment of economic activity, we could maintain a high standard of living without any need for massive nuclear development or of scraping the earth for the last of the fossil fuels (Lovins, 1973).

The potential for energy conservation was also demonstrated by the Scientist's Institute for Public Information (SIPI) in response to the proposal from the then existing Atomic Energy Commission for a massive national effort to develop liquid-metal fast-breeder reactors (LMFBRs). According to the AEC proposal, this could produce 435 million kilowatts of electricity by the year 2000 (Table 7.12). The SIPI proposal, relying

TABLE 7.12 Comparison of Proposed Fast-breeder-reactor Program with Electrical Generation and Conservation by Other Means

	PROJECTIONS TO 2000 A.D.	
ENERGY SOURCE	GENERATING CAPACITY OR SAVINGS IN MILLIONS OF KILOWATTS	PERCENTAGE OF TOTAL U.S. ENERGY DEMAND
LMFBR program (AEC)	435	23
Alternatives		
Solar energy		
Photovoltaic	140	7
Solar thermal	40	2
Solar heating/cooling of buildings	35	2
Wind generators	170	9
Bioconversion	25	1
Total solar	410	21
Geothermal	80	4
Conservation	236	12
Total alternatives	765	37

Source: Scientist's Institute for Public Information (1974).

heavily on a reasonable degree of energy conservation and development of solar energy, could reach the same goal with no construction of nuclear reactors. In fact the breeder reactor program has been stalled, with the go-ahead to proceed with the Clinch River project only being given in 1982, although funding still in doubt.

In 1974 the Ford Foundation released the results of the most thorough study of American energy policy that had been carried out up to that time. They examined three scenarios: the *historical growth scenario,* in which we were to plow ahead as we had in the past, but faster, encouraging growth and grasping everywhere for fossil fuel and nuclear power to support it; the *technical fix scenario,* in which we would seek to avoid waste and increase technical efficiency without slowing growth or changing our patterns of economic activity greatly; and finally, the *zero-energy-growth scenario,* in which the aim would be to level off the rate of energy consumption in the United States. This could be achieved without anybody being worse off materially or economically.

TABLE 7.13 "Forecasting" Energy Futures: Various Predictions Concerning United States Energy Demand in the Year 2000 A.D. All Figures in Quads·(Quadrillion Btus)

YEAR OF FORECAST	BEYOND THE PALE	HERESY	CONVENTIONAL WISDOM	SUPERSTITION
1972	125 (Lovins)	140 (Sierra Club)	160 (Atomic Energy Commission)	190 (Federal Power Commission Bureau of Mines)
1974	100 (Ford Foundation Energy Project)	124 (Ford Foundation)	140 (AEC)	174 (Electrical Energy Institute)
1976	75 (Lovins)	89–95 (Lovins; F.V. Hippel)	124 (U.S. ERDA)	140 (Electrical Energy Institute)
1978	33 (Steinhart)	63–77 (on Nuclear & Alternate Energy)	96–101 (Institute of Energy Analysis; U.S. DOE)	124 (Ralph Lapp)

Current U.S. energy demand (1982): 75 quads (Source Wasserman, 1982)

The American people and American business and industry have shown a response that would not have been predicted in the early 1970s. The increased cost of energy, and a general realization that the "energy crisis," however defined, was real, has brought a marked decline in energy use. This has confounded energy company analysts, who find themselves with more generating capacity than is in fact needed. It has led to a marked change in forecasts of future energy consumption, which is shown in Table 7.13, prepared by Amory Lovins (Wasserman, 1982). Whereas in 1972 the Atomic Energy Commission and the Federal Power Commission, along with the Bureau of Mines, were predicting levels of energy consumption in the year 2000 roughly equivalent to the Ford

REGAINING A WORLD VIEW

Heating up from Renewables

SOURCE	1980	1985	1990	1995	2000
		(Million metric tons coal equivalent)			
Renewable biomass	1189	1308	1465	1683	1955
Hydroelectric	600	710	850	1020	1200
Wind	3	5	17	90	200
Geothermal	13	27	52	87	140
Direct solar	2	6	20	69	140
Total	1807	2056	2404	2949	3635

Estimates of world energy consumption based on Worldwatch Institute. From Lester Brown (1981), *Building a Sustainable Society.* W. W. Norton, New York.

Cultures that were organized around the transformation of renewable energy sources perceived the world as a continual coming and going of seasons. The cycles of birth, life, death, and rebirth were qualitative processes. The energy sources were full of life and color. With renewable resources, the concept of order and decay was an ever-present reminder of the way the world unfolds....

Contrast the features of renewable energy sources with nonrenewable. Coal and oil are lifeless quantities. They can be divided and redivided and still the individual parts will contain the same attributes as the whole. A speck of coal is little different in composition from a chunk of coal, while the leaf of a plant is very different from the stem or roots. Nonrenewable resources represent a fixed stock. They can be easily quantified. They are subject to precise measurement. They can be ordered. Renewable resources, on the other hand, are forever changing and flowing. They are never still. They are always in the process of becoming....

Jeremy Rifkin. *Entropy: a new world view.* Bantam Books, New York, 1980, p. 95.

Foundation's historical growth scenario (160 to 190 quads) by 1978, the federal Department of Energy, and others, had dropped their estimates to 96 to 101 quads, or the equivalent of Ford's zero-energy-growth scenario. Amory Lovins was considered "beyond the pale" in 1972 when he predicted that U.S. energy usage would be as low as 125 quads by 2000 A.D. and was still considered in that "flaky" area when he predicted in 1976 that it might be as low as 75 quads. Now his estimates are considered conservative by other energy experts who think that consumption might drop as low as 33 quads—well below the 1982 level of 75 quads. Zero energy growth, or even further reductions in energy use, now seems realistic. The reason seems to lie with the ability of the American public to turn back from a no-win situation, even when the government is still beating the drums for more growth and more consumption and refuses to foreclose the "nuclear option."

SOURCES

Benjamin, Milton R., 1982. *San Jose News,* July 22, pp. 1A, 6A.

Clark, Wilson, 1975. *Energy for survival.* Anchor Press, Doubleday, New York.

Council on Environmental Quality, 1970. *Environmental quality.* CEQ, Washington, D.C.

———1980. *The global 2000 report to the president. Entering the twenty-first century.* U.S. Government Printing Office, Washington, D.C.

Darrow, Ken and Rick Pam, 1976. *Appropriate technology sourcebook.* Volunteers in Asia, Stanford, Calif.

Eckholm, Eric, 1979. *Planting for the future.* Worldwatch Paper 26, Washington, D.C.

Entwistle, Robert, 1973. The crisis we won't face squarely. *Sierra Club Bulletin* 58:9–12, 32.

Exxon, 1981. *World energy outlook, Dec. 1980.* Exxon Background Series, New York.

Freeman, David, et al., 1974. *A time to choose. America's energy future.* Energy policy project of the Ford Foundation. Ballinger, Cambridge, Mass.

Henderson, Hazel, 1981. *The politics of the solar age.* Anchor Press, Doubleday, New York.

Holum, John R., 1977. *Topics and terms in environmental problems.* Wiley–Interscience, New York.

Hughes, J. Donald and J. V. Thirgood, 1982. Deforestation, erosion, and forest management in ancient Greece and Rome. *Journal of Forest History* 26 (2):60–75.

Inglis, David, 1978. Wind power on a grand scale. *Sun,* Stephen Lyons, editor. Friends of the Earth, San Francisco, pp. 215–225.

Kristoferson, Lars, 1973. Energy in society. *Ambio* 2:178–185.

Lovins, Amory, 1973. *World energy strategies: facts, issues and options.* Earth Resources Research Ltd., London.

————1977. *Soft energy paths. Toward a durable peace.* Ballinger, Cambridge, Mass.

————1981. Statement to the 2nd International Conference on Soft Energy Paths. *Soft energy notes* 4 (1):6–7.

Lyons, Stephen, 1978. Solar cells. *Sun,* Stephen Lyons, editor. Friends of the Earth, San Francisco, pp. 246–253.

Medvedev, Z. A., 1979. *Nuclear disaster in the Urals.* Norton, New York.

————1982. Letter. *Science,* 217:200.

Morland, Howard, 1982. The meltdown that didn't happen. *Environment 82/83,* J. Allen, editor. Dushkin, Guilford, Conn., p. 63.

Nash, Hugh, editor, 1977. *Progress as if survival mattered.* Friends of the Earth, San Francisco.

Norman, Colin, 1982. Soviet radwaste spill confirmed. *Science* 216:274.

Schell, Jonathan, 1982. *The fate of the earth.* Alfred Knopf, New york.

Sinsheimer, Robert L., 1981. The presumptions of science. *The Ecologist* 11:4–11.

Trabalka, J. R., L. D. Eyman, and S. I. Auerbach., 1982. Radioactivity in the Urals. *Science* 217:198.

Wasserman, R. M., 1982. The soft path. *Environment 82/83,* J. Allen, editor. Dushkin, Guilford, Conn., p. 45.

Weinberg, Alvin, M., 1972. *Nuclear energy–18 years after.* Speech to the American Public Power Association, San Francisco.

FINDING
FOOD

We can say that man's management of the land must be primarily orientated towards three goals—health, beauty, and permanence. The fourth goal—the only one accepted by the experts—productivity, will then be attained almost as a by-product. The crude materialist view sees agriculture as "essentially directed towards food-production." A wider view sees agriculture as having to fulfill at least three tasks:

- *to keep man in touch with living nature, of which he is and remains a highly vulnerable part;*
- *to humanise and ennoble man's wider habitat; and*
- *to bring forth the foodstuffs and other materials which are needed for a becoming life.*

I do not believe that a civilisation which recognizes only the third of these tasks, and which pursues it with such ruthlessness and violence that the other two tasks are not merely neglected but systematically counteracted, has any chance of long-term survival.

E. F. Schumacher, *Small Is Beautiful* (1973)

CREATING DESERTS

In an area in the foothills north of Mexico City a story of man's relationship with the soil is written in the landscape. It was recorded by Starker Leopold in the course of his biological studies in the area (1959). The region was visited by Alexander von Humboldt in 1803. He described it as a beautiful place covered with a tall open forest of pine and oak. Only the lower slopes toward the Valley of Mexico had been cleared for agriculture at that time. But populations grew and the demand for new farming land increased. Farther and farther up the slopes the forests were cleared. First, perhaps they were cut for timber, but then the collectors of charcoal came and built their little ovens to convert the remaining woody vegetation into fuel that was easily transported to the city. The cleared lands were first planted to corn or wheat, but these give poor cover to the soil on sloping ground. The rains each year would wash some of the topsoil away and leach out the minerals on which the soil's fertility depended. Finally, corn would grow there no longer, but the soils continued to wash until only the barren subsoil remained. This, however, could grow maguey, the cactus-like agave raised for the fibers of its leaves. Maguey can grow on improverished ground, but it offers scant cover. Virtually all of the soil washed down the hill until only a bare and impervious hardpan remained and the cultivation of maguey also ceased. Still a few desert-tolerant plants could grow there, and these supported the scant grazing of goats and donkeys until they too were gone. A wasteland in the true sense of the word remains. The story illustrates a process that has been repeated again and again throughout the world, an attempt to find food, or other materials that can be exchanged for food, through exploitation of the soil, resulting in the degradation of the basic and irreplaceable natural resource on which terrestrial life depends.

The word *soil* has been used in so many senses that its meaning is sometimes obscured. Here it will be used to mean the thin layer on the surface of the lands formed by the interaction among the rocks of the earth's crust with the sunlight, the air, and living organisms. Living plants and animals make the difference between soil and the mineral substrate that can become soil through their action. All true soils are the product of life, interacting with rock, air, water, and sunlight; and they, in turn, support and are maintained by life. True soil teems with life, microscopic in size for the most part. It is thus a renewable resource, within limits, but like all such resources can be used beyond its level of sustainability and thus becomes nonrenewable.

Throughout the desert edges of the world, soil that once supported grasses, shrubs, and trees has been lost, blown by wind or washed by the infrequent but often heavy downpours of rain. Lands that were productive have become barren wastelands. We call them deserts, and the process desertification. But this is an insult to true deserts, which have their own unique flora and fauna. The extent to which these barren lands are increasing, moving at a rate of nearly 20 kilometers a year in some areas of the Sahel, the zone adjacent to the Sahara in Africa, has made desertification a matter of international concern and the subject of a major United Nations conference in 1977. The area already in the process of desertification or at serious risk from it covers 20 million square kilometers, twice the size of Canada, located particularly in Africa and Asia, but also in the Americas and Australia.

Loss of soil and productivity does not affect only the dry lands. In the humid tropics, wherever sloping ground occurs, land clearing leads to soil erosion, since heavy rains are constant in their occurrence. With soil lost the forests do not come back, or only slowly over centuries— too long for the human life span. In addition, in the productive farm lands of America and Europe, increasing demands for agricultural products and new methods of farming have led to abandonment of older soil-conserving practives. Erosion is again a major problem, and it has been estimated that soil loss from water erosion alone removes two billion tons of soil from U.S. croplands, a billion more tons than can be formed by natural soil-forming processes. Lester Brown estimates that this is like losing 781,000 acre equivalents of cropland each year (1981, p. 18).

We are as dependent on soil for our food today as we were in the Neolithic when agriculture was first beginning. But worldwide we are experiencing a loss of farming land, which some UN estimates show may equal one-third of the total now available by the year 2000.

> *A further illustration of the irresponsibility of governments has been their reaction to the findings of UNEP's highly informative Conference on Desertification, held in Nairobi in 1977. Delegates learned there that up to a third of the world's agricultural land was likely to be lost to desertification before the end of the century, while much of the world's remaining agricultural land would be subjected to serious erosion to the point that its productivity would be progressively reduced—with a corresponding increase in malnutrition and starvation.*
>
> *To counteract those fatal trends, UNEP set up a special account to raise 2.4 billion dollars for twenty years, the sum that according to its consultants was required to bring the trends to a halt. Clearly, governments, if they had had the slightest sense of responsibility, would have fought to contribute to this special fund. But the opposite has happened. By the end of 1981 only 5,000 dollars had been contributed to the special account, a donation from the government of Mexico.*
>
> Edward Goldsmith, The retreat from Stockholm. *The Ecologist* (1982), p. 98

SOIL FORMATION

Soil forms through a process known as *biotic succession* starting from a relatively lifeless surface—solid rock, volcanic ash, talus slides, lava flows, sand dunes, silt deposits, or the windblown accumulations of fine particles known as loess. Depending on the substrate and its inherent fertility (ability to supply essential nutrients to plants), succession may be rapid, as on some silts or loess, or very slow, as on solid granite rock. Always, however, it is started by *pioneer plants,* which are of necessity hardy and able to withstand severe environmental conditions, including in most cases full sunlight and extremes of heat and cold. Pioneer plants modify the inorganic base, break up rock, add humus (partially decomposed organic material) to sand, loosen up and aerate silt or clay beds, and over time prepare the ground for the invasions and establishment of less hardy vegetation. Lichens growing on rock give way to mosses and these in turn to broad-leaved herbs, ferns, or grasses. This vegetation further modifies the inorganic base, sending roots deeper, adding more plant debris to form more humus, shading the surface against direct light. The site is prepared for vegetation with more demanding characteristics.

Shrubs and small trees become established and may shade out the earlier invaders. Great numbers of animals and microorganisms add to the process. Blue-green algae and bacteria that can capture inorganic nitrogen from the air and form it into the nitrates that plants need to form proteins play an important role. Earthworms churn and mix the soil. A variety of insects and other small invertebrates each have a role to play in cycling nutrients, converting them into forms more useful to plants.

Eventually a relatively stable, but dynamic, balance is reached between the original substrate, vegetation, animals, and microorganisms, all shaped by and attuned to the local climate, including both the macroclimate or regional climate, and the climate near the ground, the microclimate. This is itself changed by the presence of vegetation, which modifies temperatures and increases humidity, and protects the ground surface from the full impact of wind and rain. What is known as a steady-state or climax community takes shape and tends to remain in place in the absence of serious outside disturbance. With this a mature soil is formed. This does not happen quickly—centuries may be involved.

The kind of soil that will be formed is determined first of all by the regional climate. Dry climates produce desert soils; less dry, grassland or steppe soils; moist climates, forest soils. But all are intricacies of life and inorganic, and all tend to be self-sustaining, growing, maintaining fertility, supporting life year after year. Differences in substrate, or slope, or exposure to the sun cause local soil differences. Seldom are soils really uniform over large areas; more commonly a mosaic of living soils with their characteristic vegetation and animal life carpets the surface of the land.

SOIL CHARACTERISTICS

SOIL TEXTURE AND STRUCTURE The size and physical characteristics of the various particles of which soils are composed, and the ways in which these particles are arranged, are among the most important properties of soil in that they influence most other soil characteritics. Soil *texture* is the term that refers to the size of soil particles. The broad classes of texture range from coarse gravel at one extreme, through sand and silt to clay at the other. The size range of particles and the way in which they group into soil textural classes can be presented in the form of a triangle in which each apex represents a different size class of soil particle (Fig. 8.1).

The textural classes to be found in a soil contribute to its *structure*, a term that describes how soil particles are grouped together into larger aggregates. Soil structure is dependent on the amount and kind of clay present and on the amount of organic matter within the soil. Clay has a large amount of surface area relative to the size of its particle and therefore the capacity to absorb water and other molecules or ions on its surface. These in turn form links between the particles and give rise to aggregates. This quality of clay is familiar to the potter, who moistens dry clay and from it forms a mixture that will hold together in whatever shape in which he molds it. Organic particles in the soil, of the same size range as clay, have a similar ability to adsorb water and link other

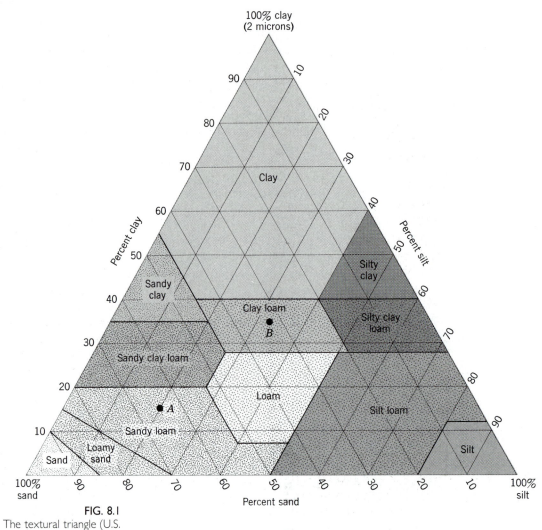

FIG. 8.1
The textural triangle (U.S. Dept. of Agriculture Soil Survey Manual).

particles together. Soils that are a mix of clay, organic substances, and coarser materials develop a combination of coarse and fine materials aggregated into crumbs, nutlike chunks, or other pieces of various sizes and shapes. Soils deficient in clay or organic materials are structureless, powdery dusts or loose sands. Soils too rich in clay may form a compacted soil mass which like baked pottery becomes virtually impervious to water or plant roots.

SOIL WATER   The water-holding capacity of soil determines its value for agriculture and the support of natural vegetation. Plants not only require water as such, but water is the solvent through which the nutrients that plants need are carried to the roots of the plant. Permanently dry soils are lifeless. Permenently waterlogged soils can support only some types of aquatic plants. Light, structureless sands and gravels are easily penetrated by water, but water quickly sinks through them to depths below where most plant roots can reach. Sand dunes, for example, even in rainy climates, can be colonized only by drought-resistant plants or those with deep root systems. At the other extreme, heavy clay soils are difficult for water to penetrate, and much of the water that does enter becomes bound to clay particles by chemical forces that make it unavailable to plants.

The soil best able to hold water and supply it to plants is one with a well-developed granular structure. Between the aggregates or crumbs of soil are channels and air spaces, and within the aggregates are smaller spaces. Water drains through the larger channels, but is held in the smaller spaces within reach of plant roots. In general, soils rich in organic matter hold more water than soils low in organic matter, both because of the capacity of humus to absorb and hold water and because of its ability to improve soil structure.

The ability of a soil to supply water to plants also varies with its surface characteristics and the local climate. Rain falling on soil must first enter it if water is to reach plant roots. Soil surfaces protected with plant cover and plant litter, and penetrated by a variety of openings— from animal burrows to channels left by decayed plant roots and stems— can take on water more rapidly than bare soils. Bare soil surfaces tend to become compacted and sealed over by the impact of rain drops. Once water enters the soil it becomes subject to evaporation and transpiration (the movement of water from the soil through plant roots, up plant stems and out into the air again through plant leaves). These are influenced by temperature, humidity, and wind velocity. Ten inches of rain in a cool, moist climate can keep a soil saturated throughout the year. In a warm, dry, windy climate, the same amount can evaporate almost as rapidly as it falls. Evaporation, however, is retarded by the same factors that facilitated the entrance of water into the soil—the cover of plant litter on the ground and the presence of layers of plants above the ground.

SOIL AERATION   Soil air is as important as soil water. Although plant leaves are engaged in photosynthesis and give off oxygen to the air, plant roots must carry out respiration, consuming oxygen and giving off carbon dioxide. Oxygen must be able to move from the atmosphere into the soil, and carbon dioxide must be able to move from the soil into the atmosphere. Soils without sufficient oxygen, such as those found in marshes and bogs or at the bottom of ponds and lakes, can support only anaerobic bacteria or other microorganisms that obtain their oxygen from the chemical breakdown of complex molecules.

Heavy clay soils become not only waterlogged but also oxygen deficient. Light sandy soils have plenty of air but do not hold water. A well-aggregated loamy soil can both hold water and still have sufficient channels for air movement.

FIG. 8.2
Soil profiles.

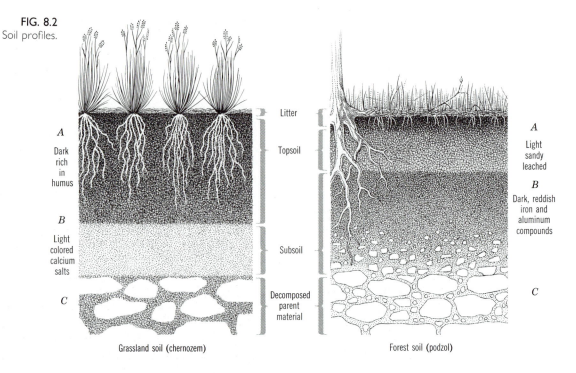

Grassland soil (chernozem) Forest soil (podzol)

SOIL PROFILE   Most soils have a more or less distinct layering when viewed in profile from a trench cut into them. These layers are known as soil *horizons* (Fig. 8.2). (The use of the word *horizon* in this sense seems intended mostly to confuse the English language still further.)

The horizons, in simplest terms, range from *D* at the bottom (unmodified parent material) to *A* at the top. However, some call the litter layer above the *A* an *O* horizon, and some interpose an *E* horizon between the *A* and the *B* layers. (The interposition of *E* and *O* in what would otherwise be an easily learned alphabetical sequence further reflects on the mental perversity of some scientists.)

The *A* horizon is commonly known as topsoil, the B is the subsoil, and the two together form the true soil. In the topsoil, organic materials become converted to humus and mixed with mineral matter. From the topsoil, through the action of rain percolating through the soil mixture, minerals are dissolved out and carried down into the B horizon, where they tend to be deposited. The A horizon is thus subject to leaching and the B to deposition of mineral compounds. The topsoil is the area for maximum abundance of soil organisms and the greatest amount of biotic activity. Deep-rooted plants serve to keep minerals in circulation, by taking them out of the subsoil and depositing them, in the form of plant litter, on top of the topsoil layer, from where they can be once again incorporated into the topsoil and made available for new seedlings or shallow rooted plants.

SOIL BIOTA   The topsoil in any moist and nutrient-rich soil will be teeming with invisible life, all of which play roles in maintaining soil fertility. The sheer
quantity of organisms in the soil is sometimes amazing. It has been estimated that there may be more than 25 million bacteria in a gram of
topsoil. The weight of these (to most people) weightless organisms can
amount to a ton or more per acre. To move to a larger life form, the
roundworm or nematode has been estimated to reach levels of nearly
650,000 per acre in the top six inches of soil. The visible animal and
plant life aboveground is usually impressive in its total weight or biomass,
but the biomass of organisms below the ground surface is often much
greater than that above.

All of these countless creatures living in the soil are busy, and their
principal task is in the breakdown, decay, and recycling of the chemical
constituents of organic matter, as well as the recombination in various
useful forms of the mineral components of the soil. Without these processes,
soil nutrients would become tied up in organic debris, soils would stag-
nate, and the production of new life would cease. Such relatively scarce
nutrients as nitrates and phosphates, in heavy demand by plants, are kept
available only by the recycling action of soil organisms. One of the most
important roles lies in capturing nitrogen from the soil air, changing it
through a series of processes involving a variety of nitrogen-fixing bacteria or algae into nitrates, in which form it becomes useful to green
plants.

One important reason for adding organic fertilizers—compost—to
the soil is the stimulation they provide for the growth and proliferation
of soil microorganisms. Chemical fertilizer alone may not be sufficient
for this purpose and may in fact inhibit it.

In addition to microorganisms, the larger living inhabitants of the
soil are also important and sometimes surprisingly abundant. The role of
earthworms in churning, mixing, and processing the soil is well known.
In the tropics in particular, soil insects can be extremely active. For
example, in one rainforest area of the Congo it was estimated that between 20 and 25 tons of plant debris were deposited on each acre per
year. Yet very little of this remained on the surface—the litter layer was
not deep. Soil insects, and particularly termites, were consuming this
plant material as it fell to the ground. In some tropical areas termites are
both abundant and conspicuous, since some species build towering
mounds. Pierre Gourou (1966) noted one area in Katanga where three
giant termite mounds occur per acre and occupy 6 percent of the land
surface. If demolished and spread around, these would cover each acre
to the depth of eight inches. Elsewhere mounds are smaller and more
abundant. Even what appears to be dry and lifeless ground will spring
to life following a rain, and small forests of tiny termite mounds will
build up overnight on dirt roads across the savannas of Zimbabwe. In
temperate-zone soils where insect life is usually less abundant than in
the tropics, it may still be impressive. In Washington, D.C., in 1970 the

17-year cicadas came up from the soil to swarm in enormous flocks on trees and shrubs. Each left a hole up to one-half inch in diameter where it emerged from the ground. Ten to 20 of these per square foot could be counted in some areas.

All of these organisms up to the size of gophers, moles, wombats, aardvarks, or badgers, which burrow in the soil, play a part in maintaining soil structure and fertility through their churning and mixing of the organic matter they add to it and their role in the interchange and circulation of soil nutrients.

SOIL FERTILITY   Fertility of soil is its ability to provide chemical nutrients for plant growth. The mere presence of these elements is not enough to make the soil fertile. They must be present in available form, meaning in solution, or be capable of going into solution in the presence of water, organic acids, and other soil solvents. Essential nutrients include those that plants require in large quantities (macronutrients), such as nitrates, phosphates, calcium, potassium, and magnesium, and also those required in trace amounts (trace elements or micronutrients), such as copper, cobalt, zinc, and manganese. Trace elements can be toxic to plants in large quantities, but are essential in minute amounts.

Under undisturbed or natural conditions, there is a constant turnover of nutrients in any area. Minerals go from soil to plants to animals, are returned to the soil in animal or plant wastes or remains, are liberated by soil organisms, and are made available for use again. In dry areas little is lost from the soil except through the slow processes of geological erosion or by animal or plant emigrants to other areas. In wet areas leaching removes minerals from the topsoil, but this is compensated, in part at least, by minerals brought from deeper in the ground by deep-rooted plants.

When people existed as natives of an area, they acted only as another link in food chains and did not remove nutrients from an area. With the advent of civilization, however, along with trade and commerce, crop plants or livestock were not always used locally, but shipped to population centers. In time cities became "nutrient sinks," draining soil fertility from all areas from which their food or fiber was produced, and slowly degrading the ability of soils to provide adequate nutrition to humans or animals.

In the humid tropics, many of the soil types appear infertile when subject to chemical analysis, since their nutrients are tied up in the living plants and animals of the tropical forests and are quickly recycled back into living systems through rapid breakdown and decomposition of dead organic material. When these forests are cleared, oxidation of organic matter and leaching of chemical nutrients takes place rapidly and soil fertility can be quickly depleted. Often crops grown will have low protein quality and contribute to human malnutrition. The abundance and luxuriant growth of tropical plants can conceal nutritional deficiencies, since it reflects only an abundance of cellulose and lignin rather than nutritionally valuable compounds.

SOIL DEVELOPMENT AND CLASSIFICATION

The soil characteristics described thus far are used in classifying soils into different types and groups, the members of which can be expected to show similar properties wherever they occur. Major soil differences, related to differences in climate and vegetation, develop from the operation of various soil development processes, each of which characterizes a widespread natural region (Fig. 8.3).

Thus, in cold, rainly climates, where coniferous forests grow, soils undergo a process called *podsolization*. Coniferous forests add little organic matter to the soil. The leaves and litter that fall are resistant to decay, reducer organisms are scarce in the surface soil, and, consequently, there is only a slow breakdown of the needles and twigs to form a humic acid. Rainfall, percolating through this litter, becomes acidic, and since the rainfall is usually high, penetrates deep into the soil. This acidic solution, therefore, can leach most of the soil nutrients from the topsoil until it comes to consist of little but quartz sand. Some minerals, mostly iron and aluminum salts, are redeposited in the subsoil, which becomes dark colored in consequence. Many important nutrients are carried deeper or are washed away. In its extreme form, podsolization occurs under heavy coniferous forest. Most forest soils in temperate climates, however, are subjected to this development process. Where broadleaved deciduous forests predominate, the process may be compensated for to some degree. Deciduous forest litter contains basic salts and minerals, and the forest floor usually supports a rich population of reducer organisms. Consequently, humus is formed and incorporated with the topsoil to restore its fertility. Such soils are less acidic and better suited to agricultural use than podsols. Nearly all of the soils in the forested regions of North America and Eurasia can be grouped together on the basis of having undergone a similar development process, although many variations result from local differences in climate, vegetation, and substrate (USDA, 1957).

In drier climates, under grassland vegetation, a different development process occurs, which has been termed *calcification*. Rainfall percolating through grass litter does not become charged with acid. Because of the relatively low precipitation, the complete leaching of minerals from the soil does not normally occur. Lime and other carbonates are dissolved from the topsoil but are redeposited in a calcified layer in the subsoil. Grasses add great amounts of organic matter to the topsoil and thus serve to replace nutrients and keep it dark and rich in humus. Calcification is best developed in grassland areas with moderate rainfall.

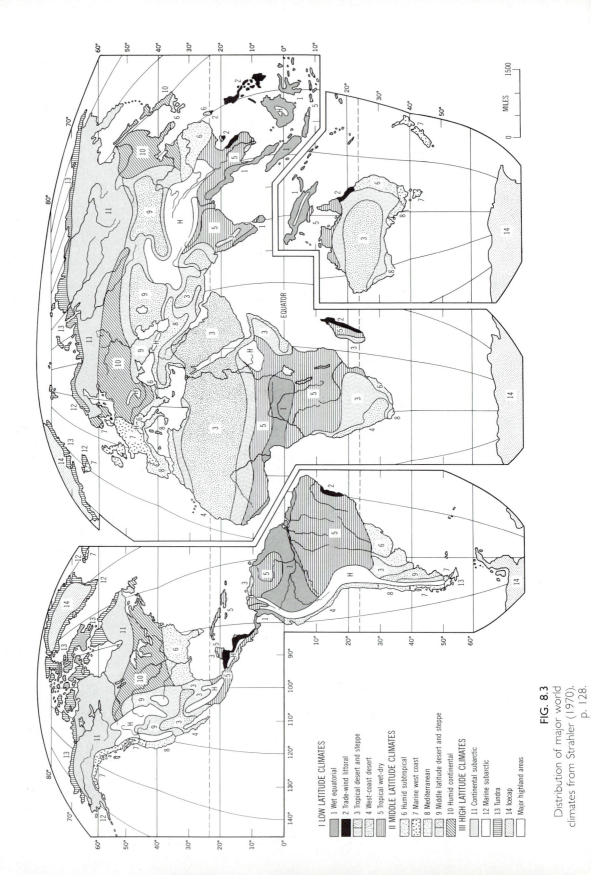

I LOW LATITUDE CLIMATES
1 Wet equatorial
2 Trade-wind littoral
3 Tropical desert and steppe
4 West-coast desert
5 Tropical wet-dry

II MIDDLE LATITUDE CLIMATES
6 Humid subtropical
7 Marine west coast
8 Mediterranean
9 Middle latitude desert and steppe
10 Humid continental

III HIGH LATITUDE CLIMATES
11 Continental subarctic
12 Marine subarctic
13 Tundra
14 Icecap
Major highland areas

MILES

0   1500

FIG. 8.3
Distribution of major world
climates from Strahler (1970),
p. 128.

188

Here the topsoil is deep and the calcified layer is well below the surface. In drier areas some calcification occurs but there is less leaching of soil materials. The topsoil may be rich in lime and basic salts but, because of the sparser vegetation, may be low in organic matter and nitrogen.

In the tropics where rainfall is heavy and temperatures are high, leaching and rapid oxidation of the surface soils results in the removal of most of the nutrients. In extreme cases, even much of the silica is removed from the topsoil. The remaining soil in the A horizon is composed predominantly of iron oxides, which, under extreme conditions, form a tough, hard layer called *laterite*. The process has therefore been called *laterization,* and the end products are variously known as *lateritic* soils, *latosols,* or, more recently, *ferralsols* because of their high iron content. Laterite is one of the hardest rocks known and is used for highway paving. It has been used in the past to construct such long-lived edifices as the temples of Angkor in Cambodia. When a lateritic crust forms in the tropics as a result of soil misuse, the land can be lost to cultivation permanently. Not all tropical soils, however, are subject to laterization.

An additional way of looking at soil development that helps to illustrate the "renewability" of soils and their continued usefulness under agricultural practices focuses on the natural processes to which soils are exposed throughout their existence. These processes may be grouped into three categories of "regimes": the weathering or wasting regime, the organic or cyclic regime, and the drift regime (Wright and Bennema, 1965).

Under the *weathering* regime the minerals from which the soils are formed are broken down to yield clay and various mineral salts or ions. The more soluble salts (e.g., sodium, chlorides, and potash) tend to wash away in any area of moderate or high rainfall, or in semiarid country they may move up with capillary water as evaporation occurs and be deposited on the soil surface. The less soluble materials, such as calcium or phosphate, are more stable, but they also move slowly from the topsoil to the subsoil or out of the soil entirely. Initially, the weathering regime favors soil fertility and plant growth through making clay and nutrients available. Over time, if it continues at a high rate because of high temperatures and rainfall, it will lead to the leaching away of most nutrients from the soil.

The *organic* regime tends to counter the weathering regime. Organic life above or in the soil not only adds carbon and nitrogen to the soil directly and incorporates solar energy within it but also keeps minerals in circulation, holds minerals in the soil, and brings them from deeper layers back to the soil surface. This organic life furthermore incorporates animal and plant residues in the soil. However, where oxidation and incorporation of organic materials is slowed down or arrested, as in podsolic soils, then the addition of organic acids to the soil water through partial decomposition of organic debris can hasten the process of dissolving out and leaching away of soil nutrients.

The *drift regime* may also counter the weathering regime. This includes those processes that disturb and mix the soil: soil churning by animals, by freezing and thawing, and by shrinking or swelling, along with the erosive process that cause the deposition of materials washed or carried by wind, water, or gravity from other areas. These processes add fresh, unweathered, materials to the soil surface with new supplies of clays and mineral salts.

The operation of these processes leads to the development of varying degrees of soil fertility and stability. Highly fertile soils in which the organic and drift regimes are operative most strongly, as in tropical volcanic soils (*andosols*) enriched periodically by ash deposit, river basin soils (*luvisols*) enriched by fertile silt deposits, and grassland *chernozem* soils may be used for intensive agricultural purposes almost indefinitely. Moderately fertile soils in which the drift and organic regimes may partially balance the weathering regime may be exploited over long periods through careful attention to the renewal of their nutrients by fertilization. The *luvisols* (gray-brown podsolic soils) of temperate deciduous forests are an example. Finally, there are low-fertility soils in which the weathering regime has been most strongly operative, or will become so when natural vegetation is cleared. These soils cannot sustain even moderate agricultural use without intensive and expensive care and management. The tropical *ferralsols* are in this category.

Although the operation of broad regional processes of soil development gives rise to many similarities among the soils in any major climatic region, there are also major differences within any region. Each soil develops from a particular kind of parent material. This is acted on over time by the weather and climate of the area, which may be quite different from the regional climate. Each soil will support a particular kind of vegetation and animal life, which acts to modify it, and these factors, in turn, may change with time as various disturbing processes act on them. It follows, therefore, that a wide range of different kinds of soils can develop within any region which is diversified geologically or topographically, or within which different disturbing factors are operating. For example, one area might be regularly burned, changing the vegetation, whereas another might be long protected from fire. Such a wide range of soils does exist, and the task of classifying them, and of determining the purposes for which each type might best be used, has exercised the ability of soil scientists over many years. A proper classification of soils permits one to use knowledge of a particular kind of soil that has been acquired over a broad area by a great number of people for the immediate management and care of the soil in a particular place.

The basic unit of soil classification is the *soil series*. This is the soil equivalent of the species in animal or plant classification. All members of a soil series will be recognizably similar, will have developed from the same kind of parent material, and will have the same characteristics and arrangements of the horizons in the soil profile. The Hugo series, for example, is a moderately acid, well-drained soil that develops under coniferous forest cover in areas with rainfall exceeding 40 inches per year. It is well adapted to growing timber and supports excellent stands of Douglas fir. It is found in areas where hard, gray Franciscan sandstone predominates. The same sandstone in lower rainfall areas and on sites less suitable for soil formation gives rise to a developmental soil series known as Maymen soil. This is shallow, rocky, and poorly suited for any use other than the support of its natural cover, chaparral (Weislander and Storie, 1952).

Soil series are generally grouped into higher units of classification, of which the category of *Great Soil Groups* is best known and most widely used. These tend to correspond with regional climates and vegetation. A partial listing of these groups is presented for North America in Fig. 8.4, using terminology still most often encountered in the literature. As the knowledge of soils throughout the world has grown, however, the older systems of classification have needed revision. It was found, for example, that the same kind of soil was often given a different name in one part of the world than that by which it was known in another, not because of language differences, but because of failure to recognize the similarity. Furthermore, other soils thought to be essentially the same throughout the world have turned out to be quite different in some areas, and to require a new terminology (Kovda, 1965).

In the subarctic regions of America and Eurasia it was once assumed the soils of the forested taiga would all tend to be podsolic, whereas beyond the forest boundary to the north, tundra soils (gleysols) would occur. In fact, it was found to be not that simple, because of local differences in climate, topography, and parent material (Tedrow, 1970). Similarly, in the tropics, soil studies have shown the early assumption that one or two great soil groups would include all of the fully developed soils of the lowland, humid tropics, does not hold up. Once again, the situation is more complex than previously expected (Richards, 1971).

Starting in 1960, the United Nations Educational, Scientific, and Cultural Organization (UNESCO), the Food and Agricultural Organization (FAO), and the International Society of Soil Science joined together in a joint project to produce a world soil map. An internationally accepted terminology has been agreed on that permits a uniform approach to soil classifications. This new terminology makes use, insofar as possible, of the older Great Soil Group terminology. Both terms are shown in Figure 8.4, whereas the Great Soil Group terminology is shown in Table 8.1. A more detailed soil map of the United States is shown in Fig. 8.5 (Dudal, 1969).

SOILS AND AGRICULTURE

The amount of land on earth with soils well suited to agricultural use is difficult to estimate. Soil surveys have yet to be carried out in many areas. Many lands are still cultivated by shifting tropical agriculture. It has been estimated there are 14 million Km^2 of such land. However,

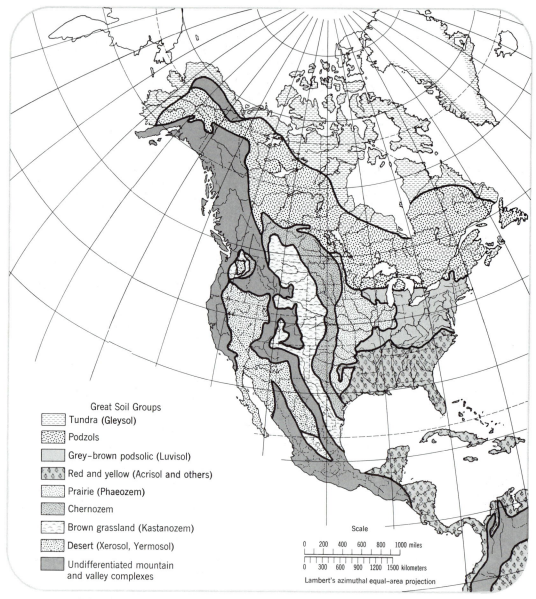

FIG. 8.4

Distribution of zonal soil groups of North America. (Adapted from Finch and Trewartha, 1942, after C. E. Kellogg, *Yearbook of Agriculture,* 1938.)

3000 Km² are lost each year to urbanization. Considering losses to erosion, desalinization, and other causes, it has been estimated that one-third of the total cropland will go out of production by the year 2000 (IUCN, 1980).

A comparison of the distribution of the major soil groups with the distribution of cropland in the United States indicates that agriculture is still largely restricted to certain soils. The chermozem, phaeozem, and kastanozem grassland soils are the great centers of cereal grain production and yield the bulk of the food, not only wheat and corn for people,

TABLE 8.1   Classification of Soils

Zonal Order	
Suborders	Great Soil Groups

Light-colored podzolized soils of forested regions	Podzol Soils
	   Brown podzolic soils
	Gray-Brown Podzolic Soils
	Red-Yellow Podzolic Soils
	   (Incl. *terra rossa*)

Lateritic soils of warm, moist subtropical, tropical, and equatorial regions	Latosols
	   Reddish-brown lateritic soils
	   Black and dark-gray tropical soils

Soils of the forest-grassland transition	Degraded chernozem soils
Dark-colored soils of the semi-arid, subhumid, and humid grasslands	Prairie Soils (Brunizem Soils) Reddish prairie soils Chernozem Soils Chestnut Soils Reddish-Chestnut and Reddish-Brown Soils
Light-colored soils of arid regions	Brown Soils Gray Desert Soils (Sierozem Soils) Red Desert Soils
Soils of the cold zone	Tundra Soils Arctic brown forest soils
Intrazonal Order	
Hydromorphic soils of marshes, swamps, bogs, and flat uplands	Bog Soils Meadow Soils (Wiesenböden) Alpine meadow soils Planosols
Halomorphic soils of poorly drained arid regions and coastal deposits	Saline Soils (Solonchak) Alkali Soils (Solonetz) Soloth
Calcimorphic soils	Rendzina Soils
Azonal Order	
Lithosols Regosols	Alluvial soils Sands (dry)

Source: Strahler, 1970 based on U.S. Department of Agriculture (1938). Washington, D.C.

but grains to feed or fatten much of the nation's livestock. Similar soils elsewhere in the world are also the primary producers of cereal grains. In the tropics two general categories of soil are particularly productive, those derived from recent volcanic deposits, particularly volcanic ash (andosols), and alluvial soils (fluvisols) derived from watersheds that yield an abundance of useful soil minerals. The older soils of the ancient granites and other crystalline igneous rocks of the tropics are low in fertility and yield alluvial soils low in fertility. Thus the deltas of the Mekong, the Ganges, or the Nile can produce continued high yields of crops because they are enriched by silts and clays washed from the

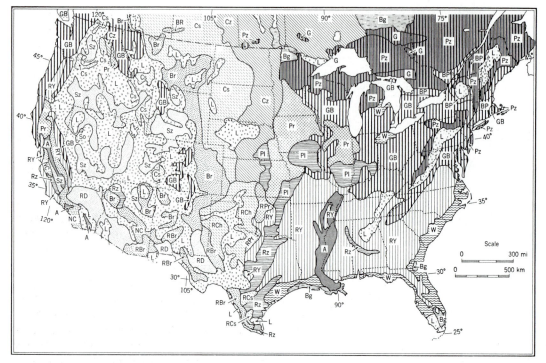

FIG. 8.5

Soils of the contiguous 48 United States and southern Canada. (*Source:* Strahler, 1970. Modified and simplified from map of soil associations of the United States by U.S. Department of Agriculture, Soil Survey Division in *Yearbook of American Agriculture, 1938,* U.S. Government Printing Office, Washington, D.C., 1938, and *Atlas of Canada,* 1957, Plate No. 35, Canada Dept. of Mines and Technical Surveys.)

ZONAL SOILS

Pz	Podzol soils
G	Gray wooded soils (Canada)
BP	Brown podzolic soils
GB	Gray-brown podzolic soils
RY	Red and yellow podzolic soils
Pr	Prairie soils
RPr	Reddish prairie soils
Cz	Chernozem soils
Cs	Chestnut soils
RCh	Reddish chestnut soils
Br	Brown soils
RBr	Reddish brown soils
NC	Noncalcic brown (Shantung brown) soils
Sz	Sierozem (Gray desert) soils
RD	Red desert soils

INTRAZONAL SOILS

Pl	Planosols
Rz	Rendzina soils
So	Solonchak and solonetz soils
W	Wiesenböden, ground-water podzol, and half bog soils
Bg	Bog soils

AZONAL SOILS

L	Lithosols and shallow soils, sands, lava beds
A	Alluvial soils

mountains of Ethopia, or the Asian highlands. But the Zambesi, draining from the Central African plateau, has no such fertile delta; nor, despite its enormous watershed, does the Amazon (Gourou, 1966). Most of the soils of the tropical forest country cannot produce sustained yields of crops even with the best of treatment, since they do not hold or respond well to fertilizer. At best, they are adapted to the shifting cultivation that allows them decades to recover fertility under the cover of natural vegetation.

In the temperate zone and into the subpolar regions, the highly podsolized soils are seldom cultivated, but certain soil types associated with them can be productive for dairying or for specialized crops. The less podsolized luvisols are intensively cultivated in Europe and Asia, and to a lesser degree in the United States. Similarly, some of the acrisols of the southeastern United States are successfully cultivated to yield a variety of crops. The heavily organic muck and marl soils, developed on formerly flooded lands in Florida and elsewhere in the subtropics, can be highly productive, but their productivity is gained at the expense of "soil mining," since the soils slowly disappear as their organic surfaces are exposed to the oxidizing effects of sun and air.

Desert soils (yermosols), in general, are seldom cultivated. Where irrigation can be made available, and where the proper balance of minerals exists, these soils can produce continued high yields of crops. But irrigation sometimes leads to the accumulation of alkaline or saline salts on the surface of former desert soils, brought up by high water tables or by capillary action as a result of the strong evaporative force of desert sunshine. Millions of acres of desert soils have been ruined by salinization and related processes.

Although it is not possible to say that agriculture has now expanded over the surface of the earth to include all of those soils most highly suitable to it, such a statement would be true with certain exceptions. There are some areas of potential high fertility and agricultural stability that have yet to be opened up and exploited, but relative to the total existing cropland on earth, these are of small extent. Efforts to expand cropland into new areas usually result only in the destruction of forests, rangelands, wilderness, or wildlife and little or no gain in total crop production. Far better results are to be obtained by using better crop varieties or better farming methods on existing farmlands. By using these improvements, production may quite easily be tripled on certain good but poorly managed agricultural lands, and no other resources are wasted.

In relation to the future of agriculture and the soil, it is instructive to review the past since, regrettably, many of the old mistakes are being repeated today. The history of agricultural use in the United States is particularly instructive.

AGRICULTURE AND FOREST SOILS

The objective of agriculture is to convert the nutrient materials of the soil into agricultural crops. Cultivation of the soil is intended to facilitate this process. Through plowing and harrowing the farmer breaks up the soil surface and the larger soil chunks, making it easier for the planting of seed and for the germinating seedlings to obtain water, air, and nutrients. In his initial cultivation also he removes competing natural vegetation or weeds and thus channels soil materials in the one direction of crop production. Through generations of experience, farmers have found the best soil structure for the production of most crops is one in which the soil is worked into relatively small crumbs and easily penetrated by water and plant roots. Cultivation aims at producing this condition.

Western agriculture in the long history of its development in the

AGRICULTURAL CHALLENGES

(a) Small-scale intensive farming such as this peasant farm near Smolensk, USSR, requires more labor but saves on expensive imported energy. This practice continues in many parts of Europe such as this farm (b) in Bavaria. By contrast, (c) a heavily mechanized wheat farm in Washington uses little farm labor but is subsidized by heavy energy inputs.

a

b

brown forest soils of Europe became characterized by those practices suited to produce the best possible agricultural structure in forest soils. It will be recalled that these soils are characterized by a layer of leaf litter and debris, a relatively leached topsoil, and a darker-colored subsoil in which the materials leached from the topsoil are deposited. Shallow cultivation does little for these soils. Deep plowing, however, tends to mix together the litter and humus, the light topsoil, and the deep mineral- and clay-rich subsoil. The resulting mixture is a stable, less erodible soil complex, with a better structure than the original forest topsoil (Jacks and Whyte, 1939). The addition of lime, which reduces acidity, and manure, which contributes nitrogen and organic compounds, further improves the structure. With care and with the standard European practices of crop rotation, cultivation can continue to improve these soils. Without this care and particularly under a system of farming based on the continued production, year after year, of a single cash crop, the structure of the soil breaks down, the soil nutrients leach out, crop yields decline, and eventually the soil becomes exhausted. If the soil lies on sloping ground, rainfall removes much of it by erosion once the structure is destroyed. When the eastern United States was settled, the European immigrants who were capable farmers continued their well-suited agricultural practices on the new lands. Where the settlers were poor farmers or interested only in production of cash crops for quick profit, the forest soils were depleted.

AGRICULTURE AND GRASSLAND SOILS

When the wave of settlement reached the grassland belt of soils, an entirely different set of conditions were encountered. The grassland soils naturally possessed the structure that cultivation over the year produced in forest soils. In their natural state they were resistant to erosion and slow to lose fertility. Because of this, many of the practices used on forest soils were gradually dropped. The new soils of the West gave continued high yields, year after year, of corn or wheat with little crop rotation. Liming and fertilization seemed unnecessary. So long as farm animals were used to pull the agricultural machinery, a certain amount of crop rotation took place to provide hay for the farm livestock, and manure was added to the soil. However, with the advent of farm machinery even these elementary soil-preserving practices were abandoned. Monoculture, emphasing high-value, high-yield grain crops in the northern plains and cotton in the southern plains, became the rule.

Despite their depth, excellent structure, and fertility, the grassland soils were not inexhaustible. Under natural conditions they were continually restored by additions of vast quantities of organic material from grass roots and stems and the droppings and remains of grassland animals, and they were maintained in structure by the mechanical action of grass roots and the burrowing of animals. Under continuous cultivation all of the factors that originally contributed toward building the soil were removed. Gradually soil structure has broken down and with it the capacity of the soil to absorb and hold water. Dry spells, which under natural conditions did little damage, became severe when the soils failed to take on and hold the rain that did fall. Yields began to decline as natural sources of nitrogen, organic materials, and mineral nutrients were removed. Farming in this region reached its lowest ebb during the decade of the 1930s.

THE DUST BOWL

In the better watered grassland soils of the East, the damage has not been so severe as that which accompanied the westward march of agriculture. In the brown soils of the arid Great Plains the most serious difficulties arose. The Great Plains region has been subjected throughout history to periodic droughts. The dry, hot areas of the southern Great Plains in particular have been plagued by long spells of below-average rainfall. Under the natural cover of short, sod-forming grasses, the droughts did little lasting damage. In the 1880s, however, the first wave of settlers moved into the southern Great Plains during a period of relatively high rainfall and lush growth. In 1890 a severe drought hit the plains and persisted for the better part of the decade. Many of the early settlers gave up and moved on to better farming lands elsewhere. In the late 1890s the rains returned, and the area again looked green and productive. A new wave of settlers arrived, plowed the plains, and planted the rich, brown soil to wheat.

In 1910 there was another dry spell and more damage. On the farmlands with bare soil exposed and soil structure broken down by cultivation, dust began to blow. An extensive area was damaged, and again many farmers gave up and moved on. In 1914 there was a great demand for wheat as the grain belt of Europe was ravaged by war. With high wheat prices, previously abandoned land looked like a good investment. Returning rains further improved the outlook. All of the land now judged suitable for agriculture was plowed, and in addition an estimated 6 million acres that should not have been plowed were put into wheat production. High rainfall and good times remained in the southern Great Rains until 1931.

In 1931 the nation was in the grip of a severe economic depression. In 1931, also, drought returned to the plains. Accentuated by previous damage to soil structure, the new drought surpassed all previous ones in severity. In the fall of 1933 began the series of dust storms that gave to the region a new name, the Dust Bowl (Fig. 8.6). Dust blew across the continent, darkened the skies, reddened the sunsets, and made the plains region almost uninhabitable in spots for man or livestock. Millions of acres of farms were damaged, with an estimated loss of topsoil ranging between two and 12 inches in places. Drifting dunes moved over farms, burying roads, fences, and even dwellings. A mass exodus of farmers, ruined by drought and unable to find work, streamed from Oklahoma,

Kansas, Texas, and adjoining areas and moved west to California or east into city bread lines. It was a period of misery and privation difficult to match in American history.

Drought, dust, and despair did what countless written and spoken words by soil scientists had failed to accomplish—it brought the nation to an awareness of the need for soil conservation. In 1935, in Washington, the Soil Conservation Service was created. The federal government and state legislatures soon passed enabling legislation that permitted the forming of soil-conservation districts. In these districts the Soil Conservation Service provided the aid and technical knowledge that farmers needed to put sound land-use principles into effect. In the Dust Bowl the process was begun of putting land back into grass where the plow should never have been used. On soil types better suited to farming, the use of conservation techniques was started.

In the 1940s the rains came again. Through efforts on the part of farmers and with the help of state and federal governments, many farms were restored to productivity. For a time it looked as though the Dust Bowl was a thing of the past, as though we had finally learned the lesson of conservation. But the 1940s also brought world war. In 1941 the German Wehrmacht swept across the rich wheat lands of Ukraine and brought the retaliatory measures of "scorched earth" and "lend lease." Grain from America went overseas to feed the allied armies and people, and grain prices in America went up. Economics and patriotism were mixed in the drive that sent the plow biting deep into millions of new

A dust storm in Colorado in the 1930's.

acres of plains grassland. The armies were fed, the Nazi war machine was broken, and the war-starved peoples of Europe were supplied. But in 1950 drought returned.

The drought of the 1950s set a new record in severity. Again the dust storms arose from eroded farms and overgrazed ranges. Crops failed, and farmers gave up trying. An emergency was proclaimed, and federal aid funds were poured into the area. That the conditions of the 1930s did not return was due in part to the generally high level of national prosperity. Farmers could afford to support their homes by working in factories in nearby cities. The land-ownership pattern had also changed. The family-sized farms that failed in the 1930s have been incorporated to an increasing extent into larger units. Fewer people were on the land to stand the brunt of the drought. In 1957 a second consequence of land misuse was felt throughout the Southwest. The rains returned, but not as gentle, life-restoring showers. Torrential downpours fell on the dust-blown eroded lands of the southern plains. Rivers swelled to flood proportions and poured over towns and cities, carrying with them the soil from once productive grassland ranges. Once again in the 1970s drought returned and ended the expectation that the United States could provide the world with all the grain needed to stave off hunger.

The Soil Conservation Service estimated in 1955 that, at least, 14 million acres in the Great Plains currently under cultivation should be returned to grass. It was pointed out that more than three-fourths of the plains cropland could be kept in crops but only if soil- and water-conservation measures were used.

The Dust Bowl was an object lesson on the effects of erosion. We have had many such lessons, from the dongas of South Africa to the gullies of South Carolina. We have had scientific studies of erosion on many soils and in many areas. The results of two such studies, in California and Missouri, tell their own story and show what happens when

TABLE 8.2   Cropping Systems and Soil Erosion

CROPPING SYSTEM OR CULTURAL TREATMENT	AVERAGE ANNUAL LOSS OF SOIL PER ACRE (TONS)	PERCENTAGE OF TOTAL RAINFALL RUNNING OFF THE LAND
Bare, cultivated, no crop	41.0	30
Continuous corn	19.7	29
Continuous wheat	10.1	23
Rotation: corn, wheat, clover	2.7	14
Continuous bluegrass	0.3	12

Average of 14 years' measurements of runoff and erosion at Missouri Experiment Station, Columbia. (Soil type: Shelby loam; length of slope: 90.75 feet; degree of slope: 3.68 percent.) From *Cropping Systems in Relation to Erosion Control,* by M. F. Miller, Missouri Agriculture Experimental Station Bulletin 366, 1936. (Adapted from Jacks and White, 1939, p. 111.)

prairie is changed to cornland or left fallow, or when land is unprotected by conservation farming practices (Tables 8.2 and 8.3). Erosion remains a major problem, from the wind erosion that brings the dust storm or the spectacular gully erosion, to the less noticeable sheet erosion that each year removes a thin film of topsoil from farms until finally all of the topsoil has gone, and the farmer is left pouring fertilizers and dollars into barren subsoil.

SOIL CONSERVATION

The most important step in soil conservation is first to hold the soil in place. If the soil remains, its other qualities can be improved. If it has washed or blown away, nothing more can be done. There are many ways of preventing erosion that can be summed up in one term: intelligent land use. In detail, they can be broken down into two major categories: mechanical or engineering methods, and biological methods.

TABLE 8.3   Effect of Cover and Conservation Treatment on Erosion Loss from a Heavy Three-day Rain Storm

AVERAGE DEPTH OF EROSION (INCHES)	EROSION PROTECTION PROVIDED				NO EROSION PROTECTION PROVIDED			
	COVER CROP	BASIN LISTING	TERRACES	NATIVE COVER (GRASS BUSH)	GRAIN	VOLUNTEER COVER	BARE	CULTIVATED (FALLOW, ORCHARD, VINEYARD)
	Percentage of area in each type of treatment that was eroded to the indicated depths, from survey of 5 areas							
No erosion	88	69	12	53	30	37	4	0
⅛ to ⅜	11	31	84	37	58	37	62	45
¾ to 1½	1	0	4	8	12	21	15	42
3	0	0	0	2	0	5	19	13

Source: Adapted from Barmesberger (1939).

ENGINEERING
METHODS

Of the engineering techniques, the first and most basic is to adapt cultivation to the contours of the land. The square field and the straight-plowed furrow have a place only on flat land. Unfortunately, our land-subdivision system has favored the square or rectangular field, and our past plowing practices have favored the straight furrow for economy of effort. It is now generally realized, if not always practiced, that when sloping ground must be cultivated cultivation should follow the contour of the land. _Contour plowing_ is a first step toward keeping soil from washing downhill. When the furrows follow the contour of a slope, each furrow acts as a check dam and reservoir to prevent water from following its normal course downhill. Excess runoff can be accommodated in grassed-over waterways or natural drainage channels.

Where slopes are greater and the danger of soil loss higher, contour cultivation needs to be supplemented by _terracing_. The flat terraces of the Far East or the old Incan lands are not suited to the farm machinery of today. In their place a broad-based contour terrace has been developed that permits contour cultivation. Behind the terrace a channel forms, which should usually be maintained in sod. This leads excess water into diversion ditches or channels that permit adequate drainage.

If erosion in the form of sheet erosion, wind erosion, or rill erosion (the incipient beginnings of gullies) is present, contour treatment of the land will help to halt it. Where gullies have cut into the land, however, they must be reclaimed. In the absence of reclamation, gullies work uphill, biting deeper into otherwise well-managed farm land. Mechanical methods of gully control involving damming are a first step. Usually, biological methods of revegetation must also be applied. In some instances old gullies have been dammed and converted into farm ponds.

BIOLOGICAL METHODS

Biological methods of erosion control are those making primary use of organisms rather than of tools and mechanical equipment. These methods are an attempt to provide through the manipulation of domesticated plants the same degree of soil protection formerly provided by natural vegetation. One biological method of erosion control on sloping ground is _strip cropping,_ the alternation of grain or other crops that give little soil protection with strips of close-grown leaf crops or grass sod, which give more adequate protection. Where grass or legume strips are alternated with crops, the soil structure, organic content, and nitrogen content may also be improved. Strip cropping is often combined with contour cultivation, or where necessary, terracing.

Where wind erosion has proved serious, shelter belts are useful. Such shelter belts consist of plantings of shrubs and trees in windbreaking barriers along the windward edges of croplands. During the conservation-conscious days of the late 1930s, shelter belts were widely planted across the Great Plains to break the wind velocity.

One of the most important factors to consider in preventing water erosion is the destructive force of raindrops. Rain falling on bare soil breaks up structure and bounces soil particles high in the air. These are

a

EROSION

Wind erosion. (a) Deserts spread on the Sahara margin when wind erosion follows overgrazing. **Water erosion. (b)** Gullies grow and spread, threatening the remaining wheat fields. **(c)** Severe gullying from water runoff in Iowa. **(d)** The same area following gully stabilization measures.

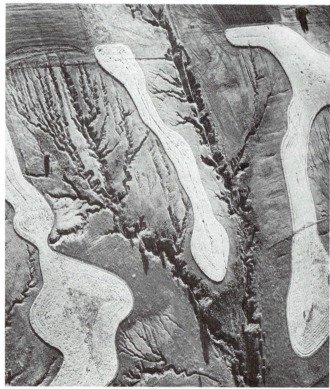

b

c

d

caught by water running over the ground and are carried downhill. Without the impact of raindrops cn the soil, runoff removes surface particles only. With raindrops new particles are continually being broken loose and added to the soil carried away. Natural vegetation and ground litter break the force of rain and prevent its impact on the bare soil. Many crop plants, however, do not provide this protection. One method, therefore, of preventing erosion is to keep crop litter and crop residues on the surface of the ground instead of turning them under in plowing. Special subsurface tillers have been developed that break up and loosen the soil without turning under the litter. Where this is not sufficient, the direct addition of mulches or plant remains to cover the soil surface may provide the necessary protection.

Crop rotation, where it involves the alternation of soil-conserving crops, such as legumes or grass, with other crops, also serves as an effective measure of erosion control, both through giving more complete protection during the period when the grasses or legumes are present and through improving the soil structure. Manuring and the use of other organic wastes also help in preventing erosion through improvement of soil structure.

MAINTAINING SOIL FERTILITY

The final step in soil conservation to be discussed is the maintenance of soil fertility. A decrease in soil fertility may be masked by increased crop yields brought about by improved varieties of crop plants. A high yield per acre may mean a much greater output of carbohydrates per acre but can disguise a reduced output of proteins, vitamins, and essential minerals. Measured in terms of energy units (calories) produced, the increased yields are comforting. But man does not live by calories alone and is selling himself short if increased yields do not mean increased nutrition (Albrecht, 1956).

Many studies have now been carried out to show the effects of soil fertility on wild and experimental animals. Crops grown on more fertile soil, although similar in appearance, give higher growth rates, stronger bones, and increased reproductive rates when fed to animals than those from less fertile soils. A greater number of animals per acre and a greater average body weight per individual can be supported on fertile soils. Experiments show that a lack of nutritional balance, such as a decrease in calcium relative to potassium or calcium relative to phosphorus, can have serious effects on animal nutrition, even where total plant growth is not affected. The absence of a single trace element such as cobalt once rendered large areas of range in Australia useless for livestock production. Addition of minute amounts of this element through a top-dressing of fertilizer has brought this range into livestock production.

Vitamin, mineral, and protein deficiencies where severe enough to take the form of human deficiency diseases are easily recognized. Where they simply add to a general, slow decline in health and vitality, they are less apparent. It is nevertheless a sufficiently serious matter for every citizen, no matter how far he may be removed from the land, to concern himself with the conservation practices that produced the food that he buys.

Many of the techniques described above are also of value in maintaining soil fertility. Techniques that maintain soil structure also prevent the excessive leaching of soil nutrients. Crop rotation, the planting of legumes and grass, and the addition of animal manures and plant remains to be soil are valuable techniques. The balanced use of chemical fertilizers, based on careful study of soil chemistry and soil needs, can help to compensate for the drain from agricultural crops. In extreme cases, complete rest from crop production under some type of soil-restoring cover may be necessary.

LAND CLASSIFICATION AND USE

The first step toward sound land use and soil conservation is land classification. Throughout the world, marginal-land farmers have attempted to squeeze a living from lands not suited to commercial crop production and have ruined the lands in the process. Elsewhere in areas otherwise suited to farming, the agricultural machinery is too often run over acres that were best put to some other use. Such areas are poor producers and can serve as focal points for damage that will spread later to the better lands. With proper classification of lands, such misuse can be avoided.

In an effort to see that land is treated according to its capabilities, the Soil Conservation Service has worked out a detailed land-classification system (Graham, 1944). This takes into account the soil types, slope and drainage of the land, the erodibility and rockiness of the soil, and all other factors that influence the capability of the land. Although the complete system is elaborate, its principal features are shown in modified form in Table 8.4. In soil-conservation districts the Soil Conservation Service is prepared to work out a land classification and use plan for each farmer who requests it. Outside of the soil-conservation districts other agencies such as the Agricultural Extension Services are usually willing to perform a similar service or to provide the information on which such a system can be based. With a classification worked out, the farmer not only can put his best lands to work but also knows what conservation measures are required to maintain all of his lands in top condition.

LAND ZONING AND ENVIRONMENTAL CONSERVATION

A second step in conservation planning follows after land classification and becomes a community responsibility. This step is land zoning, supported by adequate legislation, to prevent the misuse of land. Anyone familiar with the population expansion in the state of California or in the urbanized area of the East Coast following World War II has seen the consequences that follow on lack of zoning and planning. There is a normal tendency for cities to expand along lines of least resistance into

TABLE 8.4   Land-capability Classification

LAND CLASS	LAND-CAPABILITY AND USE PRECAUTIONS	PRIMARY USES	SECONDARY USES
	Group I. Lands Suitable for Cultivation		
I.	Excellent land, flat, well drained. Suited to agriculture with no special precautions other than good farming practice.	Agriculture	Recreation Wildlife Pasture
II.	Good land with minor limitations such as slight slope, sandy soils, or poor drainage. Suited to agriculture with precautions such as contour farming, strip cropping, drainage, etc.	Agriculture Pasture	Recreation Wildlife
III.	Moderately good land with important limitations caused by soil, slope, or drainage. Requires long rotation with soil-building crops, contouring or terracing, strip cropping or drainage, etc.	Agriculture Pasture Watershed	Recreation Wildlife Urban-industrial
IV.	Fair land with severe limitations caused by soil, slope, or drainage. Suited only to occasional or limited cultivation.	Pasture Tree crops Agriculture Urban-industrial	Recreation Wildlife Watershed
	Group II. Lands Not Suitable for Cultivation		
V.	Land suited to forestry or grazing without special precautions other than normal good management.	Forestry Range Watershed	Recreation Wildlife
VI.	Suited to forestry or grazing with minor limitations caused by danger from erosion, shallow soils, etc. Requires careful management.	Forestry Range Watershed	Recreation Wildlife
		Forestry Range Watershed Urban-industrial	Recreation Wildlife
VII.	Suited to grazing or forestry with major limitations caused by slope, low rainfall, soil, etc. Use must be limited, and extreme care taken.	Watershed Recreation Wildlife Forestry Range Urban-industrial	
VIII.	Unsuited to grazing or forestry because of absence of soil, steep slopes, extreme dryness or wetness.	Recreation Wildlife Watershed Urban-industrial	

Source: Modified from land-classification system of U.S. Soil Conservation Service, Department of Agriculture. (From Wohletz and Dolder, 1952.)
Note: The Use columns in particular depart from the usual SCS form.

lands, level and clear of heavy vegetation, on which housing or industrial construction can be carried out at minimum cost. Such lands, unfortunately, are usually also the high-value farmlands. City lots can always compete in price, if not in real value, with agricultural use of the same land. City taxes, extended to farmland, can force the most resistant farmer

CLASS VII LAND

CLASS VIII LAND

CLASS VII LAND

CLASS VI LAND

CLASS IV LAND

CLASS II LAND

CLASS V LAND

CLASS I LAND

CLASS III LAND

Land classified according to capabilities.

out of business. Industries, airports, and superhighways are all equally effective at forcing the farmer off his land. Into the orange groves of the Los Angeles basin and the cherry orchards of the Santa Clara Valley, suburban housing has moved like a crop-destroying blight. Fruit growing and crop production are forced into marginal areas of less suitable soil. That the houses might more attractively and fittingly be built on lands poorly suited to agriculture is a form of common sense difficult to hear when "money talks." Some states have taken steps to protect farmlands from urbanization and forest lands from misguided farming efforts by laws that encourage the assessment of land according to its use rather than its value if sold for real estate development, that give other forms of tax relief to farmers who choose to keep their lands in productive agriculture, and that encourage counties to zone according to land capability. In most instances, however, local zoning has not held up against severe economic pressure, and it is difficult to keep a man farming the land when by selling to a developer he could make more than he might expect in ten or more years of farming effort. Whether better effects would be achieved were the state government to take zoning power from local communities is debatable. To date, direct land purchase by the state or local government, purchase of development rights, or purchase with leaseback to a lessee who will use the land for the desired purpose have been the principal methods that have proved effective in controlling land use. Much, therefore, remains to be done to guarantee that lands

(a) Shelter belts in the Middle West reduce wind erosion. (b) Contour cultivation and strip cropping reduce soil loss from wind and water. (c) Terracing on steeper ground reduces erosion from run-off.

a

b

c

211

will be used in accordance with the best planning principles. In England, where the situation has been particularly severe, A National Town and Country Planning Act was adopted after World War II. This gave the national government restrictive control over land use and was the instrument used in accomplishing the establishment of a green belt around London and of new towns located beyond the green belt. Even this has not been entirely effective, however, and Great Britain still suffers from urban-industrial encroachment into agricultural lands and other open space.

A final step toward the planning of conservation on agricultural and other lands must be the realization that we can no longer afford single-purpose use of extensive areas. Croplands of good quality must be reserved primarily for crop production. Such farming use of these primary agricultural lands necessarily rules out for much of the year most other land uses. Even the best farming region, however, has lands not suited to crop production—for example, roadways, streamsides, rock outcrops, and steep slopes. If the entire landscape is to be considered in an environmental approach to conservation, these waste areas need attention and development also. Properly cared for they can provide recreation space, retreats for wildlife, sources of timber, and range forage, or simply add to rural beauty. Uncared for they become garbage dumps or sources of disruption of the whole land complex. If rural living is to remain a part of the American scene, its quality must be considered. The elements that once lent a wholeness to rural life, firmly established in our national background and culture, must be retained or regained. Rural factories grinding out cash crops at the expense of human values may feed an excess of people but cannot provide the qualities that make life worthwhile.

WORLD FOOD—WORLD HUNGER

A typical example of the conduct of industrial heroism is to be found in the present rush of experts to "solve the problems of world hunger"—which is rarely defined except as a "world problem" known, in industrial heroic jargon, as "the world food problematique." As is characteristic of industrial heroism, the professed intention here is entirely salutory: nobody should starve. The trouble is that "world hunger" is not a problem that can be solved by a "world solution." Except in a very limited sense, it is not an industrial problem, and industrial attempts to solve it—such as the "Green Revolution" and "Food for Peace"—have often had grotesque and destructive results. "The problem of world hunger" cannot be solved until it is understood and dealt with by local people as a multitude of local problems of ecology, agriculture, and culture.

Wendell Berry, *The Gift of Good Land* (1981)

"An empty food bowl in Asia is not easily filled by wheat grown in the American Middle West."

People can obtain food in several ways. They can take advantage of the natural bounty of unregulated nature. This is the original way in which people obtained all of their food. Wild foods are still of significant and global importance, particularly when we consider the contributions of ocean fisheries to human needs. We still use the seas of the world as "hunter-gatherers" and do not assist except in trivial ways with the productivity of these fisheries—rather the contrary. On land, and particularly in inland waters, we still take advantage of the natural bounty of wild areas. Most of our food, however, now comes from direct attempts to channel the fertility of soils and waters into directions of our choosing. At best we care for the land to make it produce more generously. At worst we exploit it, mine its fertility, in efforts to wring more yield from it than can be sustained. We have not learned the lesson of the old, old story about the goose that laid the golden eggs. We are still killing our geese to get more eggs faster.

It is possible to look at world food production in a number of different ways and to quickly get lost in a flood of misleading statistics. The work of George Borgstrom, however, starting with his book *The Hungry Planet* (1965), is a useful guide through the mazes of world food data. Some of his concepts are particularly useful for viewing world food production in an ecosystem context.

Borgstrom has used protein as an indicator of nutritional levels, in that people who obtain sufficient protein will usually have enough of the other nutrients that they require. By contrast food calories, a measure of energy content, can be misleading—since many of the calories that people consume are essentially "empty," meaning they supply energy, but not many of the nutrients needed for body structure or function. By tracing the way protein flows around the world, we can get a better view of who is feeding whom—where the food comes from and where it is consumed.

We find initially that most of the world's rich, industrial countries are not at all self-sufficient in food. Borgstrom has converted the protein in food imported into those countries into the acreage of land or water needed to actually produce that much protein and finds that many wealthy countries are in fact supported, not primarily from their own land, but by an enormous "ghost acreage," which does not show in their food statistics but represents the actual area of land (trade acreage) or water (fish acreage) that is involved in their food production. Countries that had been regarded as models of agricultural efficiency (feeding so many people from so little land), such as Japan or the Netherlands, are seen to be supported by other lands, most often located in the hungry nations of the world. The subcontinent of Europe (outside the USSR) is supported in its protein supply by a large "minicontinent" of land and water outside of European boundaries. Even countries that are important food exporters, such as the United States, are shown to be also food importers— draining food from the tropical world, including areas where hunger and malnutrition are widespread (Table 8.5).

TABLE 8.5   Ghost Acreage in Relation to Tilled Land (Amount of tilled land is considered to be 1 in each country.)

COUNTRY	FISH ACREAGE	TRADE ACREAGE	TOTAL GHOST ACREAGE
Switzerland	0.33	3.22	3.55
England	0.38	2.90	3.28
Israel	1.31	1.38	2.69
Japan	1.54	1.01	2.55
Netherlands	0.47	0.99	1.46
Egypt	0.48	0.14	0.62
China	0.23	0.03	0.26

Adapted from Borgstrom (1965).

The amount of food that flows in world trade is a small proportion of the amount of food actually consumed and produced. Rarely, and during massive famine relief exercises, food flows from wealthy food surplus countries, the rich world, to food deficit areas in the poor world. More commonly food flows from those who produce it to those who can afford to buy it—from rich to rich—and not to those who need it most.

By examining the relationship between humans and their domestic animals, Borgstrom has been able to throw a different light on the population burden actually supported by different areas of the world. Since both people and their livestock and their pets are supported by protein produced by green plants, the feeding burden that green plants must support is not just that represented by human populations, but also the human population equivalents represented by their domestic associates—the total human estate. Countries such as Australia, with relatively few people, support large numbers of domestic animals. China, on the other hand, with its billion humans, has few domestic animals. Plant protein in China tends to go directly into human mouths, whereas in Australia, most of it is first processed through cattle or sheep. In the process, of course, there is the caloric loss predictable from the second law of thermodynamics. At least 80 percent of the calories present in the green plants that are consumed will be dispersed as heat in livestock feeding, digestion, and metabolism. Less than 20 percent will remain to feed humans. Protein and other nutrients are also lost in processing plant food through domestic livestock. As noted earlier, livestock can be fed, and traditionally were fed, on foods that humans can not consume. Nevertheless, today sufficient food that humans could eat directly to allow for the support of more than two billion extra people, if livestock were cut out of the human food chain, is fed to livestock.

What keeps us from taking commonsense, direct measure to provide food for those who need it? The answers lie, in part at least, in the working of the global economic system or, more simply, in *money*. People in Peru, for example, have harvested enormous amounts of protein through their anchovy fisheries. This could have been used to solve protein deficiencies throughout Latin America. It was not, is not, and seemingly will not be used for that purpose. Hungry people have no money to buy fish. Rich people have enough money to feed anchovy meal to their chickens, pigs, cows, or whatever, and then consume less than 20 percent of the original calories in their high-protein, luxury diets. Poor countries, or rather their governments, want money to buy armaments, aircraft, automobiles, computers, and the other outputs of rich countries, so they sell food to the well fed. That's the way it is.

Much can be learned by looking at the statistics for production and trade in grain, since wheat, rice, corn, and minor grains represent the largest category of food consumed, and also since they are dry, reasonably resistant to decay, and readily transported, they can be both stored as a surplus and shipped around the world. Lester Brown has prepared statistics (1981) showing the actual area devoted to grain production around the world. This has increased from 600 million hectares in 1950 to over 750 million hectares in 1980—some 70 percent of the total cropland of the world. During the same period world grain production has increased from 631 million metric tons to 1432 million metric tons. Per capita grain production, however, which was 251 kg per person in 1950, reached a peak in 1978 of 351 kg and has since declined to 324 kg.

Surpluses of grain can either be stored as insurance against bad years—a practice as old as ancient Egypt—or be sold to those who are able to buy it. Relatively few areas of the world are really suited to large-scale grain production. These are areas of deep, highly fertile grassland soils (Chernozems, Kastanozems, and Phaeozem soils in the FAO system of nomenclature). In the past these areas were the prairies and plains of the USA and Canada; the pampas of Argentina and its neighbors; the European grasslands that extended from Hungary across the USSR into Soviet Asia; the grasslands of Australia; and the rice-growing lowlands of southern and eastern Asia.

During the period before World War II, all of these areas were producing surpluses (Table 8.6): 25 million metric tons were shipped

TABLE 8.6   World Grain Trade

REGION	Net Exports (+) and Net Imports (−) (millions of metric tons)				
	1934–38	1948–52	1960	1970	1980
North America	+5	+23	+39	+56	+131
Latin America	+9	+1	0	+4	−10
Western Europe	−24	−22	−25	−30	−16
Soviet Eurasia	+5	0	0	0	−46
Africa	+1	0	−2	−5	−15
Asia	+2	−6	−17	−37	−63
Oceania	+3	+3	+6	+12	+19

Source: Based on data from FAO and USDA.

from all other continents to the one major importing area—Western Europe—during each year. The North American contribution, 5 million metric tons, was not the largest. Soon after World War II (1948–1952), however, the Soviet bloc countries ceased to export grain, as did Africa. Asia joined Western Europe as an importer. By 1960 Latin America had ceased to be a regular exporter, whereas Africa joined the ranks of importers. By 1980 only North America and Australia/New Zealand were exporting grains. The Soviet bloc and Asia had become the leading importers, but all other continental areas had become dependent for grain upon the two exporters. To meet this market demand, the United States had expanded grain agriculture into areas previously set aside for soil conservation and restoration. Soil erosion kept pace with the increases in grain yield. The amount of grain held in storage, a reserve in case of crop failure, amounted to only 40 days' supply based on normal world rates of consumption.

The perilous state of world grain resources unfortunately is matched by the declining per capita yield of other biological resources. Data compiled by Lester Brown show per capita production of forests (wood supply) peaking in 1964 and since declining. World fish production peaked in 1970. Beef production peaked in 1976. Mutton and wool reached their peaks earlier, in 1961 and 1960. These are all renewable resources, capable of being managed for sustainable yield. But nothing can be sustained if we take more than the land can supply.

For a person living in Lima, Calcutta, Athens, or London to be dependent on surpluses produced in the American Middle West can hardly be considered a desirable state in view of the world economy, the state of biological production, and the steady eroding away of soil fertility. More and more people appear to be turning to new and improved methods for producing food at home, or near home, in order to break from the web of dependency. To consider how feasible this might be, we need to look at food production systems.

FOOD-PRODUCTION SYSTEMS

CONVENTIONAL
AMERICAN
AGRICULTURE

By usual economic standards American agriculture has been one of the world's greatest success stories. Total yields and yields per acre have been increased in virtually all sectors of food production. The number of people employed directly in agriculture has decreased markedly. This success resulted from the interaction of many factors. Before World War II most American farms were diversified. Horses were commonly used to pull farm machinery, cows were kept to produce milk and butter, and poultry was raised for meat and eggs; at least some land on each farm was used to grow feed for animals or was left in pasture. This resulted in at least a minmum amount of crop rotation. Moreover, deliberate crop rotation, using a legume to restore nitrogen to the soil and often grass

FIG. 8.7a
Trend in application of
fertilizer to U.S. farmland.
(*Sources:* USDA, 1980; Webb
and Jacobsen, 1982.)

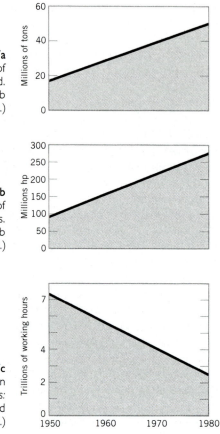

FIG. 8.7b
Trend in horsepower of
tractors used on U.S. farms.
(*Sources:* USDA, 1980; Webb
and Jacobsen, 1982.)

FIG. 8.7c
Trend in labor expended on
crop growing. (*Sources:*
USDA, 1980; Webb and
Jacobsen, 1982.)

cover to rebuild soil structure, was common. Starting in the 1920s and becoming almost universal after World War II, farm livestock was replaced by farm machinery. Work formerly done by human or animal energy was increasingly done with fossil fuel energy. This led to a greater output per person, although not necessarily more yield per acre. Yield per acre was increased by the development of new varieties of crop plants such as the various hybrid corns and wheats. These new hybrids, however, required massive fertilization if they were to reach their production potential. The use of chemical fertilizers, which were easily applied by machines, expanded greatly. Three elements in particular—phosphorus (phosphates), nitrogen (nitrates), and potassium—were used in large amounts.

The increased use of machinery, the reduction in human labor on the farm, and the increased use of fertilizers are illustrated in Figure 8.7A–C. Yields responded remarkably, at first. However, pouring more fertilizer on the land does not continue to bring the same response as one observes when fertilizer is first applied. The "law of diminishing returns'' sets in. Thus ''between 1959 and 1964, for example, each additional million pounds of fertilizer applied to cornfields in the United States brought an average of 770,000 additional bushels of corn. Between 1964 and 1970, each additional million pounds increased corn production by only 130,000 bushels, just 17 percent as much'' (Webb and Jacobsen, 1982).

All of these changes in farming practices had marked effects on the use of energy in agriculture. Whereas in the 1930s sunlight, animal power, and human labor were the principal energy inputs to food growing, by the 1980s farm machinery gulped great quantities of petroleum, and the manufacture of fertilizer, and particularly nitrogen, took great amounts of fossil fuel. The growing use of pesticides brought increased energy use to supply transport, and apply these chemicals.

Whereas in the 1930s there was a fair degree of self-sufficiency on farms, by the 1980s farms were linked into a much more extensive network of agribusiness. Work that had been performed on the farm was now performed elsewhere—in the manufacture of agricultural chemicals and farm machinery, in food storage facilities, in food processing, canning, and freezing factories, in marketing, and especially in transportation to and from the farm and the various farm-related facilities. There may have been fewer workers on the farm, but these were balanced to some degree by the great number of workers in the whole food preparation and delivery process. All of this consumed energy.

None of this seemed to matter much to the farmer until petroleum prices started their climb in 1973. Then energy analyses were applied to the agricultural process. Pimentel (1973) looked at corn production and found we were using the equivalent of 80 gallons of gasoline to produce an acre of corn, and that the ratio of energy input to energy output had become steadily less favorable from 1940 to 1970. It was pointed out that if American techniques were used to feed all of the world's four billion people, the petroleum required in farm production alone would exhaust the world's reserves in less than 30 years, with no other uses of petroleum. But corn is not a high-energy-demanding crop, and Pimentel looked only at the energy used on the farm, or processes that directly supplied the farm.

M. J. Perelman (1972) calculated that the agricultural production process in the United States involved the employment of 150 gallons of gasoline per capita to yield the equivalent in food energy of 30 gallons of gasoline per capita. Five calories were required to produce one calorie.

Hirst (1974) wrote that food production uses 12 percent of the total energy consumed in the United States, if the entire system is considered. He calculated that energy use on the farm, food processing, food transportation, food distribution, and food preparation involves an input of 8 fossil-fuel-energy calories for one calorie of food consumed. Yet agriculture is supposed to be a process in which free solar energy is converted into useful food energy, and to produce a surplus for use. Over

TABLE 8.7   Energy Use in Agriculture—Modern and Traditional

RICE CULTURE	MODERN USA	TRADITIONAL, PHILIPPINES
Input for machinery, tools, fertilizer, seeds, pesticides, drying, transport etc. Millions of joules/ha	64,885	173
Output (yield) kg/ha	5,800	1250
Energy input per unit of yield Million joules/kg	11.19	0.14

MAIZE (CORN) CULTURE	MODERN USA	TRADITIONAL, MEXICO
Input (as above)	30,034	173
Output (yield) (as above)	5,083	950
Input per unit yield	5.91	0.18

Source: CEQ (1980).

most of the world, most of the time, it has. For example, such so-called primitive agriculturalists as the Tsembaga of New Guinea are said to manage an output of 20 food calories for every calorie of energy (other than sunlight) put into its production (Rappaport, 1971). In Chinese wet-rice agriculture a yield of 50 calories for every calorie input is obtained (Lovins, 1973). These systems, of course, are labor-intensive rather than machinery-intensive ways of growing food.

Figures prepared by FAO comparing modern United States agriculture with traditional Philippine and Mexican methods of production show that the U.S. system has an energy input per kilogram of rice produced nearly 80 times greater, and an input 33 times greater for corn production (Table 8.7; CEQ, 1980).

The shift from more diversified crop growing to single crop monocultures that took place in the major food-producing areas of the United States created conditions under which insect pests and diseases could potentially thrive. This has resulted in two principle responses from the agricultural interests—efforts to breed new disease-resistant or pest-proof varieties of the various farm crops, and the increasing use of pesticides. The former approach is successful to a point—but unfortunately both disease organisms and insect pests can develop varieties able to feed on the "disease-resistant strains" just about as fast as the crop geneticists can develop new varieties. The race continues. Insects develop mutations that are not greatly affected by commonly used pesticides, resulting in the continuing production of new pesticides to which insects develop new pesticide resistance. This is an oversimplification, but the facts are that the race against plant diseases and insect pests is not being won, and meanwhile accumulation of the toxic chemicals used for crop protection has caused serious losses of wildlife along with dangers to human health.

New crop varieties are also dependent for their high yields on plenty of water being available at all periods of the plant growth and ripening cycle. This has resulted in an increased use of irrigation, not only in the drier desert and steppe regions, but also in areas where rainfall-based agriculture was the previous practice. Obtaining this water for irrigation has brought serious overdrafts on groundwater reserves along with the development of energy-demanding systems of dams, canals, and water-pumping facilities—much of which is subsidized by the public. This will be examined in more detail in the following chapter.

All of these improvements in agriculture have tended to favor the large farmowner over the small farmer, since agricultural machinery per-

Word from the Top

The Food and Agricultural Organization of the United Nations (FAO) was formed in October 1945 to address one of the major problems of the world, the increased production of renewable resources at a rate faster than the growth in world population. Its purpose and record were stated initially by Lester B. Pearson of Canada, and later by its Director-General:

1945. FAO will bring the findings of science to the workers in food and agriculture, forestry and fisheries everywhere. . . . It will assemble, digest, and interpret information to serve as a basis for the formulation of policy, national and international. It can suggest action, but only through the activities of governments themselves can the objectives be finally won.

1955. What is almost within human grasp is nothing less than the abolition of primary poverty in the last strongholds of poverty, and bringing of the low-income peoples, not to equality of income with the wealthiest peoples, but to within hailing distance, so that there is no longer a wide social and material gap between them.

1965. The outlook is alarming. In some of the most heavily populated areas the outbreak of serious famine within the next five to ten years cannot be excluded. And if food output everywhere just kept pace with population growth at the present level of consumption, by the end of this century the number of people who would be subject to hunger and malnutrition would be double what it is today.

1973. But in the name of reason, can this world of the 1970s, with all of its scientific prowess and its slowly growing sense of common purpose, go on enduring a situation in which the chances of enough decent food for millions of human beings may simply depend on the whims of one year's weather? Is this a tolerable human condition? Emphatically not.

forms more efficiently when it has lots of room to roam, costs of chemical inputs are less per acre when employed over large areas, and irrigation development tends to favor the massive scale. The costs of energy are more easily defrayed over thousands of acres than tens of acres. As a result, small farmers have been forced out of business over the past few decades, and particularly during the last ten years. The effect is stated well by Wendell Berry (1977): *I remember, during the fifties, the outrage with which our political leaders spoke of the forced removal of the populations of villages in communist countries. I also remember that at the same time, in Washington, the word on farming was "Get big or get out"—a policy which is still in effect and which has taken an enormous toll. The only difference is that of method: the force used by the communists was military; with us, it has been economic—a "free market" in which the freest were the richest. The attitudes are equally cruel, and I believe that the results will prove equally damaging, not just to the concerns and values of the human spirit, but to the practicalities of survival.*

Today, with demand for food all over the world on the increase, increasing yields from American agriculture are being relied on. But what is happening? During the 1950s yields per acre grew at a rate of 2.6 percent yearly; during the 1960s at a rate of 1.6 percent; during the seventies at a rate of less than 1 percent. For each of the last three decades growth has slowed by 50 percent, leaving a probable growth rate of .7 percent in the eighties, and .5 percent in the nineties. An increase of 2.1 percent per year is needed if projected demand for farm crops is to be met (Webb and Jacobsen, 1982).

THE GREEN
REVOLUTION

During the 1950s the Rockefeller Foundation sponsored a program in Mexico to adapt United States high-yield agriculture to Mexican conditions. Much of the effort went into developing a new hybrid dwarf wheat that would respond adequately to massive applications of fertilizer and would mature early. Through the efforts of Norman Borlaug and his associates this new variety of wheat was produced and widely planted; as a result, Mexican grain yields began to increase greatly. In 1941 Mexico produced only 50 percent of the wheat its people consumed. By 1960, despite an increase in population of 60 percent, Mexico was self-sufficient in wheat production. This was the beginning of what was to be known as the Green Revolution (Brown and Eckholm, 1974).

In the 1960s the International Rice Research Institute in the Philippines was successful in the development of new hybrid rices that also showed quick response in yield to the massive application of fertilizer. In the late 1960s and early 1970s high-yield wheats and rices were planted in many countries—the Philippines, Kenya, Pakistan, and India among them. Grain yields were tripled wherever an abundance of irrigation water, fertilizer, agricultural machinery, pesticides, and related inputs could be provided. Some agriculturalists believed the world crisis had been ended forever. American agricultural technology had gone overseas and it had won. But then the problems began (Brown and Eckholm, 1974).

Drought conditions were prevalent during the early 1970s in much of the tropical world. Without abundant water the new "miracle" grains produced less than the old native varieties. Extensives monocultures devoted to single varieties of wheat or rice proved far too susceptible to insect and disease attacks—despite, or because of, the massive use of pesticides (Paddock, 1970). Furthermore, the new agricultural systems required heavy capital investment in machines, fertilizers, and the like and essentially were not available to any except the wealthy owners of large tracts of land. The new technology carried the message from Washington that Berry states: "Get big or get out." The poor got out. Small farmers were forced off their land. Unable even to afford to eat the new high-cost grains, many of them were pushed up into the mountains or to other marginal lands where they attempted again to gain a subsistence living. Some joined the guerrilla forces. Some drifted to the slums of the big cities (Franke, 1974; Gould, 1974).

On top of all this came the jump in petroleum prices in 1973, and all agricultural development in Third World countries was hard hit. Talk about the Green Revolution faded, and with it optimism about quickly meeting world food needs. Everywhere marginal lands were being farmed, often at great environmental cost. The loss of farmlands to soil erosion, salinization, and all the other ills that result from poor management began to cancel any gains resulting from bringing new land into production. At long last some experts began to look at the traditional peasant agricultural methods to see whether high yields might yet be produced without high inputs of energy and money. It was realized that some of the older methods had been very good indeed (Allen, 1974; Omo-Fadaka, 1974; Pickstock, 1974).

AGRICULTURAL
ALTERNATIVES

There is nothing essentially wrong with an agricultural system that involves higher inputs of energy than are received in food output—providing the energy put in is cheap and essentially inexhaustible. We use fuel in much more wasteful ways than in food production, and often for no worthwhile gain of any kind. An agricultural system based on a massive input of petroleum energy cannot endure, however, since petroleum is no longer cheap and by the end of the century will scarcely be available for this use. What, then, are the alternatives? Some hope we can go on with more of the same, using some combination of nuclear power and accelerated development of coal and oil shale to keep the old system working. Others point out that it is past time to develop new systems, perhaps still with high-energy input, but making use of locally available, renewable or inexhaustible resources, such as solar, wind, water, or vegetation power in place of fossil fuel and nuclear power (Blaxter, 1974; Omo-Fadaka, 1981). Furthermore, since human labor is the one resource

a

b

FOOD AND HUNGER

(a) There could be enough food for everyone if the numbers of people are stabilized, food is produced where it is needed, and food is made available to those who are hungry. (b) In the 1980s drought and hunger again threaten the Sahelian region of Africa where this nomad family during the 1970s drought foraged for tree leaves to eat. (c) In Bangladesh also, famine still threatens millions. (d) Emergency grain shipments help reduce deaths from starvation, but world reserves are no longer abundant.

c

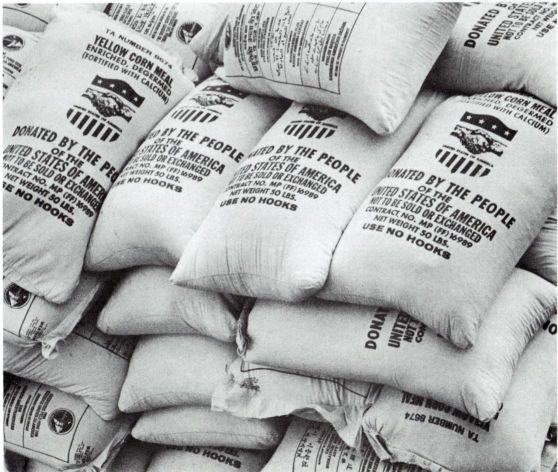

d

225

that is in abundant supply, many would urge that getting people back on the land is a first requirement. Thus, Gould has pointed out that when English farmlands, producing under the machinery–fossil fuel–chemical fertilizer system, are occupied by housing developments, food output actually goes up. The reason is the intensive hand care people give to their backyard vegetable gardens (Gould, 1974).

There are many examples of people around the world who have practiced highly sophisticated and productive agriculture without benefit of machinery or inputs from the petroleum or chemical industries. China, for example, has carried out its own "agriculture miracle" in providing food for its billion people. During the 1940s famine was a way of life and death for the Chinese people, of whom there were then only 400 million. Now, with 2½ times as many people, there is no apparent threat of starvation, and China periodically exports grain. Intensive land care, high labor input, and most particularly the recycling of organic wastes are a part of this success story. The seven million small-scale biogas generators, with their output of methane and fertilizer, tell another part of the story.

During the Cambridge symposium on the "Future of Traditional 'Primitive' Societies" in 1974, the successful agricultural practices of many people who live entirely outside the urban-industrial technocracy were reviewed. Notably successful are the Ifugao people of Luzon in the Philippines, who are noted for their elaborate terraces built on the lower slopes of the mountains they occupy. In addition to permanent, terrace agriculture, they make use of a shifting "swidden" agriculture on the higher or steeper slopes and take advantage of the great variety of natural forest crops and products from the uncultivated areas. An agriculturally supported density of 237 people per square kilometer lives in a reasonably affluent style of life. Crop diversification, intensive care of every square meter of land, and great attention to recycling of organic materials are involved in this successful land-use system (Conklin, 1974).

Many tropical root crops, of course, have much higher yields than grain crops. Thus, 30 tons per hectare of cassava can be harvested in Nigeria, using improved breeds of plants but building on traditional methods (Pickstock, 1974). This compares with 6 tons per hectare of American "high-fossil-fuel-content" corn (Brown and Eckholm, 1974), or 11 tons of "miracle rice" (IR 24 variety) on experimental plots (Allen, 1974). According to Vass (1963), in Malaya on combination hog–fish–vegetable farms as much as 15,000 pounds of pork, 1500 pounds of fish, and an unestimated quantity of vegetables per hectare are produced—admittedly with some input of energy and fertilizers. Omo-Fadaka (1981) has described similar village agricultural systems developed by George Chan for use in the South Pacific that produce biogas for energy, vegetables, meat, and fish highly efficiently with virtually no inputs from outside the system except human laobr. Klee (1980) provides a review of many of the existing traditional systems for the student who wishes to pursue this further.

In the United States, and particularly since the late 1960s, there has been an enormous upsurge of interest and effort in organic farming and gardening. This was finally recognized by the official agricultural establishment when the U.S. Department of Agriculture (USDA, 1980) reviewed and compared outputs and costs from organic farms in the United States. In general the organic farms compared favorably in output to the conventional chemical-fertilizer–and pesticide-using establishments.

According to Sale (1980), *The Amish, for example, are a perfect case study in non-mechanized efficiency. They make use of contemporary scientific information about breeding and biological pest control, but they use no internal combustion machinery whatsoever, relying wholly on animal and human labor and simple tools. Yet they consistently produce more per acre than their neighbors, various studies have shown, and of course, judged in terms of energy, harvest far more per unit of energy invested. The experience of organic farmers, too, over the last ten years—there were at least 1,500 successful organic farms in the U.S. as of 1979, most of them perfectly ordinary operations mixed in with chemical neighbors—has shown that it is possible not only to operate without chemicals and their attendant machines but to match crop yields at the same time, improve quality, and eliminate expenses. An oft-cited study from Washington University's Center for the Biology of Natural Systems that examined sixteen organic and sixteen conventional farms in the Corn Belt indicated that organic farms actually operate at about $2 an acre better than the conventional chemical farms—and use only about a third as much energy.*

There are, of course, many definitions of organic farming, but generally it is taken to mean those agricultural systems that make principal use of organic composts generated from animal manures and plant wastes in place of factory-produced nitrogen fertilizers, and that avoid the use of persistent chemical insecticides or herbicides. They range from the magical mysteries of the Findhorn garden in Scotland, through the prosaic Amish, to farms virtually indistinguishable from their chemically based neighbors in the American Middle West. Organic farming techniques have proved particularly useful in the so-called marginal areas—those not suited to large-scale, mechanized commercial agriculture—since heavy inputs of human energy and organic composts can build fertile soils starting from almost any substrate that is not bare rock or made up of toxic materials. The greatest output of vegetables and fruits, however, probably come from home and community gardens, often located within cities, where organic techniques are used.

Perhaps the most interesting feature of the organic farming movement in the United States is that it has developed with no government support, without benefit of the university-based research on which conventional agriculture relies, and often in the face of opposition from the agricultural establishment. It has nevertheless succeeded. It is only now beginning to move from the fringe areas down into the agricultural heartland. No doubt the end result will be some combination of the best elements of both conventional and organic agriculture—making extensive use of urban wastes and taking advantages of new advancement in crop genetics, including the development of more efficient nitrogen-fixing plants. Those interested in reading more about it are directed to the many publications of Rodale Press, including *Mother Earth News,* and to the books by Berry (1977, 1982), Jackson (1981), Jeavons (1973), Fukuoka (1978), Mollison (1979), Merrill (1976).

One of the problem areas for agriculture on earth has been the humid tropics. For reasons that have been discussed, permanent agriculture has been difficult to achieve within this region except where unusually fertile soils of volcanic or alluvial origin predominated. Shifting agriculture of the swidden variety has predominated throughout the prevailing soil areas, where lateritic soils rich in iron and aluminum salts predominate and the nutrients needed by plants are largely locked up in the rainforest overstory. More recently, however, experiments in the Peruvian Amazon, making use of both conventional and organic techniques, have shown some success. "Three grain crops can be produced annually with appropriate fertilizer inputs. Twenty-one crops have been harvested during the past 8½ years in the same field, with an average annual production of 7.8 tons of grain per hectare. Soil properties are improving with continuous cultivation" (Sanchez et al., 1982). Although their methods are not recommended for sloping ground, they are working with the notoriously difficult oxisols and ultisols, which heretofore have not held up under continued use. The authors state: "We believe that the continuous cropping technology can have a positive ecological impact where it is practiced appropriately, because for every hectare that is cleared and put into such production, many hectares of forest may be spared from the shifting cultivator's ax in his search to grow the same amount of food." As usual, however, one must look carefully at energy costs and government subsidies before fully accepting these results.

It is not possible to shift suddenly from those systems of agriculture now in vogue to more sustainable, ecologically based systems unless we are prepared to risk serious curtailment in food production. There is, however, an absolute necessity to move forward now, while fossil fuels and materials are still available to develop agricultural systems that are highly productive and can be permanently sustained. We cannot afford to continue practices that lead to soil erosion or to continued depletion of soil fertility. We cannot continue systems that involve the sacrifice of the productivity and resources of one area in order to support people in another. World food banks, such as proposed at the 1974 United Nations Conference on Food, are no substitute for local self-reliance in food production. Each people, each region, each nation should look to its own means for self-support. If these can produce surpluses of one commodity or another *without sacrifice of their own long-term productivity*, it will be to their advantage to do so. But surpluses gained at the expense of soil are always a poor bargain—except in the short run for the exploiter who gains a quick profit. Agricultural systems based on the continued depletion of scarce, nonrenewable resources represent a sacrifice of future well-being to present affluence. The obstacles in the way of achieving a sustainable agriculture that will produce enough food for all now living are no longer primarily technological, nor do they reflect insufficient scientific research and knowledge. They are primarily political obstacles. They will be overcome.

We do not inherit the earth from our parents, we borrow it from our children.

Slogan of the New Zealand Values Party

SOURCES

Albrecht, W. A., 1956. Physical, chemical and biochemical changes in the soil community. *Man's role in changing the face of the earth.* W. Thomas, ed., University of Chicago Press, Chicago, pp. 648–673.

Allen, Robert, 1974. New strategy for the green revolution. *New Scientist* 63:320–321.

Bamesberger, J. G., 1939. *Erosion losses from a 3-day California storm.* U.S. Department of Agriculture, Soil Conservation Service, Washington, D.C.

Berry, Wendell, 1977. *The unsettling of America.* Avon, New York.

———, 1981. *The gift of good land.* North Point Press, San Francisco.

Blaxter, Kenneth, 1974. Power and agricultural revolutions. *New Scientist* 61:400–403.

Borgstrom, Georg, 1965. *The hungry planet.* Macmillan, New York.

Brown, Lester R. and E. P. Eckholm, 1974. *By bread alone.* Praeger, New York.

Brown, Lester R., 1981. *Building a sustainable society.* W. W. Norton, New York.

Conklin, H. C., 1974. Paper presented to Symposium on the Future of Traditional "Primitive" Societies. Cambridge.

Council on Environmental Quality, 1980. *The global 2000 report to the president.* U.S. Government Printing Office, Washington, D.C.

Dudal, R., 1968. *Definition of soil units for the soil map of the world.* FAO, Rome.

Franke, R. W., 1974. Miracle seeds and shattered dreams in Java. *Natural History* 83:10–18, 84–88.

Fukuoka, Masanobu, 1978. *The one-straw revolution.* Rodale Press, Emmaus, Penn.

Goldsmith, Edward, 1982. The retreat from Stockholm. *Ecologist* 12:98.

Gould, Nicholas, 1974. England's Green Revolution. *Ecologist* 4:58–60.

Gourou, Pierre, 1966. *The tropical world,* 4th edition. Wiley, New York.

Graham, Edward, 1944. *Natural principles of land use.* Oxford, New York.

Hirst, Eric, 1974. Food-related energy requirements. *Science* 184:134–138.

International Union for Conservation of Nature (IUCN), 1980. *World Conservation Strategy,* Gland, Switzerland.

Jacks, G. V. and R. O. Whyte, 1939. *Vanishing lands.* Doubleday-Doran New York.

Jackson, Wes, 1981. *New roots for American agriculture.* Friends of the Earth, San Francisco.

Jeavons, John, 1973. *How to grow more vegetables.* Ecology Action, Palo Alto, Calif.

Klee, Gary A., 1980. *World systems of traditional resource management.* Halsted Press, New York.

Kovda, Victor A., 1965. The need for international cooperation in soil science. *Nature and Resources* 1:10–16, Unesco, Paris.

Leopold, A. Starker, 1959. *Wildlife of Mexico.* University of California Press, Berkeley.

Lovins, Amory, 1973. *World energy strategies: facts, issues and options.* Earth Resources Research Limited, London.

Merrill, Richard, editor, 1976. *Radical agriculture.* Harper and Row, New York.

Mollison, Bill, 1979. *Permaculture two.* Tegari, Stanley, Tasmania.

Omo-Fadaka, Jimoh, 1974. Industrialization and poverty in the Third World. *Ecologist* 4:61–63.

————1981. *Ecodevelopment—an African perspective.* Copy Cat Alley, Santa Cruz, California.

Paddock, William C., 1970. How green is the Green Revolution? *Bioscience* 20:897–902.

Perelman, M. J., 1972. Farming with petroleum. *Environment* 14:8–13.

Pickstock, Michael, 1974. Filling Nigeria's larder. *New Scientist* 63:452–456.

Pimentel, David *et al.,* 1973. Food production and the energy crisis. *Science* 182:443–449.

Rappaport, R., 1971. The flow of energy in an agricultural society. *Scientific American* 224:116–134.

Richards, P. W., 1961. The types of vegetation in the humid tropics in relation to the soil. *Tropical soils and vegetation,* Unesco, Paris, pp. 15–20.

Sale, Kirkpatrick, 1980. *Human scale.* Coward, McCann & Geoghegan, New York.

Sanchez, Pedro A., Dale E. Bandy, J. Hugo Villachica, and John J. Nicholaides, 1982. Amazon Basin soils: management for continuous crop production. *Science* 216:821–827.

Schumacher, E. F., 1973. *Small is beautiful.* Harper and Row, New York.

Strahler, Arthur N., 1970. *Introduction to physical geography.* Second edition. John Wiley, New York.

Tedrow, J.C.F., 1970. Soils of the subarctic regions. *Ecology of the subarctic regions.* Unesco, Paris.

U. S. Department of Agriculture, 1938. *Soils and men: Yearbook of Agriculture.* Government Printing Office, Washington, D.C.

————1957. *Soil: Yearbook of Agriculture*. Government Printing Office, Washington, D.C.

Vass, K. F., 1963. *Fish culture in freshwater and brackish ponds*. Symposium of Institute of Biology, II.

Webb, Maryla and Judith Jacobsen, 1982. *U.S. Carrying Capacity: an introduction*. Carrying Capacity Inc., Washington, D.C.

Weislander, A. and R. E. Storie, 1952. The vegetation-soil survey of California. *Journal of Forestry* 50:521–526.

Wohletz, L. and E. Dolder, 1952. *Know California's land*. California Department of Natural Resources, Sacramento.

Wright, A.C.S. and J. Bennema, 1965. *The soil resources of Latin America*. World Soil Resources Report 18, FAO, Rome.

CHAPTER
9

MOST
OF
THE
PLANET—
WATER

INTRODUCTION

If you were to throw something at planet Earth from outer space—say, an asteroid—the chances are seven out of ten that it would fall in the oceans or the seas. This is a water planet, a fact for which we are not sufficiently thankful. People are land animals and their interest and attention over the millenia of history have been directed toward the lands of the earth. The oceans, seas, bays, great lakes, and rivers have been regarded simply as spaces between the lands—to be crossed as quickly as possible in going from one land area to another. Consequently, the continents and islands are well known, whereas the bodies of water have been little known. We forget their extent and importance. All the continents put together could be fitted into the space occupied by the Pacific Ocean, and there would be room left over.

Seventy percent of the planet is covered with oceans and seas, and of the rest, a high percentage is covered by rivers, streams, lakes, ponds, swamps, and marshes. Furthermore, the continent of Antarctica and the minicontinent of Greenland, along with extensive high mountain areas, are covered by glacial ice. If all of this melted, as it has in past interglacial ages, the water area of the world would be greatly extended.

There is plenty of water on earth, and we will never run short. This is small consolation, however, to somebody dying of thirst in the middle of the Pacific. Water has the peculiar quality of being an inexhaustible natural resource that is nevertheless in short supply—meaning that water of usable quality and adequate quantity is often not in the right place at the right time for human needs or demands. Water shortages and water surpluses are problems that plague modern civilization. In earlier times people looked to the water supply before settling in an area. Often today people move into a desert and demand that water be brought to them, or settle in a flood plain and demand that water be kept away.

THE HYDROLOGIC CYCLE

The problems of water use and conservation are unusually complex, but are too often approached with simple solutions that are ineffective at best and sometimes disastrous. A look at the hydrologic cycle (Fig. 9.1) the cycle through which water moves from ocean to atmosphere to land and back to the oceans, is one way to examine some of the complexities.

The source of most of the rain that falls on the land ultimately is the ocean. Air masses lying long over the seas pick up large quantities of water through evaporation. When they move inward over the continents,

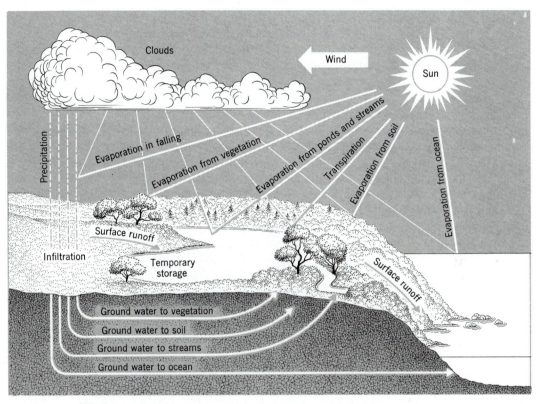

FIG. 9.1
The hydrologic cycle.

much of this water falls out as precipitation. The movement of air masses, which to a large extent controls climate and weather, is and probably will remain a natural phenomenon over which man has little or no control. The timing and distribution of rainfall may be affected in the future by human activities as techniques for inducing precipitation are improved; however, it is likely that dry climates will remain dry and we will remain unable to squeeze water from a dry air mass. Indeed, the ecological consequences of any massive attempt at weather control are so enormous and potentially dangerous that we cannot afford the kinds of blunders we have already made in the use of atomic energy or in the careless application of pesticides to the land.

When water first reaches the ground in mountain areas in the form of rain, snow, sleet, hail, or surface condensation, it becomes useful to humans. Falling on areas covered with natural vegetation it provides the soil water from which forests and range grasses must grow. Combined in vegetation it provides timber, or forage for livestock or wildlife. The excess, running off the surface or sinking in the ground to reappear in springs or as base flow in streams, again becomes useful, providing drinking water for livestock and wildlife and habitats for fish and aquatic life. Meanwhile much is returned to the air by evaporation from vegetation, soil, streams, lakes, or rivers, and by transpiration from the vegetation of the area, and this is returned once more to the ground in further precipitation in other areas. Another portion has gone deep into the ground and has moved downhill slowly through *aquifers*—underground strata of porous rock or sediments not yet consolidated into rock. This groundwater may later reappear as base flow into streams, lakes, or ponds, maintaining the flow or level of these bodies of water during the dry season when surface runoff is no longer available. Groundwater may also travel further to lie under the valleys, perhaps to keep their soils saturated and give rise to meadow or marsh or perhaps to lie deeper and provide soil water in the dry seasons or feed the deeper-rooted plants. The depth to which it is necessary to go to find saturated ground is known as the depth to the *water table.* Water tables in the lowlands are maintained by water seeping into the ground in the hills and mountains. Still other quantities of groundwater may remain for long periods in underground storage, until tapped by wells.

Water falling on farmland follows a similar course. Sinking into the soil, it provides the water from which crops are made. In the process much is transpired or evaporated back into the air. If the amount of rainfall is great and the ground porous, some water sinks through to add to underground supplies. Some will run off to add to stream flow and eventually will reach the ocean.

In the larger rivers and streams, water can supply transportation for people and their products. It also provides for additional fisheries and everywhere it lies in quantity, water provides recreation. People have always been attracted to stream or lakeside for rest and pleasure. They may seek only the scenery and beauty the water provides; they may seek the joys of fishing; or perhaps swimming, boating, and related sports will attract them. Where the water in the biosphere is located at any one time is indicated in Table 9.1. The rate at which it moves in the cycle is shown in Table 9.2.

TABLE 9.1   Where the Water Is: Distribution in the Biosphere

LOCATION	VOLUME IN CUBIC MILES	PERCENTAGE OF TOTAL
Oceans	317,000,000	97.2
Glaciers and ice caps	7,000,000	2.1
Groundwater	2,000,000	0.6
Saltwater lakes and inland seas	25,000	0.01
Freshwater lakes	30,000	0.01
Soil water	16,000	0.01
Atmosphere	3,100	—
Steam beds	300	—
Total	326,000,000	100.00

Note: It has been estimated by Vernadsky that an additional amount of water approximately equal to that in the oceans may be bound in chemical or physical combinations in the rocks of the earth's crust.
Source: Pereira (1970).

TABLE 9.2   How Water Flows: Movement in the Cycle

	GAIN (CUBIC KILOMETERS)	LOSS (CUBIC KILOMETERS)
OCEANS		
Gain		
From precipitation	411,600	
From runoff	37,300	
Loss		
From evaporation		448,900
CONTINENTS: PERIPHERAL AREAS		
Gain		
From precipitation	101,000	
Loss		
From runoff		37,300
From evaporation		63,700
CONTINENTS: LANDLOCKED AREAS		
Gain		
From precipitation	7,400	
Loss		
From evaporation		7,400

Source: Kalanin and Bykov (1969).

With the growth of civilization the course of waters has been changed from the simple original pattern. Water running from the mountains in streams is impounded behind dams. From here it may be led into irrigation canals to provide water for dry but otherwise fertile lands on which crops can be grown. It may be diverted into aqueducts and carried to meet the needs of towns and cities, or it may be used to provide electric power.

Water that reaches population centers is put to greatest use. It must first meet the living needs of the people, to provide drinking, cooking, and washing water. It is used to suppress city fires, to wash down streets, and to water lawns and gardens. It provides a means of disposing of waste products, from sewage to the vast quantities of waste created by industry. It must be used in industrial production, the processing of food, the milling of timber, and the manufacture of countless products used by humanity.

Excess water must also be coped with. Dams and levees are constructed to reduce floods. Drainage ditches and canals are built to remove excess waters from otherwise adequate farming lands.

Each portion of the hydrologic cycle and each use that we make of water present us with new dilemmas. That these dilemmas result from the way in which we have organized our societies more than from the way nature has organized the water cycle is a truth yet to be widely appreciated.

WATER AS HABITAT

AQUATIC
ENVIRONMENTS Before we look in more detail at human uses and demands for fresh water on the lands of the earth, it is worthwhile to examine the source, the water world, and to consider some of the properties of water.

Water is an unusual substance despite its abundance in the biosphere. Its characteristics make it highly suitable both as a medium in which life exists and as a component of living substance. All of the minerals and gases required by life are soluble in water and, passing through water, can be absorbed by living cells. Water has a high specific heat, meaning it takes a relatively large application of energy to raise its temperature, and once heated, it is slow to cool. Thus the aquatic environment is buffered against rapid temperature changes that occur in terrestrial environments. Furthermore, water reaches its maximum density at 4° C, four degrees above its freezing point. Water approaching the freezing point, therefore, is lighter and moves to the surface of water bodies. On freezing, water takes on a crystalline structure, and as ice, floats on the surface of liquid water, providing insulation against further temperature reduction underneath. Thus, with the exception of small bodies of water, aquatic environments provide protection against freezing for the organisms that occupy them. Furthermore, in comparison to other environments, aquatic environments are relatively uniform, and the organisms within them are sheltered against physical and chemical changes to a degree that most terrestrial organisms are not. This relative uniformity, however, makes it difficult to arrange the neat classifications of aquatic habitats and biotic communities that one is accustomed to in the terrestrial environment. Also, within any one aquatic ecosystem, food chains and webs become more complicated than those that are generally encountered on land.

Despite their complexity, aquatic ecosystems have the same basic components as those of dry land. Energy comes from sunlight. Chemicals enter the water either from the atmosphere or from the lithosphere; in particular, from the soils that surround the water body and form its *basin*. Green plants are the principal producers. Of these, the most important are the floating green plants, or plankton—commonly of microscopic size and made up, for the most part, of green algae, blue-green algae, and bacteria. The plant plankton, or *phytoplankton*, provides food for the floating animal populations of the water, also mostly of microscopic size. These, the *zooplankton*, provide food for large organisms that in turn lead up through the food chains to tunas, sharks, or billfish or the large carnivorous invertebrates. Reducer organisms play an important role and range from the scavengers that feed on and break apart carcasses to the bacteria that finally convert organic materials into their mineral components.

Among the chemical limiting factors in water, the amount of dissolved oxygen is particularly important. Cold water holds more oxygen than warm. Oxygen must enter water either directly from the atmosphere through diffusion or physical mixing, or through the action of photosynthesis. It follows, therefore, that the surface layers of water, which are readily penetrated by light and can consequently support green plants, or which are in direct contact with the air, are well oxygenated, whereas deeper layers to which light cannot penetrate and in which the decay of dead organisms most commonly takes place may have low supplies of oxygen. Were it not for the factor of mixing, and of overturns of surface and deeper water as a result of turbulence and the movement of currents, there would be continual oxygen exhaustion in these deeper, unlighted layers.

Also of importance among chemical limiting factors are the supplies of nitrates and phosphates. Where overabundant, they can cause excessive "blooms" of plankton which, on decay, exhausts the supply of oxygen. In many lakes and throughout most of the surface water of the oceans, however, these chemicals may be relatively scarce and in consequence the amount of life that can be supported is limited.

Life originated in the oceans, and animal life is adjusted to the salinities of ocean water, which are reflected in the composition of blood and other body fluids. The greatest abundance of aquatic life is still to be found in the oceans. Relatively few species have adapted to the more rigorous freshwater environments of the earth, or to inland salt lakes.

MARINE
ENVIRONMENTS
A detailed classification of marine environments would not be useful in this text. It is worthwhile, however, to consider certain differences among these environments. One factor of importance is light penetration. Sunlight can reach depths of 400 feet in the oceans, but it usually reaches less than 180 feet. The depth of light penetration is influenced by the amount of dissolved or floating substances in the water. Where nutrients, and consequently life, is abundant, light penetration is limited. Where the ocean is relatively sterile and consequently clean, light penetration reaches a maximum.

The lighted zone of the oceans is known as the *euphotic zone*. Within this all of the phytoplankton exist. Where the ocean floor is within reach of sunlight, attached plants—the *benthon* as distinct from plankton—are able to grow. These may be of great abundance and sometimes, as in the case of the giant kelp, reach enormous size. That part of the euphotic zone normally confined to continental shelves and the shallower waters surrounding islands is called the *neritic* or green water zone, as distinct from the *pelagic* or blue water zone of the open ocean. Below the lighted pelagic zone is the dark, intermediate layer of the ocean, known as the *bathyal* zone. Here may live a great variety of organisms that depend for their existence either on the downward "rain" of dead plant or animal materials from the euphotic zone above, or else on diurnal or periodic forays upward to feed within pelagic waters. Some species, and many of the whales are in this category, move freely between zones. Far below the lighted zone of the oceans, at depths of more than 2000 meters where pressure is enormous and food is necessarily limited, is the *abyssal* zone. Here in the deepest parts of the oceans life still exists, dependent on the rain of nutrient materials from the lighted zone above. In the great chasms or oceanic troughs these depths may reach to 30,000 feet or more. Only specialized creatures can exist in such deeps, and their abundance can never be great.

The topography of the oceans leads to another separate means for classifying ocean environments. Each continent is a block of lighter, largely acidic rock, floating on heavier, basic rock that forms both the floor of the oceans and the basement of the continents. Under present conditions of world climate, when glaciers occur but are not extensive, large areas of each continent are flooded by the oceans. These areas, the *continental shelves*, extend varying distances out from land to a maximum depth of approximately 200 meters. Beyond these shelfs, the continental margin plunges off steeply into the area of confluence between continental rocks and those of the deep ocean floor. The area of steep descent is known as the *continental slope*. Continental shelves represent areas where, in the neritic zone, attached vegetation can grow. They are also the areas that receive the maximum input of nutrients flowing into the oceans from streams and rivers. Consequently, most of them support a relatively great abundance of life (Fig. 9.2).

FIG. 9.2
Zonation in the ocean. (Data from Odum, 1971.)

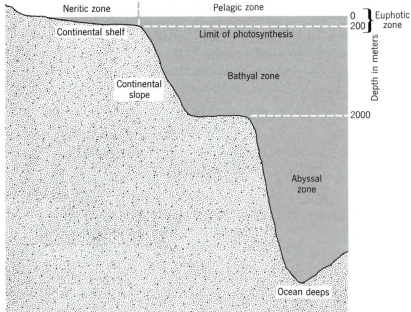

Beyond the continental shelf the ocean floor extends as a generally flat surface over long distances. It is interrupted in places, however, by the results of volcanic activity in the form of islands or submerged sea mounts. Elsewhere, oceanic rises, such as the mid-Atlantic ridge or various island chains, are oceanic mountain ranges formed by the upward thrusting of segments of the earth's crust. Where these extend upward to the euphotic zone they may support an abundance of life. In places, the ocean floor is further broken by deep chasms of oceanic deeps. These, too, are associated with areas of earth movement and volcanic activity.

The greatest variety of aquatic life is to be found in the neritic or coastal zone where the waters of the ocean mix with those flowing from land, and where marine environments give way to dry-land habitats. This is the region where tidal action is to be most readily observed.

The tides are caused by the gravitational attraction between the sun, the moon, and the earth. Water bodies, being free to move, respond to these gravitational forces more than do land masses. In consequence, as a result of the spinning of the earth on its axis, there will be, at least, one period each day when the waters of the ocean are raised to a peak by the gravitational pull of the moon (or moon and sun together), and another when they are contracted to a low point by the absence of such a force. Each separate body of water develops its own tidal rhythm in response to these varying forces. Along the Pacific Coast of North Amermica there are two periods of high tide each day, and two of low. In other areas there may be a single high and low tide in each 24-hour period. The effect of tidal movements is to expose a section of the coastal (or littoral) region to the air at times of low tide, and to flood it with water when tides are high. Organisms living in this *intertidal* zone must be able to resist dessication during the periods when they are exposed to air, and to tolerate immersion in marine saline waters during the rest of the day. Those living high in the intertidal zone are seldom covered by water; those occupying the lower levels are rarely exposed to air. The very highest area is not covered by tidal water, but is soaked each day by the splash from waves.

These influences create a wide variety of intertidal animal and plant communities. In the upper zone live creatures such as the periwinkle, certain limpets, and barnacles. In the lower zone live eel grasses or turtle grasses, sea palms, and animals such as abalones. In between one finds an enormous variety of invertebrate animals and algae that can establish themselves on rocks or can grow in mud. Further differences are interposed by the nature of the substrate. Rocky shores will support one group of species, sandy beaches another, mud flats a third, and so on. Still greater variety is interposed where freshwaters enter the oceans. In this, the *estuarine* region, is to be found enormous complexity and high productivity. To a remarkable degree, the life of the broad oceans is dependent on the continued functioning of the estuarine region.

The ability of organisms to occupy the estuaries depends on their ability to withstand salinities that diminish from the oceans into freshwater, and that fluctuate both with the outpouring of freshwater from streams and rivers and also with the inland movement of salt water in response to tidal fluctuations. Zonation of plants and animals in estuaries reflects their tolerance to decreased and fluctuating salinities. Here one may trace possible pathways over which the evolution of freshwater species occurred in past eons, just as one may trace, along the rocky intertidal zone, pathways by which certain organisms evolved from an aquatic to a terrestrial existence.

It follows from the above classification that the productivity of marine environments is highly variable. Coastal and estuarine zones are inclined toward high productivity, since they receive a constant replenishment of nutrients from the dry land. By contrast, productivity away from shores is dependent on other factors. In any open area of ocean water, as the distance increases from the influence of continental sources of nutrients, one might expect a continually diminishing productivity. Nitrates, for example, would enter from the atmosphere both directly and through the activities of nitrogen-fixing microorganisms. The input of most other nutrients depends on their rate of deposition from air currents—winds that had swept them off eroding land in continental areas. These nutrients are taken up quickly by phytoplankton, pass through food chains to larger organisms, and eventually are carried downward out of the euphotic zone on the death of these organisms. There is in consequence a steady drain of nutrients from the upper, productive layers of water down into unlighted lower layers. Were this to continue unabated, the productivity of the upper layers would be low and entirely related to the input of nutrients from the air.

Fortunately for life in the oceans such a downward drain does not continue unabated. In any large body of water, currents, both vertical and horizontal, develop. They serve to move and mix water. In all the oceans, surface currents develop in response to the rotation of the earth and movement of the atmosphere. These result in counterclockwise flows of water in the Southern Hemisphere, and clockwise flows in the Northern Hemisphere (Fig. 9.3). Interruptions of these flows by islands and continents, and interactions between the major oceans lead to complicated surface currents that move water from one part of an ocean to another and, thus, lead to a considerable degree of surface mixing. Adding to the effects of these surface currents are vertical movements of water. Cold water, being more dense, sinks to the bottom; warm water, being lighter, rises to the surface. In the tropics surface water is heated; in the polar regions in winter it is drastically cooled. Polar water, consequently, sinks and moves in ocean basins toward the tropics, where it replaces the warm, light water that moves toward the poles. A degree of vertical mixing of water therefore takes place along the edges of the polar ice caps and also in equatorial regions. This brings nutrients from deep

FIG. 9.3
Major currents in the Atlantic Ocean. These currents carry nutrients from areas of upwelling to other parts of the ocean.

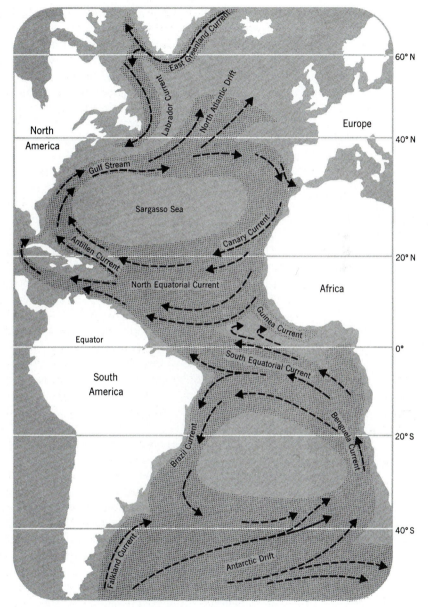

water to the surface and restores the fertility of surface waters. <u>Polar regions are often highly productive.</u>

Along the western coast of continents, in the trade wind zone, there are relatively constant winds blowing offshore that push the surface waters away from the land. This outwardly moving surface water is replaced by an <u>*upwelling* from deeper, colder layers.</u> This upwelling brings nutrients from the deeper parts of the ocean and restores surface productivity.

Thus, one of the most highly productive areas in the ocean is on the western coast of South America in Chile and Peru. Here, because of the outward movement of the trade winds, there is virtually no rain or runoff of water from the land. Yet the strong upwelling brings high fertility to the surface waters. A cold, northward-moving current, the Humboldt Current, carries these nutrient-rich waters up the South American coast into equatorial regions where they move offshore into the tropical ocean, adding to its productivity. The coasts of Chile and Peru are noted for their fisheries and for great numbers of seabirds that depend on the fish produced in the Humboldt Current. Deposition of seabird feces, guano, on the offshore rocks and islands of Peru, have made them, in the past, one of the world's great sources of nitrate fertilizer.

As a result of the variations in input from continental sources and the enrichment of surface waters by mixing and upwelling, the productivity of the oceans varies enormously. The central portions of the major oceans, such as the Sargasso Sea in the mid-Atlantic, are notoriously unproductive and have been compared to terrestrial deserts. By contrast, the areas of Antarctic mixing, and such upwelling areas as the Peruvian and California coasts, are highly productive.

MARINE FISHERIES

Human exploration of the oceans undoubtedly began with the intertidal zones. A variety of palatable and nutritious species are found there, including clams, oysters, crabs, and lobsters as well as a variety of fish. In time people learned to put out from shore in boats and exploit the fisheries along the continental shelves—the herring, cod, haddock, and plaice of the North Sea and the sardines and mackerel of the Mediterranean. As long as the number of people were few and the boats and gear used for fishing were primitive, their influence on fish populations was minor. Now, with the growth of technology, and numbers of people, this situation has changed. Human capabilities for overfishing and exhausting oceanic resources ae now well developed. However, the concept of overfishing needs some examination.

Fish, and most other aquatic animals, have a high biotic potential. Thousands of eggs are laid by each female. Although few of these eggs usually survive because of predation and unfavorable environmental conditions, the capacity for rapid growth of a population is readily expressed. People enter the marine environment as one of many oceanic predators. Usually their efforts are directed toward the capture of the larger, more mature members of a species population. Fishing is motivated by a desire either for food, for profit, or for sport. It is rarely profitable from any of these viewpoints to expend the effort necessary to pursue the last surviving members of a species. When a fishery no longer yields a good profit, commercial fishing ceases, whereas the take of a sport fisherman becomes random and incidental when fish populations are low. In consequence fishing alone is not likely to cause the extermination of a marine fish species, except under unusual conditions. Unfortunately, fishing operates in combination with a great number of other factors in marine ecosystems, and when fishing reinforces other adverse environmental factors, serious problems can develop. The example of the California sardine fishery is illustrative.

The Sardine Story

Management of ocean fisheries is plagued by the difficulties of finding facts about animal populations that cannot easily be counted or watched as they go through their life cycles. It is faced by the mysteries of a highly complex and little understood oceanic environment. To date, fisheries management in ocean waters has been largely a research endeavor, a continuing attempt to find the basic information on which a sound management program can be based. When this is discovered and the fishing industry convinced of the necessity for management, laws can be passed and agreements made that will help to perpetuate fish resources. Until then, we will continue to face crises such as the one that has confronted the sardine-fishing industry of the Pacific (Fig. 9.4; Croker, 1954; Gulland, 1970; Wick, 1974).

In 1936–1937 along the Pacific Coast of North American between San Diego and British Columbia a total of nearly 800,000 tons of Pacific sardines were landed. The sardine industry had risen to the point where it was the first-ranking fishery in North America in pounds of fish caught and the third-ranking commercial fishery in value of catch, surpassed only by tuna and salmon. The value of the take was in excess of 10

FIG. 9.4
Rise and fall of the sardine fishery of the North American Pacific coast. Since the date shown until 1982 there has been no significant recovery. (Data from California Department of Fish and Game, 1957.)

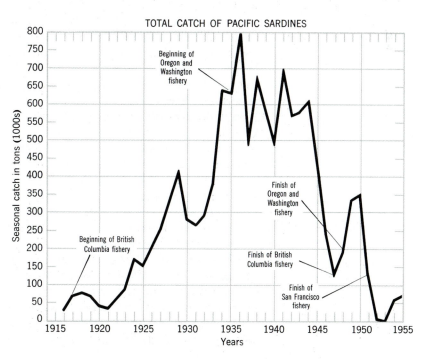

TOTAL CATCH OF PACIFIC SARDINES

Beginning of Oregon and Washington fishery

Finish of Oregon and Washington fishery

Beginning of British Columbia fishery

Finish of British Columbia fishery

Finish of San Francisco fishery

Seasonal catch in tons (1000s)

Years

million dollars annually. The sardine found its way to market in many forms, as bait for fishermen, as the familiar canned sardine, as fish meal, dog food, oil and fertilizer. Nevertheless by 1953–1954, the catch of sardines had fallen to a total of 4460 tons (Fig. 9.4). Sardine-fishing fleets were sold for other uses; canneries and reduction plants were idle. The failure of the sardine fishery illustrates many of the questions that puzzle those who depend on the resources of the sea for a livelihood and biologists who seek to maintain those resources.

The sardine fishery in the Pacific began during World War I in California, with a catch of over 27,000 tons reported in 1916–1917. In succeeding years it spread northward to the water off Oregon, Washington, and British Columbia. Soon it supported a major fishing fleet and processing industry. In 1924 the catch jumped to 174,000 tons and continued upward to its peak in 1936–1937. The fishing fleet grew to 300 vessels, each taking 100 to 200 tons of fish per day of fishing. After 1936 the take remained at a fairly high level until 1944. Biologists, however, could see that trouble was developing long before the total catch started to decline. Under heavy fishing the older fish were removed from the population, and the annual take began to depend on the yield of younger fish. The average catch per boat and per night of fishing declined. This was masked by more boats putting out to sea and fishing longer, so that the total catch held up. The symptoms of trouble caused biologists to attempt to regulate the fishing industry in order to balance the annual catch against the productivity of the population. These efforts were not successful.

The first fishery to fail was in Canadian waters. Between 1945–1946 and 1947–1948 the Canadian catch dropped from 34,000 tons to less than 500. The Washington and Oregon fisheries soon followed. After the 1948–1949 season the northern fishing fleets stopped operation, and the sardine canneries of the Northwest closed down. For a few more years the yield off California remained high. In 1951, however, the San Francisco fishing fleet returned with a disastrously low catch of 80 tons. With this, the main center of the industry closed down. Catches remained high in southern California waters for one more year, and then this fishery too collapsed.

Throughout all of this period the sardine industry remained unrestricted and refused to tolerate any limitation on its take. Whether or not such restrictions would have prevented the sardine disaster remains open to question, but it is most likely that the fishery could have been better maintained with intelligent regulation.

The collapse of the sardine industry in United States waters was associated with failure in reproduction and survival of young fish. The expected addition to the population provided by the growth of young sardines to catchable size did not occur. Offshore waters in southern California, which were major spawning grounds in the past, are no longer producing many fish. A sardine fishery still exists in Mexican waters off the coast of Baja California but has not been large enough to support a major fishing industry. Movement of sardines from Mexican to Californian waters, which occurred in the past, took place in 1955–1956 and allowed for an increase in catch in those years. However, this movement alone was not sufficient. There is evidence that changes in the condition of the ocean, resulting from shifts in currents or other causes, are involved in the depletion of the fishery. If this is true, little can be done except to hope that former conditions will return. Since overfishing and the resulting depletion of breeding populations is a contributing factor, however, there is less excuse. Overfishing can be prevented. Fortunately, in 1955 the California legislature passed its first law limiting the catch of a marine, commercial fish. This law, intended to protect the anchovy fishery, on which the former sardine-fishing pressure has descended, set a precedent for other laws that now provide needed protection for the sardine and other ocean fisheries.

A review of the situation in the 1980s, however, suggests that the former niche occupied by the sardine along the continental shelf of North America had been taken over, at least in part, by the anchovy (Fig. 9.5). By 1983, however, the sardine had started a comeback, although anchovies remained much more abundant, and some were speaking of a long-term scenario with sardines and anchovies alternating in abundance

FIG. 9.5

Anchovy catch and estimated biomass. (*Source:* 1965–1975, NOAA Technical Memorandum NMFS. California's Northern Anchovy Fishery: Biological and Economic Basis for Fishery Management, April 1980. 1976–present, Herbert Frey, Biologist, California Fish and Game Department, Long Beach, California.)

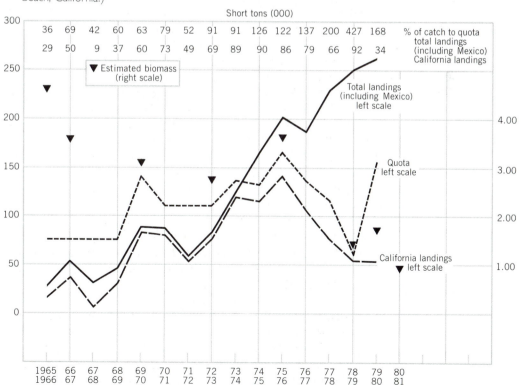

depending on changing oceanographic conditions and the degree of fishing pressure. Thus it can be seen that fishing pressure in the marine environment cannot be evaluated as a single factor. Although it may seem common sense that commercial fishing will not permanently reduce a fishery, when this is balanced against other factors operating for or against a marine species, it may have consequences far beyond those that could have been anticipated.

Experience with the California anchovy fishery reveals still more of the problems of regulating such a fishery. Overall control is now in the hands of the Pacific Fisheries Management Council, a joint Federal-State agency. California can control landings within the state, but quotas for the fishery are set by the Council. Figure 9.5 indicates both the extent to which the anchovy biomass fluctuates and the obvious lack of relationship between quota and catch. This is because the Mexican fishery is essentially unregulated and is responsible for most of the take. Regulation of the California landings has little effect when the main pressure is exerted by another country.

Marine Mammals

With sardines or anchovies the basic causes of population decline may be unclear. It is a different situation with marine mammals. Here the human factor is obviously predominant. Mammals, unlike fish, have no enormous powers of reproduction. The survival of the species depends on the survival of the one or two young produced each year.

The history of the whaling industry is one of the more colorful episodes in the human story. Initially, whaling consisted of the efforts of a few people who put out in small boats across the coastal waters to conquer and subdue the giant creatures who came from the far reaches of the ocean. In the Bay of Biscay off the Spanish coast during historical times, whaling was of this nature; the attempts to capture the right whales that came into these waters was little different from the more recent efforts of the Eskimos to capture and utilize the white whales, baluga, of the Arctic Ocean. But during the nineteenth century whaling became a much more intensive operation, and the exploits of the Yankee whalers setting out from New Bedford, Mystic, and the other New England whaling villages have passed down in history and American literature. Herman Melville's classic *Moby Dick* captures the spirit of the times. His fictional Captain Ahab of the whaling ship has been taken by some as exemplifying the entire spirit of our technological age: "All my means are sane, my motive and my object mad" (Borgstrom, 1965).

There is little doubt that the efforts of these early whalers brought some species of whales to the verge of extinction. But the greatest effects were to come. The high value of whale oil, whale bone, whale meat, and all of the other products obtainable from these animals provided an incentive to develop a more efficient technology for capturing them. In place of the hand-thrown harpoon came the harpoon gun, in place of the sail-powered whaling ship came the modern motor-driven factory ship with its satellites of hunter-killer vessels. In place of the laborious rendering of a captured whale into a compact booty of readily transportable valuables, came the capacity of reducing the entire animal, on the spot, into all of its commercially useful components. Whaling became big business, but the whales were not capable of producing in response to the new demands (Mackintosh, 1976).

The greatest impact was felt in Antarctic waters. Here the shrimplike krill, *Euphasia,* formed an important part of the zooplankton and was the food base for such giants as the blue or sulphur-buttomed whale, the largest of all mammals. We do not know how many blue whales there were in Antarctic waters, but their population has been estimated at about 200,000. To support this population it has been estimated that a total of 100 million tons of zooplankton, mainly krill, may have been required in each year. Motorized, efficient modern whaling was brought to bear on blue whale populations after the end of World War I. By 1930–1931 the annual catch of blue whales reached a peak of 29,400 animals. From then on the catch exceeded the sustainable yield from the blue whale population until it was finally apparent that if harvesting continued, even on an incidental basis, the whale would become extinct. In 1964 the blue whale was given complete protection by international agreement, and it has since shown some slight recovery.

The whaling enterprise has shifted from the larger to the smaller whales. When blue whale stocks were depleted whaling shifted to the fin whale. A peak catch of 28,000 animals was recorded in 1937–1938. From then on harvest exceeded the amount sustainable by what was an initial population of, at least, 200,000 animals. By the late 1960s the catch had declined to 3000 and the species was in danger. The humpback, also a moderately large whate, occurred in numbers that probably never exceeded 50,000 in Antarctic waters and could not support the pressure from the whaling industry. Catches of 2000 or more in a year in the Antarctic could not be sustained, since this species was also exploited in more northern waters. Pressure next descended on the sei whales, which supported catches of up to 20,000 animals in the middle 1900s but with their numbers also on the decline the catch was reduced to under 6000 in 1968–1969. Still smaller whales have been picked up in increasing numbers by the industry, and there has been talk of concentrating heavy exploitation on the small porpoises and dolphins, much to the dismay of those who regard these intelligent animals in the same category with domestic pets (Holdgate, 1970).

In 1970 the United States put a stop to commercial whaling by this country and in 1971 banned all imports of whale products into the United States. Whaling by this time was of relatively small economic importance in the United States. The United States took the lead at the United Nations Conference on the Human Environment in 1972 in calling for a moratorium on all commercial whaling. The conference agreed, but the

MARINE FISHERIES

(a) At its peak the California sardine fishery produced 800,000 tons of fish per year. In the late 1940s and early 1950s it collapsed. (b) The Peruvian anchovy fishery (producing the fish meal shown here) led the world in yield. It collapsed in the 1970s. (c) Despite the International Whaling Commission's efforts, Japanese and Russian whaling fleets still kill large numbers of whales. (d) White whales provide support from traditional Eskimo whaling in Canada. (e) The northern fur seal was restored to abundance through a treaty limiting the annual harvest.

a

b

c

d

e

conference had no authority to enforce its agreement. Responsibility rested with the International Whaling Commission, made up initially of the representatives from whaling nations. The Commission had previously provided protection for the seriously endangered blue whales, right whales, and California grey whales but balked at the idea of a general moratorium. Opposition came particularly from Japan, the Soviet Union, and Norway, which were still engaged in commercial whaling, and in the case of Japan, very actively engaged.

Whales and their conservation exemplify a problem that besets the exploitation and conservation of most marine fisheries. The oceans are effectively "no-man's land," or no-person's-water. They belong, beyond certain agreed-upon limits, to all nations and to no nation. Whoever gets there first has the right to capture and own the resources. Effective control depends on goodwill and international pressure. An international body such as the Whaling Commission can make rulings, but cannot enforce them if any one nation chooses to disregard them. Thus in 1982, after ten years of meetings, the IWC finally agreed to a moratorium on all commercial whaling, starting in 1986. Japan and Norway announced their attention to disregard the moratorium. The Soviet Union, no longer greatly interested in whaling, gained a little goodwill by going along with the agreement.

Georg Borgstrom has pointed out some of the realities of marine ecology that have bearing on the conservation of whales. Around 500 pounds of phytoplankton must be used to produce 100 pounds of zooplankton. This can, in turn, yield a maximum of 10 pounds of herring, which then provide the basis for one pound of mackerel. Should tuna in turn feed on the mackerel, an ounce and a half of tuna might be produced. Thus a tuna weighing 100 pounds would represent a phytoplankton production of 500,000 pounds. The ratio of 5000 to 1 represents a high caloric loss. By contrast, the blue whale feeds on zooplankton directly and converts it into useful meat. If we have as a goal the production of protein useful to man from the oceans, we would go far to find a more handy and efficient plankton converter. We could be cultivating blue whales and their relatives as marine livestock equivalent to cattle on the land and taking from them an annual sustainable crop. Instead we have treated them as we once did the American bison, and talk glibly about building plankton harvesting devices that at their best would be less efficient than the whales. Many find it abhorrent, however, for us to treat these large-brained ocean giants as simply another source of food for people.

The inadequacies of human behavior have affected many kinds of marine mammals other than whales. Some, such as the Steller's sea cow of the Arctic, became extinct. Others, the manatees and dugongs and the monk seals of the Mediterranean and Caribbean, have been pushed to near extinction. Others, although once depleted, have been brought back to healthy levels. An outstanding example is the northern fur seal that hauls out to breed on the rocky Pribiloff Islands off the Alaskan coast. This species was once exploited by Russians, Americans, and Japanese and pushed to danger of extinction. One of the first international agreements affecting marine resources was signed by Russia, the United States, Japan, and Canada in 1911. Since then, the fur seal has been harvested annually on its breeding ground, but within a sustainable yield. It has increased from small numbers to a population that exceeds one million animals. It can continue forever to yield skins and other by-products for human use. It remains, however, a center of controversy, since many object to the use of seals to supply "luxury" items such as fur coats for people who could easily get along without them.

Anadramous Fisheries

Particularly vulnerable to human pressures are the fish that migrate from fresh to salt water, spending a part of their life cycle in each environment. These species, known as anadramous fish, must face not only the hazards of ocean life but also the dangers to be found in streams and rivers. One example is the Atlantic salmon. Originally this was an abundant species that spawned and spent the early stages of its life cycle in the streams and rivers round the North Atlantic in Europe and America. As mature fish, they were found at sea and here they were commercially exploited. Within the fresh waters of Europe and America they received the attention of sport fishermen and were highly valued by anglers. A combination of dams and other obstacles constructed in their home streams and the ever-growing level of pollution in these waters led to major declines in fish populations. Those fish that successfully ran the gauntlet of hazards in fresh water were then subject to further decimation in the oceans. Concern for the future of the species resulted in increasing attention being given to its conservation. As a result of the pressure by conservationists, the commercial fishing of this species by northern European nations was discontinued in 1971. However, the continuing pressure on its home streams gives rise to no optimism about its future recovery.

In Pacific waters the Pacific salmon of several species compete with tuna for first place among commercial fish. Heavy exploitation by commercial fishermen combined with heavy sports fishing occurs, but it cannot be considered the major cause of depletion. This is to be found in the fresh waters. The construction of Grand Coulee Dam on the Columbia blocked the upper reaches of the river to Chinook salmon spawning. Shasta Dam and other high dams on the Sacramento River and its tributaries have cut off most areas of spawning ground in California. To partially replace the reproduction lost by blocking off these spawning areas, fish hatcheries have been constructed on several river systems, and these have helped to maintain the fishery. The continuing demand for water for power or irrigation, however, or for the control of floods will soon result in the damming of all of the main rivers of California, more dams in Oregon and Washington, and increasing dam construction in Canada and Alaska. These developments must force a dependence on the few remaining open streams and a much greater effort to develop and improve habitat conditions in these waters if salmon fishing is to be perpetuated.

Fisheries and World Food

Optimism that the ocean fisheries of the world could make increasing contributions to meeting growing demands for food was widespread during the 1950s and 1960s. Fisheries play a particular role in contributing protein, chronically deficient in the diet of a high percentage of the world population. Georg Brogstrom calculated that the world fisheries' yield in the middle 1960s represented protein equivalent to all the cattle in the world. Between 1950 and 1970 the average increase in world fisheries catch was estimated by FAO at 7 percent per year, from a total of 21 million metric tons in 1950 to 70 million in 1970. It was widely believed that this increase could continue, up to a potentially sustainable yield of 100 million metric tons (Schaefer, 1965). However, subsequent events have affected this optimisim.

In the past the northern oceans yielded most of the world's fish catch, and the technologically advanced nations took most of the harvest. More recently, many developing nations entered the marine fisheries business, and emphasis shifted to other waters. Between 1958 and 1968, for example, the fisheries yield of the Northeast Atlantic, traditional for European fishing, declined by half. In the same period the yield from the southeast Pacific increased 42-fold. Increased fisheries yield resulted in part from the development of more efficient fishing technology, the entry of new fishing fleets into the business, and the harvesting of species lower in the food chains than those previously taken (Gulland, 1970).

What seemed to be ignored in the general optimism about oceanic fisheries was that much of the gain in the world harvest came from one fishery, the Peruvian anchovy. In 1970 it contributed over 12 million of the 70 million metric tons. In 1971 the anchovy fishery began to collapse, and from 1971 to 1974 world fisheries yields went down. Although some increase has since occurred, the catch in 1980 was below 80 million tons—far less than had been hoped (Fig. 9.6).

The anchovies off the western coast of South America thrive in the nutrient-rich waters of the Humboldt Current. For centuries they yielded a minute part of their substance for the support of the Indians who occupied the nearby coasts. A far greater portion went to support the abundant sea birds that nested on rocky offshore islands.

In 1953 a small anchovy fishery was developed in Peru, which yielded a total of 37,000 pounds of fish. Thereafter, as the California sardine fishery collapsed, the Peruvian fishery was progressively developed. The fishing fleet increased, and processing factories that could reduce these small fishes to a dry fish meal were constructed on the

FIG. 9.6
World Fish Catch. (*Source:*
CEQ, 1980; Webb and
Jacobsen, 1982.)

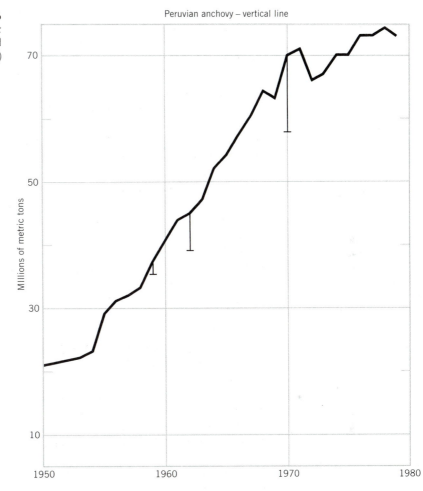

FIG. 9.6
World Fish Catch. (*Source:* CEQ, 1980; Webb and Jacobsen, 1982.)

mainland. By 1959 the annual yield had been increased to 1,909,000 tons, by 1962 to 6,275,000 tons, and finally by 1970 to 12 million tons. FAO has estimated that the sustainable yield of this fishery was 9.5 million tons, but in four of the years ending in 1970, the catch was in excess of this limit. By that time many of the symptoms of overfishing that characterized the last years of the California sardine fishery were in evidence—lower catch per unit of effort, increasing proportions of juvenile fish in the catch, and failures of the less efficient enterprises (Loftas, 1972).

The collapse of the anchovy fishery, however, would have taken place in the absence of overfishing. It was caused primarily by a phenomenon known as *El Niño,* a change in the pattern of upwelling and in the flow of the cold Humboldt current, which has occurred before at unpredictable intervals. The big question, however, is whether or not the anchovy will recover when the normal upwelling and current flow is resumed, or whether, as with the California sardine, the combination of overfishing and current change will have brought a more lasting decline. By 1983 there was no evidence that the earlier abundance of anchovies would be restored. It is obvious that we know far less about oceanic fish populations than we should, and in far too many cases fisheries failures, apparently influenced by overfishing, are taking place. There is no cause for optimism about ever-increasing fisheries yields or major contributions of fisheries to world food sources.

What is particularly ironic about the Peruvian anchovy fishery is that, even at its peak yield, it made little contribution to feeding the protein-hungry people of the Third World. Georg Borgstrom has pointed out that the anchovy fishery could have provided all of the people in South America with an adequate protein diet. It could have met the minimum protein needs of 413 million undernourished people. Yet with small exceptions it has not gone to hungry people at all. It has gone to the well-fed nations of the rich world and has been used mostly to enrich the diet of domestic animals. Said Borgstrom (1971): *The Peruvian-Chilean protein aid to the satisfied world overshadows, both in absolute and relative terms, anything done in the postwar period to alleviate the shortages of the Hungry World. . . . A similar tapping of invaluable protein resources but on a much more modest scale (approximately 100,000 tons) is taking place along the Atlantic Coast of South Africa. This protein also bypasses the protein-short continent of Africa in order to support largely European animal production. On the whole, close to one-half of the marine fish catch is channeled via fish meal and oil into the hopper of the satisfied world.*

If it were possible to increase world fisheries yields to 100 million tons or more, who would benefit? Would we even begin to solve the world's protein hunger? The Peruvian experience is not encouraging.

MARINE POLLUTION
Among the most common and persistent of human attitudes toward the ocean has been the view that it is the ultimate answer to the problem of waste disposal. This idea of the ocean as a dump has been encouraged by its apparent vast expanse and depth relative to the needs of man. Anything toxic or obnoxious, from atomic wastes and old war gases or ammunition, down to junked cars, sewage, and general urban debris has been placed in the oceans with a confidence that we have seen the last of it. Added to this, all of the outpourings of pollutants from streams and rivers reach the oceans, and much of the debris polluting the urban air eventually is deposited in ocean waters.

But the ocean is not a limitless dump, and it has become apparent that this attitude toward it is likely to create limitless problems. Perhaps more than anything else, the wreck of the *Torrey Canyon* off the coast of England in 1967 brought the situation into focus. The *Torrey Canyon* was one of a new generation of giant oil tankers used to transport oil from the fields of the Middle East or Latin America to refineries in Europe or the United States. In March 1967 it ran aground off the coast of Cornwall in England and proceeded to spill its cargo of 36 million gallons of petroleum into the seas. The Cornish coast of England is a favored vacation spot and its beaches are highly valued. With the summer tourist season coming on, resort owners and all of those dependent on the tourist trade were faced with the prospect of an end to their prosperity. Oil-soaked beaches and oily waters guarantee that potential visitors will spend their holidays elsewhere. Furthermore, seabirds by the thousands became entrapped in the oil and died despite rescue efforts. In spite of a campaign on the part of the British government and local volunteers to clean up the oil, using detergents, napalm, and virtually everything else that could be thought of, damage was done. The oil spread along the coasts of England and reached the beaches of France, across the Channel. Investigations were launched to determine the extent of damage to fisheries, intertidal life, marine mammals and birds, and to recreation values generally.

Not long after the *Torrey Canyon* storm had died down, the world was given another example of the problems of ocean pollution. In the blue and placid Santa Barbara Channel off the coast of southern California, in another favorite tourist and recreation center, an oil well used to pump from the fields that lay deep beneath the channel waters began to leak. Oil poured upward to the surface of the water, formed an enormous slick, and began to move toward the beaches of Santa Barbara and adjoining communities. Again the *Torrey Canyon* pattern was repeated. Despite all efforts, great damage was done. In this case the federal Department of Interior, the agency most concerned with conservation, was held to blame for having issed leases to the oil companies that permitted them to drill in this vulnerable locality.

The news from around the world continues to record the wrecks of oil tankers, the flushing of oil bunkers by ships at sea, the leakage from undersea oil wells, and other continuing sources of oil pollution. In 1970 Thor Heyerdahl made one of his exploratory voyages in a papyrus ship from Africa to the West Indies—to prove that the Egyptians could have made the journey and thus influence the development of Amer-Indian civilizations. He reported encountering floating petroleum or tar almost throughout his Atlantic voyage. Other reports have added to the picture of a growing global problem that requires continued internation attention. Griffin and Steele (1980) have pointed out that fear of environmental damage from oil pollution is exaggerated. Crude oil is biodegradable and the oceans are large. Tanker accidents, even including such as the *Torrey Canyon,* or the larger *Amoco Cadiz,* which went down off the coast of France, only add 9 percent of the total oil release of 1.5 million tons that goes into the oceans each year. Offshore drilling accidents, even such spectacular ones as the oil well blowout off Yucatan in the late 1970s, which spread oil north to Texas, average only 34,000 tons annually.

Runoff from oil operations on shore, however, provide around a half million tons annually, whereas the bulk of the oil entering the sea comes from the routine flushing out of tanks from those ships that take on sea-water as ballast after delivering their oil cargoes. They further point out that natural oil seeps from the ocean floor add as much oil to the oceans as all other pollution sources.

The immediate damaging effect of oil pollution near shore to marine birds and mammals, shellfish beds, scenic and recreational resources, and potentially to the entire near shore biota is nevertheless significant. It is little consolation to those who live in areas affected by pollution to be told that the oceans are large and long-term effects will be small.

Oil is only one of many marine pollutants. Pesticide residues are now being recorded from all parts of the oceans. A die-off of seabirds in the Irish Sea in 1969 was believed related to the heavy discharge of another industrial pollutant—polychlorinated biphenyls (PCBs)—produced and used in a variety of manufacturing processes. Mercury levels considered to be dangerous to man were found in tinned tuna and frozen swordfish. Since these species feed across broad areas of the open ocean this led to the conclusion that mercury contamination had also become a global phenomena. The need for regulation and control of the discharge of pollutants into the oceans has become clearly apparent, but the means for accomplishing this remains unclear. The use of the oceans is still largely uncontrolled. Regulation is an international concern, but the difficulties of reaching agreements among sovereign nations are great, indeed, and the problems of enforcing such agreements are even greater. In 1972 a convention restricting ocean dumping was signed by many nations, but in fact dumping continues. The Law of the Sea agreement among most nations was rejected in 1982 by the United States, even though it could only be considered a first step toward proper management.

ESTUARIES AND
COASTAL WATERS

Compared to the pressures put on the resources and the environments of the open oceans, those affecting coastal and estuarine waters are much more severe (Hedgpeth, 1978). The history of the twentieth century, particularly its latter half, has been marked by man's movement to the sea. The coastal areas of America continue to attract a steady stream of immigrants from inland states. In Europe and in many other parts of the world a similar trend is evident. The coastline is an attractive place for living—recreation, in theory, at least, is available in one's front yard in the form of boating, fishing, swimming, and a variety of other shoreline or water sports. Coastal areas have naturally attracted industry and commerce through the appeal of cheap, waterborne transportation and the apparent availability of large quantities of water for industrial uses.

Use of the coastal zone, however, has seldom been planned to take into account the vulnerability of the environment. Instead, virtually every form of environmental affront has taken place. Thus, estuarine marshes and coastal swamps form a source of nutrients of great importance to marine aquatic life and also provide shelter and a nursery ground for a wide variety of otherwise oceanic species. They are not only highly productive themselves but are vital to the maintenance of productivity in a much wider oceanic area. To the developer, however, they represent areas to be dredged and filled in order to form platforms on which houses or other coastal accommodations can be built, or areas through which boat canals can be dredged to allow boat access to a new residential areas.

Efforts to drain marshes along the coast have further resulted in the cutting of canals that move fresh water quickly to the sea. Where previously runoff moved slowly through a variety of winding channels, picking up nutrients and slowly mixing with salt water, the new canals create massive outpourings of fresh water after each rain. This can disrupt the aquatic life in the bays or channels into which it is poured. Rapid drainage of fresh water has also caused a movement of salt water inland through what were formerly freshwater aquifers. This has caused a salting up of water supplies needed by the new seashore communities.

Rivers and streams bring into the estuarine zone all of the pollutants and excess nutrients they have picked up in their flow across the lands. Added to this, new coastal communities often pour pollutants directly into the sea. Coastal and estuarine biotic communities suffer all the effects resulting from the concentrations of toxic substances and excessive fertilization. Undesirable planktonic blooms are balanced by the loss of more desirable species of aquatic life.

Dredging, draining, and the construction of coastal installations have changed offshore currents with the consequent erosion of existing beaches and deposition of sand in other areas where it is not wanted. Many efforts to correct this problem by the construction of groins and breakwaters have only accelerated the damage.

Many of the most valuable and interesting biotic communities occur on or near the coast. Pressure on the coastal zones often leads to their complete destruction. Coral reefs are blasted or plundered by those who seek fish, coral, or shells. Tidal pools and tidal marshes—where not polluted, dredged, or filled—are often devastated by those who collect marine life for fun or profit.

In the United States many steps have been taken to ensure better protection and management of those coastal resources that were not already destroyed, but it is late in the game. Elsewhere in the world little is being done and devastation accelerates. Marine parks and reserves are badly needed. Many are now in existence, but only a small percentage of the coastal environment is thus protected. Effective protection for coastal lands, waters, and resources beyond the boundaries of any foreseeable system of parks and reserves is equally important. The health of the entire ocean can well hinge on the care we take of the waters near the coast and the lands in contact with them.

THE COASTAL ZONE

(a) The intertidal zone. In this meeting place between land and sea a great diversity of marine life is to be found. Sandy beaches, mud flats, or rock outcroppings each support a distinct group of marine organisms. (b) Mangroves line the estuaries of tropical coasts and provide a nursery ground for many marine animals that spend their adult life at sea. In addition, they support a specialized biota that is largely restricted to the mangrove habitat. (c) Life in the coastal zone reaches its greatest diversity in the coral reefs of shallow tropical seas.

a

b

c

261

INLAND WATER
ENVIRONMENTS

To a greater extent than marine environments, the aquatic environments of the continents and islands are highly diversified and marked by a wide range of physical and chemical conditions. Physical conditions vary from those of the boiling lakes of volcanic regions to permanently frozen bodies of water in polar or high mountain areas. Chemical extremes are represented by the clear lakes of certain high mountain and polar areas that contain few nutrients, and the lakes and inland seas of interior drainages that are so saline that only a few highly specialized forms of life can make use of them. A similar range is to be found among rivers and streams.

Lakes and Streams

Lakes vary according to their age, their depth, their size, and with the conditions of their watersheds. Two broad categories are recognized, based on the relative levels of dissolved nutrients in their waters. One group of lakes is known as oligotrophic and includes the clear, cold lakes of high mountains and of glaciated subpolar regions. These lakes commonly have rocky bottoms and rest in barren, infertile watersheds. Low water temperatures result in a high degree of oxygenation, but the lack of dissolved nutrients prevents an abundant growth of plankton. Rooted vegetation has difficulty becoming established on their rocky edges or bottoms. The level of life that can be supported is therefore low. There is a gradation from these nearly sterile lakes through to moderately fertile lakes. Such clear, cold lakes as Tahoe in the Sierra Nevada of California–Nevada and Baikal in Siberia are considered as oligotrophic, but nevertheless they support a relatively abundant life. Tahoe, which connects through the Truckee River with Pyramid Lake in Nevada, supports a distinctive fauna. Baikal, long isolated from other water bodies, but of great size, supports a completely unique and highly varied fish fauna.

Associated with these lakes are the clear, cold streams of high mountain and subpolar regions, which are also of low-nutrient, oligotrophic character. Lakes and streams alike support many of the most highly valued sport fish—the cold-water fisheries of rainbow and brook trout, muskellunge, and northern pike. These often reach large size individually but, because of overall limitations in their food supply, seldom become abundant.

At the opposite extreme among fresh waters are the *eutrophic* lakes. These are usually warmer and characteristically have muddy or sandy bottoms, rounded contours, and gently sloping shorelines. Usually they are surrounded by watersheds in which soil has developed and matured and in consequence supplies the lakes with abundant nutrients through runoff or subterranean flow. Warm water causes an acceleration of life processes, and the abundance of nutrients encourages plant growth. Such lakes support abundant submerged, emergent, or floating aquatic vegetation. Throughout the lighted portion of their waters plankton blooms during the warm season of the year. Populations of invertebrates and fish, as well as aquatic amphibians and reptiles, are generally abundant and diversified. In temperate regions, where winter freezing normally occurs, these lakes develop seasonal problems. When ice and snow cover their surface, photosynthesis is inhibited or ceases. The decay of plant and animal life along with continued respiration by animals can cause oxygen exhaustion and die-offs of animal life. In subtropical and tropical regions where growth and photosynthesis can continue at a high rate throughout the year, lakes of this kind are among the most productive of ecosystems and yield a continuing abundance of fish and other aquatic life.

Over long periods of time most lakes will evolve from an oligotrophic to a eutrophic condition, as soils in their watersheds mature, as erosion occurs, and as nutrients become more abundant. But this is normally a slow, geologically timed process. *Accelerated eutrophication* of water bodies is a result of man-caused pollution and can bring serious damage to water bodies that have been valued either for their clear, cold water and the recreational and esthetic values associated with this attribute or for their sustained, high productivity, which can be swamped out by excessive supplies of nutrients and excessive growth of certain plants, followed by high rates of decay and oxygen depletion.

The "ideal" eutrophic lake in the United States is one that supports an abundant population of black bass, lake perch, or the various sunfish. When such a lake becomes choked with plant growth, grows warmer, and develops a more variable oxygen supply, however, it becomes the home for catfish or carp. Still further eutrophication can lead to conditions unsuited to any fish and eventually to an environment suited only to blue-green algae or anaerobic bacteria.

The conditions described for lakes also apply to streams. Most large rivers that drain fertile watersheds are eutrophic with a high nutrient level and have many of the characteristics and problems of eutrophic lakes.

Zonation occurs in lakes as in the oceans, but to a lesser degree (Fig. 9.7). Large, deep lakes have a *littoral zone* around their margins within which rooted vegetation can grow—reeds and rushes, pondweeds and duckweeds. Beyond the littoral zone and lying over the deeper water is a *limnetic zone*, the lower limits of which are defined by the limits of light penetration and within which active planktonic growth can occur. Below the limnetic zone is the dark, *profundal zone* where no photosynthesis occurs. This may still support abundant life, but it is dependent for its food on either the lighted waters above or the littoral region of the shore. Particularly in temperate regions and in deeper lakes, zonation is further accentuated by *thermal stratification*. Surface waters are heated by the sun in summer and, as a result, become lighter and less dense than the deeper layers. The deeper layers may be maintained at a maximum density and constant temperature of 4° C. As one moves from surface to deeper waters, a sharp temperature gradient, or *thermocline*

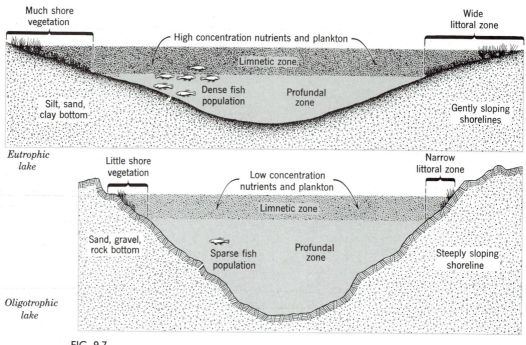

Much shore vegetation

Wide littoral zone

High concentration nutrients and plankton

Limnetic zone

Dense fish population

Profundal zone

Silt, sand, clay bottom

Gently sloping shorelines

Eutrophic lake

Little shore vegetation

Narrow littoral zone

Low concentration nutrients and plankton

Limnetic zone

Sand, gravel, rock bottom

Sparse fish population

Profundal zone

Steeply sloping shoreline

Oligotrophic lake

FIG. 9.7
Cross sections through oligotrophic and eutrophic lakes.

occurs. If the thermocline corresponds with or is below the level of the limnetic zone, than all photosynthesis occurs in the warmer waters and the profundal zone, as the summer progresses, may face oxygen depletion with its consequences for life. In the autumn, as the weather cools, surface temperatures of the lake will decline and eventually reach the 4° level of the deeper waters. The thermocline disappears and the water from the two zones mixes freely, restoring oxygen to the deeper layers. As winter progresses the surface water cools and ice forms, and once again a stratification and thermocline is set up, although less severe than in summer. This again brings dangers of oxygen depletion if the winter remains cold. Spring warming of the surface once again restores equal temperatures, a spring overturn occurs, and the waters are once again mixed. Both zonation and temperature stratification have consequences for the distribution of aquatic life and create separate ecologic niches within a water body, allowing for a greater variety of life. When lakes are managed for intensive fish production, these characteristics must be recognized and compensated for to maintain high levels of yield.

Fisheries Conservation and Management in the United States
The fisheries of the freshwater lakes and streams of North America attract annually an army of anglers numbering well over 20 million. Dangling a hook and line into a quiet pond or flashing a trout fly over a splashing stream is a form of recreation with a traditional, and almost irresistible,

appeal to a large segment of the American population. Because it is a form of sport open to participation by all ages of people, it has a much larger group of followers than the more strenuous sport of hunting.

Beginnings. The history of freshwater fisheries in America can be traced through a period of early abundance, when streams ran clear and fish could be easily taken, to a time of serious depletion. The causes of depletion were basically the same as those that have affected other natural resources. Forests were cut, and streams that once supported abundant fish life deteriorated. Farmlands were mismanaged and erosion silted up lakes and streams. Debris, washed from overgrazed slopes, choked stream channels below. Pollution from mill or factory wiped out fisheries for miles below the source. Eventually, the situation became serious enough to cause alarm and action. In the 1870s the federal government entered the picture when a Bureau of Fisheries, forerunner of the present United States Fish and Wildlife Service, was created. State governments began to form fish-conservation commissions or agencies to look into the problem of restoring and improving fisheries.

The conservation of fisheries went through a period of emphasis on protection through restrictive laws and of concern with the control of wild predators and then moved into the field of artificial propagation and the introduction of exotic species. Most of the early state fish commissions were charged initially with the task of setting up fish hatcheries, where fish could be reared and then released to stock streams and lakes. They were also charged with looking into ways of improving fisheries through the introduction of new species from other areas. Only much later did an ecological approach begin, with attention to providing suitable habitat for existing fish populations and research toward discovering actual causes of fisheries depletion.

The effect of the hatchery program on freshwater fisheries was far reaching. Whereas a good share of America's land birds and mammals are still truly wild animals reared in more or less natural habitats, America's freshwater fisheries are increasingly artificial. A wild fish in natural stream or lake is becoming more difficult to find, except in the still existing wilderness of Canada and Alaska. The early history of fish conservation saw the mass movement of species from one side of the continent to the other, plus the introduction of many additional kinds from Europe and Asia. Even those streams that still support native species of fish are often stocked with hatchery-reared fish or their descendants.

Fisheries Management. In earlier days of fish conservation, the approach to the management of warm-water fisheries was much the same as for cold-water or trout fisheries, with increasing restrictions on angling that limited gear, seasons, and numbers and size of fish that could be legally caught, combined with the development of a hatchery program. After a time, experience began to show that this approach did not make sense. Some lakes, heavily stocked with hatchery fish, began to produce less

266 a

b

FRESH WATER HABITATS

(a) Cold trout stream in Colorado. (b) Oligotrophic lake in New Hampshire. (c) Eutrophic lake in Connecticut.

c

than other unstocked lakes. Fish populations which increased without reference to the food supply, were stunted in size and provided little incentive for angling. Some restrictions on take are obviously necessary—dynamite, poisons, and nets can finish off any population. Once a general rule was established limiting sports-fishing gear to hook-and-line, however, further restrictions were often unnecessary. Studies in the reservoirs of the TVA and of various warm-water species in Midwestern lakes and ponds, where hatchery stocking and rigidly enforced seasons and creel limits had been the rule, showed that these measures were unnecessary. It was found that these lakes could be fished as heavily as anglers wanted to fish them and would still yield an abundance of fish from natural reproduction alone. The question was raised whether a warm-water lake could be overfished when recreation was the only incentive. With these studies came a shift in the emphasis of management, from artificial propagation and restrictions on take to the improvement of habitat and relatively unrestricted fishing (Klingbiel, 1953).

Since fish have a remarkably high rate of reproduction, given adequate spawning grounds, proper water conditions for hatching, adequate food, and enough weedy cover for protection, natural reproduction will produce increasing numbers of catchable-size fish. If the habitat is adequate, hatchery progation of fish is unnecessary. If the habitat is protected and improved, nature will supply the fish.

With trout and other cold-water fish, it has also been realized that too much emphasis has been placed on hatchery production and not enough on habitat improvement. Nevertheless, trout fisheries often present a different problem, since the demand for fishing and the capacity of the habitat often do not coincide. With the best of management, natural propagation cannot meet the demands placed on some of the heavily fished cold-water lakes and streams. Although it is generally true that these waters are not "fished out" in the sense that the last fish have been caught, they can be "fished out" in the sense that all of the easily caught fish have been hooked. When this happens they no longer provide adequate recreation to fishermen. To meet popular demand, fish and game departments are forced to remain in the hatchery business, stocking streams and lakes with trout on a "put-and-take" basis. Trout are reared in hatcheries to legal or "catchable" size and then released in suitable places before the start of the fishing season. It is not necessary that these fish be able to survive permanently in the stocked waters but only that they survive long enough to be caught. Heavily fished areas may be restocked several times in a single season. Similarly, intermittent streams, sterile lakes, and reservoirs that could not support permanent fish populations can be stocked. These fishing grounds, if located near centers of population, will attract fishing pressure that would otherwise fall on the natural fish populations of productive lakes and streams. The more remote areas are thus preserved for the enthusiast who prefers more natural conditions.

Deterioration of streams and lakes through failure to practice conservation on watershed lands remains a major problem. Logging in some areas, despite laws to the contrary, often results in the choking of streams with debris or the pollution of streams with organic wastes. Industries and cities still contribute to stream pollution. Poor farming practices, overgrazing, mining, and lumbering still cause increased erosion with consequent deterioration of watercourses. In addition, many practices advocated in the name of conservation have caused much damage to fisheries. As discussed previously, the construction of high dams on rivers creates impassable barriers to migratory fish. Admittedly, the reservoirs formed behind the dams can provide a different type of fishing, which may have equal or greater value, but this does not always occur. Low dams can be bypassed by fishways and ladders; high dams such as Shasta in California and Grand Coulee in Washington cannot. Although mature fish can be lifted over these dams by one device or another, young fish returning downstream experience high mortality during the trip over the dam. In addition to dams, irrigation canals prove a major hazard to fish life. Where possible these must be screened off to prevent fish from entering them and perishing. Unfortunately, the design, installation, and maintenance of adequate fish screens is expensive.

Farm Ponds and Food Fish. One of the important developments that has come with the rise of the conservation movement has been an interest in farm fish ponds. Small ponds developed on farming lands not only serve in water conservation but, when stocked with fish, can be a permanent source of recreation, food, and sometimes income to the landowner. Many farm owners have developed their own home fishing grounds, stocked with bass or sunfish.

In most other parts of the world, fish are important for food rather than recreation. Where populations are dense and space for livestock limited, much of the animal protein in the diet comes from fish. Fish ponds, and the use of fish in conjunction with other land use, such as growing fish in rice paddies, and the use of poultry, pigs, and fish in various combinations have resulted in very high yields from small areas. Fish ponds in southeast Asia have yielded 13,500 pounds of fish per acre. The practice of fish culture, aquaculture, is growing in importance, and is now practiced widely not only with freshwater species but also in marine environments. Estuaries and coastal lagoons appear particularly well suited for aquaculture.

WATER AS A RESOURCE

The rise of Western civilization has been associated with the ability to manage water, to use it for irrigation while avoiding problems of flooding. Modern industrial civilization, more than any preceding it, places heavy demands on water. Exceptional demands are placed by high-energy intensive agriculture, which can rarely be satisfied by rain alone. Industries engaged in processing raw materials require great quantities of water for their functioning. Water is needed in the energy business, not just waterpower as such, but the large amounts used in fossil-fuel-fired or nuclear-powered generating plants. Cities are totally dependent on water collected from distant hills and mountains, the watersheds from which rain fall drains into rivers and lakes or sinks into underground storage basins. Because we have great engineering ability and centuries of experience in capturing and transferring water from one place to another, we have located cities and industries without reference to water supply, counting on water being brought from some other place to meet whatever demands we can generate. A particularly striking example of this proclivity is illustrated by the cities of coastal southern California, in particular Los Angeles.

THE LOS ANGELES STORY
An example of the unbalanced distribution of population and water supply characteristic of the western world is provided by the coastal plain of southern California. Here on one-eighth the area of California live more than half the state's people. Los Angeles alone is the second largest city in the United States. The warm, dry Mediterranean-type climate, with its prospects for outdoor living throughout the year, the miles of bathing beaches and recreational grounds, and the employment offered by industry have attracted people from afar. Early in the twentieth century the motion-picture industry moved to the Los Angeles area, attracted by the clear air and a climate favorable for year-round open-air photography. The air is no longer clear, but the industry remains in a diminished state. Aircraft and other industries, since attracted to the region, have provided employment for the people and have, in turn, attracted more people.

The same climate that brings people to southern California does not bring water. The rainfall may be between 10 and 20 inches annually, on the average, over most of the coastal plain and only reaches a more adequate 30 to 40 inches in restricted areas of the higher coastal mountains. The rainfall is erratic, dry cycles alternating with wet, and much of the annual rainfall may come in a few gully-washing storms. The area receives less than 1.5 percent of the state's total water. By contrast the sparsely peopled northwest coast of California receives more than 38 percent of the total rainfall (Dolder, 1954).

Water problems are not new in southern California and cannot be related entirely to misuse of the land. Between 1769, when the Spanish first arrived, and 1955 there were an estimated 25 major floods, alternating with long periods of drought and crop failure. In the late nineteenth century an effort was made to bring the local water supply under reasonable control through the construction of dams and aqueducts and through the placing of timber and brush-covered mountains in federal forest reserves for the protection of the watershed cover. Underground water supplies were tapped by drilling numerous deep wells.

By the early 1900s it was realized that local water supplies were inadequate for the growing population. Los Angeles city began to reach out for water, first to the Sierra Nevada in the north. After much controversy with the local residents, Los Angeles obtained control of the Owens River watershed, draining the east slope of the Sierra 250 miles away. A great aqueduct carried the first water from this region to Los Angeles in 1913. With further population growth, this supply proved inadequate, and the city reached farther north to tap the Mono Lake watershed in the period between 1934 and 1940. Realizing that even this supply would be insufficient, Los Angeles next looked to the waters draining from the western slopes of the Rocky Mountains into the Colorado River. In 1933 work was begun to impound the Colorado at Parker Dam, 155 miles south of Hoover Dam (p. 275), and to carry this water across the desert 242 miles to Lake Matthews in southern California (Kahrl, 1979; Nadeau, 1950).

Other southern California cities and communities, faced with similar problems, have engaged in equally heroic efforts. With evergrowing populations, southern California had to look still further afield. In 1951 a project was approved to bring water from Feather River in the north Sierra Nevada through some 567 miles of conduits to the south. As part of the California state water plan the Feather, the Trinity, and other northern rivers are tapped to provide water for urban populations and irrigation farming in the drier southern regions of the state.

The Colorado River region, unlike California's Owen's Valley, is not susceptible to the kind of strong-arm pressure that Los Angeles Metropolitan Water District has employed. Many states use its water, as does the northern part of Mexico. One of them, Arizona, has felt that too much of the Colorado's water was being captured by southern California, to the detriment of Arizona's development. After long legal wrangles the Supreme Court agreed with Arizona and told southern California that it had until 1985 to share its Colorado River water with Arizona. Los Angeles next began to draw much more heavily on the Mono Lake watershed, and this precipitated a new kind of controversy. Mono Lake is a heavily saline lake with a unique fauna. On its islands were found the nesting sites for tens of thousands of California gulls—most of the state's population of this species. With little water from the tributary streams escaping from the Los Angeles pumps and aqueducts, the lake began to evaporate. Islands became peninsulas, coyotes and other predators crossed from the mainland to attack the nesting gulls. Meanwhile, the lake salinity increased to the point that the gull's food supply diminished. In 1981 gull nesting attempts largely failed. Efforts to halt the channeling of water southward have not been entirely successful although a court ruling in 1983 opened new hopes for a compromise between urban needs and the natural values of Mono Lake. Heavy rainfall in 1982–1983 has given further respite. In 1983 attempts were being made to establish Mono Lake as a national mounument. Some hope that the threatened earthquake and volcanic activity in the Long Valley caldera south of Mono Lake will come to the rescue—but those are grim hopes.

The most recent California water battle has centered on the proposed Peripheral Canal, intended to channel waters from California's northern rivers around the delta of San Francisco Bay and ultimately into the California aqueduct heading toward the southern San Joaquin Valley and Los Angeles. The June 1982 elections brought a resounding defeat for this proposal, with northern California voters almost unanimous in opposition. But nothing is really solved, and undoubtedly the south will try again.

The Los Angeles problem is by no means unique, and in various degrees is shared with many other areas. Good farming soils, good industrial sites, and centers for commerce often do not coincide with the availability of abundant water. Populations grow and water demands increase. Governments are asked to respond by launching huge water development schemes. One could, of course, encourage the development of industry and population growth in areas where water is abundant and limit growth where it is scarce. This seems to go against the cornucopian philosophy encouraged by the global economic system. In conventional economics resources are *supposed to be* limitless, just as oceans are supposed to be bottomless sinks for the deposit of wastes.

URBAN WATER NEEDS AND DEMANDS

Water that reaches a city for human use should be clean and pure. Water that leaves a city, after human use, is often dangerously contaminated. The provision of adequate water is often difficult, the disposal of wastes equally so. In much of the heavily populated part of the world, however, the water that reaches a city is contaminated, and the water leaving it is even more so. The more technologically advanced cities have installed elaborate purifying systems to remove various pollutants and make the water somewhat safe for human consumption. In less advanced areas, people take their chances and often pay the costs in health. Few people except those living high on the watersheds or in unpopulated regions have the privilege of drinking "new" water, fresh from the air or from the ground, uncontaminated by prior use. For most city folk, the water used today has been used before—it has gone through somebody's kidneys or somebody's industries first.

Water uses are either consumptive or nonconsumptive. Consumptive uses, such as agriculture, lead to direct loss of water from the useful part of the hydrologic cycle, either through evaporation, transpiration, or incorporation into some other substance such as plant or animal tissues or industrial products. Most urban-industrial uses are relatively nonconsumptive. Kalinin and Bykov (1969) estimated that one-sixth of the water used for domestic purposes and one-tenth used for industrial purposes is consumed. The rest is restored to streams or underground storage for later use, although usually in a polluted state.

TABLE 9.3   Expected World Demands for Water: 2000 A.D.

| | WATER REQUIRED (CUBIC KILOMETERS) | |
FORM OF USE	TOTAL	AMOUNT LOST IN USE (EVAPORATION)
Irrigation	7,000	4,800
Domestic	600	100
Industrial	1,700	170
Dilution of wastes	9,000	—
Other	400	400
Total	18,700	5,470
Total available supply: 37,300 cubic kilometers.		

Source: Kalanin and Bykov (1969).

The amount of water used in urban-industrial processes is large. Landsberg (1964) has calculated that each urban resident in the United States uses 110 gallons of water per day. Of this 60 gallons is used in the home for gardening, air cooling, laundry, cooking, bathing, washing, and drinking (the latter amounting to one gallon per day). Eisenbud (1970) reports that per capita use of water in New York City is 150 gallons per day. This is far less than the nearly 1900 gallons per day withdrawn from U. S. water resources, per capita, and the actual consumption of approximately 440 gallons per day. The difference is in the use of water by agriculture, which is the greatest consumer of water (Pimentel et al., 1983). (See Table 9.3.)

The extent to which a city will go to meet its domestic and industrial water needs has been exemplified by Los Angeles. Other problems that may be encountered in the drier parts of the world are pointed up by the experience of another California city, Santa Barbara. Santa Barbara is built on a narrow, coastal plain backed up by high, chaparral-covered mountains. From its early days it has had difficulty in obtaining water. In 1920, Gibraltar Dam was built on the Santa Ynez River in the mountains behind the city, and water from the reservoir was carried through the mountains in a tunnel four miles long (p. 274). Shortly after the dam was built it became obvious that the reservoir was filling with silt and losing its storage capacity. To stop silting, two additional dams, Mono and Caliente, were built upstream (p. 274). Within two years their reservoirs were completely filled with silt and debris. In 1946–1947 siltation had reduced the capacity of Gibraltar reservoir to one-half, and it was necessary to build the dam higher. In 1948 a severe water shortage hit the city and caused great restrictions and inconvenience. To obtain additional supplies a new and larger dam, Cachuma Dam, was completed on the Santa Ynez River below Gibraltar Dam. The expense of all of this construction has been considerable, and yet no permanent solution has been achieved if population and industrial growth are to continue, since in time Cachuma will also fill in.

a

WATER AND WATERSHEDS

(a) Gibraltar reservoir near Santa Barbara. The steep, chaparral-covered slopes erode readily when fire removes the vegetation. (b) Mono reservoir near Santa Barbara. This dam was built to stop silt from flowing into Gibraltar reservoir. In this 1938 picture the area behind the dam had completely silted in. (c) In this 1949 picture the old reservoir site had grown an open woodland. (d) Before a brush fire burned the area in the southern California mountains enclosed by the dotted line, a single storm drain handled the runoff in this orchard. (e) Following the fire in 1941, runoff from a light rain filled the orchard with debris. (f) Hoover Dam on the Colorado River, part of the system that provides Los Angeles with water.

b

c

d

e

f

The Santa Barbara problem is one shared by many arid regions. The watershed cover in the mountains is highly inflammable. Despite extreme efforts at protection, including the closing of the entire watershed to public use during the dry season, fires start and sweep over vast acreage. Burned-over slopes erode badly, and the resulting debris fills reservoirs (p. 275).

Thus the provision of adequate water to a city involves the careful management of vegetation in sometimes distant mountains. Such watershed management must include the control of erosion with consequent siltation and also the provision of optimum quantities of usable water. Natural vegetation, while maintaining soil, preventing erosion, and regulating runoff from watersheds, can also be a source of much water loss through water transpired from leaf surfaces. Some transpiration is an unavoidable cost of the protection and other values vegetation provides. However, there is much difference in the amounts of water transpired by different types of vegetation. Replacement of one type by another could be one way to increase water yields from a watershed without loss of benefits provided by well-covered hillsides. Where the natural vegetation, like chaparral, is highly inflammable, the danger of fire and resulting erosion loss could be minimized if it could be replaced by a less inflammable type. The danger in such management, however, comes when one set of values such as high water yield is placed above all others such as timber, forage, wildlife, and recreation values, which may contribute to an enrichment of the lives of people in the area concerned.

To meet urban-industrial water requirements in semiarid and arid lands today, a variety of approaches may be required. Manipulation of vegetation on the watersheds is one that has already been discussed. To be available at need, however, water must be stored in some way, and surface reservoirs have been the usual approach to this problem. Such reservoirs suffer from siltation, which cuts down their useful life and storage capacity, from pollution, and from serious problems of evaporation. Some success in retarding siltation and pollution has been achieved, although in very few places, as a result of careful management and regulation of use in the watersheds. Evaporation losses have been reduced by the use of films of heavy alcohols such as hexadecanol, which are floated on the surface of the reservoir. For small ponds, these films can be quite effective, but for large reservoirs, subject to mixing and churning by wind, they are relatively ineffective. Attempts have also been made to increase water yields and to cut down on siltation by sealing off the soil on small watersheds by the use of asphalt, plastic sheets, silicone resins, or even rubber sheets. As yet, these efforts have been confined to small areas, but they do produce remarkable results. The only problem is that virtually all other values in the lands of the watershed are sacrificed to the single purpose of water production. This seldom can be justified.

An approach to urban water storage that has high merit is the one that makes use of underground reservoirs. Water is allowed to soak or is pumped into natural aquifers beneath the ground and is held in these permeable layers of rock or of alluvial materials. Most natural underground supplies, in areas of high water demand, have been depleted. Indeed, excessive pumping of underground water has in some areas caused a sinking of the land surface and in coastal regions has often led to an invasion of the aquifers by salt water from the sea. Recharging aquifers by pumping in fresh water, during times of high rainfall and runoff, or by holding runoff where it can soak into the aquifers through permeable soil, not only restores the underground supplies but is a way of keeping water where it will not be subject to siltation or evaporation and where, with care, it can be kept free from pollution.

WASTE DISPOSAL   The disposal of sewage and other wastes produced by human activities is a problem that has confronted the human race since populations first concentrated in towns and cities. Satisfactory solutions were seldom attained. Conditions in ancient Rome have been described by Lewis Mumford (1961). Despite the engineering skills of the Romans and their inclination toward plumbing, most people lived under highly unsanitary conditions, and some of their refuse dumps were still highly obnoxious when excavated more than 1000 years later. Nevertheless, neither Rome nor any other ancient city had much effect on the total environment. The quantity of water, air, and land available to dilute and break down waste products was sufficient to rule out any more than local pollution problems.

Sir Arthur Bryant (1968) has described the conditions of pollution in London during the seventeenth to nineteenth centuries. The small streets and byways and the streams that drained through the city were often stinking and foul. Yet the Thames flow was sufficient to dilute the wastes, and it was not until the twentieth century that it became too polluted for salmon or for swimming. (Its quality has since been restored.) However, it was also not much more than a century ago that sanitary sewers began to be used extensively to carry urban wastes into watercourses. Many cities had sewers before them, but these were storm drains intended to prevent flooding rather than for the disposal of wastes. It was not until 1855 that the first comprehensive sanitary sewer system was constructed in the United States, in Chicago.

Motivation toward the construction of sanitary sewers was provided to a large degree by the prevalence of disease. Diarrhea and dysentery, typhoid fever, and cholera, all transmitted by human wastes, were notorious killers up until relatively recent times and remain so in areas where sanitation is inadequate. The water dispersal of wastes, and more particularly the purification of urban water supplies have done much to remove these diseases as serious causes of death in industrialized countries.

The initial gains obtained by water disposal of wastes continued only so long as the supply of water was relatively large in relation to the numbers of peoples and industries—that is so long as dilution was great and the water was sufficiently well-oxygenated to enable biological decomposition of wastes to proceed normally. However, certain disadvantages appeared initially: organic matter carried down the stream was lost to the land, and in many areas soil fertility and structure had been maintained through the return of these manures to the soil. As time passed and populations grew, the load of waste materials in the streams and other water bodies began to exceed the capacity of water to disperse dilute or provide the means for breaking down these materials. New health problems developed from polluted waters. The recreational value of these waters disappeared—they were ugly, odoriferous, and unpleasant to be near. Furthermore, the excess of nutrients provided to these waters created a condition known as *accelerated eutrophication*—meaning an excessive enrichment by such nutrients as nitrates and phosphates. This disrupted biological balances, causing undesirable "blooms" of algae that on dying placed an excessive demand on the oxygen supply of the water. Oxygen deficient or anaerobic conditions developed in which only anaerobic forms of life could exist.

To meet these difficulties, cities installed sewage-disposal plants. In them the solid organic matter is separated from the liquid through various washing, skimming, and settling processes. These solids, when processed, disinfected, and dried have potential value as fertilizer. Unfortunately, the great reliance of agriculture on inorganic chemical fertilizer, because of its relatively low cost and the ease with which is applied, has limited the demand for treated organic solids from sewage. Furthermore, the liquid effluent, still highly charged with nutrient materials, must be disposed of. In a few instances, cities have used this effluent for industrial processes. In the city of Baltimore, for example, sewage effluent water has been piped to the steel mills of the Bethlehem Steel Company. There it has been used in large quantities in the manufacturing and processing of steel. By this method the normally high water demand of the steel mills has been reduced and a pollution problem alleviated. In general, this sensible approach has not been followed because of the relatively high initial cost for piping and pumping the wastes.

Disposal of wastes from canning and food-processing industries presents difficulties similar to the ones of sewage disposal in that high concentrations of organic matter are carried in the waste waters. Lumber mills and other industries also have waterborne wastes that are highly charged with organic materials and that can cause serious stream pollution. One means of disposing of these wastes is to spray them on lands covered with natural vegetation. Such land disposal, however, is seldom feasible in large urban-industrial areas. Ways for concentrating and removing wastes and of finding uses for them (*recycling*) must be found.

Mills, mines, chemical industries, tanneries, and other industrial concerns often have waste waters containing highly toxic or objectionable chemicals that can render large streams unfit for any further use. Some pulp mills, which may have highly toxic wastes, have devised recirculating systems whereby the waste water is processed, the chemicals reclaimed for further use, and the water rendered pure enough for reuse. These systems, although expensive to install, cut down on the freshwater requirements of the mill and make it possible to operate where water supplies are limited. Similar processes are needed for all polluting industries. Yet they are slow to take effect. The extent of the danger that can result from the failure to act is exemplified in the mercury story.

In 1953, people in the vicinity of the city of Minamata in Japan fell ill from a mysterious disease. Before it could be identified, 105 had either died or were seriously incapacitated, their nervous systems badly damaged. Mercury poisoning had long been known but had not been expected here. Nevertheless, the cause of the trouble was mercury that was dumped into the water by a large chemical factory, passing then through food chains and becoming concentrated in the bodies of fish on which many of the local people relied for their protein. In the mid-1960s, mercury poisoning was identified in Sweden and dangerous concentrations of mercury were found in freshwater fish. The source here proved to be primarily pulp mills, which had been treating their logs with a mercuric compound to prevent fungal growth and damage to the wood. This came through in the pulp-mill effluent and became involved in the concentrating mechanisms of aquatic food chains. The Swedes took drastic action, closing down fisheries and forcing the pulp mills to seek new means for protecting their logs. But few other countries took notice.

In the late 1960s and the 1970s mercury was found to be widespread in North American waters. Pulp-mill chemicals, agricultural seed dressings, and a variety of other mercury sources were identified, and vigorous action was taken to close down on obvius polluters. But in 1971 the world was shocked by the discovery of high levels of contamination in tuna and swordfish products. Tuna and swordfish feed across the open oceans on other fish, which feed on the floating oceanic plankton. For these fish to be contaminated meant that mercury, like DDT, had become a global pollutant, but we are still arguing about how dangerous it may be.

Thus, it has become obvious that all efforts at water pollution control have been inadequate. In the 1970s people were disturbed to hear that a Great Lake, Lake Erie, was "dying from excessive eutrophication. Yet it was to be expected. Lake Erie absorbs the wastes from the factories of Detroit, Toledo, Cleveland, Erie, Buffalo, and other cities, and the sewage from an even greater range of towns. Much of this has received little or no treatment. In addition, the runoff, laden with pesticides and excess fertilizer from a great area of Midwestern farmland, spills into the lake.

Lake Erie lost its normal complement of aquatic life, supported great algal blooms, and had a growing percentage of oxygen-deficient water inhabited only by anaerobic organisms. Niagara Falls, over which Lake Erie drains, had become the nation's most spectacular sewer outfall. Yet Lake Erie was only one of many problems. (The reports of its "death" were exaggerated and its quality is slowly being restored.)

Lake Tahoe, high in the Sierra Nevada, faced a sewage problem brought about by a combination of unrestricted growth and an initial complete lack of attention to sewage treatment. Lake Geneva, once a clear, blue lake in the Swiss mountains, was clear and blue no longer, but polluted from sewage. Even remote Lake Baikal in Siberia, unique for its distinctive aquatic fauna, was threatened by the effluent from new Soviet pulp mills. It was obvious, world over, that despite the brave words of earlier years, most factories, socialist or capitalist, had not installed recirculating or waste-reclaiming systems; most communities had not provided adequate sewage-treatment systems, and siltation, from accelerated erosion, was still going on at a disturbingly high rate.

In the United States, congressional and administrative action was taken by the federal government, and equivalent moves were made by most states and many cities. In 1966 water pollution control was moved from the Department of Health, Education, and Welfare to the Department of the Interior, in recognition that it was a general environmental problem and not primarily one involving human health. Then, because of the belief that it was being insufficiently emphasized at the urban level, a new Environmental Protection Agency (EPA) was established in 1970 with a responsibility for the control of all forms of pollution. A bill passed in 1965, the Clean Rivers Act, required all states to develop water quality standards, subject to federal approval, in order to restore the nation's rivers and streams. In 1966 Congress appropriated $3.6 billion for the development of waste treatment facilities. Each year more and more money has been directed toward these ends. New York City alone has appropriated $2 billion toward the alleviation of pollution. In 1981 a federal "superfund" of $1.6 billion was established for use by EPA in cleaning up toxic waste dumps. In effect the average citizen must pay more for the clean water she once considered free and part of her heritage. She is paying for lack of foresight, for the cost of doing the job right many years ago would have been only a fraction of the cost of changing a system built to provide short-term benefits at the expense of long-term costs.

On the international level all industrialized countries have been forced to face the same problems as the United States. This has led to many new conferences and programs. Unfortunately, many developing countries in Asia, Africa, and Latin America, feeling less involved in pollution problems, have shown a willingness to accept pollution as part of the price of development and have welcomed those industries fleeing from the increasing environmental controls of the technologically advanced countries. Such an attitude shifts the location of the problem but guarantees it will continue to grow more severe on a global scale.

WATERPOWER   Waterpower has been discussed previously but needs further comment here. The need for waterpower, in addition to the needs for municipal water supplies, irrigation waters, and flood control, has spurred on the building of dams. Furthermore, the sale of electric power from federally constructed water projects to private power companies or to municipalities has helped to pay, in part, the costs of dam construction.

The sale of waterpower has provided an economic justification for the construction of projects that might otherwise appear less feasible. In 1966, for example, the Bureau of Reclamation proposed that two dams, Marble Canyon and Bridge Canyon, be constructed in the Grand Canyon. These not only would have detracted from the wild quality of one of the nation's most important scenic resources but would have backed water into the area of Grand Canyon protected by the National Park Service. The sole justification for these dams was the production and sale of hydroelectric power for income to be balanced against the cost of other facilities, designed to bring irrigation water to central Arizona. Fortunately, an outcry from conservation organizations caused the Department of the Interior in 1967 to withdraw its plans for these dams.

Perhaps one of the greatest "boondoggles" proposed under the justification of hydropower production has been the Rampart Dam on the Yukon River in Alaska (Stegner, 1965). This immense structure, to be built at a cost of over a billion dollars in the Yukon wilderness, would have flooded 8 million acres of land and have done almost incalculable damage to fish and wildlife resources. It would have generated an excess of power beyond any foreseeable needs within Alaska. Fortunately, a study sponsored by the National Resources Council and conducted under the leadership of Stephen Spurr of the University of Michigan revealed the high costs and doubtful benefits of this project before plans for it had become too far advanced. It was shown that Alaska's power needs could be met by smaller dams closer to its centers of population (Spurr, 1966).

On a worldwide basis, the future development of hydroelectric power sources can only partially satisfy anticipated power needs, because many areas lack the combination of elevated lands and fast-flowing rivers needed for hydroelectric development. Yet for many countries and areas, which have not yet developed their waterpower potential, such development can bring gains in living standards. Unfortunately, what appears to be in part the "prestige" value of tall hydroelectric dams and the availability of great quantities of electric power had led some countries to make a disproportionate effort toward their construction. Egypt's High Aswan Dam has as its primary justification irrigation, but power yield is also important. Serious environmental problems have resulted from its construction, including erosion of agricultural lands in the Nile Delta, decline of eastern Mediterranean fisheries, and an increase in waterborne disease. In Zimbabwe, Kariba Dam brought environmental problems both before and after its construction—the displacement of native peoples, the need for an internationally supported rescue effort to save the wildlife, the rapid spread of water weeds, the consequent failure of the fisheries to develop in the manner expected, and others. Ghana's Volta Dam, completed in 1964, provides power for the development of the aluminum industry, but has brought accompanying environmental problems of considerable consequence, including the displacement of peoples and the spread of the disease "river blindness" to an increasing number of people (Lawson, 1970). The Ivory Coast's $100-million dam, the Kossou, on the Bandama River, has displaced a hundred thousand people and undoubtedly, will bring a spread of waterborne diseases, for dubious gains in power and irrigation. One is inclined to question, whenever a major dam and reservoir is proposed, whether or not the same ends could not be reached in some way less destructive to the environment.

IRRIGATION

Throughout the drier parts of the world there is a great demand for water to be used in irrigation of farming lands. To provide such water, highly expensive dams and water-diversion projects have been built and are being built in many places. In general, areas with less than 20 inches of rainfall annually can be farmed only at a risk of crop failure unless irrigation water is available. There are complicating factors, such as temperature and evaporation rates and the regularity and dependability of the rainfall, which make farming successful in some areas with less than 20 inches of rain, but these are exceptions. The soils in the drier lands, because of the low rainfall, are relatively unleached and therefore rich in surface materials. Where water can be made available in quantities sufficient for washing out excessive accumulations of salts, even the soils in dry, desert lands can become highly productive.

One of the most successful irrigation projects in the United States is the Imperial Valley of southern California. Here some 500,000 acres were brought into cultivation through the private and doubtfully legal construction of the all-American canal from the Colorado River, which provided the necessary water. Because of the warm climate, crops can be grown in seasons when they are unavailable elsewhere in cooler areas, and subtropical crops such as dates and citrus fruits can be produced in quantity. Other areas throughout the southwestern United States have also been brought into production. Their value is high, yet their benefits and costs need careful study.

Successful irrigation of dry land requires the continual exercise of skill and vigilance. The irrigation system of Egypt in preindustrial times was, for the most part, successful because it was based on a relatively simple plan, involved the use of an excess of water, and took advantage of the natural drainage system established when the Nile River subsided within its banks at the end of the flood season. The irrigation system in

About 64 million acre-feet of water a year—over two-thirds of groundwater withdrawals—are used to irrigate 32 million acres of crops in the United States. Groundwater levels are declining beneath at least 15 million of those acres, one-third of our irrigated cropland. As water levels fall and energy costs rise, farmers will not be able to afford to pump the water. USDA projects that irrigation will become impractical on over six million acres of cropland in the next 30 years. Indeed, many farmers in the High Plains of Texas have already turned off pumps that once drew water from the rapidly depleting Ogallala aquifer.

Maryla Webb and Judith Jacobsen, *U.S. Carrying Capacity* (1982), p. 25–26.

Mesopotamia failed because it was a complex system requiring a high degree of human control and likely to go wrong when human society became disorganized. Furthermore, the distribution of relatively limited amounts of water through canals exposed it to an illness that has plagued all irrigation efforts—the salinization of the soil. This occurs when water tables are raised or when water moves upward through the soil by capillary action in response to evaporation from the soil's surface. As water evaporates, it is converted into vapor and leaves behind on the surface the salts dissolved within it.

When water is abundant and the conditions of drainage are favorable, the excess of salts is leached from the soil and carried away by subsurface drainage. When water is scarce or drainage is impaired, the movement of salts is upward; they accumulate on the soil surface, and eventually form surface layers in such quantities that the soil becomes unsuited for anything except salt-tolerant plants.

Roger Revelle (1966) has described the problems that developed in West Pakistan. Here the British performed a major task of land transformation in the valley of the Indus River. What was once desert was changed into highly productive irrigated land through the construction of a series of barrages (low dams) that diverted Indus water into an intricate system of irrigation canals. About 23 million irrigated acres were brought into production and, in the early part of this century, Pakistan produced a surplus of food. Soon, however, trouble developed. No shortage of water was involved but, instead, the reverse. Because of inadequate drainage, the water table was raised to a point where some areas were virtually drowned out. With the high water table and rapid surface evaporation, salts were deposited on the surface and made the soil unsuitable for crops. By the 1960s Pakistan's population had grown and its lands were going out of production. In place of food surpluses, there were major food scarcities. The problems are not irremediable, but the cure is expensive. The irrigation canals must be sealed so they do not leak water and raise water tables in the areas through which they pass. Drainage

a

b

c

WATER USES AND PROBLEMS

(a) Mechanized, highly fertilized farming systems require a much greater input of water throughout the growing season. Here corn crops are irrigated by a sprinkler system. (b) Moving Colorado River water westward to irrigate the Imperial Valley resulted in the refilling of the Salton Sea. Here the Alamo River, a drainage ditch from the Imperial Valley, empties into the Salton Sea. (c) Efforts to bring more fresh water to dry areas has led to the building of desalinization plants such as this test facility near San Diego. (d) Efforts to prevent excess water from flooding farmlands, such as this one in Pennsylvania, or cities has led to the building of expensive dams and other flood-control structures.

d

canals must be established to move off the excess water. An abundance of water must be provided to leach out the excess salts, which can then be carried off in the drainage canals.

This same type of problem is common to all irrigated areas. In some places, where excess water and drainage could not be provided, it has forced land abandonment. Even where drainage is handled well and salinization is under control, the problem remains of where to put the drainage water. At this stage in human history, agricultural drainage water is far from being an innocuous substance. Generally, it is loaded with excess pesticides, herbicides, and other agricultural chemicals in addition to the great quantities of minerals leached from the fields. Dumped into a river, it can make the water unsuited for further irrigation downstream. Dumped into a bay, a lake, or an estuary, it can cause the difficulties associated with eutrophication plus those caused by the accumulation of toxic chemicals in food chains. In the 1980s California's San Joaquin Valley was suffering from salinization, leading to demands for construction of a "big ditch" to drain irrigation water northward to be dumped in its highly polluted state into coastal waters.

It is increasingly obvious that the difficulties associated with irrigation should give pause to individuals who view it as an easy way out of the world's food dilemma. Unfortunately, the demand for higher and higher production to match ever-growing human numbers favors a willingness to ignore the risks.

EXCESS WATER

The spread of people over the face of the earth has been accompanied since early times by attempts to settle in areas where an excess of water was a problem. Low-lying seacoast lands, marshlands, and alluvial plains have attracted them as potential agricultural or urban sites. In each such area they have sought ways to dispose of the surplus water. One of the most heroic efforts in this direction has been the reclamation of land from the sea in the lowlands of the Netherlands and Belgium. Here an elaborate system of dikes, drains, and pumps has been put to work to reclaim over a million acres of land for urban and agricultural use from the Zuider Zee.

In the United States reclamation of marshlands has long seemed a good way to bring new areas into agricultural use. Drainage of marshes has in some instances succeeded in providing first-class farming land. In other instances unfavorable consequences of marsh drainage have become obvious. Marshes, through providing areas of storage and later slow release of excess water, can be of great value in regulating stream flow and preventing floods, in increasing the quantity of groundwater and keeping water tables high, and in providing a habitat for vast numbers of waterfowl and other wildlife. Drainage not only has brought wildlife destruction but also has contributed to increased floods and lowered water tables. In many cases the damage has overbalanced the gains.

One of the worst examples of a conflict between drainage projects and other environmental values has been in southern Florida. Here irreplaceable natural areas are being sacrificed to bring additional land into housing or agriculture by drainage and the impoundment of water. The same process may be observed over much of the eastern seaboard.

Unfortunately, coastal marshes and swamps are frequently regarded as wasteland to be drained or filled in for "useful" purposes. Yet, repeatedly, studies have shown them to be some of the most highly productive ecosystems on earth. Not only do they support great quantities of waterfowl and have high recreational value, they have a key role to play in aquatic food chains, providing nutrients on which coastal and oceanic fisheries may depend and often providing shelter for young or larval stages of species that later move out and contribute to the richness of ocean fisheries. The pink shrimp fishery of the Gulf of Mexico is an example. This multimillion-dollar fishery is dependent on the "nursery" function of the mangrove swamps of the Everglades, estuarine regions where the developing shrimp spend a critical part of their life cycle before moving as adults into open marine waters.

Where people have settled in the floodplains of rivers, they have run the risk of being drowned out. In ancient Egypt they learned to live with the Nile floodwaters, allowing them to rise each year, deposit their thin layer of silt, and retreat once more to the river channel. In America we have seldom adopted this reasonable way of living with nature but have, instead, sought to control and confine the rivers. Such control has brought gains in increased crop yields, has permitted the building of cities and residences on the flood plains and in general, has permitted more intensive land utilization, but at a cost (Leopold and Maddock, 1954).

Along the lower Mississippi and other major river systems, one method of controlling floods has been to build levees that keep the river in a restricted channel. The normal tendency of the river is to rise over its banks in flood time and often to deposit silt on the flooded areas. Confined by levees, the silt load may still be deposited but within the river channel. Each year the river may build its bed higher, and the next year's flood is consequently raised. To meet this threat, levees have been built higher until finally in some areas the river, confined by levees, flows well above the rooftops of cities and towns along its bank. Sooner or later comes the big flood the levees cannot hold, and the results are disastrous. In a spectacular flood in 1852 the Yellow River in China broke through such elevated levees, took millions of lives, and found a new channel to the sea. Along the Mississippi Valley similar catastrophes, but with less loss of life, have happened in much more recent times. In the great California floods of 1955 the Feather River poured through a levee break to do millions of dollars in damage and take many lives in Yuba City. In 1965 hurricanes and high water combined to send water over the Mississippi River levees in New Orleans and do millions of dollars worth of damage. To prevent this type of damage, spillways and bypasses are built along with a levee system to allow excess floodwaters to pour through channels across bottom lands, which can otherwise be used at nonflood times for agricultural purposes. However, even with these devices, levees break, and flood damage still takes place. Many examples have been apparent during the wet winters of 1981–1983, during which flooding has become too frequent to be fully covered by the news media.

To give further flood control the tendency in the United States has been to emphasize large multiple-purpose dams. These dams, when built in a suitable location, can reduce floods as well as provide water for power, irrigation, and other uses. There are few conservation questions, however, about which more controversy has raged than the question of the value of these multiple-purpose dams. The most elaborate series of dams in the country thus far has been built along the Tennessee River, under the jurisdiction of the Tennessee Valley Authority. These have converted much of the river into a chain of freshwater lakes. The TVA has provided flood control, irrigation water, electric power, navigation, and water for domestic and industrial use through the dams built as part of a project to restore the badly eroded lands and to reorganize the damaged economy of the Tennessee River watersheds. The TVA has served as a model for many other nations and yet has been the target of more criticism than most other government agencies have received, in part because it was considered to represent a major federal intrusion into an area that had been previously the domain of private enterprise, but more recently because it has been a cause of destructive strip minning, air pollution, and an advocate of nuclear power.

Along the Missouri, the Columbia, and the Colorado, series of dams and reservoirs have grown to provide flood control, power, irrigation, or these and other functions in combination. Virtually every river in California has been dammed or will be under the state water plan. As a nation we seemed committed, perhaps somewhat unwittingly, to the principle that dams are worthwhile and, since they channel federal funds and employment into local areas, it is seldom politically desirable for local congressmen to oppose them.

Objections to the big dams on our river systems are many, and some of them have been discussed previously. Dams are expensive. They flood lands at the reservoir site; they lose water through evaporation from the reservoirs; they destroy fisheries. Wilderness, wildlife, and recreational values are often sacrificed to dam construction. Dams may catch water heavily laden with silt. This silt normally settles to the bottom of the reservoir, and silt-free water is released at the outlet. Such silt-free water often has unanticipated damaging effects of the stream channel below the dam, scouring and eroding the river banks and picking up a new silt load, which is then deposited in some previously slit-free area. In addition, siltation of the reservoir may threaten the life of the structure and, in some instances, may result in the creation of a new alluvial plain at the former reservoir site. Water storage in reservoirs, with the consequent decrease in stream flow, can cause invasion of salt water in delta areas, creating new problems for agriculture in these regions.

It must be realized also that large dams do not prevent downstream floods. Each dam is built with a certain reservoir capacity and with the realization that, under certain known flood conditions, flood waters will be in excess of what the reservoir can hold. Complete flood prevention, if it could be accomplished, would be so costly that it is not even contemplated for any major drainage area. At best, dams are planned to hold back flood waters up to a certain rate of flow and to minimize damage from floods that exceed that rate. Yet because they control most floods, dams encourage development on floodplains thus partially protected. In consequence, when floods do occur the damage far exceeds what might have been expected had no dam been present (Kates, 1964).

Opponents of large dams indicate that the same objectives can be accomplished at less expense by "stopping floods where they start," at the headwaters of streams. There is something to be said for this point of view. Under natural conditions of forest and grassland vegetation, soils in the watersheds of streams were protected by a spongelike layer of litter and humus, and the structure of these soils favored water penetration and retention rather than runoff. Destructive use of headwater lands has increased the amount of runoff and in many areas has increased the frequency and severity of floods. Attention to proper conservation use of headwater lands would cut down on flood danger. Thus, along the Wasatch Front in Utah, heavy summer rains in 1923 and 1930 caused severe flooding in many areas. In two adjacent canyons, however, the flood picture was quite different. Both watersheds received equally heavy rain, yet the watershed of Parrish Canyon produced severe floods, whereas the adjacent Centerville Canyon produced little or no flooding. Investigation showed the Parrish Canyon watershed was heavily overgrazed, whereas the Centerville Canyon watershed was protected from excessive grazing. With this realization, the Parrish Canyon watershed was brought under protection from heavy grazing and fires, and the vegetation was restored. This has prevented further flood damage. A dam in Parrish Canyon would not have helped. With the excessive erosion taking place it would soon have filled with silt, and the flood damage would have gone on. In this area the answer to floods was protection of the watershed (Colman, 1953).

In southern California in 1933 a chaparral fire burned seven square miles of land in the San Gabriel Mountains. In the following winter a severe rainstorm occurred, and it was followed by a flood that caused an estimated $5 million worth of damage. The flood issued from the burned-over watershed and had a peak flow estimated at 1000 second-feet per square mile. Nearby unburned watersheds that received the same amount of rainfall had peak flows measured between 20 and 60 second-feet per square mile and experienced little damage. In this area, vegetation protection rather than dams is the way to prevent such floods.

To demonstrate the effectiveness of watershed management as a means toward flood control, the Soil Conservation Service has undertaken a series of watershed projects aimed at stopping floods high in the drainage basins, preventing erosion and siltation, and also providing a better quality of land use. To date, these efforts have met with considerable success in some directions. Lands have been improved and made more productive and stable. Erosion has been cut down, and with this the silt load of streams has been decreased in some areas. Small local floods have been eliminated, and larger floods reduced to some extent. Flood damage to lands located in the upper watershed has been greatly reduced. However, land management practices alone have not accomplished all of these objectives. Flood control is still provided in part by dams but, in these projects, by many small dams on tributary streams. In the aggregate these small dams are expensive and can be subjected to many of the criticisms also directed against the large downstream dams. Furthermore, against certain types of floods they are ineffective. For example, in December 1955, heavy general rains fell for many days over much of northern and central California. Nearly every stream and tributary reached flood stage, and the major rivers poured into many cities and towns and inundated vast areas of agricultural land. In all, the damage was measurable only in hundreds of millions of dollars. Watershed treatment and small upstream dams would not have controlled these floods, although they would have alleviated much flood damage. The severity of the floods was reduced by the presence of the giant multiple-purpose dams at Folsom and Shasta. Such heavy rains as this can saturate the best-managed soils and can exceed the water-holding capacity of the best-treated drainage basin. Similar rains caused great damage along the central California coast in 1981–1982 and again in 1982–1983.

It must be realized that long before civilization appeared on the scene there were floods and that regardless of how much land-use practices are improved and whether we build small dams or large, floods will still occur. There is no single panacea to flood problems. In some places large dams alleviate flood damage; in others they are ineffective, and watershed management offers most promise. Lands must be preserved, and erosion must be prevented for reasons other than flood control. As long as we continue to build high-value structures, subject to damage by flooding, in areas where floodwaters naturally accumulate, we will continue to experience damage from floods. To control this damage we seem committed to spend somewhat fantastic sums of money for dams and levees, upstream and down, but we cannot economically eliminate this damage so long as cities and industries remain on the floodplain. Under these circumstances, it seems reasonable to consider an alternative. Areas subjected to frequent flooding can be zoned to prevent their use for purposes that might involve excessive loss of property or life when floods occur. Such zoning can prevent the construction of additional structures in these areas. Outright purchase and removal of existing structures by government agencies would be less expensive, in some cases, than the efforts now directed toward flood control. Such lands could then be devoted to other uses less likely to be adversely affected by floods. Such floodplain zoning has been tried in a few areas, and its use is being forced by circumstances in areas subject to frequent flooding. The possibility has been suggested also that, in place of spending money for flood control, governments should offer flood insurance to those using areas subject to flood damage. The cost of the insurance to the floodplain user could be adjusted to the type of use and the likelihood damage will be experienced. Such insurance costs could effectively prevent certain types of use for land subject to frequent flooding, although the willingness of people to gamble on the chance of not being flooded appears to be very strong. Far too often it is the people who cannot afford to live elsewhere who are hurt most by flooding.

NAVIGATION

Another major use of water is for transportation—the movement of goods and people. During the early history of civilization, water transportation was generally cheaper, more efficient, and faster than land-borne transport. The balance shifted with the coming of the railways and shifted even further with the development of rapid highway and air travel. Nevertheless, the importance of water for transportation remains, particularly with materials that are bulky and are required in quantity, but for which speed of transport is not vital. Furthermore, navigation on water provides a satisfying form of recreation of growing importance. The use of water bodies for navigation is entirely nonconsumptive and should not necessarily involve any impairment of their quality, but the maintenance of navigation channels frequently involves dredging or other modification of waterways, and this can have an impact on aquatic life and its productivity. The disruptive effect of waterborne transportation on natural or wild areas is often considerable. Increasingly, also the presence of waterborne transportation adds to water pollution.

RECREATION

Water-based recreation is now big business in America. In many places new towns and communities are planned around artificially created bodies of water in the expectation that they will make the site more attractive to the prospective home buyer. Waterfront property has become a scarce and expensive commodity. The costs of new dams and reservoirs are partially justified on the basis of the recreation use they will attract. In a survey of America's outdoor recreation preferences, the water-based sports of swimming, fishing, boating, ice skating, water skiing, canoeing, and sailing ranked in the top 20 pursuits. There is no doubt that the demand for access to recreation water is high and growing.

The need for natural bodies of water, untouched by development of any kind, is also great. Natural streams, lakes, and seashores that can be maintained in a near-primeval condition, now scarce in America, have a value not only to those seeking a high quality of outdoor recreation but also for the study of hydrology, ecology, and other environmental sciences. These areas form needed reference points for comparison with those areas man has changed.

There is a tendency in water development projects to underestimate the value of an untouched stream or other body of water and to overemphasize the benefits in irrigation, urban water, power, or other quantifiable benefits to justify the construction of engineering facilities. Unless this practice can be reversed, America stands to lose much that is priceless and irreplaceable in outdoor resources.

RECAPITULATION

In dry years, in the name of water conservation people are urged to save water—to bathe less often, flush their toilets less often, not wash their cars, turn off the taps, and so on. The impression is given that these little savings taken collectively will somehow save the day. Yet all of the use of water for urban and industrial purposes represents only about 17 percent of the water withdrawn from water resources and consumed. The other 83 percent is used by agriculture and this mostly for irrigation. If water savings are to be made it is in the agricultural sector we must make them. This does not mean that city folk can afford to be wasteful. Often their water supply comes from limited sources, and these do run dry if withdrawals are too great. But it does mean that most of the costly water supply installations are primarily for the benefit of agricultural users.

Savings in water can be made by changing methods of irrigation from sprinklers, or ditches, to drip systems using underground pipes that deliver water to plant roots as needed. Savings can be made, in dry areas, by shifting from water-demanding crops—rice for example—to crops with lower water needs, and by shifting from crops that require freshwater to those that can tolerate some degree of salinity. Savings can be made by ceasing to devote large areas of dry farmland to irrigated production of pasture or fodder crops intended primarily for livestock feed.

The conflict for water will grow worse, and particularly so if we decide to develop coal and oil shale resources in the arid Western United States. Such development could increase water demand for energy production from fourfold to 30-fold over present levels of water use (Pimentel et al., 1982). As noted in Chapter 7, such desperate striving for more fossil fuel energy is hardly justified.

Nevertheless, water problems look different when viewed from the top down, nationally or internationally, than when examined from the bottom up, locally. For example, if we accept the figure of 60 gallons a day as representing home use of water per capita (and this certainly exceeds actual needs), and multiply this by one million, we have a problem for government to find 60 million gallons of water per day for a city of a million. On the other hand, in an area with an annual rainfall of 36 inches, a collecting surface of 100 square feet could gather 2400 gallons of water in a year, and a house with a 2000 square foot roof area could harvest 48,000 gallons in a year, enough to supply 130 gallons of water a day.

The practice of collecting rainwater from rooftops and running it into household storage tanks was once common, and still is in some areas. Reliance on massive water developments and regional supply systems, however, has caused people to give up such do-it-yourself practices and has changed a non-problem into a national problem.

Similarly, the problem of disposing of sewage and household wastes can be either a national dilemma, or the same waste can become a local asset. Composting toilets use little water and produce as end products useful fertilizer. A further step is the biogas or methane-generating unit described earlier. China has probably done more than most nations toward eliminating the whole concept of "waste," through making maximum use of all materials at the local level.

One cannot pretend that all problems of water management and conservation can be met by paying greater attention to local efforts to solve local problems. New York's water problems will not be solved by putting in roof collectors. It is certain, however, that many water conservation problems would be alleviated and some would disappear if individuals would once again assume greater responsibility for their own welfare, and if small communities would work together to find local solutions to their difficulties. We have gone much too far toward mass organizations, government or private, assuming responsibilities for supplying all things to all people.

Shifting now to the more global viewpoint of water conservation, we must see to it that water-conservation plans are fitted into an overall pattern of environmental conservation and not treated in isolation. They must always include attention to proper land conservation in watershed areas. Better soil conservation on farming lands will lead to better use of soil water, better storage of soil water, increased filtration to subsurface water supplies, and a lessened demand for irrigation water. Through soil conservation, erosion can be slowed to a tolerable rate, and problems of downstream siltation reduced. Better land use in forest and range areas brings increased water filtration, stabilized runoff, and improved year-round water yields. Each region must take responsibility for its own watersheds, streams, and rivers. Individuals, communities, municipalities, and industries must be held responsible for reducing water pollution to tolerable levels.

All needs for flood control, irrigation, electric power, and municipal water cannot be met by sound land management and local initiative—at least not the way societies are organized today. State and federal governments necessarily become involved in the broader issues. Yet the expenditure of great sums of money for somewhat doubtful gains in flood control, irrigation, or hydropower cannot continue. Each day decisions made on the use of water involve the sacrifice of one value for the enhancement of another. Too often the values sacrificed are those that make life worth living for many people, and the values enhanced are those that increase profit for the few.

SOURCES

Borgstrom, Georg, 1965. *The hungry planet.* Macmillan, New York.
————1971. Ecological aspects of protein feeding—the case of Peru. *The careless technology,* John Milton and Taghi Farvar, editors. Natural History Press, New York.
Brown, Lester R. and E. P. Eckholm, 1974. *By bread alone.* Praeger, New York.
Bryant, Sir Arthur, 1968. *Set in a silver sea.* Doubleday, New York.
Colman, E. A., 1953. *Vegetation and watershed management.* Ronald Press, New York.
Croker, Richard, 1954. The sardine story—a tragedy. *Outdoor California* 15:6–8.
Dolder, Edward F., 1954. Water—California's lifeblood. *Conservation—concern for tomorrow.* California State Educational Bulletin, pp. 45–63.
Eaton, F. M., 1949. Irrigation agriculture along the Nile and the Euphrates. *Scientific Monthly* 48:33–42.
Eisenbud, Merrill, 1970. Environmental protection in the city of New York. *Science* 170:706–712.
Griffin, James B. and Henry B. Steele, 1980. *Energy economics and policy.* Academic Press, New York.
Gulland, J. A., 1970. *The fish resources of the ocean.* FAO, Rome.
Hedgpeth, Joel, 1978. Man on the seashore. *Wildlife and America,* H. Brokaw editor. Council on Environmental Quality, Washington, D.C.
Holdgate, M. W., editor, 1970. *Antarctic ecology.* Academic Press, London.
Kahrl, William L., editor, 1979. *The California water atlas.* Governor's Office of Planning and Research, Sacramento.
Kalanin, G. P. and V. D. Bykov, 1969. The world's water resources, present and future. *Impact of science on society.* UNESCO, Paris, 19:135–150.
Kates, Robert W., 1964. *Hazard and choice perception in flood plain management.* Department of Geography, University of Chicago.
Klingbiel, J., 1953. Are fishing restrictions necessary? *Wisconsin Conservation Bulletin* 18:3–5.
Landsberg, H. H., 1964. *Natural resources for U. S. growth.* Johns Hopkins, Baltimore.
Lawson, G. W., 1970. Lessons of the Volta—a new man-made lake. *Biological Conservation* 2:90–96.
Leopold, Luna and T. Maddock, 1954. *The flood control controversy.* Ronald Press, New York.
Loftas, Tony, 1972. Where have all the anchoveta gone? *New Scientist* 28:583–586.
Mumford, Lewis, 1961. *The city in history.* Harcourt, Brace, World, New York.
Nadeau, Remi, 1950. *The water seekers.* Doubleday, New York.

Pimentel, David, et al., 1983. Water resources in food and energy production. *Bioscience* 32:861–867.

Revelle, Roger, 1966. Salt, water and civilization. *Food and civilization.* U.S. Information Agency, Washington, D.C., pp. 83–104.

Schaefer, Milner, 1965. The potential harvest of the sea. *Transactions of the American Fisheries Society* 94:123–128.

Spurr, Stephen H., 1966. *Rampart Dam and the economic development of Alaska.* University of Michigan Press, Ann Arbor.

Stegner, Wallace, 1965. Myths of the western dam. *Saturday Review,* October:29–31.

Webb, Maryla and Judith Jacobsen, 1982. *U.S. carrying capacity—an introduction.* Carrying Capacity, Washington, D.C.

Wick, Gerald, 1974. Fishing off California. *New Scientist* 61:564–565.

CHAPTER
10

THE WILDER LANDS: FOREST AND RANGE

INTRODUCTION

Out beyond the farm fence or away from the cleared and planted patch in the jungle, the wilder areas of the land begin. Sometimes the transition is fairly obvious, as when you leave the irrigated wheat fields of the Dakotas and move into the short-grass prairies where the Herefords and black Angus cattle take the place of farm machinery. Sometimes there is a mosaic of farm and forest, cultivated land and natural pasture. It is obvious that you are not entering wilderness: evidence of human use is easy to find, but the predominant vegetation is native grasses, shrubs, and trees, growing more or less as they have always done, and wildlife is to be found—deer or antelope, coyotes and foxes, prairie dogs, and other species not welcomed on the farmed land.

This is productive land in an economic sense, contributing its products for direct human use—lumber and other forest products, livestock, wildlife for the hunter. It is also contributing in less direct ways—fresh water for the rivers, clean air, outdoor space. In western North America, much of it is under government control in the form of National Forests, Provincial and State Forests, Public Domain under Bureau of Land Management control—a small bit is even recognized as belonging to the Indians, who used to have it all. In eastern North America, most of it is under private ownership, but there are sizable blocks of public lands.

The wild species of plants and animals that occupy it are managed, to some degree. Trees are cut and planted. Fire is used deliberately to modify vegetation, or wildfire is controlled. Livestock and wildlife use is monitored to keep the better forage plants productive. Some of it is intensively managed: trees of better quality for lumber are planted, or forage grasses from other countries are seeded in. Some of it is poorly managed and shows signs of severe erosion or of invasion by those pioneer species we call weeds.

The two dominant forms of commercial use of these areas, which depend on management of the vegetation, are forestry and livestock production. These have always been to some extent in conflict with one another, and decisions must be made by public agency or private owner which shall predominate in any particular area. Cows and sheep prefer the low-growing grasses and forbs (broad-leaved herbs) that come in when forests are pushed back by fire or clearing. Wood growers want to keep as much space as possible in tree growth. Both are adversely affected when the miners come in, and in the United States at least these people are given precedence over God and nature to seek their fuels and minerals everywhere. It is impossible to entirely separate forest and rangelands since the categories overlap. Closed forests are all too readily, if temporarily, converted to pastures. Nonetheless, because of the different approaches and problems associated with these forms of land use, it is easier to consider them separately.

THE FOREST LANDS

Attitudes of people toward forests have always been somewhat ambiguous. This may be because people were not originally forest animals and were not at home in forests. It is true that there are forest peoples who have learned to adapt to the ways of the forest, but the dominant tribes who have taken over most of the earth have come from more open lands. When they occupy forest, they clear it. Their attitude has been one of invader and aggressor, mixed in the past with fear and superstition. Read the fairy tales—the "good guys" do not live in the deep woods. Part of the reason for our general failure to adapt to forest life is in the nature of forest vegetation. Forests are great storehouses of carbohydrate, in particular cellulose. But they are not great producers of accessible protein. Ground-feeding animals that depend on grazing and browsing are always scarce in comparison to their relatives that live in more open lands simply because the nutritional quality of the accessible, shade-grown vegetation is inadequate. The successful forest animals live in, on, or within the trees. In the rich tropical forests the nutrients are largely locked up in the forest vegetation and not in the soils. Protein deficiency has plagued people who live in tropical forests. They can grow starchy food, but to find protein they must be ingenious.

Compared to other vegetation, forests have a high degree of complexity and diversity. Even the northern forests where a few species of trees dominate over large areas still support a variety of other plants at the shrub or ground level, and often a diverse biota within the soil. All of these species interact, and we have yet to unravel all of their specific roles and their relative importance to the forest system. The tropical forests are the most diverse, often with hundreds of species in a square kilometer. Frank Golley (1978) found 120 species of trees alone in an Amazonian plot 5 meters wide and 50 meters long. He asks: "Are all species significant or are there redundant species in these forests? Is the mixture of species a chance phenomenon or is it due to organizational principles of the living system? Is the behavior of the forests dependent upon the richness or not?"

One of the striking characteristics of forests is the longevity of the dominant trees. Even transient successional forms, the birches and aspens that occupy the land for a time following a fire, are long-lived by human standards, whereas some of the conifers live for millennia—a European yew for more than 2000 years, redwoods for more than a 1000. The giant sequoias, at 3000 years, were growing where they are when

FORESTS ARE NOT JUST TIMBER

(a) In Zaire this forest is clearly a home for wildlife. (b) These ancient bristlecone pines in California's White Mountains are not a renewable resource. (c) Forests hold the mountains together in West Africa and create scenes that enrich the human spirit.

b

c

ancient Athens was thriving. Bristlecone pines, growing at the upper limits of tree growth in western America, have survived for more than 4000 years, whereas in the arid Hoggar Mountains of the Algerian Sahara, a Mediterranean cypress (*Cupressus dupreziana*) has lived for 4700 years (Gabriel 1969; Ovington, 1965).

Diversity and longevity bring difficulties for human management of forests. The human mind is ill at ease with problems that present too many variables, and we have traditionally preferred to simplify things down to "manageable proportions." Yet the greatest challenge to environmental management is the challenge of diversity, and this could yield the greatest rewards. Simplifying the complex usually sets in motion forces of instability, as the natural order seeks to reestablish itself. We create our own weeds and pests and problem species.

We have preferred to manage biotic resources in such a way that they produce a sustained yield—a new crop each year equivalent to the one harvested the year before. With certain types of fast-growing trees, this sustained yield principle has been successfully used, and it can apply anywhere to the production of *wood*. Yet we are deceiving ourselves if we talk of the sustained yield of *forests* that have taken centuries or millennia to develop. It would be possible to manage ancient forests on a long-term cycle so that there would always be ancient forests. But have you tried to get economists and politicians to develop a "thousand-year plan"? Perphaps they don't expect the human race to last that long. Without the long-term plan, they may be right.

THE STATUS OF FORESTS

Derreck Ovington (1965) has estimated that the existing forested area of the world represents approximately one-half of the "original" forest area. Forests have certainly vanished in the face of human onslaught with fire, axe, saw, and bulldozer. Most of Europe's forests are gone, although the remaining forest area is considerable. The Forest Service has estimated that there were 900 million acres of forest in the United States. About one-third of that has been cleared.

It is unusually difficult to compare the forest areas remaining today with those that have existed in the past. At best the earlier estimates were based on the area of "forest land," land that could be expected to support forest because of its geographical locations and climate. There was little information on the amount of forest actually occupying that land. Furthermore, the question of what should be called forest, as compared to woodland, savanna, scrub, or deforested land, was not made clear in early as compared to more recent figures.

One of the first attempts to put together a realistic world picture of the area of the world actually forested was prepared by FAO in 1948 and presented by S.B. Show in the U.S. Department of Agriculture yearbook *Trees* (1949). This indicated a total forest area of nearly 4 billion

TABLE 10.1   Area of the Forests and Woodlands of the World

FOREST TYPE	1973 AREA (MILLIONS OF HECTARES)
Tropical rain	568
Tropical seasonal	1112
Temperate coniferous and temperate deciduous	448
Boreal	672
Woodland, shrubland and savanna	1000
Total	3800

Source: CEQ (1980). Data from Persson (1974).

hectares. Later Whittaker and Likens (1975) estimated that the world forest area in 1950 was 4.85 billion hectares—not counting open woodland, savanna, or scrub. Persson (1974) and others estimated the area of "closed forest," actually occupied by forest cover, in 1973 was 2.66 billion hectares. This excluded land where tree cover was less than 20 percent of the area and lands used for purposes other than forestry. Assuming that the bases are roughly comparable, this would suggest a decline in area of closed forest of over 1.5 billion hectares—resulting presumably from forest clearing (see Table 10.1).

There is no generally agreed-upon figure for the amount of net annual deforestation over the globe. The governments of tropical countries suggested that the annual rate during the 1975–1980 period was in the neighborhood of 6 to 7 million hectares; however, these governments have an interest in concealing the truth. Although these figures were published by FAO, the Director General of FAO stated in 1978 that the rate was 10–12 million hectares a year. The United States CIA, not usually considered pro-environmentalist, estimated that the rate between 1978 and 2000 would average 18–20 million hectares per year (see Table 10.2). The upper limit was used in the Global 2000 forecasts reported here, with the following explanation:

TABLE 10.2   Estimates of World Forest Resources, 1978–2000

	AREA OF CLOSED FOREST (MILLIONS OF HECTARES)		
	1978	2000	CHANGE
North America	470	464	−6
Europe	140	150	+10
USSR	785	775	−10
Japan, Australia, New Zealand	69	68	−1
Subtotal: Industrial world	1464	1457	−7
Latin America	550	329	−221
Africa	188	150	−38
Asia and Pacific LDCs	361	181	−180
Subtotal: Developing areas	1099	660	−439
Total, world	2563	2117	−446

Source: CEQ (1980), p. 134.

"The substantially higher estimate used in this study takes into account the common disparity between the official designation of areas as forests and the actual use of the land by farmers, as well as the disparity between official intentions and actual accomplishments in the tropical nations."

If this suggests that governments lie, or are careless with the truth, or do not know what is going on in their own countries, or do not want you to know, that is because all of these inferences are correct. Anyone who puts in much time in intergovernmental meetings of the United Nations or other organizations has experienced these contradictions. It makes it difficult to really know what is going on in the world.

The estimates presented in Table 10.2 identify rather clearly where the problems lie. During the last two decades of the twentieth century the forests of the industrialized regions of the world are not expected to decrease substantially in area. The greatest decrease is expected to occur as a result of future development within the Soviet Union, the country that supports the largest area of closed forest. This is equaled, however, by an expected increase in the closed forest area of Western Europe. By contrast all of the developing or nonindustrialized areas of the world will suffer severe losses in forest, with a net loss of 439 million hectares between 1978 and 2000 A.D. The forests to be lost are the humid and subhumid tropical and subtropical forests of the world—the richest, most productive, most diverse, and least understood. Table 10.3 needs to be examined in this respect since it shows the change from the original forested area of the humid tropics up until 1976, an overall reduction of

TABLE 10.3 Decline of Humid Tropical Forests

REGION	TOTAL HUMID TROPICAL FOREST CLIMAX AREA (ORIGINAL FORESTED AREA)	ACTUAL AREA OF HUMID TROPICAL FOREST REMAINING 1976	DECREASE IN FOREST AREA	PERCENT DECREASE
	MILLIONS OF HECTARES			
East Africa	25	7	18	72
Central Africa	269	149	120	45
West Africa	68	19	49	72
African total	362	175	187	52
South America	750	472	278	37
Central America/Caribbean	53	34	19	36
Latin American total	803	506	297	37
Pacific region	48	36	12	25
Southeast Asia	302	187	115	38
South Asia	85	31	54	64
Asian total	435	254	181	42
Humid tropics total	1600	935	665	42

Source: Adrian Sommer (1976), p. 24.

42 percent. Although the figures are not entirely comparable, the data from the two tables suggest an overall decrease of tropical forest from 1600 million hectares to 660 million hectares—a loss of nearly one billion hectares. This is a loss of forested area greater than the entire land area of the United States. The implications of this are examined more fully in the next chapter, since the areas involved have been truly the wildest lands.

It should be borne in mind, however, that *cutting* forests and *losing* forests are not the same thing. Most of the forests of Western Europe and many in North America have been cut, logged, many times. They have regrown. Loss of forest means that the land is converted to some other purpose—farmlands, grazing lands, wastelands, urban-industrial areas. Up to a point loss of forest land to some other productive and stable form of use is a positive gain to the human race: much of our productive farm land and the communities where we live was once forest, and we would not care to give it back to growing trees. When the change is from productive forests to temporary, soil-depleting and soil-eroding forms of use that have no hope of permanency, however, then the loss of forests is truly to be deplored. Much of the change in the tropical world appears to be in this direction. To add to the problem, tropical rain forests have been defined as a nonrenewable resource by Gomez-Pompa et al. (1972), who state: *"All the evidence available supports the idea that, under present intensive use of the land in tropical rain forest regions, the ecosystems are in danger of a mass extinction of most of their species. This has already happened in several areas of the tropical world, and in the near future it may be of even greater intensity. The consequences are nonpredictable, but the sole fact that thousands of species will disappear before any aspect of their biology has been investigated is frightening. This would mean the loss of millions and millions of years of evolution, not only of plant and animal species, but also of the most complex biotic communities in the world.*

NORTH AMERICAN FORESTS

The situation in that area of North America north of the Mexican boundary—sometimes called Anglo-America with apologies to all the non-Anglos—is considerably more hopeful than in the tropical world (Table 10.4). That is not to say that forests are necessarily well-managed, but that the forest area has been largely stabilized and there is no likelihood that much of it will be lost to other uses. The decrease of 6 million hectares predicted in Table 10.2 is a lot of forest, but less than 2 percent of the total area. How things will actually go depends on decisions to be made by all of the forestland owners, from the federal government to individuals who have a few acres. The governments, however, can provide incentive for good forest management (Fig. 10.1).

TABLE 10.4   North American Forest Resources—1970–1973

CATEGORY	USA (1970)	CANADA (1973)	TOTAL (ANGLO-AMERICA)
	AREA IN MILLION HECTARES		
Stocked commercial forest	194	220	414
Unaccessible productive forests (Alaska)	5	0	5
Reserved forests (national parks, etc.)	8	15	24
Total productive forest	207	235	442
Unstocked commercial forest	8	17	26
Open woodlands and forests of extreme low productivity	103	73	176
	VOLUME IN BILLION CUBIC METERS		
Net annual growth on commercial forest land (underbark)	527	270	797
1975 fellings (underbark)	358	147	505

Source: CEQ (1980). Data from U.S. Forest Service, Canadian Forestry Service, FAO, and others.

FOREST MANAGEMENT

There are many ways to manage forests, and one is to leave them alone. This is the obvious approach in areas where one wishes to follow the course of events as they would occur without human interference and is appropriate to various reserves to be discussed in Chapter 11. Usually, however, one wishes to use a forest for some other purpose, and some degree of change within the forest ecosystem is deemed desirable. If one is concerned primarily with the protection of watersheds to insure good infiltration of water to underground aquifers, and a high sustained yield of water to streams with a minimum of siltation, it may be desirable to maintain a virtually undisturbed forest. If water yield is a principle objective, however, and is to take precedence over all other uses, it may be important to modify the vegetation, to replace those species that transpire more water with others that are less water demanding. If the objective was to maintain a diversity of native species, offering a maximum number of ecological niches to wildlife, one would institute a management system favoring a wide variety of successional stages of forest growth in balance with areas of climax vegetation. Within the latter, one would be particularly careful to maintain old trees, dead trees, and fallen trees, since these provide a habitat for particular kinds of animals. A forest to be managed for public recreation may be kept more open than one managed for other purposes, to allow easy access and scenic vistas as well as a variety of habitats for wildlife.

Management for timber production, as an important or primary objective, also can involve many different approaches. Trees grow faster

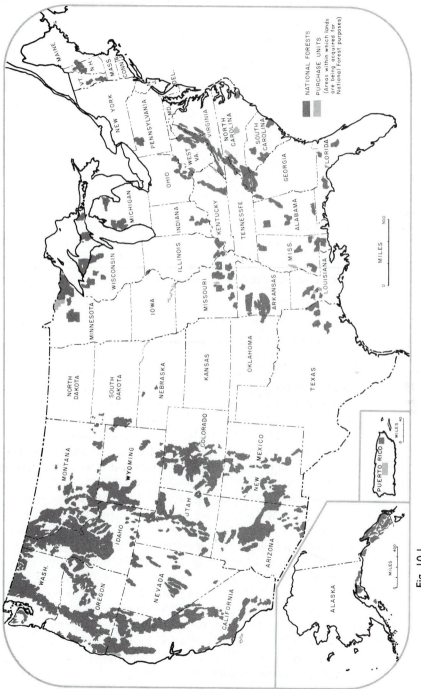

NATIONAL FORESTS

PURCHASE UNITS
(Areas within which lands
are being acquired for
National Forest purposes)

Fig. 10.1

National forests of the United
States (map by U.S. Forest
Service).

and produce more cellulose per acre when young than when mature. If the need is for pulpwood or wood chips, or for firewood, then areas will be kept in young forest reproduction and trees will be cut before their growth begins to slacken off with approaching maturity. If the need is for high-quality lumber, than a maximum area devoted to mature trees will be required. For certain species, only the very old trees produce the higher quality lumber. The redwood lumber that has traditionally reached the market from California forests is the product of old trees. Youngsters only a century or two old do not produce it.

One of the oldest forms of silviculture (tree culture) is *coppicing*. In this, mature trees having the capacity to sprout from their stumps are cut back. Sprouts come up in abundance, are allowed to grow to the required size, and are then harvested. The stump will then produce additional sprouts and the process is repeated. Oaks, ashes, chestnut, alder, and other hardwoods will sprout in this way. The products of coppices were used for poles, firewood, charcoal, and other special needs. A modified coppice system was known as *coppice with standards*. In this some single-stem, tall trees (standards) were left to provide shade for the coppices and to produce ship's timbers. Coppicing is not longer widely used, although it has value wherever needs for small wood products exist (Ovington, 1965).

Where a sustained yield of wood is expected, it is important to carry out a forest survey and inventory as a first stage of management. In this volume of timber in an area is determined, broken down by location, species, age classes, condition of trees, and other criteria. When this is available, a management plan may be worked out, usually involving a system of rotation cutting, to enable a regular harvest and to provide for regular growth to replace the trees that are cut. Where mechanical equipment must be moved about to reach trees and to haul them out of the forest after they are cut, a network of roads must be planned and constructed before logging actually takes place. Skill and care taken in locating and constructing roads to avoid erosion or other forms of forest damage are as important to forest perpetuation as other aspects of the activity.

Three basic systems of cutting are now in use in forests managed for timber: clear cutting, shelterwood cutting, and selective cutting. The first is particularly appropriate to forests in which the trees are of relatively uniform age and are made up of commercially useful species. All the trees are cut from a block or strip, leaving open ground. The debris and litter left after logging may also be removed, burned, or concentrated, and the ground left suitable for seedling growth. If the trees in uncut blocks or strips can provide an abundant supply of seeds, no artificial planting may be required. Otherwise the area may be reseeded or planted to nursery-grown seedlings.

Selective cutting is appropriate to forests of mixed age classes or containing several species of unequal commercial value. Mature trees of the desired species are harvested. Young trees are left to grow to maturity. Great care must be taken not to damage the trees left in the process of removing the ones to be cut.

Shelterwood cutting is intermediate between the above two systems. In this, part of the tree stand is removed in the initial cutting, and in particular those trees of poor form or quality are taken out. This is essentially a thinning operation that opens up the forest floor to light. The best quality trees are left to cast seed and provide shelter for the growing seedlings. After a good seed crop has been distributed, a heavier cut is made of the remaining trees, leaving some to provide shelter. In a third stage after seedlings are well established, the remaining mature trees are removed.

In all of these systems, the yield from the forest must be balanced against ecological requirements and economic conditions. Cutting will be less when market conditions are poor and heavier when good market conditions exist, but in no case should the existence of good markets permit deviations from the system to the degree that growth and reproduction are seriously reduced.

Systems of clear cutting commonly leave ugly and unnatural openings in a forest, particularly where operators insist on following straight lines or contours and leave sharp lines of demarcation between the cutover and unlogged forest. Where forest debris, including major parts of the tree not wanted as saw logs, is left on the ground, the results are unattractive. Systems of selection or shelterwood cutting leave a more natural appearance to the forest and are preferred by those who favor multiple use and wish to use forests for outdoor recreation. Clear cutting is also more likely to encourage erosion, and it may leave stream beds choked with debris following logging. Nevertheless, some types of forest do not regenerate well following selective cutting, since the seedlings may thrive best on soil from which the debris and litter have been removed and which is exposed to full sunlight. Careful forest management requires a balancing of all of the various values obtainable from the forest and the selection of systems that will perpetuate them. Care for forest regeneration is equally important with skills used in forest cutting and timber removal if the forest is to be maintained. In intensively managed forests, trees may be thinned and pruned to obtain the best growth and yield. Diseased and damaged trees may be removed and dense stands of young trees opened up. Lower branches may be taken off to improve lumber quality. In the forest of many age classes and species, some form of cropping can be going on at all times and a steady income can, theoretically at least, be produced.

Prevention of waste is another important part of good timber management. Full utilization of a tree for lumber is not possible, but remnant parts may have value for other uses. The development of the pulp industry, producing paper and other products, and the plastics industry, based on cellulose, has created a demand for almost the entire tree.

Recent developments in these industries have made possible the use of many species of trees previously not utilized and, in fact, almost any kind of cellulose can now be used in one or another forest-based industry.

FOREST PROTECTION

Individuals who manage forests to obtain a sustained yield of wood or for maintenance of other values have long been concerned with preventing or suppressing those factors in the environment that are destructive to forests. These factors are many. Fire has received the most publicity and prominence but is easily surpassed in its effects by forest diseases and forest insects and, at times, by damage by vertebrate animals, floods, avalanches, hurricanes, storms, or other unusual weather conditions. All of these are natural and have been operative for as long as forests have been on earth. None can necessarily be classified as ''problems'' in themselves. They become problems because of the values people place on certain areas of forests, and their consequent desire to maintain these areas in a particular state.

The effect of fire and the role fire plays in forest ecology can be considered to vary along a climatic gradient. The highly humid forests such as tropical and some temperate rain forests are virtually fireproof in their natural state. Although people have used fire to open up or clear these forests they can burn only after the vegetation has been cut and allowed to dry; even then, burning must be done during brief dry periods in the generally humid weather. The extremely dry forests at the arid end of the climatic gradient are dry enough to carry fire at any time. Because they are slow-growing and produce relatively little plant debris however, they may not accumulate enough fuel at the surface of the ground to carry a fire. When they do burn they are slow to recover, and may be permanently replaced by vegetation more suited to arid conditions.

Those forests most suited to fire grow in climates with a pronounced dry season but also with enough rainfall to permit abundant plant growth. In such areas, fire has been a constant factor in forest history, and forests are to some degree conditioned to its presence. Fires may start from lightning, in the absence of people; however, humans have been around a long time and have been using and misusing fire for a good share of that time. Thorn forest and monsoon forest alternate with savanna in accordance with the prevalence of fires. Pine forests, redwood forests, and mediterranean sclerophyll forests are all adapted in varying degrees to fire. Redwoods, for example, have an unusually tough and fire-resistant bark. When they do burn they have the capacity to sprout vigorously from what appear initially to be blackened and lifeless trunks.

During the early development of forestry in the United States as well as in many other countries, a decision was made to protect forests as completely as possible against fire. Although this decision was difficult to carry out, skill in the prevention, detection, and suppression of forest fires was gradually developed, and many areas of forest were protected for long periods of time. Unfortunately, this (Smoky the Bear) policy had unanticipated effects. Litter accumulated on the ground in quantities that would not have built up in the absence of human intervention. Dense stands of tree reproduction and brush grew wherever light penetrated the canopy. When a fire eventually entered such a protected forest, it was a different kind of fire than what would have occurred under natural conditions. Generating intense heat from the abundance of fuel, it could quickly change from a ground to a "crown" fire sweeping through the woods at a terrifying rate of speed. Under some circumstances, fire "storms" developed, devastating great areas and impossible to suppress until all fuel had been consumed or rainstorms had saturated the ground.

Gradually a shift in attitude toward fire has occurred. Prescribed burning is now used more and more widely as a forest management tool. In this practice, fires are started at a time of year when they will burn slowly and will not generate intense heat. They are used to thin the layer of forest litter and open stands of brush and young trees. A forest managed by fire in this way can be made secure against devastating wildfires.

During recent decades, however, the prevention and suppression of wildfires has remained and certainly, for some time to come, will remain a major burden for forest protection agencies. It has not been unusual in the United States to lose a billion board feet of timber to fires in a single year. Acreage burned annually is in the millions, and expenditures for fire protection are generally in excess of $100 million a year.

Disease has been less-publicized, but much more destructive than fire. Disease- and insect-killed timber is commonly salvaged by logging, but much is not used, and management plans are impaired. Among the more spectacular forest diseases in the United States have been chestnut blight, blister rust, and Dutch elm disease. All are caused by parasitic fungi. Chestnut blight, introduced accidentally from the Orient early in the twentieth century, quickly spread through the eastern hardwood forests. Within a short time it had almost completely eliminated the once abundant and highly valued chestnut tree. No effective way of controlling this disease has yet been found. Fortunately, other species of chestnuts are resistant, and it has not done equivalent damage in other continents. White-pine-blister rust was accidentally introduced from Germany. It has prevented the eastern white pine from becoming reestablished in areas from which it was eliminated by fire and logging. It has spread into forests of western white pine and sugar pine and has done great damage. Since this fungus must spend part of its development cycle on gooseberry or current bushes (*Ribes* spp.), it can be controlled through the laborious process of eliminating these plants from the vicinity of white pine or sugar pine forests. The Dutch elm disease is carried from tree to tree by insects. It threatens the elm-tree component of America's deciduous forests.

a

FOREST MANAGEMENT AND PROTECTION

(a) Fires may move from the ground up tree trunks to become devastating crown fires. (b) Repeated burning changed this forest to low-value brush. (c) Controlled burning can reduce the danger of wild fires through removal of fuel and may help to maintain certain types of forest in a productive condition. (d) In block cutting, seed trees are left to favor regeneration. (e) Early clear-cut-and-burn logging brought ruined landscapes. (f) In selective cutting in western pine forests, younger trees are left to produce a new crop. (g) An intensively managed forest in Sweden.

b

c

d

e

f

g

313

Thus far the best hope for controlling diseases lies in sound forestry practices, including the removal of trees likely to become infected and the prevention of injury to young trees. Encouraging forest diversity is the best forest insurance. Disease spreads more quickly and has greater effect where one species of tree dominates the ground in closely ranked stands. Interspersion of species allows for slower spread and easier control. If one species is lost, others remain to fill the gaps and maintain the forest.

Insect pests represent the most serious threat other than people to forest—and because of human reaction to them, a serious threat to entire ecosystems. Daniel Janzen (1970) has pointed out that a plant has three major external defenses against herbivores: (1) weather inimical to the insects or other plant-eaters; (2) predators and parasites that feed on the herbivores and at times control their numbers; and finally (3) forest diversity with scattering and interspersion of individuals of a species. In temperate zone forests, management practices that cut down on species diversity remove the third defense and interfere with the second. Weather, however, remains a controlling factor, so that insect outbreaks are periodic and do not take a constant toll. In tropical forests, diversity provides a high degree of protection, and there is an unusual variety of predators and parasites for any insect that feeds on plants. The first factor is not operative, however; weather is always favorable to outbreaks of any kind of species. Hence, when tropical forests are simplified into single-species plantations, all of the defenses against herbivorous enemies are removed, or seriously reduced.

Insect pests particularly destructive in Northern Hemisphere forest include the spruce budworm, which at times sweeps through northern forests with devastating effects, the larch sawfly, which can destroy great areas of larch or tamarack, the pine weevil, which attacks those white pines that escape blister rust, and the pinebark beetle, which devastates forests of ponderosa pine in the western United States.

With insects as well as disease, sound management aimed at maintaining healthy, vigorous trees, good soil conditions, and the maximum diversity commensurable with the goals of management provides the best protection. Pesticides fail in the long run to control pests, but they succeed too well in reducing populations of species preying on the pests. Since these pesticides accumulate in food chains, they destroy great numbers of animals. The ideal pesticide to control insect pests would be one highly toxic to the pest, but to nothing else. In the absence of this ideal, balanced chemical controls, using the least dangerous pesticides, become essential at times, where good management and biological control have not succeeded.

TIMBER SUPPLY AND DEMAND

North America, including only the United States and Canada, leads all other continents and regions in the production of wood products. The

United States, however, in addition to being one of the greatest timber producers, leads also in consumption. Particularly in the consumption of paper, the United States is far ahead of other nations. Thus the average consumption of newsprint was approximately 41 metric tons per 1000 people. The nearest rival was Sweden, which consumed 36 metric tons per 1000 people. Anyone who has compared the giant-sized United States newspapers with the small ones produced by most other countries can understand the reason. It has been estimated that the Sunday edition of *The New York Times* for one year requires 125,000 tons of newsprint, which requires the annual growth from 1250 square miles of Canadian forest land. The wasteful consumption of paper and the problems that result from the disposal of paper wastes have led to increased interest and activity in recycling or reusing paper.

According to Webb and Jacobsen (1982): *If current trends continue, demand for wood from U.S. forests is likely to surpass supplies by 1990, according to U.S. Forest Service projections. A growing imbalance between supply and demand could nearly double the price of some wood products by 2030, it concludes, and bring about "continuing and substantial increases in the relative stumpage prices for most species and sizes of timber and for most timber products."*

There is good reason to believe that demand may exceed these projections. Per capita use of fuelwood in homes could more than triple by 2030. In 1900, before the widespread use of oil and gas for heating, annual per capita fuelwood use was 18 times what it is today. As households and industry move away from expensive oil and gas, per capita consumption could approach those levels, bringing total wood demand above 28 billion cubic feet a year.

. . . The widespread substitution of wood for oil in the manufacturing of plastics and other synthetic materials could drive demand even higher than the level projected by the Forest Service.

Despite these dire predictions, the timber industry has in fact been in a slump, and demand, with the recession/depression of the early 1980s, has been low. While predicting a timber famine for the future, timber companies are busily exporting logs and lumber to whoever will buy them and no doubt will continue to sell to the highest bidder even if the shortage of timber in the United States does materialize.

FORESTRY IN OTHER COUNTRIES

Outside of the United States the nations of the world represent all extremes in forest resources and forestry practices. Canada is most like the United States. It is a timber-exporting country and likely to remain in this category for sometime to come. Particularly favorable to the practice of forestry is its land ownership pattern. Over 90 percent of its commercial forest land is in federal or provincial ownership.

Europe has led the world in the development of forest science and forest management. This has resulted partly from the drastic reduction that took place in its total forest area as land was cleared for agriculture or other more intensive uses. Although most of Europe was once forested, only 29 percent is forested today, and much of this is in Scandinavia. In Great Britain, which was once largely forested, only slightly more than 7 percent of the land is now in forest. In France only 20 percent remains in forest. In 1664 the realization that forests were rapidly disappearing caused John Evelyn, one of the founders of the Royal Society of London, to recommend the establishment of forestry as a science and as a concern of the Royal Society. Shortly thereafter Colbert, minister to Louis XIV of France, produced the *French Forest Ordinance of 1669* in which sound forestry and land management rules were promulgated. Gifford Pinchot learned his forestry at the French forestry school at Nancy, and most of the pioneer foresters in America were influenced by French and German forestry concepts.

The total forested area in Europe, outside of the USSR, is 140 million hectares compared to 470 million in North America. However, the total production from European forests was over 300 billion cubic meters compared to 500 million from North America. The yield per hectare, therefore, was more than two times greater in Europe than in North America. The difference reflects the intensity of care and the skill in management. Trends in forest management in Germany are of particular interest. After 1840 German foresters engaged in a highly artificial form of forest management. Forests were clear-cut and replanted to the species of trees that were in greatest demand, mostly to pure stands of spruce and pine. It was believed that by doing this the highest yields could be obtained from each acre without wasting soil productivity on growing "weed" trees or brush. The former broad-leaved and mixed broad-leaved and coniferous forests were replaced by uniform, even-aged stands of conifers. In time it was found that the continued production of these single-species forests damaged the soil through increasing the rate of podsolization and by breaking down the circulatory system of soil minerals. Losses to insects, diseases, and storms increased. Then the second and third generations of pure spruce and pine began to decline in yield per acre as both growth rate and timber quality fell off. In consequence, after 1918, there was a swing in Germany back toward a more natural type of forest. Mixed forests were planted, as comparable as possible to the original forests of the area. Clear cutting was replaced by selective cutting, using logging methods that did as little damage as possible to the remaining stands of trees. Under this system of management, known as *Dauerwald*, yields have increased and forest lands have been improved (Lowenthal, 1956).

In Switzerland, most forest land belongs to the communes or the cantons, but management rules have been laid down by federal law and affect all forest owners. Clear cutting is not allowed nor can forest land be converted to other uses without federal permission. Great Britain, in an effort to restore the productivity of land and to reduce its reliance on imports, has instituted a major reforestation program. Areas of the Scottish highlands long ago depleted of trees and then burned and grazed into ruin, are now once again supporting healthy stands of Scots pine.

Southern Hemisphere countries such as Australia, New Zealand, and South Africa were deficient in conifers originally and faced the need to import most of the softwood timber required for construction. To remedy this situation, extensive coniferous plantings over millions of acres have been undertaken, relying particularly on California's Monterey Pine. In Australia great areas of native *Eucalyptus* forest have been cleared to make way for pine monocultures. Such plantations are depressing to anyone but a wood producer, but initially, at least, they have produced high yields in a remarkably short space of time. Whether these yields will continue or the German experience will be repeated remains to be seen. It must be recognized, however, that such plantations are most comparable to agricultural croplands and represent a sacrifice of wildland values to commodity production.

RECAPITULATION

Long before forests were regarded as commercial resources, they were of great value. These values remain even in areas where the need for wood products is high. Forests hold the land together and keep water cycles functioning. They are regulators of the atmosphere and areas where people can go for recreation and renewal of spirit. They are the homes for the greatest diversity of plant and animal species that can be found in any region on earth.

Planning for sound forest management requires the recognition of all forest values. In some places and some times it is necessary to emphasize one value over others—wood or water may take precedence. Over any broad region, however, we cannot afford to sacrifice too many forest values. Perhaps the lesson of environmental conservation is to recognize that forests are far more than trees. In our concern to see more trees, we must not lose sight of the forest.

> When you've seen one redwood tree, you've seen them all.
>
> Remark attributed to an immigrant from Illinois visiting northwestern California

RANGE LIVESTOCK IN THE UNITED STATES

BEGINNINGS   The first livestock probably reached America when the Norsemen landed in Vinland in the eleventh century. Neither the Vikings nor their livestock survived. It was not until the time of Columbus when livestock were again brought to the Americas, and it was probably Cortez who first brought cattle and sheep to the mainland of North America in the early sixteenth century. Livestock spread rapidly under Spanish methods of handling. Cattle and sheep came to New Mexico in the sixteenth and seventeenth centuries and spread through California in the latter part of the eighteenth century. The horse must have escaped from Spanish missions and settlements in the seventeenth century, for by 1680 the Pueblo and Apache Indians had the horse, by the 1750s the horse had reached Montana, and before 1800 Canada.

The livestock industry in the United States has had its most colorful history in the area known as the western range, the arid grassland, sagebrush, and scrub country lying westward of the 100th meridian, which bisects North Dakota and runs southward through Dodge City, Kansas. It should not be imagined, however, that the western range supports most of the livestock in the United States. The area east of the 100th meridian supports far more beef and dairy cattle than the area to the west, and it is only in sheep numbers that the West has a slight edge. The livestock business had its beginnings in the eastern United States with animals brought from Europe by early colonists. From early colonial times livestock were pastured in forest clearings along the westward fringes of agricultural lands. From here the animals were moved back into farm fields and pastures for fattening and from there to market in towns and cities. As agriculture spread westward, the pastoral fringe of land moved ahead of it until the prairie states were reached.

In the eastern United States, livestock had a profound influence on vegetation. With grazing pressure native grasses and forbs were displaced from pastures and fields. In their place came a mixture of exotics that had followed the settlers from Europe. The most important of these was Kentucky bluegrass, a perennial that has followed agriculture and pasturing throughout its long history in Eurasia and that helped to stabilize the pasture lands of western Europe. Bluegrass is an excellent forage grass for livestock and well able to hold up under heavy grazing. With its aid the soils on eastern pastures were held in place and their condition improved.

TEXAS CATTLE   While livestock were gradually spreading with the American colonies, a major center of stock raising had grown up in the Spanish domain of Texas. Spanish land grants were liberal and favored the establishment of large ranches needed for the maintenance of a range livestock industry. The cattle in this region were the Texas longhorns, a breed originally developed in Spain, long legged, rangy, hardy, and well suited to foraging in a half-wild condition on the open range (p. 324). When Texas entered the Union there was little change in land-ownership policy. Texas retained ownership of public lands within its boundaries and continued to follow the Spanish practice of disposing of them to encourage range livestock production. As a result the livestock business thrived. With abundant grassland range and little need for hay or pasture land, costs of operation for cattlemen in Texas were low. Markets were difficult to reach, and many cattle were butchered for hides and tallow. Nevertheless, stock raising remained profitable. In the 1840s trail herds of Texas cattle were driven to market in Louisiana and later to Ohio. With the California gold rush, a number of drives of Texas cattle to California were carried out.

In 1860 Texas is estimated to have held more than 4½ million cattle. Following the Civil War, a greatly expanded market for beef led to the series of trail drives of Texas cattle immortalized in western song and story. Most of the cattle trails were developed to meet shipping points on the new railroads that were being built westward in the 1860s. These shipping points, Abilene, Newton, Dodge City, and others, soon developed into the wild and lawless cow towns of western legend. During the 20-year period between 1865 and 1885 an estimated 5½ million head of cattle were driven northward from Texas, some to market, others to stock the newly opening rangelands to the north.

The settlement of the grassland ranges in the central and northern prairies and plains was retarded for a time by the Plains Indians. A few pioneer stockmen established ranches in the North in early times; the biggest expansion, however, took place in the 1870s, as the Indians were subdued and the herds of bison on which they had depended reduced and finally eliminated. In 1870 it is estimated that there were between 4 and 5 million cattle in the 17 western states; by 1890 there were over 26½ million.

SHEEPHERDING   Sheep brought to New Mexico in the sixteenth century were to form the basis for the sheep industry in the West. In the seventeenth and eighteenth centuries sheep ranches were established in New Mexico, Texas, Arizona, and California. Along with cattle, sheep spread westward in front of American colonists from the eastern seaboard. The greatest expansion of the sheep business in the plains and prairie states took place after the cattlemen were well established. The extent of this expansion is indicated by the figures for 1850 when there were 514,000 sheep in the West and 1890 when the numbers had reached 20 million. The greatest increase in the northern plains came in the 1880s when cattle numbers were beginning to decline. Wyoming carried 309,000 sheep in 1886 and over 2,600,000 in 1900, during which period the number of cattle declined by half a million. In Montana there was little increase in cattle between 1886 and 1900, but sheep increased from somewhat less than 1 million to over 3½ million.

In California sheep spread with Spanish missions, *ranchos,* and later with American settlers. Great bands of sheep were moved westward to stock California in early days—more than a half million between 1852 to 1857, and later equally vast bands moved eastward to stock ranges of the Great Basin states. Many early sheepmen in California used to carry on the old Spanish practice of nomadic or migratory sheep grazing.

One route regularly followed took the sheepherders up the east side of the Sierra Nevada, across the high passes of the central mountains, and back southward along the western slopes. The numbers of sheep on these long drives were large, and the damage has been made memorable in the writing of John Muir, who described the devastation in the Yosemite region, and in the findings of later surveys, which described the almost complete destruction of ground vegetation in the Mt. Whitney region. The spread of sheep in the West did not take place without arousing bitter feelings among the cattlemen. Cattlemen, with established home ranches, particularly resented the passage of migratory bands of sheep across ranges, using forage they had hoped to reserve for their own cattle. The bitterness broke out into the open cattle–sheep wars in some areas.

PUBLIC LANDS

The history of livestock in the West cannot be understood without considering the land-disposal policy of the federal government. As a result of numerous transactions, the United States government had obtained claim to approximately 1½ billion acres of land within the boundaries of the contiguous United States (Fig. 10.2). The policy of the government was to dispose of these lands as rapidly as possible. The philosophy of Thomas Jefferson dominated land-disposal policies. He believed lands should be used to encourage settlement and development of the nation and thus to strengthen it against its enemies rather than sold for immediate gain to the treasury (Fig. 10.3). A variety of acts were passed by

FIG. 10.2

The original public domain of the United States. (*Source: Bureau of Land Management.*)

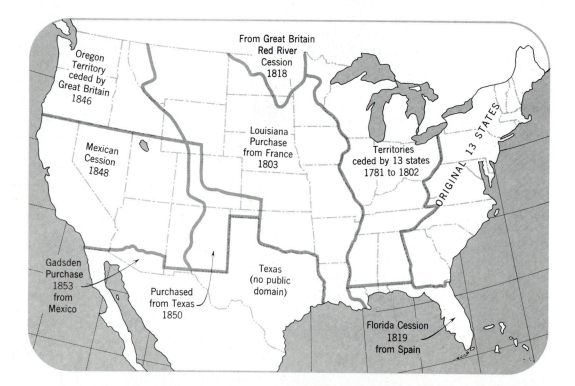

FIG. 10.3
Additions to and disposals of
the public domain.

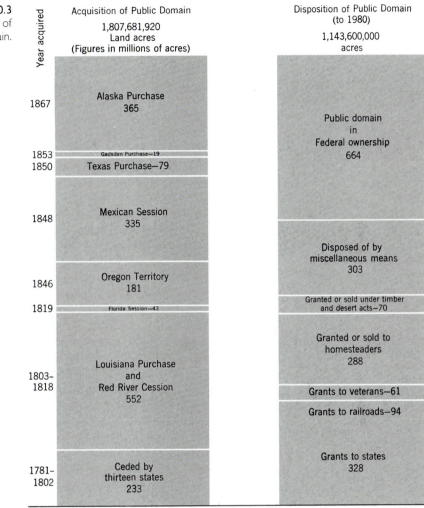

Year acquired

Acquisition of Public Domain

1,807,681,920
Land acres
(Figures in millions of acres)

Year acquired	
1867	Alaska Purchase 365
1853	Gadsden Purchase—19
1850	Texas Purchase—79
1848	Mexican Session 335
1846	Oregon Territory 181
1819	Florida Session—43
1803–1818	Louisiana Purchase and Red River Cession 552
1781–1802	Ceded by thirteen states 233

Disposition of Public Domain
(to 1980)

1,143,600,000
acres

Public domain
in
Federal ownership
664

Disposed of by
miscellaneous means
303

Granted or sold under timber
and desert acts—70

Granted or sold to
homesteaders
288

Grants to veterans—61

Grants to railroads—94

Grants to states
328

Congress providing for the sale or homesteading of federal land. Noteworthy was the Homestead Act of 1862, which provided title to 160 acres of land, free of charge, to legitimate settlers after five years of residence on the land. The 160-acre limitation proved to be a major difficulty. In the farming lands of the East, 160 acres is more than adequate to support a family. In the arid West, where agriculture is not possible, 160 acres is insufficient for the raising of livestock. The acreage limitation, for the West, was later raised to 320 and then to 640 acres in 1916. However, even 640 acres does not provide adequate space for commercial stock raising. Much unfortunate publicity about farming opportunities in the West, accompanying the passage of the various homestead acts, encouraged settlers to cultivate land that should never have been plowed. Ultimately this led to failure and land abandonment but not without hardship to both land and settler.

When the livestock industry expanded into the West, it moved into federal land. In favorable locations, stockmen established headquarters and attempted to obtain for themselves adequate range for their livestock. The limitations of the Homestead Act were evaded in various ways: by having friends or relations take up homesteads on adjoining areas and eventually dispose of them to the central ranch owner or by homesteading land in the areas where water was available and thus obtaining use of the surrounding, drier ranges. By one device or another, many ranch owners obtained title to considerable areas of land. Still, many were dependent on unpatented federal land, the public domain, for a large part of their range forage.

The invention of barbed wire in the middle 1870s brought a measure of stability to western grazing lands by making it economically feasible to fence off areas of private range and thus exclude the migratory herder or trespassing livestock. Some ranchers, however, undertook to fence in large areas of public domain as well and had to be restrained from this by federal order. In the absence of fencing, ranch owners decided to respect each others' rights to graze certain areas of public land and joined together to exclude trespassers.

With the establishment of the forest reserves in 1891 and the National Forest system in 1905, additional stability was brought to western grazing lands. The land removed from the public domain and reserved as National Forest included much valuable mountain grazing land. Initially, misunderstandings led to efforts to eliminate livestock from forest reserves. Later, however, local stockmen were allowed grazing privileges on National Forest land, being charged a nominal fee per head of livestock grazed. Difficulties arose when the Forest Service attempted to improve National Forest ranges by restricting livestock numbers or seasons when grazing was permitted. Many stockmen resented what they believed to be unwarranted government interference with their rights.

After the National Forests were established, much federal land still remained as unreserved public domain. Much of this was suitable for grazing. In 1934 the Taylor Grazing Act was passed by Congress as a measure to bring this federal range under proper management. Eighty million acres of public domain land were placed into grazing districts to be managed jointly by the federal government and committees of local stockmen. The Grazing Service was established to administer the new grazing districts. From the start, however, it was handicapped by the opposition of stockmen, who resented interference with long-established practices, and by lack of support from other federal agencies. In 1946 its functions were taken over by the Bureau of Land Management, which since that time has had responsibility for both the Taylor grazing districts and the other unreserved public-domain lands. This agency has responsibility over 160 million acres of federal land in western grazing districts and has been attempting to restore them to productivity (Table 10.5).

TABLE 10.5   Public Lands and Administrative Agencies, 1980

AGENCY	AREA CONTROLLED (MILLIONS OF ACRES)
Bureau of Land Management	398
U.S. Forest Service	226
National Park Service	71
Fish and Wildlife Service	43
Department of Defense	30
Other agencies	2
Total federal	770
State lands	135
City and county lands	20
Indian lands	52
Private lands	1315

Source: Statistical Abstract of the United States, 1981.

Since the 1880s western stockmen with access to federal land have been dissatisfied with its administration. Since the time when they were ordered to remove all fences from public-domain land, they have attempted to bring pressure to bear on Congress to make it possible for them to obtain outright leases of federal land for grazing purposes. Grazing privileges on National Forests and the more liberal grazing allowances on Taylor grazing lands have not been sufficient to satisfy those who want permanent grazing rights. Stockmen's associations, with a powerful lobby in Washington, have brought pressure in many sessions of Congress to have grazing lands removed from the jurisdiction of the Forest Service and other federal agencies and turned over to the use of cattle and sheep interests.

The 1970 report of the Public Land Law Review Commission reflected an effort in this direction, recommending the "dominant-use" principle as a means for giving livestock grazing priority above all other uses on certain lands, and recommending the disposal of certain lands to livestock owners (Pyles, 1970). Although it was not implemented, the pressure to gain more local livestock-owner control continued into the '80s with the so-called sagebrush rebellion, which was financed by grazing, mining, and energy interests, and seeks to have federal land "returned" to the states. The fact that it has never belonged to the states is considered beside the point.

RESTRICTION OF THE WESTERN RANGE   The westward movement of agricultural settlement rapidly cut down on the amount of land available for grazing. Originally the rich chernozems, prairie soils, and the deeper brown soils of the Plains States supported range livestock. Early livestock owners in the northern grasslands once

a

b

THE WESTERN RANGE

(a) Angus cattle on a Colorado range. (b) Texas longhorns. (c) The cowboy tradition—moving out herefords in Idaho. by 1890 there were over 26 million cattle on the western range. (d) Sheep survived where cattle died. From 1850 to 1890 sheep increased on the western range to 20 million.

c

d

found forage so abundant and nutritious that cattle could thrive on it throughout the year. Some reported cattle were able to gain weight on natural feed during the winter and become fat enough for market in early spring. But as the better soils were taken by farmers, livestock were forced into drier lands and less fertile upland soils. This, combined with deterioration of the vegetation, made it no longer possible to carry live-stock through the year on natural forage. Furthermore, the market for grass-fed beef began to decline as the cornbelt states were settled and corn-fed cattle were shipped to market. A relationship developed between western cattle owners and the mixed farm-livestock economy of the corn belt. Cattle were shipped young from the western range, fattened to market age on corn and other forage, and moved to market. This practice, in turn, led to a change in the type of cattle in the West. The hardy Texas longhorns could thrive on rough range forage but failed to fatten into choice beef in the corn lot. They were gradually replaced on the western ranges through shipment of other breeds from the East—Herefords mainly, but also Aberdeen-Angus, Shorthorns, and others. The newer cattle breeds required more care and were less able to fend for themselves. The rancher with a permanent establishment and available hay or irrigated pasture lands was favored over the older type who depended entirely on native forage. Western sheepmen, primarily interested in wool production, were less dependent on the farming states. The Merino sheep, a wool breed, came with the Spanish and for long remained the preferred sheep. Later, a new Merino-type sheep, the Rambouillet from France, became popular for wool production. In the farming states, generally, the emphasis shifted from wool to mutton breeds as the industry became established.

DAMAGE TO THE
WESTERN RANGE

Severe winters, drought, and the uncertain market conditions of the late 1880s and the 1890s put an end to the great expansion of the livestock industry. During this expansion the western United States was settled, but at a high cost to the nation. This cost was revealed in the first general survey of the western range carried out by the Forest Service in the early 1930s. (Forest Service, 1936). This survey showed that the original capacity of the native range vegetation to support livestock had been cut in half during the few decades that the range had been grazed. The original capacity of the native vegetation was estimated at 22½ million animals units (1 animal unit equals 1 cow or horse or 5 sheep or goats). As a result of overgrazing by livestock, the vegetation had deteriorated to the point where in 1930 the range capacity was only 10.8 million animal units. However, in 1930 the western range was still carrying 17.3 million animal units instead of the 10.8 million that it could have supported without further damage. The damage was therefore continuing. If stocking were reduced to a level below the range capacity, it would take approximately 100 years to restore the ranges to their original condition. In about 60 years of use, therefore, enough damage had been done to require a century to repair.

The survey also found that of the 728 million acres of range in the West, 589 million acres were suffering from serious erosion, thus both reducing their future productivity and adding to the silt load of the streams. Only about 95 million acres were found in satisfactory condition, and these, for the most part, were either privately owned or National Forest lands. The lands in the worst condition were the public domain, the no-man's lands of the West that had received neither administration nor care. This Forest Service report was received with great distaste by stockmen, who admitted local overgrazing but denied the widespread severity of the damage and labeled the report as seriously biased. However, both sides would admit that much was needed to restore or build up the grazing capacity of western rangelands.

Factors that have contributed to overgrazing of rangelands are several. First, in the early days, was ignorance. Stockmen from the East, inheritors of European traditions, were familiar with livestock management on well-watered pasture lands. They had no experience with the arid West, where the capacity of the land to support livestock is often extremely low. The Spanish, experienced with arid ranges, had learned mostly how to exploit them, not how to conserve them. As permanent ranches were established and people settled down to the business of earning a living on a long-term basis, some proved to be good observers and managers. They learned to recognize the better forage plants and the conditions that favored such plants and handled livestock accordingly. Through practical, trial-and-error management ranchers developed systems that later-day scientific range managers were to adopt or modify. Others, less capable or more handicapped by economic or environmental circumstance, failed to learn the lessons and continued to try to carry more livestock than the range would support.

Climate has been, and remains, a cause of range damage, although it is often blamed for human mistakes. Droughts are normal on western ranges, and grazing capacity fluctuates with wet years and dry. A range properly stocked for a high rainfall year may be dangerously overstocked if drought follows. With dry years, livestock numbers must be reduced, or supplemental feed in the form of hay or food concentrates must be purchased to carry them without pressure on range forage. A widespread drought, however, often brings falling market prices and higher prices for hay or grain. If the rancher is short of cash, there is a strong temptation to try to hold excessive numbers of livestock in the hopes that better conditions will return. Damage always results.

Economic factors contribute to range damage. High prices for beef, mutton, or wool encourage heavy stocking; falling prices make it difficult to dispose of animals without great financial loss. Ranchers, like others, are in business to make money.

RANGE ECOLOGY AND MANAGEMENT

CARRYING CAPACITY   Much range damage has occurred because of failure to realize that each area of range has a carrying capacity. This can be defined as the number of animals that can be carried on it and kept in good condition without damage to the range forage. Carrying capacity depends on the soil and climate, the type of native vegetation, and the ability of the vegetation to hold up under grazing. It varies from one site to another, being high in well-watered areas with deep soil and extremely low on rocky, arid ranges.

Grass can stand only a limited amount of grazing pressure. Each perennial grass plant produces each year a certain surplus of growth that can be safely grazed without injury to the plant. Each plant also has a *metabolic reserve*, a certain minimum area of leaves and stems needed to carry out the necessary photosynthesis to build and store foods in the crown or root system. Annual grasses, which die each year and regenerate from seed the following year, could theoretically be cropped off to the roots once seed has been cast without damage to future generations. Actually, with annuals as well as perennials a certain minimum amount of leafage and stem must be left on the ground to provide soil protection and a more favorable bed in which seeds will germinate. The number of animals to be carried safely on the range depends, therefore, on the surplus of leafage and stems put on by vegetation. If too many animals are held, not only the surplus is eaten but also the reserve portions of the plant. If this process is repeated for long, plants weaken and die.

Species of range plants differ greatly in their ability to withstand use. The taller grasses of climax vegetation of the prairies are not able to withstand heavy grazing. Under heavy cropping they disappear, and their place is taken by more resistant, often sod-forming, grasses, which have leaves and stems that grow more nearly horizontal to the ground surface and are, therefore, less easily cropped (Fig. 10.4). With continued heavy use even these sod-forming grasses disappear. On the resultant bare ground, relatively unpalatable weeds of various kinds seed in. If the range is protected from fire, woody plants of less palatable varieties will move into former grassland areas.

In a widely used classification, put forward by Dyksterhuis (1949), range plants are placed into three categories: *Decreasers,* the tall climax grasses, are nutritious and highly preferred by livestock, which decrease in number under moderate grazing. *Increasers* are species also present in the climax but in a lesser amount or subordinate position. They are often sod formers and are also nutritious and eaten well by livestock but better able to stand up to grazing use. These species increase in number or in space occupied as the tall climax grasses diminish. With very heavy grazing pressure, even the increasers are killed out, and their place is taken by *invaders,* native or exotic weeds or woody plants of low forage value, little used by livestock and generally not as well adapted to main-

FIG. 10.4
Growth forms of grasses:
(a) annual; (b) sod forming;
(c) bunch.

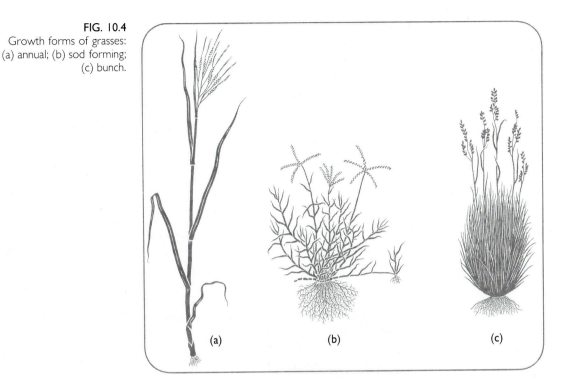

(a)　　　　　　　　(b)　　　　　　　　(c)

taining or holding the soil as the original vegetation. Proper range management includes maintaining a balance on the range between increasers and decreasers and keeping the invaders to a minimum (Table 10.6).

In terms of plant succession, overgrazing leads to a replacement of climax species or species high on the successional scale by plants low

TABLE 10.6   Successional Changes with Grazing and Protection on the
North American Prairie

		Decreasers	
Climax	Grazing	Big bluestem (*Andropogon gerardi*)	No grazing
		Little bluestem (*A. scoparius*)	
		Lead plant (*Amapla canescens*)	
Middle succession		Increasers	
		Kentucky blue grass (*Poa pratensis*)	
	Grazing	Blue grama (*Bouteloua gracilis*)	No grazing
		Yarrow (*Achillea millefolium*)	
		Invaders	
Early succession		Western wheatgrass (*Agropyron smithii*)	
		Plantain (*Plantago spp.*)	
		Russian thistle (*Salsola kali*)	

Source: Weaver (1954).

on the successional scale or pioneer species. Conversely, absence of grazing pressure if the damage is not too great will usually allow successional processes to operate and permit climax species to regain the ground.

RANGE CONDITION
AND TREND

Range managers are trained to judge ranges on the basis of *condition,* which on many range types is simply a way of measuring the extent to which a range has departed from a climax stage toward lower successional stages as a result of grazing use, and *range trend,* which determines whether under existing conditions of management the range is returning toward a climax condition or deteriorating further.

In the Soil Conservation Service system, five classes of range condition are recognized, varying between excellent and very poor. An example of the criteria used is provided in Table 10.7. Notice that in the bottom row of this table the acres required per animal unit month, that is, the acres needed to support one cow or five sheep for one month, vary between 0.75 for a range in excellent condition and more than 5.0 for a range in very poor condition. Obviously then, a rancher who keeps his ranges close to excellent condition will be able to carry more livestock and make greater profits than a rancher who allows his ranges to deteriorate. It should be remembered, however, that range condition is a measure of the degree to which a particular type of range approaches its maximum potential yield of forage. It is something quite apart from range and soil type. Thus, a well-watered prairie range with tall climax grasses on deep soil, rated in excellent condition, would have a higher carrying capacity than a range in excellent condition in the desert grassland region of the Southwest.

RANGE PESTS

Although it is true in general that in the absence of grazing or with a reduction in livestock numbers ranges will improve in condition, there are many exceptions. Some of the invaders that occupy depleted ranges are not native plants and occupy no place in normal successional processes. Under some circumstances these invaders will continue to hold the ground even when the range is completely protected. Normal successional processes are halted, and the cover of exotics is said to form a *disturbance climax.* Thus, in California, the exotic grasses and weeds that arrived with the Spanish now form a disturbance climax that maintains itself. Studies at the San Joaquin Experimental Range in California have shown that even with complete protection from grazing over a long period of years, native perennial grasses do not replace the exotics. Elsewhere in the West, large areas of rangeland have been covered by a blanket of cheat grass *(Bromus tectorum),* which has completely replaced the original vegetation. Both its soil-holding ability and forage value are low compared to the native grasses, but it maintains itself effectively even in the absence of grazing.

Along with an invasion of weeds following overgrazing comes an invasion of animal pests. Under climax conditions in grasslands a variety

TABLE 10.7   A Range Condition Score Sheet

FACTORS EVALUATED	EXCELLENT	GOOD	FAIR	POOR	VERY POOR
1. Relative potential forage yield (in percent)	90–100	75–90	50–75	25–50	0–25
2. Important desirable forage plants (percentage of ground surface covered by each species): Wild oats, *Avena* spp. Soft chess, *Bromus mollis* Calif. bunchgrass, *Stipa pulchra* Cutleaf filaree, *Erodium cicutarium* Bur clover, *Medicago hispida,* etc.	85–100	65–85	35–65 "DECREASERS"	10–35	0–10
3. Less desirable forage plants (percentage of ground covered): Ripgut brome, *Bromus rigidus* Annual fescue, *Festuca megalura* Foxtail, *Hordeum murinum* Yarrow, *Achillea millefolium* Blue dicks, *Brodiaea capitata,* etc.	0–15	10–30	15–50 "INCREASERS"	25–65	40–90
4. Undesirable forage plants: Medusahead grass, *Elymus caput-medusae* Nitgrass, *Gastridium ventricosum* Star thistle, *Centaurea melitensis* Dwarf plantain, *Plantago erecta* Tarweed, *Hemizonia* spp., etc.	0–15	5–20	10–40 "INVADERS"	25–75	40–100
5. Plant residue or litter per acre	Abundant	Adequate	Moderate	Scarce	Very scarce
6. Erosion	None	None to slight	Slight to moderate	Moderate to severe	Severe
7. Acres per animal unit month	.75–1	1–2	2–3	3–5	5 plus

Source: For California Annual Grass Range in North-Central California. Adapted from Grover (1945).

of rodents and other types of animals live without creating serious problems. When low successional weeds replace the climax, a different group of animal species also moves in and usually increases in numbers. The kangaroo rat *(Dipodomys)*, jack rabbits *(Lepus),* and ground squirrels *(Spermophilus)* are among the range invaders. Vast amounts of money and time have been spent on their control, often under the theory that the rodents were the cause rather than an effect of range damage. However, numerous studies have shown that the most effective means of control is a barbed-wire fence, which keeps out livestock. When grazing is excluded, and grass grows tall and dense, ground squirrels, jack rabbits, and kangaroo rats must either move out or perish.

RANGE CONDITION AND MANAGEMENT

(a) Fencing is an essential tool for controlling livestock.
(b) Excessive overgrazing around waterholes is often an indication of poor management of livestock.
(c) Nebraska prairie in excellent condition.
(d) Oregon rangeland in very poor condition.

b

a

c

d

RANGE PROBLEMS IN OTHER COUNTRIES

Throughout the world, in prairie, steppe, pampas, and veld, ranges are still being damaged and deserts are encroaching on formerly useful land. The more productive ranges with high carrying capacities usually receive adequate care, but the more arid and marginal rangelands are frequently exploited with little apparent concern for the future. Abuse of rangelands carries not only the consequences of lowered carrying capacity and a diminished economic return from the land but affects all other natural resources as well. In some areas a valuable wildlife resource is destroyed to make room for livestock; the range is then damaged so that it is no longer suited for either wildlife or livestock. Such damaged areas are a source of erosion and disruption of watersheds, which can, in turn, affect still wider areas than those originally damaged.

In many areas of Africa among pastoral peoples, cattle have a traditional social value that far exceeds any market value that they may have. Traditionally, the worth of a person has been measured by the number of cattle he owns. The animals are killed and eaten only on ceremonial occasions and are not regarded as a source of meat, although their milk is used. Under such circumstances the usual incentives for animal husbandry or for careful management of range and pasture are lacking. Under primitive circumstances, livestock numbers were limited by predators and a variety of other natural causes. With civilization, however, many of these limiting factors have been removed and numbers of livestock have increased rapidly. With this has come widespread overgrazing and severe erosion. Large areas of Africa in the past have been rendered uninhabitable to cattle by the presence of the tsetse fly, some forms of which carry human sleeping sickness, but which more commonly carries the livestock disease *nagana,* fatal to cattle. Efforts to extend grazing land through elimination of the tsetse fly have involved bush clearing and the use of insecticides. Since wild species of African game serve as hosts for the tsetse fly, however, campaigns have been directed against the wild game, and hundreds of thousands of head of spectacular and valuable wild mammals have been slaughtered in the name of fly control. Ironically, more recent studies have shown that the game animals being removed have a higher economic value and produce more meat than the livestock with which they are replaced. The most economically efficient utilization of the dry, rough rangelands of Africa in the future will probably prove to be some combination of use by existing domestic breeds and species of grazing and browsing mammals that are at present wild.

In India, as in Africa, the noneconomic value of cattle has handicapped range-management progress. The cow, introduced by the invading Aryans over 3000 years ago, is an object of religious veneration to many Hindus. Sacred cows, unrestricted and unconfined, damage both range and agricultural lands. India is a country that normally would support forest. But over much of the peninsula, forests have been completely eliminated to make room for grazing or cropland. Overgrazing, combined with gathering of vegetation for fuel, has done further damage so that, in an area that would have supported productive vegetation, barren desert exists and is spreading. George Schaller (1967) has stated: *India had an estimated 204 million cattle and buffalo and 94 million goats and sheep in 1956, of which 21 million of the former and 13 million of the latter grazed exclusively in the forests. . . . Livestock is permitted to graze without restrictions in virtually all forests and most sanctuaries, and serious damage to the vegetation culminating in widespread erosion is common particularly in the thorn and deciduous forests.*

Efforts on the part of the government to reduce the numbers of cattle have caused riots and the threat of political upheaval.

In the Middle East and the Saharan region, deserts have been spreading and becoming more barren through overgrazing. Writing of Iraq, Bryan and Springfield (1955) have described the virtual elimination of vegetation from the rangelands. Larson (1957) has described devastation in the Libyan desert, and sees no hope for range improvement until such time as the numbers of livestock moved about by nomads can be brought under some control.

In 1978 many of the nations that share land on the southern edge of the Sahara Desert joined in requesting United Nations assistance toward halting the southern march of the Sahara. Yet in virtually all places where a southern extension of the desert has been observed, the cause is the same—failure to control the numbers and distribution of livestock. Planting, reseeding, water development, and virtually every other available means toward improvement of range and livestock are bound to fail unless this control can be exerted. Indeed, most development efforts that have been attempted in this region have aggravated the problem rather than cured it. Water development in areas previously protected from livestock use because of the lack of water brings destruction of these in addition to the destruction of the ones previously grazed.

Australia has been a world leader in the management of pastures in its better watered lands but, in the semiarid lands of the interior, rangelands have been allowed to deteriorate extensively. The presence of exotic pests has handicapped range improvements in many areas. At one time the prickly pear cactus, introduced from Mexico for livestock feed, overran millions of acres of range, forming dense, impenetrable thickets. All efforts at control failed until a biological method was attempted. An insect enemy of the prickly pear was brought in, which fed on and destroyed the cactus. Its extent was thus reduced to manageable proportions. In 1928 and 1930, several million eggs of the *Cactoblastis* moth were brought from Argentina and the larvae hatched out in prickly pear territory. By 1933 the last big area of prickly pear had been cleared out (Ratcliffe, 1947).

The introduction of the European rabbit to Australia greatly aggra-

LIVESTOCK AROUND THE WORLD

(a) Some see hope in new domestic species adapted to extreme environments, such as these reindeer in Sweden's arctic tundra. (b) But livestock have other values; for example, India's "sacred cows" have great religious significance. (c) In the high Andes of Peru, llamas take the place of lowland species. (d) Overgrazing is a problem everywhere. Here goats have cut a network of trails near Baghdad in Iraq.

c

d

vated range problems. Originally brought in by those who felt nostalgic for the rabbit hunting of the Old World, the rabbit spread rapidly throughout much of temperate Australia. Free from the predators and other limiting factors of its homeland, it had no difficulty displacing the native, marsupial mammals. On the arid ranges of the interior the combination of sheep and rabbit grazing was more than the vegetation could withstand. Drifting sand dunes and blowing dust marked the eastward march of the desert into the already narrow belt of productive land. Great sums of money were spent on rabbit control. A fence was built completely across the border between New South Wales and Queensland in hope of confining the rabbit. The effort failed. A new answer was then sought, a biological one. Myxomatosis, a virus disease endemic among cottontails in South America, but fatal to the European rabbit, was introduced. Spread from one rabbit colony to another by mosquitoes, it proved to be initially highly effective in reducing the rabbit population. Undoubtedly tens of millions of rabbits died. Rangelands, held back by rabbit grazing, began to recover. But the rabbit did not disappear. Here and there rabbits survived, apparently disease-resistant, and these are building up a new strain of hardier rabbits against which some new more virulent strain of the disease will undoubtedly be applied.

With rabbits temporarily under control, their place on the arid lands was taken by the native kangaroos, the red kangaroo in the steppe, the grey kangaroo in the scrub, the wallaroo or euro in western Australia. A war against kangaroos was underway before the war against rabbits had ceased. Arid lands are unstable ecosystems. Further simplication of their biota from grazing pressure of domestic livestock increases their instability.

It would be possible to go on for pages, reciting stories of successes and failures in managing rangelands. It is enough, perhaps, to emphasize that, throughout the world, livestock have a place in balanced land use. With increasing populations this place will grow in importance. It becomes urgent therefore to institute effective range management in all lands, before rangelands are pushed downhill on the successional scale to a point of no return.

SOURCES

Bryan, H. M. and H. Springfield, 1955. Range management in Iraq. *Journal of Range Management* 8:249–256.

Dyksterhuis, E. J., 1949. Condition and management of rangeland based on quantitative ecology. *Journal of Range Management* 2:104–115.

Council on Environmental Quality, 1980. *The global 2000 report to the president.* U.S. Government Printing Office, Washington, D.C.

Forest Service, 1936. *The western range.* Senate Doc. 199, Washington, D.C.

Gabriel, Alfons, 1969. The geography of the Sahara. *Sahara,* Putnam, New York.

Golley, Frank, 1978. *Proceedings of the U.S. Strategy Conference on tropical deforestation.* U.S. Department of State, Washington, D.C.

Gomez-Pompa, A., C. Vazquez-Yanes, and S. Guevara, 1972. The tropical rain forest: a non-renewable resource. *Science* 177:762–765.

Grover, D. I., 1945. *Range condition, a classification of the annual forage type.* Soil Conservation Service, Washington, D.C.

Janzen, Daniel, 1970. The unexploited tropics. *Bulletin of the Ecological Society of America* 51:4–7.

Larson, F. D., 1957. Problems of population pressure upon the desert range. *Journal of Range Management* 10:160–161.

Lowenthal, David, 1956. Western Europe. Haden Guest, et al., editors, *World geography of forest resources.* Ronald Press, New York.

Ovington, J. D., 1965. *Woodlands.* English University Press, London.

Persson, R., 1974. *World forest resources.* Royal College Forestry, Stockholm.

Pyles, Hamilton, 1970. *What's ahead for our public lands.* Natural Resources Council, Washington, D.C.

Ratcliffe, Francis, 1947. *Flying fox and drifting sand.* Angus and Robertson, Sydney.

Richards, P. W., 1952. *The tropical rain forest.* Cambridge University Press, Cambridge, U.K.

Show, S. B., 1949. The world forest situation. *Trees.* Yearbook of Agriculture, Washington, D.C.

Schaller, George, 1967. *The deer and the tiger.* University of Chicago Press, Chicago.

Sommer, Adrian, 1976. Attempt at an assessment of the world's tropical forests. *Unasylva* 28:5–25.

U.S. Department of Commerce. Bureau of the Census, 1981. Statistical Abstract of the United States. Government Printing Office, Washington, D.C.

Weaver, J. E., 1954. *North American prairie.* Johnson, Lincoln, Neb.

Webb, Maryla and Judith Jacobsen, 1982. *U.S. carrying capacity—an introduction.* Carrying Capacity, Washington, D.C.

Whittaker, R. H. and E. L. Likens, 1975. The biosphere and man. *Primary productivity of the biosphere,* Lieth H. and R. H. Whittaker, editors. Springer-Verlag, New York.

CHAPTER
11

THE WILDEST LANDS

CHANGES

They were always out there, for as long as people have been on earth—
the lands across the river, the other side of the mountain, those places
up in the hills where people did not usually go, the frontier. Throughout
the entire human story there has been a backdrop of wilderness against
which the action of farm and homestead, village and city has been played.
It seemed there were always more lands, more timber, more pastures,
more wild animals to give substance to the myth of inexhaustible resources.

For Americans, even after most of the country was settled there were
still the areas yet untamed, the wild mountains, or southern swamps, or
the deserts. But beyond that there were the more magic places, names
to excite the adventurous spirit—Africa, the Arctic, the Himalayas, the
Amazon, the really wildest lands. We want to believe they are still there,
just as we want to believe there are "Pacific paradises" that we have not
yet spoiled. Television fosters the myth, with its never-ending wild animal series, hovering near "prime time," occasionally even invading it.

But in those "magic places," the people who have always lived
there still believe the myth also—even though in their latest excursion
into the rainforest or the desert they have encountered the villages or the
herds of those who had moved in from the other side. People cannot
accept the rate of change that is going on; it is too fast and it takes place
within the lifetime of those who were brought to adulthood in a seeming
changeless land. Nobody before had to worry about taking care of the
forest, or the wild animals—they took care of themselves, or God watched
over them. They had not been human concerns. It is asking too much
for people to believe that in just 5, 10, or 20 years all the rules have
changed, that what "always was" is no longer.

Increasingly we are drawing lines on the map, attempting to separate
the wild from the tamed. We designate lands as wilderness areas, nature
reserves, national parks, and we say that these are no longer places
where people can live, or take from, or use in any way except the way
of the visitor who comes to look, but not to inferefere. This is difficult
for people who have always lived in wild country and consider themselves a part of it.

There may have been areas on earth, rich and teeming with life,
that were seemingly devoid of people. But most such areas in reality
were visited at least seasonsally, or occasionally, by hunting or gathering
parties; or they were used by the shamans or the young people on a
"vision quest." The really barren, lifeless areas of the poles, the most
arid deserts, the highest mountains were not occupied by people, and

> *We did not think of the great open plains, the beautiful rolling hills, and winding streams with tangled growth as "wild." Only to the white man was nature a "wilderness" and only to him was the land "infested" with "wild" animals and "savage" people. To us it was tame. Earth was bountiful and we were surrounded with the blessings of the Great Mystery. Not until the hairy man from the east came and with brutal frenzy heaped injustices upon us and the families we loved was it "wild" for us. When the very animals of the forest began fleeing from his approach, then it was that for us the "Wild West" began.*
>
> Chief Luther Standing Bear, of the Oglala Sioux. Cited in
> T. C. McLuhan, *Touch the Earth*, 1972.

in some of these places no visitors came. But they are still pretty much that way today. Most of the land we designate as formal wilderness or set aside in national parks is land passed on to us by people who considered it, in part at least, their homeland. We considered it to be of national park quality or worthy to be designated a "World Heritage Site" because they, the original inhabitants, did not treat it the way we do land, did not treat its animals the way we have treated wildlife. They cared. So they have gone, and our formal designations, our wardens and partrols, take their place. Something seems to have gone wrong somewhere along the way (Dasmann, 1982).

> *We were lawless people, but we were on pretty good terms with the Great Spirit, creator and ruler of all. You whites assumed we were savages. You didn't try to understand. When we sang our praises to the sun or moon or wind, you said we were worshipping idols. Without understanding, you condemned us as lost souls just because our form of worship was different than yours.*
>
> *We saw the Great Spirit's work in almost everything: sun, moon, trees, wind, and mountains. Sometimes we approached him through these things. Was that so bad? I think we have a true belief in the supreme being, a stronger faith than that of most whites who have called us pagans. . . . Indians living close to nature and nature's ruler are not living in darkness.*
>
> *Did you know that trees talk? Well they do. They talk to each other, and they'll talk to you if you listen. Trouble is, white people don't listen. They never learned to listen to the Indians so I don't suppose they'll listen to other voices in nature. But I have learned a lot from trees: sometimes about the weather, sometimes about animals, sometimes about the Great Spirit.*
>
> Tatanga Mani (Walking Buffalo). Stoney Indian. Cited in
> T. C. McLuhan, *Touch the Earth* 1972.

PROTECTED AREAS

Since the protection of Yosemite Valley in 1864 and the establishment of Yellowstone National Park in 1872, interest in the establishment of protected areas, available for recreation and visitation, but not for exploitation, has grown, not only in the United States but throughout the world. In Canada, in South Africa, and in the British and French colonial areas, which then extended around the world, national parks were set aside during the late nineteenth and early twentieth centuries. In Europe proper, however, the American idea of a national park has not attracted a great deal of support. There are many protected areas, but mostly these have criteria different from the national parks of the United States. In England, for example, what is called a national park is quite open to settlement and use for farming, grazing, wood-cutting, dam-building, and so on under agreed-upon controls. It is a tourist area, but not really a nature reserve. What is called a nature reserve, however, is essentially a national park—although tourism may not be encouraged to the same extent as in North America.

The International Union for the Conservation of Nature (IUCN) has been trying for many years to sort out and classify the various kinds of protected areas established in the different countries of the world. The results are presented in Table 11.1. They range from the strict nature reserves, which may be entered only for authorized scientific study (which will not disrupt or disturb natural conditions) to multiple-use areas, which are similar to the national forests of the United States. The name and the reality, however, often do not resemble each other. Some reserves, although legally established and vouched for by the authorities, in reality are fully occupied by "illegal" settlements. People have moved in and the authorities fear to push them out, not wanting political repercussions. In other countries the authorities charged with administration of parks

TABLE 11.1   Protected Areas

Group I. Areas important for nature conservation, either as a first priority, or among priority uses.
  1. Strict nature reserve/scientific reserve
  2. National park
  3. Natural monument or landmark
  4. Managed nature reserve/wildlife sanctuary
  5. Protected landscape
Group II. Areas important for general environmental conservation
  6. Resource reserve/interim conservation unit
  7. Anthropological reserve/natural biotic area
  8. Multiple use area/managed resource area
Group III. Internationally recognized for special protection
  9. Biosphere reserve (UNESCO)
  10. World heritage site (UNESCO)

Source: Adapted and modified from IUCN (1978).

TABLE 11.2   World Distribution of National Parks and Nature Reserves

BIOGEOGRAPHICAL REALM	NO. OF AREAS	AREA IN HECTARES
Nearctic	308	138,807,800
Palaearctic	726	44,669,119
Afrotropical	361	112,520,047
Indomalayan	382	22,349,480
Oceanian	37	3,417,513
Australian	372	31,112,883
Antarctic (incl. New Zealand)	108	2,706,156
Neotropical	324	44,611,738
Total	2618	400,193,736
Selected major biomes		
Tundra	32	101,266,252
Tropical dry forests, savannas	544	83,306,109
Deserts and semideserts	226	76,742,567
Subtropical and temperate forests	930	57,757,000
Tropical humid forests	335	44,999,157
Mixed mountain systems	397	29,577,946
Temperate grasslands	76	4,553,341
Mixed island systems	69	1,564,141

Source: IUCN (1982).

and reserves seldom leave the capital city. Thus they are saved from any bruising encounters with reality.

The United Nations List of National Parks represents an attempt by IUCN to separate the wheat from the chaff and to give recognition to those parks that are both in fact protected and of significant size (more than 1000 hectares except for island parks). The list is impressive—over 2600 in 1982 (Table 11.2 and Fig. 11.1). There are also some 354 marine parks (not all listed). But on second look the impressiveness diminishes. Although we hear a great deal of opposition to the idea of "locking up" large areas for the purpose of protecting nature, in fact the area that is protected is deplorably small, probably about 3 percent of the land area, worldwide. We have attempted to analyze this situation in greater detail for Africa, using 1980 data (Table 11.3).

The situation in Africa is revealing of the overall picture in the Third World. Africa has a higher percentage of its area protected in national parks and reserves than either Latin America or Asia. There has also been more money, coming from private and government sources in the industrialized world, going to Africa to help in the development and maintenance of African parks and reserves than has been spent in either of the other tropical regions. The reason for this rests primarily in the worldwide appeal of the spectacular wildlife of Africa. Nevertheless, the situation in Africa is depressing. Less than 3 percent of its land area is included within national parks or nature reserves that meet United Nations standards. This means that 97 percent of the area is available for

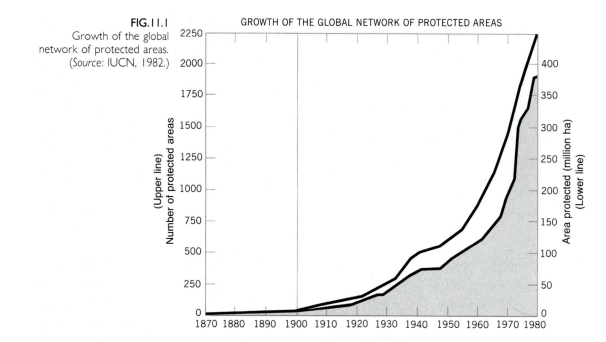

FIG.11.1
Growth of the global
network of protected areas.
(*Source:* IUCN, 1982.)

GROWTH OF THE GLOBAL NETWORK OF PROTECTED AREAS

direct use and exploitation in ways that involve extraction of minerals, harvesting of timber, conversion to agriculture, or other uses intended to directly benefit humans. One would think, however, from the statements of many African delegates at international meetings that the strain of maintaining 3 percent of the land free from exploitation was more than their people could bear. This despite the fact that tourism based on national parks and reserves has been an important source of foreign exchange to all of those countries that have attempted to capitalize on their wild heritage.

Africa is by no means a uniform continent, and attitudes toward the protection of the environment are as various as the governments and people. Southern Africa has the best overall record in establishing and maintaining protected natural areas. Botswana has a higher percentage of its land (17 percent) in national parks and reserves than any other country. Namibia (under South African administration), Zambia, and Zimbabwe have 8 percent of their land in national parks and reserves. Eastern Africa is second in its overall record of protection of natural areas; however, only three countries—Rwanda, Tanzania, and Uganda, each with 12 percent of their land area protected—have earned that second place. Uganda, however, has been so torn apart by war and internal turmoil that its natural areas can hardly be considered protected. It is noticeable that Kenya, which makes the most money from tourism based on its national parks, is not one of the African leaders in percentage of land protected.

The most disturbing record is that of Northern Africa, which shares with most of the Islamic world an apparent disregard for the protection of nature and for environmental conservation in general. Less than 1 percent of its area is protected. Much of this is contributed by one very large reserve in Chad, which in fact was never very well protected, and now as a result of continued internal wars is probably not protected at all. Chad and the Sudan contribute what little nature protection occurs in the Moslem part of Africa, and their reserves are for the most part located outside the Islamic area of Africa.

Most, but not all, of Africa is still going on with a system of parks and reserves set up under colonial administrations—British, French, Portuguese. They have not yet officially disbanded these reserves, but neither do most countries do much to protect them. There are the exceptions, and some are outstanding—Cameroons, Ghana, Botswana, Zambia, and Zaire to mention a few—where reserves have been expanded since independence and are for the most part taken seriously. But these are still exceptions. Unfortunately, the whole truth will not be heard in United Nations meetings, nor will it even be spoken by supposedly private and independent organizations such as the International Union for the Conservation of Nature or the World Wildlife Fund. They depend too much on the goodwill of governments. (See Table 11.3 on pp. 348–349)

The idea behind the establishment of nature reserves and similar areas should be an attempt to put things back together, to integrate the conservation of human cultures with the conservation of the natural world. This should be done in part to encourage those who have cared for the land in the past to continue to do so, and in part to encourage those who have not cared to begin to take an interest in conservation of nature, to realize that their future is tied in with the future of the natural environment and with the proper use of the lands and resources on which they depend for their livelihood.

In fact, the national parks, nature reserves, and other protected areas of the world have most commonly been established without the advice or consent of the people most likely to be directly affected by their establishment. Without the support or at worst acceptance by these people, the future of any protected area cannot be considered secure, since in their search for the means for their own survival, the temptation to take wildland resources from the area or to encroach upon its boundaries will tend to be irresistible. Furthermore, the prospect for extending any system of protected areas to take in new lands or waters becomes increasingly dim where popular support for protection of nature is lacking.

INDIGENOUS PEOPLE

In attempting to work with people who live in or near areas that have been designated as having protected status by the government of the

TABLE 11.3   National Parks and Nature Reserves of Africa

	NUMBER	AREA IN 100 km²	TOTAL LAND AREA 100 km²	PERCENT OF LAND AREA PROTECTED
SOUTHERN AFRICA				
Angola	5	481	12,467	4
Botswana	9	1,046	6,004	17
Lesotho	1	1	304	<1
Malawi	3	52	1,185	4
Mozambique	4	159	7,838	2
Namibia	9	628	8,232	8
South Africa	25	326	12,222	3
Swaziland	4	4	174	2
Zambia	18	594	7,526	8
Zimbabwe	18	289	3,906	8
Total/Mean	96	3,576	58,850	6
EASTERN AFRICA				
Burundi	0	0	278	0
Djibouti	0	0	230	0
Ethiopia	2	9	12,219	<1
Kenya	15	293	5,826	5
Rwanda	2	27	263	12
Somalia	1	33	6,377	<1
Tanzania	17	1,146	9,451	12
Uganda	16	170	2,359	12
Total/Mean	53	1,679	37,003	5
CENTRAL AFRICA				
Central African Republic	3	56	6,226	1
Cameroon	12	224	4,754	5
Congo	9	103	3,420	3
Equatorial Guinea	0	0	281	0
Gabon	1	36	2,677	2
Sao Tome/Principe	0	0	10	0
Zaire	7	803	23,454	3
Total/Mean	32	1,221	41,121	3
WESTERN AFRICA				
Benin	2	78	1,126	7
Cape Verde	0	0	40	0
Gambia	0	0	113	0
Ghana	5	105	2,385	5
Guinea	1	1	2,459	<1

country concerned, or areas that are considered worthy of some form of legal protection, there is danger that we will confuse ourselves by our own terminology. If we designate some people as "indigenous" and consequently worthy of special consideration, we leave other people in the category of "nonindigenous" and consequently not worthy of special consideration. I do not believe we can risk such a dichotomy, which

TABLE 11.3   National Parks and Nature Reserves of Africa (*Continued*)

	NUMBER	AREA IN 100 km²	TOTAL LAND AREA 100 km²	PERCENT OF LAND AREA PROTECTED
Guinea-Bissau	0	0	361	0
Ivory Coast	9	180	3,225	6
Liberia	0	0	1,114	0
Nigeria	5	185	9,238	2
Senegal	6	101	1,967	5
Sierra Leone	1	2	717	<1
Togo	3	6	560	1
Upper Volta	4	46	2,742	2
Total/Mean	36	704	26,047	3
NORTHERN AFRICA				
Algeria	0	0	23,817	0
Chad	3	841	12,840	7
Egypt	0	0	10,020	0
Libya	2	14	17,595	<1
Mali	1	8	12,397	<1
Mauritania	2	118	10,307	1
Morocco	0	0	4,466	0
Niger	2	48	12,670	<1
Sudan	14	367	25,059	2
Tunisia	2	1	1,642	<1
Western Sahara	0	0	2,660	0
Total/Mean	26	1,407	133,500	<1
AFRICA TOTALS				
Total/Mean	243	8,578	296,521	3

SUMMARY

PERCENTAGE OF LAND AREA PROTECTED	NUMBER OF COUNTRIES
0	12
1–2	18
3–4	5
5–6	5
7–8	5
9–10	0
11+	4
Total	49

Source: IUCN (1980).

from the outset establishes two classes of citizens, one with special privileges, and the other presumably to be kicked around as usual.

In one sense there are no indigenous people—all have ancestors who have come from somewhere else. At some time every native group was an invader, an exotic coming from some other place. There are, however, marked differences in how long each of us has been in a

NATIONAL PARKS AND OUTDOOR RECREATION

National parks, at their best, protect undisturbed areas and secure them for the future. Much of the justification used to finance the national park system, however, is based on the role they play in attracting tourism to a region, or in meeting popular demand for outdoor recreation. Conservation and mass tourism may conflict within a national park. (a) The future of the cheetah is not secure. In Africa's national parks it is vulnerable to disturbance by tourists.

d

(b) In the American national parks backpacking is a means for reaching the wilderness—but only the hardy and fit can go that way. (c) Rocky Mountains National Park retains wilderness values near the metropolis of Denver. (d) Mass recreation, such as skiing, has many followers but is disruptive to national parks. (e) In the Great Smoky Mountains National Park, the wilderness has been restored following a long period of human settlement.

e

particular place and the degree to which we have adapted our ways of life to that area. Some can trace their ancestry in a particular area back over centuries; others have just arrived and do not intend to stay. Some are entirely dependent on the resources of a particular area; others come to visit, to trade, or to raid, and have their source of livelihood elsewhere. Attitudes toward land and resources can differ depending on background, tradition, and degree of allegiance to a particular living area. There are therefore real differences between people in relation to their response to the need to manage or protect the resources of an area. These, however, cannot be resolved by a simple native/non-native dichotomy. Some natives only wish to go somewhere else; some non-natives deeply desire to become natives and to cherish and care for the land they occupy.

duty to be loyal

Earlier we have attempted to distinguish e*cosystem people* as those who live within an ecosystem or several adjacent and related ecosystems and are dependent on those resources for their existence (Dasmann, 1974). Such people must over time learn to live within the ecological limitations of their home area if they are to survive. Although individually they may not have a strongly developed ecological consciousness, culturally they are committed to sustainable ways of life that are essentially sound in ecological terms. By contrast, *biosphere people* are those tied in to the *global economy*, whose livelihood is not necessarily dependent on the resources of any one particular ecosystem. No dichotomy is intended with this terminology, but rather an indication of the extremes of a cultural continuum. Much of the difficulty encountered in attempting to achieve ecologically sustainable ways of life comes from people who are in transition from one extreme to the other: their cultures have been disrupted or destroyed, and with that their means of working with the natural environment to which their ancestors were adapted, but they have not yet achieved any firm foothold in the global economy.

From the viewpoint of cultural conservation, it is obvious that the ecosystem people are the most likely to be adversely affected by contact with representatives of the more dominant culture, including those who come with the intention of establishing nature reserves. They are also the people who have in the past maintained the ecological conditions that today are favorable to the establishment of nature reserves. Does this mean that they should be given favored status? Does their past record of occupancy of the area, including care for the wild species within it, entitle them to remain in place even when the interests of the national government and the international community dictate that nature conservation should be given first priority in that area? If the answer is yes, should this entitlement remain even after they adopt the ways of the dominant society—when automatic weapons replace bows and arrows? (Goodland, 1982).

We would suggest that all people who live in an area and consider it to be their home must have similar rights and be given equal consideration when planning for nature reserves or other protected areas. The question to be asked is not whether or not they are indigenous, but whether or not their ways of life are compatible with the objectives and goals of conservation. Hunter-gatherers who have traditionally been conservative in their use of wildlife and plant resources and who constitute no threat to the future of wild species in that area should be encouraged to remain within a nature reserve and to participate actively in its protection. This arrangement can work, however, only so long as their numbers and their resource utilization remain in balance with the productive capacity of the area. As Brownrigg (1982) has pointed out, in "protected areas planning must also anticipate population increases and culture change. It is unrealistic to expect a group to atrophy, or worse, to return to some traditional technology long ago discarded in favour of a more modern alternative." Agreement must be reached, however, for population surpluses to be accommodated elsewhere, and for resource utilization, whether traditional or modern in its technology, to remain within prescribed limits. Otherwise the goal of nature conservation is sacrificed.

Hunter-gatherers, fisherfolk, hunter-gardeners, shifting cultivators and pastoral nomads could in theory all be accommodated within protected areas, providing they agree to the limitations already described. But the same rules must apply to nontraditional peoples who occupy areas of high priority for nature conservation, including those primarily involved in raising cash crops for export. If their ways of using the land do not conflict with nature conservation priorities, and if they agree to limitations on their numbers and their use of resources, they can equally be welcomed within a protected area and be asked to join in the activities of protecting and managing the reserve.

To say these things is easier than to do them. If the doors of the national parks and reserves are to be opened to some people, perhaps under carefully defined conditions, then what about others who also claim rights to the land or resources of the area? Are those with ownership rights that have been formally recognized by the government to be treated differently from those with traditional rights dating back into the distant past that are not formally recognized? What about those, such as many American Indian nations, that once had formal rights, established by treaty, but have lost their land to others or to the government despite these agreements? Furthermore, are we to agree to one set of conditions governing the establishment of protected areas in the nonindustrialized world that do not also apply to the industrialized world? Are the Sioux in the Black Hills to be treated differently from the Yanamani in the northern Amazon basin? Do we need a uniform code for the treatment of peoples whose cultures or means of livelihood are likely to be affected by the establishment of protected areas? It can be one that takes into account the special problems of endangered peoples, just as wildlife laws become more restrictive when a species is endangered. It must be flexible enough to recognize that some people can be compensated in cash for the lands or resources they may be asked to sacrifice but that others cannot. Those who cannot are not only those with traditional rights or communal ownership but all those who closely identify with the land and the natural environment where they live—the new natives on whom the future may depend.

NATURE RESERVES AS ISLANDS

Since the work of MacArthur and Wilson (1967) there has been increasing interest in the concepts of island biogeography as these apply to the size, shape, and distribution of national parks, nature reserves, and other protected areas. The prospect that areas designated for nature conservation may in the future exist as islands surrounded by lands used intensively for the production of food and other necessities for human survival has caused serious concern that these areas may be inadequate to provide for the survival of the species originally contained within them. The basis for this concern has been explored in books by Soulé and Wilcox (1980) and Frankel and Soulé (1981). (See Table 11.4.) To counteract any tendency toward insularization of nature reserves, the UNESCO Biosphere Reserve project (UNESCO—MAB, 1974) has proposed that such reserves consist of a fully protected core area (strict nature reserve) surrounded by buffer zones that may be used for recreation (national parks) or compatible forms of resource exploitation (managed forests, rangelands, hunting areas, etc.) grading outward to more intensively used areas. Although many designated biosphere reserves do not fit these criteria, those national park systems that have been reasonably successful for nature conservation, such as those of the United States and Canada,

TABLE 11.4 Effects of Insularization (estimated number of extinctions since time of island formation related to island size)

ISLAND	AREA, km²	INITIAL NO. OF SPECIES	PRESENT NUMBER	PERCENT EXTINCTIONS
		Land mammals		
Borneo	751,709	153	123	20
Sumatra	425,485	139	117	16
Java	126,806	113	74	35
Bali	5,443	66	19	71
		Land birds		
Ceylon	65,688	239	171	28
Hainan	33,710	198	123	38
Trinidad	4,834	350	220	37
Fernando Po	2,036	360	128	64

Data from Wilcox, Terborgh, and Winter in Soulé and Wilcox (1980).
These examples illustrate the general tendency for survival to relate to the size of the island. Since these islands are not comparable in land use or human population, rates of extinction vary for reasons not entirely related to island size.

do have *de facto* buffer zones surrounding and often connecting the national parks. These are for the most part federal, state, or provincial areas in which use is controlled and managed with a view toward sustainability. Furthermore, even beyond these protected areas the general level of land management is reasonably good, and the common attitude of the human population is at least indifferent and benign, and at best highly favorable to nature conservation. As a result many towns and cities are *de facto* bird sanctuaries, supporting an unusual abundance and diversity of wild bird species as well as a surprising variety of small mammals.

In those parts of the United States where nature conservation is most successful, it is not the nature areas that are islands, but the human communities. The pattern of human use is such that cities, towns, and intensively used rural areas form a pattern of large and small islands connected by transportation corridors, but surrounded by much larger areas within which native vegetation and animal life survive very well.

The future of no country is likely to be secure, and certainly no system of parks and reserves will survive, if we attempt to set up systems of protected areas—no matter how well distributed—within a system of land use that otherwise is contributing to the degradation of soils and the declining productivity of renewable resources and is relying on heavy inputs of agricultural chemicals including pesticides to compensate for a deteriorating resource base. In considering the relationships of people to protected areas, therefore, we must look well beyond the boundaries of those areas and work with the local people to create ecologically sustainable systems of land and resource use. Nature reserves must be seen as parts of those systems, not separate from them. Obviously, people must see the opportunity for economic stability in a context of ecological sustainability before they will take a serious interest in protecting the wild environments of protected areas.

Without in any way denying the importance of strict nature reserves, national parks, or other closely protected areas, equal attention must be paid to universal rules of land use and nature protection that apply throughout the country. In various calculations of minimum population size needed to maintain the genetic diversity within a wild animal species and the minimum area of a protected reserve needed to maintain that population, it becomes apparent that we will never have a system of nature reserves or national parks adequate in themselves to protect all wild species (Soulé and Wilcox, (1980). We must be able to rely on the rational use and management of lands outside the reserves. (Swanson, 1978).

To protect wolves and caribou the magnificent system of national parks and nature reserves in the state of Alaska is likely to be inadequate. For those species alone we need virtually the entire state of Alaska. Fortunately, we *have* the entire state of Alaska, for the wildlife laws of that state, which apply to all areas, will, if enforced, offer the necessary degree of protection. Attention to rules of land use and nature conservation that apply everywhere and not just to areas within or near protected natural areas is required. We need to recognize that planet earth was originally established as a nature reserve, the only one we know of in the entire universe. We need to keep it that way.

ESTABLISHMENT OF PROTECTED AREAS

SUGGESTED PRINCIPLES OR GUIDELINES

As a contribution to the World National Parks Conference, held in Bali, in 1982, the following principles and guidelines were prepared (Dasmann, 1982):

General Principle
The conservation of nature is fundamental to human existence and is the concern of all people everywhere. It is not to be accomplished only by the setting aside of specially protected natural areas, but must be practiced in all places at all times. All areas must be protected areas to some degree, since even the most heavily urbanized areas provide suitable living spaces for many wild species.

Ownership, Tenure, and Resource Use
The rights of land ownership, tenure, or resource use do not include the right to land degradation or resource abuse. Recognition of such rights by governments should be dependent upon agreements for reasonable care and stewardship over the land and its resources.

Protected Natural Areas
The establishment of protected natural areas intended to provide for the conservation of biotic communities or wild species can be of direct benefit to the peoples and communities in surrounding or adjacent areas, but without adequate attention to the interactions between people and the natural environment such establishment can also have adverse effects on their economies or cultures. To provide for long-term positive interactions, the following guidelines are potentially useful.

Use of Local Knowledge. People who have a long history of use or occupancy of areas to be considered for protection also have a familiarity with its species, communities, and ecological processes that cannot readily be gained through surveys, inventories, or base-line studies by experts from elsewhere. In particular long-term trends or fluctuations in abundance and distribution of wild species, past influences and changes, values, and usefulness for human purposes can be determined most easily from local people. Consultation with these people is essential to gain the knowledge important for both conservation and the avoidance of conflict.

Local Involvement with Planning of Protected Areas. Planning of protected areas should involve those people who are most likely to be directly affected, positively or negatively, by implementation of protected area status. Every effort should be made to achieve the desired conservation objective with minimum disruption of traditional ways of life and maximum benefit to local people. Boundaries of protected areas and regulations governing their protection and use should reflect the actual conservation objectives to be accomplished and the ways in which these can be achieved through local cooperation, rather than attempting to adhere to internationally approved categories. A simple conservation rule that has local adherence and support may accomplish more than a national park that has not.

Local Involvement with Management and Conservation. Insofar as possible local people should be involved with management and conservation practices within a protected area. All of them, at best, should take an active interest in protection of the area. At the least, they should provide the guards, wardens, rangers, and laborers.

Use of Protected Areas to Safeguard Native Cultures. People who have traditionally lived in isolation from the dominant cultures within a country may be protected from unwanted outside interference by establishment of a protected area that includes all of the lands they have traditionally used—giving them the authority to exclude outsiders and to manage the lands as they see fit. Protected natural areas are also useful as buffer zones surrounding the traditional lands of isolated cultures. Outsiders are in this way controlled by the protected-area authorities. Neither of these options is intended to exclude interaction or travel on the part of the native group. The reserve boundary or buffer zone has a "one-way screen" keeping out unwanted visitors but not holding people inside who wish to leave.

Economic Benefits. Economic benefits derived from a protected area from tourism or other forms of use must be shared with local people according to agreements and contracts reached before the protected area is established. For existing protected areas, renegotiation with local people will be important to give them a greater role in maintaining the protected status of the area.

Definition of "Local People." The people directly affected by the establishment of a protected area often include many who are not permanent inhabitants of the area or its vicinity. Other groups may use the area seasonally—migratory hunter-gatherers, nomadic pastoralists, and the like. Still others may use the area only occasionally, but those occasions may have great importance in relation to religion, ceremony, or long-term subsistence needs; that is, the area may already be a "reserve" for people who do not live there permanently. All of these people must be considered in reserve planning, conservation, use, and economy.

Planning and Development of Surrounding Areas. Planning or development of protected areas must not be undertaken in isolation from planning and development of the lands surrounding the protected areas to provide a viable and sustainable economic future for the people involved. The principles of agroecology and agroforestry as well as wildlife management should be considered in the planning and development of these areas. The basic principles of ecodevelopment should be applied. The *conservation unit* approach developed by W. J. Lusigi (1978) for Kenya may provide a useful model, as well as the biosphere reserve model by UNESCO—MAB.

UNITED STATES RESERVES AND NATIONAL PARKS

The United States took an early lead in the establishment of areas protected in order to maintain natural environments in relatively pristine conditions with its establishment of the first national parks. According to the IUCN list published in 1982, there were 37 national parks ranging in size from Denali (Mount McKinley) in Alaska (2,356,000 hectares) to the Hot Springs of Arkansas (2358 hectares). Listed also were 41 national monuments, also administered by the National Park Service. These are sometimes as effectively protected as a national park, but some are open to grazing, mining, or other restricted uses. The largest of these was the Wrangell–St. Elias area in Alaska (4,825,238 hectares), one of the largest protected areas in the world. Also administered by the National Park Service are national seashores, lakeshores, and recreation areas. Although primarily intended for outdoor recreation, and often including farms or ranching activities, these provide considerable protection for wild species. Thirty such areas were included in the IUCN list.

The United States Fish and Wildlife Service protects the National Wildlife Refuges and other wildlife areas, of which 127 are included in the 1982 list, including the 7,306,596-hectare Arctic National Wildlife Refuge. These are protected to the degree necessary to assure that the wild animal populations contained within them continue to thrive. Hunting may or may not be excluded, but is always controlled. Other uses—mining, grazing, wood cutting—may be permitted if they do not interfere with wildlife protection.

Congress in 1964 passed the Wilderness Act, which established a national wilderness system. This was intended to provide additional protection for those areas still remaining in a natural state, without roads or other major disturbance. Wilderness status rules out the use of motorized transport, including airplanes, within the area and prevents logging or other major modifications of the vegetation or landscape although grazing may be permitted, and in some wilderness areas some mining has been allowed. All of the areas included in the wilderness system were already protected by the Forest Service, Park Service, Fish and Wildlife Service, or Bureau of Land Management. Wilderness status, however, provides another layer of protection that cannot be set aside by administrative decrees.

As noted earlier, all of these more strictly protected areas benefit from being surrounded by the protected, multiple-use areas administered by the Forest Service or Bureau of Land Management. They are located in states where fishing and hunting are carefully controlled by state regulation. They are not islands.

The Alaska National Interest Lands Conservation Act passed by Congress late in 1980 and signed by President Carter totally changed the statistics for many categories of protected areas. One hundred and four million acres were added to protected categories. The National Wilderness System increased to over 80 million acres. Over 43 million acres of national parks were established (some had been national monuments). Nearly 54 million acres were added to the national wildlife refuge system and 13 new rivers were added to the national wild and scenic rivers system. Among the new wilderness areas was the Wrangell–St. Elias National Park of 8.7 million acres. This adjoins the Kluane National Park of Canada, over 5 million acres in size, to make it the second largest protected wilderness on earth. Only Greenland's national park is larger, but it consists mostly of glacial ice.

WILDLIFE

People began worrying about the disappearance of wild animals from their vicinity long before they worried about the condition of wild country in general. We find from the earliest days of civilization a tendency to establish hunting preserves, where the king and the nobility could hunt. Presumably these took the place of the general wild environment that was there before the cultivated lands and the domestic livestock began to occupy much of the space around the city. Accounts of successful hunts fill some of the earliest records of the comings and goings of monarchs. This would fit with Mumford's idea that the rulers of the first cities came from hunting peoples rather than the agriculturalists.

We have postulated in an earlier book (Dasmann, 1981) that human attitudes toward wild animals changed with the first dependence on domesticated plants and animals. The deer, antelope, or elephants that were admired and tolerated by hunter-gatherers took on a different aspect when they began to raid the gardens and fields, and perhaps consume in a single night what people had planned to use as their food for the year. Certainly the large predators ceased to be mere competitors for meat, and only sometimes enemies, and took on a more sinister role when they began to feed on chickens, pigs, sheep, goats, or cattle. The division between wild and tame must have become marked, way back at the beginning (Shepard, 1982). It happens to people today, normally inclined to like all animals, when the deer first come into the young orchard, or the gophers remove the year's supply of artichokes. Suddenly their furry coats and big brown eyes lose their appeal. But the attitude of the hunter-gatherer persisted alongside that of the farmer. Wildlife was wanted, but not too close to home.

We find all kinds of strange attitudes and superstitions growing up around wild places and wild animals. Certainly the deep, dark woods—the still mostly undisturbed wilderness that surrounded the villages of ancient and medieval Europe—was feared by many of the farming folk. They became the haunts of trolls and goblins, of witches and elves. Anything might live there—and not just fierce wild animals. But fierce wild animals became even fiercer in the imagination. Wolves became demonic beings, even though evidence of wolf attacks on people is hard to find (Lopez, 1978). They were transmuted into werewolves, just as in other lands people imagined leopards that became men, grizzly bears that were transformed humans, or were-tigers roaming the jungles of Burma.

But despite this there was a positive concern for the future of wildlife—particularly mild, noncarnivorous wild animals. It was not a concern for all wild animals—that is still hard to find today—but for those more visible, and usually more attractive-looking animals that in America are usually included in the term *wildlife*. (The term has been taken up in England to mean all wild animals and plants, but that serves only to confuse Americans). In Europe this concern, following the aristocratic tradition, resulted in the nobility and landed gentry setting aside reserves where animals were generally protected. In the American colonies the concern resulted in the passage of protective legislation. Most of these laws had little initial effect.

The reality of the settlement of America was for many years a war against nature, with forests being cut and wildlife being slaughtered. Some species became extinct; the passenger pigeon, once present in the tens of millions, is the most familiar example. But the rate of extinction of species was not high. The worst effects were on the elimination of local populations and a great decline in wildlife abundance.

In American law, inherited from the British, wildlife belonged to the sovereign. In England this meant simply the king or queen. In America it was interpreted to mean the sovereign people of each *state*, and not the sovereign people of the United States. Since wildlife was the property of its people, the state through its government had responsibility to protect or dispose of wild animals. States were not quick to take on this responsibility, however, leaving the situation that wildlife belonged to everybody and therefore to nobody—while it was alive. Legally, however, wild animals that were killed became the property of the killer—so long as no laws were broken during the process. This encouraged mass slaughter by commercial meat hunters, plume hunters, egg gatherers, and anyone who figured out a way to make a little money from wildlife exploitation. Legally, also, property owners had a right to protect their property against wildlife—which meant that when cattle or sheep owners began to move their flocks and herds into the public land of the western United States, they were entitled to eliminate any threatening predatory animal. More than that, however, since wildlife was publicly owned, it could be claimed that the public had a responsibility to protect private property from damage caused by its wildlife. Thus the federal and state governments were brought into the business of predatory animal control, resulting in great reductions of numbers of wolves, mountain lions, bears, bobcats, and coyotes (although the latter two were to regain their abundance).

> *Perhaps the first awareness of diminishing wildlife came when early settlers noted a reduction in numbers of the highly visible grazing herds, or the availability of deer near settlements, or a reduction in shad runs into local streams. Without doubt, the absence was first ascribed to a movement of the animals away to some less-disturbed pastures or forest groves or spawning streams. No one would have believed that humans could exterminate so many. But at last, as it finally was with the Bison, the wagonloads of Buffalo hunters came to realize that the lost herd was never going to be found just over the next hill or in the next valley; the towering piles of Buffalo bones at the railheads across the plains, awaiting shipment to the fertilizer makers back East, were testimony to man's predatory prowess. Perhaps never before in human history had so many animals, of different species, been killed in so short a time.*
>
> Thomas L. Kimball and Raymond E. Johnson, *Wildlife and America* (1978), p. 8.

ECOLOGICAL IDEAS

THE KAIBAB STORY
In northern Arizona, in the Grand Canyon country, lives a herd of Rocky Mountain mule deer that has achieved international fame. Here in the Kaibab National Forest the deer are not different in appearance from their relatives elsewhere in the West. What distinguished them was their phenomenal rate of increase and equally rapid decline many decades ago. They were one of the first American wildlife populations to put on a demonstration of what has since been called a population *irruption*. Thus they achieved a measure of immortality in conservation annals.

Before 1906 there were not many deer in the Kaibab country. Nobody knows how many, for sure, but the best guesses say about 4000 animals. Supported in part by this deer population was an abundant population of predatory animals, plains wolves and coyotes, mountain lions and bobcats, and some bears. Sharing the range with them were sheep and cattle in addition to various other wild animals. In 1906, President Theodore Roosevelt, acting in the name of wildlife conservation, proclaimed the Kaibab region a federal game refuge. To make room for more game, the livestock were moved out. To allow the game to increase, trappers were put to work removing the predatory animals.

Operating with great efficiency these men exterminated the wolf and greatly reduced the numbers of other predators.

Without further livestock competition for forage, with complete protection from hunting, and with few remaining natural enemies, the deer population responded. At first the forest rangers and others noted with satisfaction a healthy increase in the number of deer. Soon, a different note was sounded in the Forest Service reports. There were deer everywhere. Tourists could count hundreds in a short walk. Shrubs began to take on a heavily hedged appearance, as though overefficient gardeners had been pruning them. On the aspen trees a browse line was noticed, with all the leaves and small twigs removed as high as a deer could reach. Next, timber-tree reproduction began to suffer and to be killed out from heavy deer browsing. Forest Service reports sounded a warning and requested the deer population be reduced in numbers.

Elsewhere in the country, conservationists and sportsmen were waging what they sometimes thought was a losing battle to save wildlife from extinction. The idea that there could be too many deer, anywhere, was strange and frankly unbelieveable. The Forest Service reports were ignored, even by the game department of Arizona. Meanwhile, the Forest Service was becoming desperate in its efforts to prevent forest damage and what seemed to be inevitable mass starvation for the deer herd, and they attempted to initiate a large-scale hunt to eliminate the excess deer. A wrangle about the rights of the federal government over wildlife as opposed to states' rights developed and went to the high courts of the land. While the controversy went on the deer problem solved itself: the deer died.

Between 1906 and 1924 it is estimated that the Kaibab deer herd may have increased from 4000 to 100,000 animals (Fig. 11.2). Between

FIG. 11.2
The Kaibab deer irruption (from Rasmussen, 1941).

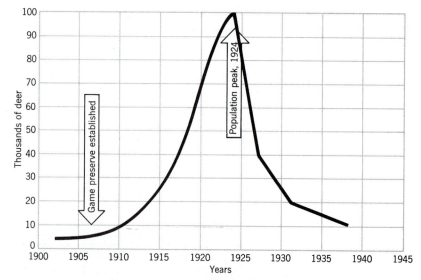

1924 and 1930 perhaps 80,000 deer died from starvation. Between 1930 and 1939 further die-offs reduced the herd by another 10,000 (Rasmussen, 1941).

SOME POPULATION DYNAMICS

The Kaibab example taught some people that protection for wildlife can be carried too far. It demonstrated to game biologists some facts about animal populations that have since been confirmed by numerous studies. One basic fact is that most animals have high reproductive rates. Given favorable conditions an animal population can multiply rapidly. In nature a balance is reached between reproductive capacity and the drains on the population by all of the many factors that bring loss. The number of animals present at any one time depends on the balance between two forces: the *biotic potential,* or maximum rate at which a species can increase if unchecked, and the *environmental resistance* (Fig. 11.3), the sum of all the forces that cause death or lower reproductive gains. If the environmental resistance is lowered, in one way or another, animal populations increase. If a species, such as the Kaibab deer, is freed from natural checks by a great expansion in its habitat or reduction in the

FIG. 11.3
Theoretical population growth curve showing the increase in a deer population in a new environment with a carrying capacity for 500 animals.

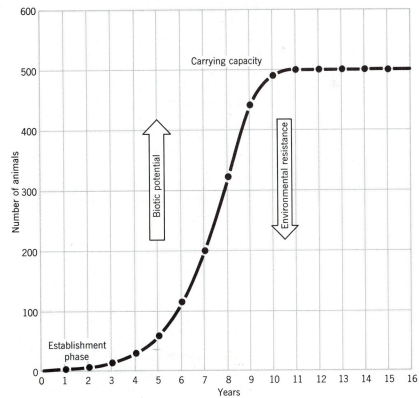

numbers and kinds of enemies, it can increase for a time at a rate determined only by its maximum reproductive ability.

Every habitat, for wildlife as well as for domestic livestock, has its *carrying capacity,* which sets limits on population increase. No wild-animal population can be maintained permanently at a level above the carrying capacity, which is determined by the available food, cover, water, and other essentials for life. Yet each year, a population at carrying capacity will produce young. This crop of young will represent, therefore, an excess above what the environment can support. Either the young must perish or older animals must die to make a place for them. The annual crop of young, therefore, represents a surplus number of animals that cannot be maintained by the environment. This surplus each year may, in theory, safely be harvested by man, without in any way decreasing the numbers of animals the environment will maintain. If man does not harvest it, natural causes will bring about the reduction. However, the surplus also provides food for all the predators, scavengers, and decomposers. It is part of the fuel for the ecosystem—and if totally removed by man, the ecosystem will change.

The carrying capacity for any species in a complex, climax environment may be relatively stable from year to year and, consequently, the number of animals will not change greatly. If the environment is generally favorable for the support of a great variety of animal species, then there will be predators, parasites, diseases, and competitors present in numbers adequate to remove the excess produced annually by one species population. In the more simplified environments in cold or dry ecosystems, carrying capacity can be expected to fluctuate greatly. Following wet years in an arid region an abundance of plant life may be produced and provide a high carrying capacity for a species such as the Chukar partridge, which will build up to a high population level. In such areas, dry years follow wet, and at such times the carrying capacity for most species may drop to an extremely low level. Thus we see great fluctuations in the numbers of animals that inhabit arid regions, and we cannot count on any particular level of abundance being maintained.

In successional environments the carrying capacity changes from year to year in a direction either favorable or unfavorable to a particular species. Thus the habitat may absorb the annual surplus of young produced during the time when succession is proceeding in a direction favorable to that species. Once a turning point is reached and plant succession is no longer in a direction favorable to the animal species, carrying capacity will decline in each succeeding year and die-offs in the population will follow.

Among the various kinds of animals, some species in some environments appear to control their own numbers. These are the *territorial animals.* A *territory* is now generally considered to be an area inhabited by an individual or group of animals of a given species and maintained for the more or less exclusive use of that individual or group. Other individuals or groups are excluded either by direct aggression toward them, or by various behavioral devices that lead to mutual respect of each other's territories. Some animals (the robin, for example) maintain territories during the breeding season but then come together in large flocks for migration and the winter. Other animals, the wren-tit for example, maintain territories throughout the year. Some species, such as many of the colonial-nesting seabirds, have territories that consist only of the immediate area surrounding the next. Others, such as the California quail, include within their territory feeding, nesting, roosting, and escape cover. The roe deer, in some environments, maintains a territory for the exclusive use of the single family group. The wolf maintains a pack territory within which all members of the pack may breed and rear their young. In all species that are territorial, this form of behavior results in spacing of individuals and thus a limitation of the numbers of individuals permitted within a particular environment. Excess individuals, unable to find a suitable territory, are driven out or otherwise are forced to move out from the particular area.

Among nonterritorial animals, some appear to be controlled in numbers by various predators or by some combination of predation, parasites, and disease so that their numbers remain fairly stable as long as their natural enemies are present. If the enemies are removed by man's activities or by some natural catastrophe, then populations of such species may increase for a time to high levels before other environmental factors, food shortage, lack of cover, adverse weather, and the like, operate to cause a decline in their numbers. Many of the smaller game animals, quail, pheasants, cottontails, tree squirrels, appear to have their overall levels of abundance controlled in these varied ways. Those that are to some degree territorial assist through their own behavior the operation of other limiting factors in their environment. The animals that cannot *find* suitable territories become more vulnerable to predation, adverse weather, or other causes of death.

Among animals such as the mule deer or white-tailed deer, territorial behavior is at best weakly developed. Where natural enemies are reasonably abundant, they can exercise some control over numbers. Where man has removed most natural enemies, however, these species soon begin to increase to a point where they press on the food supply of their environment. Thus the Kaibab deer increased to a level beyond the carrying capacity of their area, overbrowsed and destroyed the shrubs and other food plants on which they depended, and thus ultimately crashed to a much lower level than might have been maintained if their numbers had been controlled by man.

HABITAT NEEDS

A major task of wildlife management, if we are to have wildlife at all, is creation or maintenance of suitable wildlife habitats. Habitat needs vary for each species. Failure to understand these needs has led to many mistakes. A study carried out in British Columbia helps illustrate this point.

R. Y. Edwards (1954) has told the story of Wells Gray Park and its caribou herd. Before 1926 this was a primitive area, of high, glacier-topped mountains, breaking off southward to foothills and valleys. The valley floor and lower mountain slopes were covered with a dense, humid, cedar-hemlock forest. At higher elevations this was replaced by a drier, boreal forest of spruce and fir, breaking way at about 7000 feet into alpine tundra. On dry, south slopes at lower elevations was a forest of Douglas fir, with grassy openings.

The original animal life was varied but without excessive numbers of any one species. The mountain caribou were the most spectacular animals present. They wintered in the damp cedar-hemlock forest, where they fed on the abundant supply of lichens that grew there, and in summer traveled to the higher tundra and spruce-fir forest. There were a few mountain goats at higher elevations and a small number of mule deer that wintered in the dry, Douglas fir forest and grassland. A few mountain lions and coyotes followed the deer. Small numbers of black and grizzly bears were present, as were wolverines and martens in the heavy forest. Beaver were well distributed but not abundant.

In 1926, the scene changed. A fire started in the Douglas fir forest and spread northward along the river valleys sweeping into the cedar-hemlock forest. The fire was intense and destroyed the humus of the forest floor, and even burned out the large stumps of trees. Over 200 square miles of forest were destroyed. After the 1926 fire, another 80 square miles burned in 1930 to 1931 and another 100 in 1940. Together these fires reduced the great extent of climax forest to early successional stages. On the burned area fireweeds and willow invaded, followed by birch and aspen. A completely new habitat was created, with a much simplified type of vegetation. In this habitat a different type of animal life was favored, not the rich abundance of many species that had been present but great numbers of a few adapted species.

Deer became numerous in the burn, and with the increase in deer the mountain lion and coyote increased also. White-footed mice and ground squirrels invaded the burn and increased to high levels. Beaver and black bear, favored by the successional growth, increased and thrived. Most strikingly, moose, previously unknown in the area, colonized it four years after the first fire. Favored by the abundant willow, birch, and aspen browse, they became numerous. With the moose, timber wolves invaded the area. By contrast, all of the species that had been favored by the climax forest growth decreased. Most striking was the decrease in the caribou. The decline started in 1926, was noted with alarm by 1935, and was accentuated by the 1940 fire. In the early 1950s only a small remnant of the caribou herds existed, and these animals were to be found in winter in the three small remaining patches of mature, cedar-hemlock forest. They were absent from the burn. With the fire had gone the dense cover and abundant growth of lichens and other climax plants on which they had depended for food.

Throughout North America, the decrease in numbers of caribou in recent decades has been a matter of concern to wildlife conservationists. In Alaska and Canada the barren-ground caribou of the tundra have declined in numbers (Leopold and Fraser Darling, 1953). The woodland caribou has vanished from the forests of the northeastern United States and has decreased greatly in Canada. Wolves have been blamed for the decrease, climate has been blamed, competition with moose and deer has been blamed. It is now generally recognized, however, that the basic cause is fire or fire plus logging. Fire has destroyed the lichen-covered forest over great areas of caribou range. With the climax forest the caribou have gone. At the same time the great increase in moose in both Canada and Alaska has caused comment. Fire, with the successional growth of willow, birch, and aspen, is a basic cause. Conservation efforts aimed at decreasing losses from hunting or eliminating predation by wolves have had little effect on numbers of moose or caribou. Habitat is the controlling factor.

If the list of wildlife species now extinct or threatened with extinction is examined, it will be found that a high percentage of these species are like the mountain caribou. They are wilderness animals, dependent on the maintenance of climax or near-climax habitat conditions. The now-rare fur bearers of the United States, the wolverine and fisher, appear to be among these forms. They are now scarce in most areas of their former range, despite almost complete protection from hunting or trapping. For such wilderness animals it is now apparent that maintenance or restoration of their numbers depends, with our present knowledge, on maintenance of extensive wilderness areas in which they can survive. As we learn more of their habitat requirements, we may be able to single out those special features that favor their survival and, through management, to increase these habitat features. Until then protection of wilderness is the only answer.

The species of wildlife that form the bulk of our huntable game populations and those that have become pests of farmlands, forest lands, and rangelands are the successional forms. They have been favored by our use, and misuse, of the land and have exercised their biotic potentials in expanding into newly created habitats left by fire, loggers, or excessive numbers of sheep and cattle.

Looking at the wildlife situation now through the eyes of ecologists, we can easily see the importance of habitat and the capacity of game populations to expand when habitat is provided. Yet through the long years of effort toward wildlife conservation, these facts were not obvious.

With the work of MacArthur and Wilson (1967) and subsequent elaboration by many others, the mysteries of why some species (climax and wilderness forms) tend to become scarce, whereas others become more abundant when exposed to human influences, has been clarified. The concept of r-selected and K-selected species, discussed in Chapter 4, is worth reviewing at this point.

THE ROLE OF PROTECTION

Protection from hunting once seemed to be all that was needed to bring game back to previous levels of abundance. We know now that all of the protection in the world cannot lead a game population to increase when the habitat is not adequate. For wilderness animals, strict protection from hunting or trapping is required if they are to remain in the few remaining areas where they survive. But protection will not increase them; for that, we need more wilderness.

Waterfowl, while not climax species, have been hard hit by the expansion of settlement. Their migratory habits and tendency to congregate in large flocks have made them particularly vulnerable to hunting. Veritable armies of duck hunters set forth each year in pursuit of waterfowl. Without rigidly enforced game laws, the numbers of ducks, geese, and swans would soon be reduced to the vanishing point. Many waterfowl breed in the pothole country of the Canadian prairie and the still largely undisturbed tundra of the Arctic. From breeding grounds they migrate along well-defined routes, or flyways, to wintering grounds in the southern United States or Central or South America (Fig. 11.4). Those wintering in the United States have been affected by the drainage and reclamation of formerly extensive marsh or slough areas. In California, a major wintering ground for the Pacific flyway, high land values have resulted in the drainage of much of the former winter habitat. Flocks of geese and ducks concentrate on the few ramaining water areas and move out to feed on rice, barley fields, and truck gardens, causing extensive damage. Management has attempted to provide, through land purchase and development, more extensive wintering grounds and feeding areas apart from the croplands.

Drainage and urban development have removed large areas of marsh along the East and Gulf coasts, wintering grounds for birds of the Atlantic, Mississippi, and Central flyways. Some of these birds are also affected by the disappearance of breeding grounds. The ducks and geese of the Mississippi flyway breed in large part in the marshes and potholes of the North Central United States and Canada. The great land-reclamation program of the federal government in the early decades of this century led to the drainage of many important breeding areas. Waterfowl-conservation measures have included reflooding of formerly drained marshes, where these are of low agricultural value. Rigid protection from excessive hunting remains important if waterfowl are to be preserved, but protection alone will being no great increase in numbers. The habitat holds the key to increase. Further development of breeding, resting, and wintering

FIG 11.4
Simplified waterfowl flyways.

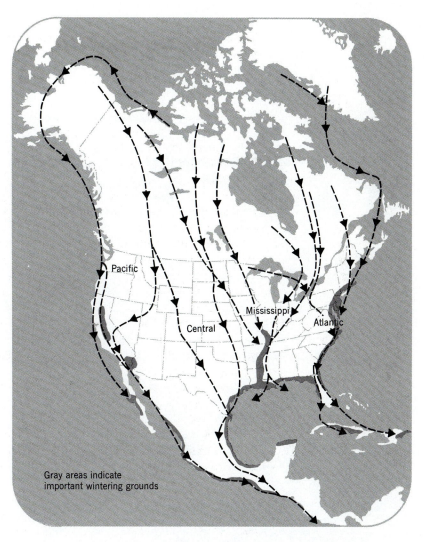

Pacific

Mississippi

Central

Atlantic

Gray areas indicate
important wintering grounds

areas is needed to bring the great flocks of former years back to the flyways.

With the great bulk of our now-abundant game animals, protection has been carried too far. We have created what is almost an excess of the successional type of habitat in which most game animals thrive. Into this habitat, quail and grouse, deer and rabbits, pheasants and doves have expanded. With a minimum of protection their numbers could be maintained, and their annual increases could provide recreation for many. But the public has been sold on the idea of protection and it is difficult to convince them that there can be too much of it. This has been most obvious with the deer, which have increased to the level of becoming a pest of forest land, rangeland, and farmland in many areas of the country. With deer, early in wildlife-conservation history, hunting was restricted

a

b

c

CHANGES IN WILDLIFE ABUNDANCE

(a) The bison have survived the "march of progress" and have regained abundance in protected reserves. (b) Caribou, seen here on an Alaskan tundra, decline in numbers as fires burn over their winter ranges in the taiga. (c) But the same fires bring in the successional vegetation on which moose thrive. (d) Early abundance of sea birds is still reflected in this Mexican island rookery. (e) Depsite the advances of civilization, the red deer of Europe thrive in many wild areas from Scandinavia to the Mediterranean.

d

e

to the male sex only. This was done with the realization that under normal levels of hunting enough bucks would survive for reproductive purposes. The female animals, protected from hunting, could produce enough young to permit the population to increase. The law protecting does was a measure to provide for population growth, not a measure of chivalry. A tradition has grown among sportsmen, however, to the point that the doe deer has been elevated to the position of "America's sacred cow." Some simple mathematical calculations will show that removal of part of the bucks each year will never keep a deer population from increasing. Yet it has been extremely difficult to obtain the necessary changes in hunting laws essential if excess deer populations and the consequent die-offs are to be prevented.

More so than protection from hunting, the importance of predator control has been oversold to the public by zealous conservationists. It is difficult to find records of any serious studies that show where predator control has accomplished anything of value. Where livestock are concerned, it can be a different matter. Major predators may have to be thinned out where sheep are to be run free on the range. Smaller predators can be an expensive nuisance when overly abundant in farming areas. But where game alone is involved, predators are part of the ecological balance. Predators help to remove the annual increase and thus to keep populations from overrunning the food supply of their habitat. Predators help to eliminate the old, the sick, and the weak from a population and make room for younger and more vigorous animals. Above all, predators have a place in a balanced biota, as part of the natural scene. Their recreational value and esthetic worth is immense. Wildlife to be worth preserving should be wild, and to remain wild it should be rich and varied, with predators as well as prey. If wildlife management is to concentrate on the sheer production of meat, eliminating all that conflicts with or feeds on the cherished herbivores, it becomes then only another form of animal husbandry, a useful and profitable pursuit, but lacking those qualities associated with the word *wild*.

AN ENVIRONMENTAL APPROACH

We have passed through two major phases in wildlife conservation in America. Initially, preservation and restocking dominated thinking. This led to confusion and bafflement when carefully protected species declined or liberated animals from game farms failed to survive. Next we moved into the age of the wildlife specialist, when emphasis on habitat management and population dynamics led to some spectacular gains and to a greatly widened understanding. But this period has also been the age of the hunting-license buyer, the hunter who demands an ever-increasing supply of those species he prefers to shoot. Using the new techniques, the game specialist has been able to produce great crops of deer, pheasants, or ducks but at a cost. In dollars alone this cost is excessive. Game departments are supported entirely by income from hunting-license fees. Too often the sportsman who buys a $10 license expects to shoot a brace of pen-raised pheasants that cost $20 for the game department to produce and still get his deer, ducks, and quail shooting thrown into the bargain. Sometimes, also, the gain in shootable game has been at the expense of other natural resources. Increasingly it has been at the expense of wildlife itself, neglected or destroyed in the effort to increase numbers of already too abundant game.

It is necessary to reexamine basic thinking about wildlife problems and to enter a new era of wildlife conservaion, of the conservation of balanced biotas in place of specialized concentration on increasing numbers of huntable game. It should be an era in which the needs of the people as a whole, for natural environments with abundant and varied animal life, are given precedence over the wants of the hunter.

In the past, wildlife has been relegated in the thinking of conservation workers in other specialties to those land areas not suited for more economically valuable products. We realize now that wildlife, like all life, requires deep, rich soils and does poorly on areas where soil nutrients are lacking. If wildlife is to remain abundant, it must be fitted into farm plans, range plans, and forest plans. Only a small percentage of our lands can reasonably be reserved for wildlife alone. Moreover, it is *wildlife* that must be fitted into land-use plans, not an unhealthy monoculture of a favored game species.

VANISHING HERITAGE

In any discussion of environmental conservation it is natural to emphasize the issues of direct and present concern to most people, in particular those factors with an immediate bearing on human survival. Yet to do so is to create a false impression of relative priorities, because some of the more important aspects of conservation have little relation to our quantitative needs, no obvious or immediate bearing on human survival, and are scarcely known to most people. Nevertheless, if they are not attended to, and soon, the long-term chances for human survival may be impaired, and the quality of life will be damaged. There is far more to conservation than the efficient and sustained production of species or things of economic value. There are qualities of the environment that must be considered without reference to any increment that they might add to the gross national product, or to any fluctuation that they might create in the indices of economic growth. There is a need in the human environment for wild nature, untouched or little modified by human activities. There is a need also to maintain the physical records of our cultural past if we are to better evaluate the prospects for the future. A heritage of diversity exists on earth, natural and man-made, which we cannot afford to lose.

a

WILDLIFE RESTORATION

(a) The wild turkey, once seriously threatened, has been restored to abundance by protection, habitat management, and restocking. **(b)** The trumpeter swan has been brought back to a secure population level by protective measures. **(c)** Rated as "dangerous to man" the grizzly bear holds on in national parks such as Yellowstone, and Glacier, despite the efforts of those who want all dangerous animals destroyed.
(d) Long feared and hated because of false ideas, the wolf is now becoming a popular animal and its future in North America is becoming more secure.

b

c

d

We must recognize the value of nature in itself, apart from any value it may have for future exploitation. A need exists to protect areas only for the purpose of having them available for future knowledge about the natural world. There is a need to set aside natural communities solely for the quiet, esthetic appreciation some people may gain by viewing them. There is also a need to set aside other places only for the sake of the wild creatures who live, unstudied and unpraised, within them. There is room on earth for all such areas and purposes. We must be prepared to grant the right of existence to species other than homo, without being threatened by the obvious truth that our own survival may ultimately depend on them.

ENDANGERED SPECIES

Although the United States is a world leader in wildlife management, the emphasis of this profession has been directed toward producing game for the hunter rather than the protection and restoration of animals not available for sport. Early in history, some species (the passenger pigeon, Carolina parakeet, heath hen, and California grizzly among them) became extinct. Today many species are rare and in a highly endangered status. Other once-abundant species are decreasing for reasons not understood.

A concern for endangered species has led to acceptance of responsibility over them by the United States Fish and Wildlife Service, and active interest and protection by private groups such as the Audubon societies. For some, strict protection from hunting or other disturbance seems the only measure needed to bring back populations. For others, habitat restoration is essential. The establishment of a Federal Wildlife Refuge system, starting with the Pelican Island in Florida in 1903, and since extended to 386 refuges by 1980, has been an important step.

Good success has been achieved with some species. The trumpeter swan, once near extinction, is now relatively secure. The sea otter of the Pacific Coast, once thought to be extinct, is once more abundant. The Key deer of southern Florida is, for the present at least secure. The wild turkey and the Alaskan fur seal are now abundant, although they were not long ago considered endangered.

Among the many species for which special protection is still required are the California condor, black-footed ferret, ivory-billed woodpecker, whooping crane, grizzly bear, Everglades kite, Hawaiian geese, Florida panther, timber wolf, and red wolf. Continued vigilance is extended over the small remnant populations of condors, cranes, and Hawaiian geese. Equal vigilance must also be extended to other species if they are to remain on this earth.

As in most areas of environmental conservation the prospects for preservation of natural environments and wild species are far less promising in most of the world than they are in the United States. The critical nature of the problem has been brought into focus by such organizations as the International Union for the Conservation of Nature, which starting in 1966 has published Red Data Books that list hundreds of rare and endangered species the world over. The International Biological Program has also helped focus world attention on the need to set aside areas of undisturbed vegetation and animal life for future scientific study, and IUCN is helping to carry out this activity.

In an attempt to find some better way to preserve the outstanding wild areas of the world, Russell E. Train, then president of the Conservation Foundation, proposed the creation of a World Heritage Trust. This could channel private and public money toward an effort to purchase and provide adequate protection for outstanding examples of the world's wild country and wildlife. The idea has been developed over several years, and currently it is an arrangement, under UNESCO, by which nations may dedicate their outstanding natural areas or cultural sites to the long-range benefit of mankind as part of a World Heritage system. In return, apart from the prestige and publicity, they will receive assistance from a World Heritage Fund in achieving or maintaining proper standards of protection and management.

There are great numbers of proposals at both the national and international level to do something about the problems of the Human Environment. In 1970 at its General Conference, UNESCO approved a program known as Man and the Biosphere, intended to initiate and coordinate international research aimed at discovering the information essential for the proper conservation and management of the world's living resources. Many of the projects of this program could do much toward maintaining the heritage of wild nature. In 1970 the International Council of Scientific Unions (ICSU) launched a new program under the aegis of SCOPE (Special Committee on Problems of the Environment) intended, among other activities, to provide for a worldwide system of monitoring the changes in the environment caused by human activity. All of these programs have great potential importance. None of them as yet has received any significant amount of financial support. None of them can operate without adequate money. This becomes most obvious when we consider what is happening to the tropical areas of the world.

TROPICAL FORESTS AND SPECIES EXTINCTION

The story concerning what has happened and is happening to the tropical forests of the world has already been told in part in the preceding chapter. The possible effects of this massive deforestation on the survival of species on earth is presented in Table 11.5, prepared by Thomas Lovejoy for the *Global 2000 Report*. It is significant that we do not know whether there are 3 million or 10 million species on earth—scientific collection

a

b

c

THREATENED SPECIES

Critically endangered. (a) Essentially exterminated in the wild, captive populations of the Arabian oryx have increased to a point where restoration of wild populations can begin. (b) The California condor, reduced from thousands to twenty, will hopefully be restored by captive breeding in zoos. **Endangered.** (c) The mountain gorilla's survival depends on Africa's national parks. **Threatened.** (d) Hide hunting has reduced populations of alligators and crocodiles. (e) Lions and (f) black rhinos depend for their survival on protected areas.

d

e

f

a

b

c

A WORLD HERITAGE

An international convention in 1975 created a system for protecting the world's heritage of cultural and natural areas. Part of the new system is shown by (a) Angkor in Cambodia, (b) the Galapagos Islands of Ecuador, (c) Machu Picchu in Peru (a royal tomb) and (d) the Acropolis in Athens.

d

TABLE 11.5 Impact of Tropical Deforestation and Other Habitat Change on Extinction of Species—Animal and Plant (Projected to 2000 A.D.)

	PRESENT NUMBER OF SPECIES (1000S)	AMOUNT OF DEFORESTATION (%)	LOSS OF SPECIES (%)	EXTINCTIONS OF SPECIES (1000S)
	Low Rates of Deforestation			
Tropical forests				
Latin America	300–1,000	50	33	100–333
Africa	150–500	20	13	20–65
Asia	300–1,000	60	43	129–430
Subtotal	759–2,500			249–828
All other areas	2,250–7,500		8	188–625
Total	3,000–10,000			437–1,453
	High Rates of Deforestation			
Tropical forests				
Latin America	300–1,000	67	50	150–500
Africa	150–500	67	50	75–250
Asia	300–1,000	67	50	150–500
Subtotal	750–2,500			375–1,250
All other areas	2,250–7,500		8	188–625
Total	3,000–10,000			563–1,875

Calculations by Thomas E. Lovejoy, in CEQ (1980), p. 331.

and taxonomic study has not been able to keep up with the wealth of material available from the land areas of the tropics and the world's oceans. We know that the humid tropical forests are the world's greatest collection of wild species. We probably will not know how many there were since the process of extinction has started. If Lovejoy is correct we stand to lose between 437,000 and 1,875,000 species within the next 20 years. That could average 50,000 species a year, or somewhere around 5 species per hour becoming extinct, every hour, every day from now until 2000 A.D., with no termination of that process in sight. Gerald Barney has looked at similar data and estimates that one-quarter of the world's biota lives in these tropical forests, and with the likelihood of two-thirds of those forests being cleared, we could stand to lose one-eighth of the species on the planet (Barney, 1978). Depending on whether the species total is 3 or 10 million, his figures come out as comparable with Lovejoy's. But we just do not really know. The change is happening fast and we do not know what was in the areas being logged or what is left, or what can come back from other areas.

Of course it won't be just the strange and unfamiliar species that disappear. A good share of America's bird species winter in the tropics, and many of them depend on tropical forests. When they do not come back next spring, you will know something happened to their habitat. Two species of warblers (the hooded and Kentucky) are already showing a decrease (Fitzpatrick, 1982). As for the others, you might not miss them since you do not know their names. But perhaps when the results are in you will miss them very much.

SOURCES

Barney, Gerald, 1978. *Proceedings of the U.S. strategy conference on tropical deforestation.* U.S. Department of State, Washington, D.C.

Brownrigg, Leslie A., 1982. *Native cultures and protected areas: management options.* World National Park Conference, Bali. Mimeo.

Council on Environmental Quality, 1980. *The global 2000 report to the president.* U.S. Government Printing Office, Washington, D.C.

Dasmann, R. F., 1974. Difficult marginal environments and the traditional societies which exploit them: ecosystems. Symposium on the future of traditional "primitive" societies. *Survival International News* 11:11–15.

———1981. *Wildlife biology.* John Wiley, New York.

———1982. *Indigenous peoples and protected areas.* World National Park Conference, Bali. Mimeo.

Edwards, R. Y., 1954. Fire and the decline of a mountain caribou herd. *Journal of Wildlife Management* 18:521–526.

Fitzpatrick, John W., 1982. Northern birds at home in the tropics. *Natural History* 91:40–47.

Frankel, O. H. and M. E. Soulé, 1981. *Conservation and evolution.* Cambridge University, Press, Cambridge, U.K.

Goodland, Robert, 1982. *Tribal peoples and economic development.* World Bank, Washington, D.C.

IUCN, 1978. Categories, objectives and criteria for protected areas. IUCN, Gland, Switzerland.

———1980, 1982. United Nations List of National Parks and Equivalent Reserves. IUCN, Gland, Switzerland.

Kimball, Thomas and R. E. Johnson, 1978. The richness of American wildlife. *Wildlife and America,* H. Brokaw, editor. Council on Environmental Quality, Washington, D.C.

Leopold, A. S. and F. Fraser Darling, 1953. *Wildlife in Alaska.* Ronald Press, New York.

Lopez, Barry Holstun, 1978. *Of wolves and men.* Scribners, New York.

Lusigi, Walter J., 1978. *Planning human activities on protected natural ecosystems.* J. Cramer, Vaduz, Germany.

MacArthur, R. H. and E. O. Wilson, 1967. *The theory of island biogeography.* Princeton University Press, Princeton, N.J.

McLuhan, T. C., 1972. *Touch the earth.* Pocket Books, New York.

Rasmussen, D. I., 1941. Biotic communities of the Kaibab Plateau. *Ecological Monographs* 3:229–275.

Shepard, Paul, 1982. *Nature and madness.* Sierra Club Books, San Francisco.

Soulé Michael E. and Bruce A. Wilcox, editors, 1980. *Conservation Biology* Sinauer Associates, Sunderland, Massachusetts.

Swanson, Gustav A., 1978. Wildlife on the public lands. *Wildlife and America,* H. Brokaw, editor. Council on Environmental Quality, Washington, D.C.

UNESCO—MAB, 1974. *Criteria and guidelines for the choice and establishment of biosphere reserves.* UNESCO, Paris.

FOUR

WHERE DO WE WANT TO GO?

CHAPTER 12

HOW TO MAKE THE EARTH UNINHABITABLE

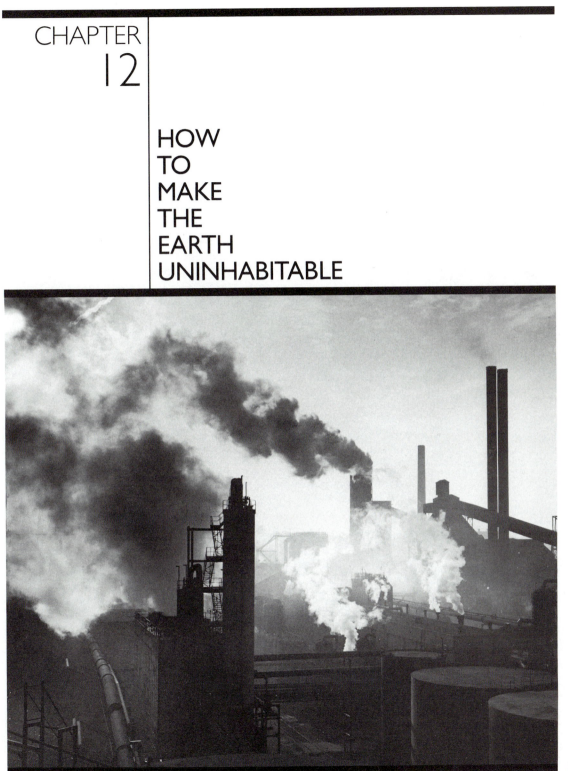

> *It is not so much that we are systematically annihilating life on this planet, but that there is nothing really being done about it, and worse still, nobody cares. "For want of interest, the future has been cancelled" ran the title of Paul Ehrlich's film that appeared about a decade ago.*
>
> *Indeed for governments throughout the world, the environment is little more than an embarrassment. Their main preoccupation is to earn the necessary foreign currency required to assure the economic development on which their prestige, power and future must depend. To this end they will sacrifice anything—their forests, their land, their topsoil, not to mention their traditions, their culture, their religion, indeed all that their ancestors, for countless generations, held to be most holy.*
>
> Edward Goldsmith, The retreat from Stockholm. *The Ecologist* (1982), p. 98.

POISONING A PLANET

One of the characteristics of the human animal is a wide range of environmental tolerance, the ability to continue to exist under conditions from which most species would flee. This has enabled human societies to spread over the face of the earth, to increase and multiply despite what would appear to be a great number of physical handicaps. People cannot fly without machines, they cannot run very fast, they are not very strong—but they have an incredible ability to "take it," to endure. A few other species—rats, mice, starlings, pigeons—seem able to tolerate the conditions under which people live, and they accompany mankind around the world. Fleas, lice, and house flies also qualify. This human trait, however, seems to be one that would actually permit people to destroy the biosphere. The ability to accept thoroughly unwholesome conditions can permit these conditions to finally build up to the danger point. There is no doubt, if nothing else works, that pollution can set the final limits to human growth and expansion. There are limits to the amounts and kinds of poisons the living systems of the biosphere can tolerate, before they begin to unravel and fall apart so that life on earth begins to disappear. We do not know precisely where those limits are, and this is what encourages people to gamble. We take a risk whenever we add to the earth's burden of pollution, but if the stakes seem reasonably high, if a profit can be made, there are always people willing to take the risk. So we go on playing Russian roulette with the environment, hoping that nobody has put extra loaded cartridges into the cylinder.

Pollution has been a theme running through this book, and some aspects of it have already been discussed at length. This chapter looks at other aspects of the problem, and perhaps we can find ways in which it can be all tied together. There is little doubt that pollution usually results from a failure to realize and act on the knowledge that in the biosphere the rules of physics apply—all actions have equal and opposite reactions.

PESTICIDES   In the desperate race to produce food faster than populations would grow, humanity has resorted to some desperate measures. In Chapter 8 we noted that a characteristic of American agriculture since World War II, and of most agriculture in the developed world, has been the employment of pesticides. This has been forced by the spread of monocultures that leave great areas planted to a single variety of a single crop species, and by the extent to which mechanical and chemical devices have replaced human labor on the farm. Starting during World War II a whole new variety of pesticides were produced by the chemical industries, and the use of these has gone hand in hand with the new agriculture, spreading with the Green Revolution into the countries of the Third World.

The first of the new pesticides was DDT, developed on a large scale during the war when it proved effective in controlling populations of lice, fleas, and other disease-bearing insects. The initial impact of this chemical on both public health and agriculture was so encouraging that it was adopted and widely used with little investigation of its side effects. The use of DDT virtually eliminated malaria in some parts of the world. The use of this and other related insecticides knocked back populations of crop-destroying insects and contributed to the gains in agricultural yield. But, unfortunately, biotic communities are complex and not amenable to such simple solutions to human problems.

Insect pests initially can be controlled by an application of a pesticide such as DDT at a level not harmful to birds and mammals. Control, however, is not eradication, and some insects always survive. Frequently, these will be individuals most resistant to the pesticide. If this resistance is inheritable, a DDT-resistant population of cinch bugs, bag worms, scale insects, or other pests will breed following several applications of this chemical. It then becomes necessary to increase the dosage or find a more lethal chemical. Eventually, control efforts may lead to applications of poisons at levels toxic to birds, mammals, or man himself. Insects breed rapidly and produce large numbers of offspring. It takes relatively little time to develop pesticide-resistant populations. The slower breeding vertebrates are not so fortunate. But this is only part of the problem.

In 1962 Rachel Carson attracted national attention to pesticides with the publication of her book *Silent Spring*. In her words the consequences of our continued careless use of pesticides might result one year in the arrival of a springtime in which "There was a strange stillness. The birds, for example—where had they gone? Many people spoke of them, puzzled and disturbed. . . . On the mornings that had once throbbed with the dawn chorus of robins, catbirds, doves, jays, wrens, and scores of other bird voices there was no sound; only silence lay over the fields and woods and marsh." *Silent Spring* has been accused of scientific inaccuracy, but Carson's emotional approach accomplished what a thousand scientific papers could not do—awakened the people to an awareness of the hidden dangers of pesticides. Later, more sober accounts, but equally valid indictments, were to appear (Rudd, 1964; Van den Bosch, 1980).

The pesticides that have been effectively and widely used in recent decades are organic in nature. One group, the chlorinated hydrocarbons, include DDT, DDD, dieldrin, chlordane, and endrin, among others. The other group, the organophosphates, includes malathion, parathion, and TEPP. Of the two, the first group has presented the most problems. DDT, for example, persists on soil and vegetation long after it has been applied. Repeated dosages may therefore be consumed by animals. It is also a broad-spectrum pesticide, meaning it effects many kinds of animals other than the particular insect for which it was intended. It is a cumulative poison; animals store it in their fatty tissues and may build up high concentrations in their internal organs even though the initial field concentration was at a level not toxic to most species. The organophosphates, although highly poisonous, are generally not cumulative nor do they as a rule persist on the ground (Table 12.1).

As a method for control of pests, the most widely employed pesticides have this disadvantage: since they affect the entire community and not just the pest species, they kill off the predators and parasites that normally feed on the insect as well as the pest itself. They thus simplify the biotic community and generate instability. Lacking effective enemies, the pest species can increase more rapidly and to higher levels, before the populations of its former predators and parasites can recover sufficiently to again exercise some control. The control chemicals thus tend to create a continuing demand for more or better control chemicals. The agriculturalist who seeks to protect his crops is likely to make this demand. If other methods were available, he might turn to them, but chemical control seems simple, cheap, and initially at least, effective.

An example of the kind of problem that has developed has been presented by Rudd (1964). In the 1930s a reddish fire ant was accidentally introduced into Alabama and, thereafter, spread widely throughout the southern states. These ants built earth mounds that interfered with crop cultivation, they were capable of delivering a stinging bite, and they reportedly did some damage to crops and livestock. In 1957 the United States Department of Agriculture took action against them in cooperation with the states involved. A major program of control started using the chlorinated hydrocarbons dieldrin and heptachlor. During 1957–1958

TABLE 12.1   Relative Toxicity of Pesticides

PESTICIDE	LD[50] IN MILLIGRAMS PER KILOGRAM BASED ON WHITE RATS[a]	LC[50] AT 11°C IN MILLIGRAMS PER LITER OF WATER BASED ON FISH[b]
CHLORINATED HYDROCARBONS		
Aldrin	40.0	0.0082
Dieldrin	46.0	0.0055
DDT	250.0	0.005
Endrin	12.0	0.0044
Heptachlor	90.0	
Lindane	125.0	n.e.[c] at 0.03
Toxaphene	69.0	0.0022
Endosulfan	110.0	
Telodrin	4.8	
ORGANOPHOSPHATES		
Malathion	1500.0	0.55
Parathion	8.0	0.065
Methyl parathion	15.0	
Azinphosmethyl	15–25	0.055
TEPP	1.6	
Mevinphos	6.0	0.83
Ethion	208.0	0.42
Temik	1.0	
Trichlorphon	450.0	n.e. at 1.0
CARBAMATES		
Carbaryl	540.0	
Zectran	15–36	n.e. at 1.0

[a]Dose required to kill 50 percent of population.
[b]Concentration in water required to kill 50 percent of population.
[c]No effect.
Source: Shea (1969[b]).

over two and a half million acres were aerially sprayed with these chemicals. As a result, "Fish, wildlife, livestock, and poultry suffered losses; the destruction of wildlife bordering on catastrophic." Outbreaks of other insect pests, presumably stimulated by the destruction of their natural enemies, took place. Fifteen million dollars was spent on the control program. The fire ant remained in the South.

At Clear Lake, California, the use of DDD to control a gnat population caused a reduction to near elimination in the population of the western grebe, a diving bird for which the lake was famous. Subsequent studies revealed that the grebes concentrated the chemicals in their tissues to a level 80,000 times as great as the amount originally applied to the lake. Elsewhere, control programs against spruce budworms and gypsy moths, insects that do serious damage to forests, caused significant wildlife losses from DDT poisoning. Dieldrin and aldrin, used against Japanese beetles, caused wildlife mortality. Elsewhere in the world, in Japan for example, losses of wildlife to a point of near extinction for some species have been reported. In Ecuador massive fish kills followed the spraying of banana plantations with a fungicide. In Malaya the use of insecticides in oil palm plantations stimulated much more serious outbreaks of the bagworm pest than those that occurred before the pesticide was used. In the tropics generally, where biological controls are normally more operative, the potential hazards from continued use of pesticides are known to be high but have yet to be fully assessed.

Perhaps, the basis for the trouble is illustrated in this small table based on studies in Lake Michigan:

	DDT CONCENTRATION (PARTS PER MILLION)
General environment Lake bottom sediments	0.0085
Small invertebrates (zooplankton)	0.41
Fish	3.00 to 800
Herring gulls	3,177.00

Since DDT is not broken down appreciably by biological action (it is not strongly biodegradable), it accumulates as it passes up the food chain from one organism to another. Initially low concentrations in the environment become very high, indeed, when they reach the terminal organisms in the food chain, the meat-eating or fish-eating organisms.

In England birds of prey began to decline in numbers starting in the early 1950s. The cause was not known. A little later a similar decline was observed in the United States. Slowly the story began to unravel.

It was not until 1967 that investigations began to focus on the cause of loss of the birds of prey. In that year Derek Ratcliffe (1967) in England found that eggshell weight and thickness had decreased 8–24 percent in birds of prey in England between pre-1947 (when DDT came into wide use) and the post-1947 period. The next year, Joseph Hickey (1968) and his associates reported similar findings in raptorial and fish-eating birds in North America. This was then related to findings by D. B. Peakall in New York showing that DDT or dieldrin caused a rapid metabolism and breakdown of sex hormones in birds. Data than began to accumulate from many directions. By 1970 there was no longer the slightest doubt that DDT and its relatives, through interfering with the sex hormonal regulation of metabolism in birds, was leading to the production of thin-shelled eggs, or eggs without shells, and was further interfering with the survival of any young that escaped the breakage of eggs during the process of nesting. In 1970 disturbing reports came in from the Channel Islands of California: a virtually complete failure of the brown pelican to bring any nests through to a successful hatch as a result of DDT accumulation. Pelican eggs contained 2600 parts per million of DDE (a product of the metabolism of DDT). The double-crested cormorants, pelagic cormorants, common murres, and common egrets along the California coast showed similar effects. Plankton in the coastal waters was contaminated with DDT, which thus entered the food chain. Catches of mackerel off the California coast were seized and condemned when it was shown they contained 20 times more DDT than the allowable "safe" level for human consumption.

It became increasingly apparent that we were in danger of losing all of the birds that are high on food chains—hawks, eagles, falcons, owls, herons, egrets, and seabirds—and that there was no reason to expect the effects of pesticides to stop there. Fish and aquatic invertebrates of many species proved to be particularly vulnerable, and great damage has been reported to food fish production in some areas. Deaths and reproductive losses of marine mammals have also been attributed to accumulations of organochlorine pesticides, of which DDT is the most widespread. George Woodwell (1967) has estimated that as much as one billion pounds of DDT alone might be circulating in the biosphere. It has been found from the Antarctic to Greenland—in areas where it has never been employed but has drifted on air or water currents. Charles Wurster (1968) found that, at a level of 100 parts per billion in seawater, DDT could drastically reduce photosynthesis in plant plankton, the base of all oceanic food chains.

Studies carried out by the University of Miami revealed that oil slicks in the ocean appeared to concentrate oil-soluble pesticides such as DDT and dieldrin. One oil slick investigated off Miami revealed 10,000 times more dieldrin in the thin surface film of oil than in the water immediately below. This could, of course, bring great danger to surface-feeding marine life, including the animal plankton. Studies carried out by the National Science Foundation and the National Ocean and Atmospheric Agency revealed the widespread distribution of petroleum in the form of tar balls throughout the oceans. Again these were found to contain dissolved organochlorine pesticides as well as the equally dangerous PCBs (polychlorinated biphenyls) in high concentrations. Since these tar balls attract marine organisms, probably for shelter, the likelihood of their poisoning is increased.

We have once again put ourselves into a dilemma. The World Health Organization, faced with controlling malaria and other insect-borne diseases, does not want to abandon DDT, which is relatively cheap and still effective enough against some disease vectors. Agricultural and forestry departments, seeking to increase yields, do not want to give up these tools. But the end results of these activities could be disastrous.

Action has now been taken in the United States and many other nations to ban the use of DDT and its relatives. But in the developing nations of the world the use of these pesticides is still expanding. If they would stay in place, this might not be so bad, but stream flow, ocean currents, and air movements take them everywhere.

With the crackdown on the use of DDT many of the birds of prey have begun to recover. The Peregrine falcon, which was most threatened, is on the way back thanks in part to captive breeding and restocking carried out by the federal Fish and Wildlife Service, state wildlife agencies, and such universities as Cornell and the University of California at Santa Cruz. The California brown pelican and other sea birds off the West Coast have bounced back from the difficulties of the early 1970s, as a result of a crackdown on a chemical factory that was releasing DDT-laden effluent into coastal waters. Not only has the brown pelican been successful in raising crops of young, but it has spread from what seemd to be its last stronghold on Anacapa Island to breed on other Channel Islands as well. Unfortunately, those American birds that migrate into Latin America encounter all of the pesticides that are banned at home. On their journeys back to the United States they bring the pesticides back with them.

Part of the answer to pesticides is improved land use, encouraging diversity and restoring natural ecological processes. Studies in the Soviet Union (Gilyarov, 1968) have shown that where DDT is used, the soil fauna is knocked out and may take four years to recover. The same soil fauna, as well as flora, is needed to restore soil fertility. Encouraging the nitrogen-fixing microorganisms in the soil can reduce the need for massive applications of energy-wasting nitrogen fertilizer. Experience in many parts of the world has shown that with a high crop diversity, the need for pest control is greatly reduced. Biological controls, using predatory insects or disease organisms that attack pest insects, has been highly effective against Japanese beetles, scale insects, and other problem insects, but this activity still receives far less support than goes into the development of new poisons.

Unfortunately, whenever you think that some problem is on the way to solution, reality rises up and hits you. In 1980 the Mediterranean fruit fly was discovered in the Santa Clara Valley of California, an area that before extreme suburbanization took place had been one of the major fruit-producing centers of the country, and even in 1980 still had many orchards. The Medfly is a destructive little creature that attacks many fruits and vegetables.

The State of California, under the leadership of Governor Jerry Brown, took what appeared to be a well-thought-out and moderate approach to the problem—stripping fruit from trees and hand-spraying with malathion in the area surrounding the Medfly discovery. To further cope with the infestation, sterile fruit flies were brought in and released—a standard method of biological control. One can suspect that sabotage and political chicanery played a part in the failure of these methods, since Governor Brown is not popular among conservative agriculturalists, or conservatives in general. Some of the "sterile" fruit flies, probably thousands of them, were not sterile. The Medfly spread, finally appearing in southern California and the agricultural heartland of the San Joaquin Valley. At this point the U.S. Department of Agriculture aided by full federal authority, cheered on by many farmers, and of course cheered most loudly by the chemical industry, demanded aerial spraying. Spray planes flew up and down the air lanes covering all possible areas of fly infestation. Thousands of gallons of malathion were sprayed on property, people, domestic animals, everything. The cost jumped to over $100 million. By 1982 the Medfly was reported to be wiped out. What else was wiped out we may not know for some time.

Malathion is one of the milder pesticides, but it could just as well have been one of the worst. What was totally depressing is that the people of the area concerned were completely put down by what resembled a military attack. It did no good for towns, cities, counties or even the state to oppose the aerial spraying. All protests were ignored. Some of us will remember.

> For the first time I realized that I and other university researchers had virtually no influence over pest-control policymaking. It had been rudely brought home to me that over the years we university types had simply been puppets playing silly little games while the pesticide establishment called the shots in pest control. The hope of developing integrated control was a vague dream, and scientific pest control a farce.
>
> Robert van den Bosch, *The Pesticide Conspiracy* (1980)

AIR POLLUTION There are many experts who give air pollution first rank among conservation problems because of its potential for threatening the life and health of millions of people, and ultimately perhaps, all life on earth. It is not a new problem, except for its present global dimensions. People have been affected seriously and have been killed by polluted air ever since the Industrial Revolution, or before.

Particulate matter in the air, in the form of dust or smoke, has caused problems to human health and comfort in some places at some times throughout history. To this was added, starting with the Middle Ages and increasing ever since, the by-products of the combustion of coal and later of petroleum. In this century the internal combustion engine has become a major source of air pollutants. Since World War II, radioactive elements from nuclear explosions and power plants and the wide range of new chemical pesticides have joined the list of poisons in the air. To these can be added a whole range of other materials produced by industry or transportation: dust from cement factories, fumes from pulp mills, exhausts from jet planes, aerosols from spray cans, PCBs and heavy metals from other industrial processes, and so on. We are adding new and potentially dangerous chemical pollutants to the air faster than we can analyze the effects or dangers from the existing ones. In many places

a

b

c

POLLUTION: HOW MUCH IS TOO MUCH?

(a) Smog. Do we really want fresh air? **(b)** Where do the children play when fish can't live in the water?

(c) Spraying pesticides on corn—the wrong way to go.

(d) Pesticide consequences.

(e) Oil slick surrounds the Statue of Liberty in New York Harbor. **(f)** Radioactive wastes being covered at Barnwell, South Carolina, awaiting the day when "safe" disposal becomes possible.

we have reached a crisis stage. A new word, *smog,* has been added to the language to describe the poisonous mixture that has taken the place of what was once harmless fog and haze.

The recent history of air pollution disasters starts with the Meuse Valley in Belgium. In December 1930 a heavy concentration of smog in this area killed 60 people. In October 1948 Donora, Pennsylvania, experienced a high concentration of air pollutants, which caused widespread respiratory illness resulting in 17 deaths. In London a long period during which there were many minor disasters caused by the cities infamous "black fogs" culminated in December 1952, when 4000 people were believed to have died from breathing polluted air. In all of these disasters, the primary blame was placed on high concentrations of sulfur dioxide, a by-product of coal combustion or of the burning of fuel oil with a high sulfur content. The polluters were both the ordinary citizens, burning coal or fuel oil to heat their houses, and the factories and other industrial plants that burned large quantities of these fuels.

There has been more than a little success in cleaning up the visible, particulate pollution resulting from coal and fuel oil combustion. In Pittsburgh, which was once known for its dirty air, the factories no longer pour out visible smoke and ash, and the buildings are no longer coated with soot. In London the black fogs are a thing of the past. Sulfur dioxide, however, is more difficult to remove. It is invisible, and people are less likely to complain about it. Nevertheless, it combines with the moisture in the air to form sulfuric acid droplets. Starting in the 1960s and becoming steadily worse, sulfur dioxide, without the particulates that used to partially neutralize it, is falling out as "acid rain" in Scandinavia, the eastern United States, and elsewhere.

Robert Risebrough (1978) has identified acid rain as "the most consequential environmental toxicant" over broad areas of eastern North America. The Canadian east has been particularly hard hit by pollution drifting in from the industrial centers of the United States along the Great Lakes. The acidity of the rain has been increasing and sometimes is more acidic than vinegar. Hundred of lakes in the northeast are now lifeless in the sense that fish, frogs, salamanders, zooplankton, and phytoplankton have been killed. The lakes are beautifully clear—but essentially dead. Stream flow is similarly polluted. In Canada forest reproduction as well as the growth of older trees has been badly affected. Similar effects are noted in Scandinavia, where the acidity derives from the industrial centers in Germany and Great Britain. Thus far the United States had not responded to Canada's plea to do something to stop the pollution. The factory owners say they cannot afford it. One wonders if they can afford to stay alive.

Urban air pollution crises usually result from weather conditions. Normally daytime air temperatures will decrease from the ground upward. Warmed air, near the ground, will rise, and as it does so will cool. This upward movement of air will carry pollutants away from the zone where people live. Wind will carry them away from their area of origin, disperse them, and mix them. Under certain conditions, however, the normal air temperature gradient changes. For example, a mass of warm air may move in with a weather front and overlay the cooler air below. A *temperature inversion* will result. Inversions also occur as a result of the cooling of the air near the ground during winter. This creates a stagnant layer of cold air, and the familiar winter mists of the countryside. On seacoasts, also, there may be a movement in summer of cooler air from over the ocean, which will force the warm air inland upward; the cool air may then be held for long periods near the ground until it becomes warmer than the air above. With such inversions, the upward movement of air is prevented and pollutants are trapped within the zone where human activities are concentrated.

Inversions frequently persist for several or more days during times when there is little horizontal air movement to carry pollutants away from their source. The frequency at which inversions occur varies from one place to another. New York, which produces enormous quantities of air pollutants, escapes disaster because inversions are relatively infrequent and seldom persist for long. Los Angeles, with a lower total output of pollutants, has frequent inversions and long periods of heavy smog.

Air pollution is regarded primarily as a threat to human health. It has been estimated by Lave and Seskin (1970) that if air pollution were reduced 50 percent there would be a saving to the United States of over $2 billion just from the time lost in work and the medical expenses from bronchitis, pneumonia, lung cancer, cardiovascular diseases, and other related sicknesses. However, air pollution also directly damages buildings and other structures. The cost of repair and prevention runs into additional hundreds of millions of dollars and becomes critical when architectural masterpieces or historical monuments of great value are involved. Air pollution affects all plant and animal life. Pine trees are particularly susceptible and have been damaged greatly in the mountains around Los Angeles, as well as elsewhere. Lichens, which dominate the arctic tundras, are highly vulnerable to sulfur dioxide pollution. The cutflower industry and many kinds of agricultural crops have been pushed out of the area of heavy air pollution in southern California.

Throughout the United States the automobile has risen to first place as a cause of air pollution, and in California it has long held this position. It has been estimated that 42 percent of air polluting emissions in the United States are produced by transportation. Los Angeles, one of the first cities faced with a major air pollution problem, has done many things to try to solve it. In 1947 the California legislature passed an enabling act assigning the authority to California counties to control stationary sources of air pollution. Los Angeles County moved to control the emissions from industrial plants and to stop the burning of refuse in municipal dumps. Next, a more difficult step was taken through forbidding the burning of trash in home incinerators. Space heating of buildings was the next target, and the use of high-sulfur fuels was forbidden. Despite all of these controls, smog problems grew worse. In 1955 the California legislature passed an act creating multiple-county Air Pollution Control Districts, thus providing for uniform regulations in counties sharing a common airshed. By that time in southern California it had become apparent that the major offender, the source of 80 percent of pollution, was the automobile, and this could not be controlled by a local district. In 1960 a state Motor Vehicle Pollution Control Board was established. Through the action of this board, it is now mandatory that all new motor vehicles registered in the state be equipped with devices that reduce the quantity of pollutants in automobile exhausts. These devices, however, are still inefficient, and the pollution problem remains, and grows worse. In the 1980s the smog problem continues to reach critical levels. "Stay inside and try not to breath much" is not a good answer.

Automobile-caused air pollution is a symptom of a sick transportation system. It will probably not be solved by tacking more and more expensive devices on automobile exhaust systems. It could be solved by providing a healthier form of transportation. Yet the federal government can provide $40 billion to build an interstate highway system for automobiles and trucks, while doing very little to promote relatively non-polluting and energy-efficient rail or other rapid public transportation systems. It has been known for years how to develop relatively nonpolluting engines that burn renewable fuels. Yet billions of dollars go into devising new varieties of gasoline engines that waste energy, pollute the air, and end up in the category known as "solid waste." It is argued that the American people do not wish to give up their motor vehicles. It is undoubtedly true that Americans and others like to have private, high-speed vehicles for personal transportation. But they have not been given much choice.

NOISE POLLUTION

Most primates are noisy animals and man is no exception. Anyone who has listened to a pack of baboons getting settled for the night in Africa develops a better perspective on the racket frequently heard in human gatherings. It is no news that cities are noisy places. The fact has been commented on since the Towers of Babel were first constructed. But in the technologically advanced sections of the world, noise pollution has reached new dimensions. Some ideas of the magnitude of the problem are shown in Table 12.2 prepared by the Council on Environmental Quality. The decibel scale shown is a measure of the energy level of sound. The scale is logarithmic, meaning a level of 130 decibels is 10 times as great as one of 120 and 100 times as great as one of 110. In a quiet environment the sound level will be about 50 decibels or less; at 80 decibels the sound level becomes annoying. Nevertheless in the cities, people are commonly exposed to levels of 110 decibels or more—that of nearby riveting machines, jet takeoffs at the airport, or those mind-deadening institutions known as discotheques.

TABLE 12.2   Weighted Sound Levels and Human Response

DECIBEL LEVEL[a]	REPRESENTATIVE SOURCES OF SOUND	HUMAN RESPONSE TO SOUND LEVEL
150		
140	Aircraft carrier deck jet flights	Painfully loud
130	Limit of amplified speech	
120	Jet takeoff at 200 feet	
	Discotheque	
	Auto horn at 3 feet	
110	Riveting machine	
	Jet takeoff at 2000 feet	
100	Shout at 0.5 feet	Very annoying
	New York subway station	
90	Heavy truck at 50 feet	Hearing damage (8 hours)
	Pneumatic drill at 50 feet	
80		Annoying
	Freight train at 50 feet	
70	Freeway traffic at 50 feet	Telephone use difficult
60	Air conditioning unit at 20 feet	Intrusive
	Light auto traffic at 50 feet	
50		Quiet
	Living room	
40	Bedroom	
	Library	
30	Soft whisper	Very quiet
20	Broadcasting studio	
10		Just audible
0		Threshold of hearing

[a]Weighted sound levels based on frequency response of human ear.
Source: Council on Environmental Quality (1970) from Department of Transportation.

Steady exposure to sound at levels of 90 decibels or more is believed to cause loss of hearing. Other effects of noise on man are only now being pinpointed, but they include direct physiological as well as psychological effects. There appear to be individual differences in tolerance to noise and wide differences in tolerance to different kinds of noise—high-frequency whines are more difficult to withstand than dull roars, sudden and unexpected sounds cause more reaction than those that are regular or anticipated.

Although much more research on the effects of noise must be conducted before we can speak with any certainty, there seems no good reason for putting up with as much noise as is now forced on urban dwellers. Many cities and some states are attempting to enforce anti-noise regulations and to force manufacturers to build machinery and equipment with lower noise ratings. The federal government is now moving into this area with the setting of standards and with research on acoustical problems.

Probably the greatest national attention to the subject of noise was directed toward the plan to develop the supersonic transport. The SST, like all planes that fly faster than the speed of sound, creates a sonic boom all along its flight corridor. This noise level would be intolerable to those who would have to live with it and, in addition, is capable of creating structural damage. Furthermore, the SST would create a much higher level of airport noise, even flying at subsonic, than any existing jet plane. Although the federal administration had guaranteed the SST would not be permitted to fly over inhabited areas, the opponents to the project were skeptical about such promises. Opposition to noise, as much as any other factor, helped contribute to the defeat in Congress of the proposal to develop an American SST.

SEWAGE AND AGRICULTURE
The problems related to the disposal of human and animal organic wastes have been partly discussed in preceding chapters. We have cities that must find some way of getting rid of sewage and other wastes produced by millions of people. We also have agricultural soils being depleted of organic material by monocultural practices, which forces the employment of excessive amounts of energy-demanding nitrate fertilizers, as well as other chemicals. The fertilizers, washing from farmlands and into streams, lakes, or estuaries, create an additional pollution problem. The system is obviously disrupted, and what could be a healthy recycling does not take place.

The magnitude of the urban sewage problem cannot be dismissed lightly. New York City must do something with 5 million cubic yards of sewage sludge—the end product of its sewage treatment plants—each year. It has tackled the problem by hauling it in barges 11 miles offshore and dumping it. The sewage dumping ground has long been an unhealthy part of the ocean, since about 15 square miles of ocean bottom are now covered with a concentrated mass of sludge and can support only anaerobic forms of life. In theory this sludge is supposed to work its way down a submarine canyon into the ocean deeps. It has not obliged, however, and recently has been working its way back toward the beaches. Properly processed and returned to the land, this could be valuable fertilizer. Left alone it is a menace to marine life and a health threat to people.

Chicago, by contrast, has attempted to solve its problem in a more rational way, using its wastes to restore the soils of about 36,000 acres of marginal farm lands and strip-mined areas. Although the digested and chemically treated sludge represents no menace to health, citizens in the recipient areas have filed suit against the city of Chicago to prevent further dumping, since they fear that some unknown disease hazard may creep upon them. The belief that anything organic is filthy is widespread among Americans—an unfortunate by-product of mishandled health education and a direct product of advertising campaigns by those who sell disinfectants and deodorants to the gullible. The principal health hazard in sewage sludge from urban areas results from concentration of heavy metals. This is a result of the failure to separate chemical and industrial wastes from household sewage and can represent a formidable problem where sludge is used in food plant production. However, all of the cities' sewage could be used on soils that are not being used in food production, until such time as the separation of organic and nonorganic wastes can be effected. The nation's strip-mined areas alone could absorb all of the urban sludge and would be at least partially restored as a result.

One of the most absurd sewage disposal problems has been that resulting from new methods of livestock production. The concentration of great numbers of animals in small areas of feed lots, poultry batteries, and the like results in the production of large quantities of manure, which must then be removed. For some time this has been dumped into streams, thus adding to the burden of stream and lake pollution. It obviously belongs back on the farm, where it would enrich and improve the soil, but with farms mechanized and chemicalized, the bother of collecting and spreading manure has been too great for the landowners. Now, with the high cost of chemical fertilizer, one can expect a greater interest in obtaining manure, and some reports indicate that this particular pollution problem may be a thing of the past. One major feedlot, as of 1982, is using its manure stacks for methane generation.

A POTPOURRI Many books have been filled just by listing some of the various kinds of pollution and the problems resulting from them. No attempt is made here to be comprehensive, and some additional points deserve mention. During studies of the possible effects of the SST on the atmosphere, it was discovered that the nitrogen oxides in the exhaust of these big planes, released in the stratosphere at the altitudes used for supersonic flight, had the potential for destroying the ozone layer of the stratosphere. This is the chief atmospheric barrier to ultraviolet radiation. A great increase in ultraviolet radiation reaching the earth's surface would do more than just cause sunburn. It could create a serious hazard for many forms of animal life and vegetation. More recently it was discovered that the explosion of hydrogen bombs in the atmosphere would produce similar results if many of them were to be set off. Still more recently it was shown that the fluorocarbon gas used in pressurized spray cans, refrigeration, and various other processes could also produce similar effects. None of these things—SSTs, hydrogen bombs, or pressurized spray cans—can be considered essential to a high standard of living or even important to the "American way of life."

The poisoning of many people in Japan with methylmercury, in the Minamata case described in Chapter 9, was followed by the realization that fish and people in Sweden and other Baltic Sea countries were being exposed to excessive amounts of organic mercury. You might have expected that the use of mercury salts as a fungicide for the protection of agricultural seeds might have been abandoned as a result of this, but it

a

TECHNOLOGICAL COSTS

(a) A toxic waste dump in Massachusetts. Cleanup is underway, but new toxic wastes are being produced every day. **(b)** Total devastation was caused in Tennessee by fumes from copper smelting. **(c)** Copper mining and smelting in Arizona—will it create a new wasteland? **(d)** Worker's dwellings in the most polluted area near a steel mill in Wales. Should the poor always pay for "progress"? **(e)** The junk pile continues to grow in Alaska.

b

c

d

e

was not. In Iraq in 1973, 6000 people were poisoned by eating seed grain treated with methyl mercury (Bakir, 1973). In 1974 it was necessary to kill 50,000 calves in Italy, 30,000 in Holland, and additional numbers in other European countries because phenyl mercury acetate became mixed up in their feed. Heavy metals of other kinds continue to pile up in the human environment despite their known hazards. Heavy cadmium concentrations have been found in sea otters off the California coast and high concentrations of arsenic in crabs along the Canadian Pacific coast. Tetraethyl lead is spewed from automobile tail pipes around the world although even relatively low concentrations of lead have been associated with nervous and behavioral disorders, whereas high concentrations are fatal. The simple concept that people should not be allowed to poison other people, even though it is very profitable and convenient to do so, has apparently not been accepted by all the people. Those who are not made noticeably ill, or who have not had their friends and relatives poisoned, prefer not to get involved.

Donella and Dennis Meadows et al. (1972) have summed the situation up well in *The Limits to Growth*: *Virtually every pollutant that has been measured as a function of time appears to be increasing exponentially. . . . It is not known how much CO^2 or thermal pollution can be released without causing irreversible changes in the earth's climate, or how much radioactivity, lead, mercury or pesticide can be absorbed by plants, fish, or human beings before the vital processes are severely interrupted.*

In the late 1970s and early 1980s still another pollution problem came to light with the realization of the extent of toxic waste dumps and the hazards associated with them. Industries had been storing toxic wastes of all varieties, from the most extreme poisons such as cyanide to potential cancer-causing and mutation-causing chemicals such as PCBs. Some of the storage was in ordinary oil drums stored on the surface of the ground. Some of the wastes had been buried. In some areas housing had been built on top of what had been a toxic dump. One of the most widely publicized incidents was in the Love Canal area near Niagara Falls, where serious health problems developed as a result of leakage from a dump site, polluting air and water. The entire small community had to be abandoned and the people moved. As a result of investigations by the Environmental Protection Agency and state environmental agencies, it has begun to appear that such dumps are to be found in hundreds of places around the United States. Many are leaking. Often the company that originally left the waste has gone out of business or moved away. Holding industry responsible for its "past sins" in this way has not been popular among industrialists—and indeed the potential cost of removing and burying wastes in "safe sites" (whatever they are) will run into hundreds of millions of dollars. But the alternative is worse. Congress responded to this crisis by establishing a $1.6 billion "superfund." But the EPA has shown an unwillingness to either crack down on polluters or clean up the dumps. In 1983 the town of Times Beach, Missouri, had to be evacuated because of contamination by the highly poisonous chemical dioxin. Similar contamination has been found in a number of other towns in the Middle West.

> Can we overcome our corrupt ways and marshal our efforts to collaborate with Nature as her brightest child and shepherd of Earth's life system? If not, it is almost certain that things will worsen for Nature, but even more so for us. Then, at a certain point in time we may no longer be able to cope with the adversity and we will perish. But Nature will survive, and so, too, will the insects, her most successful children. And as a final bit of irony, it will be insects that polish the bones of the very last of us to fall.
>
> Robert van den Bosch, The Pesticide Conspiracy (1980)

THE URBAN-INDUSTRIAL-TECHNOLOGICAL TRAP

In the 1980s people belonging to the biosphere cultures control the world. The biosphere cultures are centered in the metropolitan areas of the world. Each metropolis depends, not on any local ecosystem, but on the resources of the biosphere. Food and drink come in from everywhere: coffee from Colombia, tea from Sri Lanka, bananas from Panama, olive oil from Italy, oranges from South Africa, pineapples from Hawaii, and so on. Fuel may come from Saudi Arabia or Venezuela. Minerals come from Zambia, Jamaica, Zimbabwe, Chile, and Peru. Manufactured goods flow out from the metropolis to change and influence all parts of the world. Money and technology also flow out to dominate and control. In the United States more than three-quarters of the people are urban—not city people, necessarily, but more likely suburban, or living in the satellite towns that surround the big cities. It is in the cities where the greatest achievements of humanity are to be found, and also the worst failures. It is in the cities where the greatest conservation battles are being fought, and it is city people who decide the fate of other areas.

One of the most disturbing features of life in a modern city is the feeling of helplessness and dependence. The larger and more complex the metropolis, the less able is each individual to help himself. One is totally dependent on the continued functioning of the urban society for everything—food, clothing, water, transportation, light, heat—all of the necessities for survival. Self-sufficiency and independence are only words. Instead one must rely on some unknown or impersonal "them" who are responsible for providing everything. When things go wrong, when the garbage is not hauled, or the sewage lines break, when water does not flow and telephones do not work, it is always "they" who are to blame, but nobody knows who "they" are. They may be identified with city government or the big corporations, but both are equally impersonal, and both seem totally interrelated. This helplessness and dependence may account for the great flight to the suburbs and then to the exurbs, which has characterized the years since World War II. There, at least, one can have a plot of ground, a home workshop, and less of a feeling of being hemmed in. But as the suburbs expand outward, those in the inner rings begin to develop the same trapped feeling.

In the 1980s in many large American cities, the city heart has deteriorated, with slum conditions widespread. The metropolitan edge has deteriorated with the unplanned spread of suburbs, most of which offer a minimum of environmental amenities. The spread of unplanned highway "strip towns" and the development of an urban fringe area—neither farm nor city but of neglected land in transition—has made the situation worse. Traffic congestion in and around cities has become extreme. In an effort to solve this problem freeways, parking lots, and other automobile-oriented enterprises have cut into and often shattered the earlier city framework, sometimes destroying scenic and historical areas as well as urban open space in the process. Pollution of air and water has become chronic. In many areas water shortages exist or are threatened.

Yet the greatest problem may be presented not by the existing situation but by the prospect of future growth. If some forecasters prove correct we will have to build accommodations for double the present urban population within 35 years. If they are correct we must build the equivalent of metropolitan Washington each year. However, there is nothing inevitable about this process. We could decide to live in a different way.

If the American situation is depressing, the world situation often appears hopeless. According to the United Nations, the rate of urbanization is most rapid in developing countries. Whereas in 1920 the urban population was 100 million, it is predicted that by 2000 the urban population will be 2 billion. The Secretary-General of the United Nations has pointed out (UN, 1969): *However, in most areas, governments have neither prepared for, nor have they been able to cope with, the mass migration into urban areas. In the large cities, slums of the most wretched nature often become the environment of people who once lived in greater dignity and better health on rural lands. Pollution of air, water, and land, concentrated in urban areas, have become universal problems, threatening man's health. Diseases associated with urban living in developing nations has increased greatly despite advances in medicine. Noise and congestion in urban areas add to physical and mental distress.*

It is paradoxical that the greatest creations of humanity—the cities—have become the places least suited to human occupancy. But the paradox is caused by the history of cities and the sudden shattering of their frameworks by too rapid growth. A city adequate for the needs of pedestrians cannot be adjusted quickly to accomodate hordes of motorists. A city built to house 50,000 people within a circumscribed space cannot be stretched to accommodate five times as many without serious disruption of its former framework. For many years American city planners made pilgrimages to Europe and came back shaking their heads in amazement at the ways in which European cities had resisted the disruptive forces that plagued those of America. They do so no longer.

The supposedly greater environmental wisdom of the older civilizations of Europe vanished as soon as population pressure, and particularly economic affluence, reached critical levels. It was then realized that the European did not necessarily love his quaint old dwelling; nor did he ride a bicycle instead of an auto by personal choice. Today historic and picturesque quarters of London and Paris are mushrooming with high-rise buildings all too reminiscent of Omaha or Kansas City. New towns in France exemplify the worst in "plastic modern" architecture. The traffic congestion in Rome must be experienced to be believed. Air pollution from Milan blots out the landscapes of Lake Como. The Swiss mountains are invaded by ugly developments to accommodate tourists, and many of the once-distinct towns and villages are merging together in a continuous urban sprawl. But, despite the now obvious problems, the situation in Europe, where population growth is slow, seems idyllic compared with that in developing countries. The Secretary-General of the United Nations reported (UN, 1969): *In most developing nations it has rarely been possible to provide in advance the urban planning and design. . . . Migration into cities is often associated with the importation of disease such as trachoma, tuberculosis, parasitosis, and skin diseases. The influx of people tends to bring enormous pressure on water supplies and arrangements for waste disposal, with the consequent appearance of diarrhoeal diseases. Overcrowding of premises and sites is typical. Inadequate housing accommodation is accompanied by shanty-type construction and further unsatisfiable demands are made upon water supply and waste disposal facilities. Food supplies may be inadequate, badly distributed or prepared, and sold under unhygienic conditions. . . . In rapid urbanization every form of publicly provided service, including transport and education, tends to be overloaded. Schools are heavily overcrowded, and as a result attendance tends to fall, and juvenile delinquency becomes more common. Social change often leads to disintegration of the family and other primary institutions of society. . . . The stress that often accompanies accelerated change results in emotional tension and a feeling of insecurity. These may find their expression in mental breakdowns, psychosomatic manifestations, suicide attempts, increased frequency of crime, drug dependence and anti-social behavior. . . . The magnitude of the problem in some developing nations appears to defy solution by anything less than a massive national and international effort.*

a

TECHNOLOGICAL BENEFITS?

(a) The endless city—Los Angeles—is bigger better? (b) Paris destroys itself—new office tower in Montparnasse. (c) The freeway and the city—no answer to urban transportation needs. (d) Urban renewal—is this the way? Are new towns the answer? (e) A Danish example and (f) an English new town.

b

c

d

e

f

411

Most of the world's people are sustained by growing their own food, tending their own animals in rural areas, and living in small, cooperatively run villages and settlements or as nomads following herds, harvesting wild crops, fishing, and hunting in economies based on barter, reciprocity, and redistribution of surpluses according to customs such as feasts and potlatches. One of the aspects of the crises of industrial development is that it begins to suck all such informal, use-value production and consumption into the monetized economies, drawing populations into the cities, denuding rural agricultural areas, dissolving the cultural glue of village life and reciprocal community systems of food-sharing, care of the young and elderly, and folk medicine, and destroying inherited cultural wisdom learned in coping with diverse eco-logical conditions. . . .

The industrial model in its mass-consumption, global-advertising stage of titillating rural populations with visions of city lights, cars, flashy clothes, cigarettes, booze, Coke, and rock music now creates mass migrations throughout the planet in search of money, jobs and status symbols. At the same time, traditional values of sharing, respect for nature, and reciprocal unremunerated services appear old-fashioned, boring, and backward, described by Marx, who despised peasant culture, as "the idiocy of rural life." But after tempting every rural community on the planet that can be reached by mass media and transistor radios with the consumer model of the industrialized "good life," industrialism is caught in a cruel hoax: it cannot deliver. It can deliver for only some of the population at the expense of others—and as we are now seeing, it can deliver only some of the time (while there are cheap, abundant environmental resources to be used up). But it cannot work in the long run.

Hazel Henderson, *The Politics of the Solar Age* (1981), pp. 25–26

PATTERNS AND PROBLEMS

It is impossible here to do more than give an outline of some of the problems facing metropolitan areas. Most of our towns and cities grew originally with little overall planning or control. They reflect thousands of individual decisions and hundreds of partial plans. These have con-tributed in some areas to a rich texture of interesting urban diversity, in others to ugliness and confusion. Past efforts to achieve some order in the cities have to a large extent taken the line of separating urban func-tions through zoning. Zoning laws have separated the industrial areas where people work in producing goods; the commercial areas where people shop or work at office jobs; and the residential areas where peo-ple sleep and carry out much of their social life. The latter are further divided into areas of single-family detached homes and areas of multiple-family housing represented by high-rise apartments or other high-density housing. Such a separation of urban functions was inhibited originally by transportation facilities. In the nineteenth century and earlier, it was necessary to be within walking distance of work and shopping areas. With the development of individual transportation by private automobile, however, it became possible to separate these urban functions widely. Thus the development of residential suburbs, extending often in uniform patterns for many miles beyond the former city boundaries, occurred.

Cities, by their very nature, present problems of transportation. They are areas in which agricultural produce is processed or consumed and areas in which the various products of industry are manufactured. There must be a constant flow of goods into and out of the city. The modern industrial city often grew up around the railroad junction. The central railway station was in many American cities the focus around which hotels, entertainment centers, stores, and offices were grouped. The railway line was later the axis along which the city expanded into the countryside, the means by which city people traveled to seek recreation, the basis for the existence of satellite towns, resorts, and other urban-oriented developments. Within the city, public transporation systems, horsecars or, later, electric trolleys served to move people from the industrial, or commercial centers to the residential districts. With the rise of the private automobile and the gasoline- or diesel-powered truck, however, this old framework of the city was disrupted. New urban centers, more readily accessible by automobile, arose, and the area around the railway station disintegrated into a "skid row" or slum district. Highways, rather than rails, provided the new avenues for urban expansion into the countryside. Public transportation facilities disintegrated.

With ever-growing numbers of automobiles, traffic jam became a permanent part of the urban scene. The difficulties of reaching the city center and of parking when there, along with other factors, led to a breakdown of the central city. Business and industry followed the people to the suburbs. New centers of work and commerce, dispersed widely around the periphery of the urbanized area, began to replace the old centralized urban core. The central city became a place where the poor concentrated, where ethnic minority groups were forced to live, and where housing, schools, and all other urban facilities deteriorated. Cities, in the old sense of vital, thriving centers of human activity and interest, appeared to be dying.

The suburbs have been the subject of many sociological studies since the end of World War II and have been blamed for many of the ills of modern society. Yet there is little doubt that most people who have moved there from the central city have gained a marked improvement in living conditions. The suburbs have become the established center of the American middle-class family, since they offer security and space for the raising of children in congenial surroundings. They have been consistently rejected by the adolescent and young adult who find them restrictive and dull. They have little appeal to the intellectual. In one form or another, however, they are likely to remain part of urbanized America.

There have been many different approaches to urban renewal. Some center on the belief that the automobile is here to stay and seek, through the construction of freeways and adequate parking facilities, to develop new patterns of automobile-oriented urban centers and residential areas. Others believe that the automobile is by its nature inimical to healthy cities and seek the development of clean, attractive, high-speed public transportation systems that will replace the private car, combined with pedestrian-oriented centers of shopping, business, and entertainment. Some seek to retain and rejuvenate the old urban residential areas, now frequently deteriorated into slums. This approach has been followed with marked success in Georgetown in the nation's capital, in the North Beach area of San Francisco, Greenwich Village in New York, the French Quarter in New Orleans, and elsewhere.

A more common approach to urban renewal is demolition and re-development. The old congested centers of Philadelphia, Pittsburgh, southwest Washington, D.C., and other cities have been replaced by gleaming new towers of office buildings and high-rise apartments. Such an approach is frequently disastrous for those people who lived in the old areas, but cannot afford to live in the new.

The garden city concept, for which Ebenezer Howard was the best known early advocate, has many followers today. The new towns of Reston, Virginia, and Columbia, Maryland, essentially follow this patern, with a major emphasis on the clustered development of housing around recreation lakes and surrounded by green areas of open space. In both of these towns and in many other developments, emphasis has been placed on the formation of what is essentially an urban village within an urban town in a city. It is hoped that such small, unified communities will give the individual greater opportunity and scope for activity in the affairs of his society, and a greater feeling of personal identity.

No one approach to urban development or renewal provides the answer for the cities of the future. Indeed, it is to be hoped that no single urban pattern will be allowed to prevail to the same extent in the future as, for example, the uniform, detached-house suburban pattern was allowed to prevail after World War II. Our understanding of cities, and of people, is far from complete, and we would do well to be skeptical of those who would offer us packaged solutions for all of our urban problems. Indeed, the preservation or creation of urban diversity, to provide different ways of living, old and new, in different kinds of cities, for people of differing tastes, and thus to allow a maximum degree of individual choice, is the most human approach to the future development of urban environments.

TRANSPORTATION   For most of man's history, travel within a city was on foot, and transportation of goods was conducted by human porters or domestic animals drawing carts of various kinds. Travel between centers of population was, for people "of importance," by carriage of one sort or another, or by boat. The famous Roman roads, which are still in use today, were laid out to facilitate travel by chariot between the capital and regional centers of the Italian peninsula, but travel to the far reaches of the empire was

> ... *Marxist theory holds that socialism is simply a later stage of capitalist development and would grow out of the processes of capitalist production and accumulation. In fact, the new vulnerabilities of industrialism itself have now produced an even greater irony: that the fierce and supposedly fundamental debate between Marxism and capitalism of the nineteenth and early-twentieth centuries has turned out to be a surface argument. Both systems are systems of industrialism, dedicated to maximizing material production and narrowly conceived technological "progress"; both short-change the considerations of ecological tolerances and the fundamental needs of human beings that go beyond material sufficiency to needs for philosophical meaning and concerns of the spirit.*
>
> Hazel Henderson, *The Politics of the Solar Age* (1981), p. 2

usually by water transport. Proximity to navigable waters determined the location of many of the world's great cities and favors their continuance today. Transportation is not exclusively an urban concern, but it is in and around our urban centers that transportation problems have become hopelessly snarled.

Methods for improving water-based transport showed their greatest enhancement during the period from 1870 to approximately 1940, with the replacement of a dependence on sails or oars by steam- and then diesel-powered engines. Speed of transportation was increased somewhat, although the sailing clippers at times made the transatlantic run nearly as quickly as did the diesel-powered liner; but, more important, reliability was markedly improved. In more recent decades there have been some radical advances—hovercraft moving on a cushion of air now regularly cross the Channel between France and England, nuclear-powered submarines can stay at sea and remain submerged for much longer periods of time and move faster than their petroleum-driven predecessors, giant supertankers have capacities not believed possible in the recent past. Nevertheless, the average level of ocean transport has shown little improvement. Travel by ship across the ocean has now become a luxury for those who feel they can afford to spend extra time in their travels or simply wish to spend a completely restful vacation. Others, who once were forced to take this time, now crowd their schedules with other activities.

As noted earlier, the greatest problems of land-based transportation have resulted from the shift from railways for intercity transport, and the shift from surface trolleys and underground subways for inner-city transport, to a one-sided dependence on the private automobile and motor truck. Highway construction, favored by taxes on petroleum that were earmarked for this specific purpose, has been carried out in ways completely disproportionate to human needs. All other systems of transport have suffered from neglect with the exception of the air transport, which has also undergone one-sided development.

The comfort and convenience attached to the private motor car, as well as the sheer pleasure derived from its ownership and operation, cannot be ignored. Nevertheless, the automobile, as it is presently constructed and used, is completely impractical for movement within high-density urban areas. The needs of the cities for rapid, convenient, and comfortable mass transit systems have long been obvious; not that these systems are the single answer to urban transportation problems, but they are an obviously important part of any answer.

> Whether we are faced with a new, paradisical era or a catastrophe like the Norse Ragnarok is still unclear, but there can be no lengthy period of compromise between past and future in an ambiguous present. The reconstructive and destructive tendencies in our time are too much at odds with each other to admit of reconciliation. The social horizon presents the starkly conflicting prospects of a harmonized world with an ecological sensibility based on a rich commitment to community, mutual aid, and new technologies, on the one hand, and the terrifying prospect of some sort of thermonuclear disaster on the other. Our world, it would appear, will either undergo revolutionary changes, so far-reaching in character that humanity will totally transform its social relations and its very conception of life, or it will suffer an apocalypse that may well end humanity's tenure on the planet.
>
> Murray Bookchin, *The Ecology of Freedom* (1982), p. 18

Opposition to the construction of airports near the city reached a high level during the late 1960s and early 1970s. In Tokyo farmers and students fought pitched battles with the police to prevent construction of new airport facilities. In London's outskirts similar battles are threatened by those who oppose the destruction of residential areas, urban areas, or valued nature reserves to make room for an additional airport. In Florida the plans to construct a giant jetport in the Big Cypress Swamp, north of Everglades National Park, intended to serve the cities of Miami and Tampa, were brought to a halt after $13 million had been expended. The opposition of conservationists, based on the damage the jetport would cause to the Everglades and Big Cypress environments, was sufficient to stop construction.

The opposition to the construction of new airports, however, does not solve the problem. Existing airports, saturated with plane traffic, are both dangerous and inefficient. The inefficiency is related particularly to the failure to integrate air terminals with any effective form of surface transportation. It has long been a complaint that one can spend more time getting from the city to the metropolitan airport than it takes to fly across the country. Inattention to the comfort and safety of passengers has been accompanied by greater attention to larger and faster planes—in other words to what has been the most efficient part of the system.

This led to investment by airlines in jumbo jets and, most peculiarly of all, to a drive to develop an unneeded and generally unwanted supersonic transport. Fortunately, in 1971 Congress decided to veto any further federal support for the SST. In France and the USSR, however, where governments seem strangely entranced by technology, SSTs have been built and attempts are being made to get them into regular service. The fact that the first Russian SST crashed at the Paris Air Show did not help their cause greatly. Today the Anglo-French Concorde SST is regarded as a financial disaster.

Urban centers require efficient and flexible transportation systems. Precisely what form these systems should take is difficult to predict in advance—but their use of nonrenewable fuels must be eliminated before many years have passed. There is not the slightest doubt that the present reliance on petroleum-drive motor cars and airplanes as an answer to transportation needs must be abandoned. A recent review of the problem and a proposed solution are provided by Swan (1981). This combines light rail transport, eventually to be solar powered, with various uses of buses, minibuses, vans, and bicycles to form a transportation network. No major new technologies are required but only intelligent fitting together of now separated transportation parts.

THE URBAN SYSTEM It is generally accepted, in theory, that urban communities represent systems within which the various parts necessarily interact. They have many features in common with natural ecosystems, but also marked differences. The modern metropolis is a supraecosystem—a system that affects and is affected by a wide range of natural ecosystems and cannot be circumscribed within anything less than the entire biosphere. All modern cities are tied together by networks of transportation and communication, so that Paris and New York are more closely interrelated and interacting today than Philadelphia and New York were in colonial times.

Urban systems are necessarily built up from a network of subsystems—transportation being an example. These are tied together in various ways. The subsystems through which food, water, and materials move into a city, and the one through which wastes move out or are, hopefully, recycled, are obviously related to subsystems of transportation and communication. Increasing size and complexity in urban systems lead to greater fragility, that is, to greater dangers of disruption from disturbance. Thus a breakdown somewhere in the electrical power grid covering the northeastern United States brought the city of New York to a total halt in 1965, since there were no adequate buffering or compensating devices. A strike by sanitation workers disrupted many years of progress in the system for sewage disposal in England, and led to unacceptably high levels of water pollution. The work of a few hijackers has affected and slowed the world's air transport system. Part of this vulnerability and much of the confusion in urban existence results from the failure to treat urban communities for the systems they are and to plan accordingly. Part of it, however—perhaps the most important part—is the result of excessive centralization of control and of power.

In the first of these causes, it is too common for those concerned with one subsystem—and transportation is the notorious example—to work in isolation from all other subsystems. Builders of suburban tracts commonly work without consideration of the effect of their community on transportation, sewage disposal, water supply, schools, and all of the other parts of the broader urban community to which the new tract will belong. It is the job of the metropolitan planners to be aware of these things, but many planners are not environmentally trained, and all are ruled by politicians, who often reflect special interest pressures.

Perhaps the greatest failure in urban planning and development is the tendency to get carried away by the technological game of building and developing and to forget that the city is intended to be the home for a particular type of animal, the human being. This is a species noted for individuality and diversity, for aggressive and territorial tendencies in behavior, and is frequently characterized by bad temper and destructiveness. Thus the new and shiny housing developments intended to improve the lot of slum dwellers are commonly hated by those who are forced to live in them. They seldom function in the way the designers had intended. Studies of what the people concerned really want seldom precede the development of mass housing that people are then forced to accept. Studies of how people react to new towns and communities are rarely financed, since it is embarrasing to the developers and government officials to consider past failures. It is easier to go on building tomorrow's failures.

The energy crisis will force a restructuring of urban areas. There is no doubt that a high degree of self-sufficiency could be developed within small, urban-suburban neighborhoods. Attention to local development of renewable energy supplies, solar, wind, or whatever is most available, would unhook these communities from complex and centrally directed power webs. Community systems for handling organic wastes with the generation of methane and the production of fertilizers are feasible. Community gardens for food production could do much to remove dependency on outside food sources. There are many things that could be done—all involve opening up the urban network, decentralizing its functions, developing local sufficiency and reliance and, perhaps most important, developing a *sense of community*.

There is no good reason for supinely accepting continued urban growth. Much of this takes place because nothing is done to encourage people to remain on the land, and because villages and small towns suffer from public neglect. A move toward strengthening the rural settlement pattern and for providing in village and town the means of livelihood and centers for intellectual and cultural advancement could be accomplished by government action. It could also be accomplished by individuals, if they have the will to do so, whether or not government shows much interest; in the 1980s this is a developing trend. Someone has suggested that Los Angeles be set aside as a "national degradation preserve" in which all efforts to protect or improve the environment would be forbidden, and only uncontrolled economic growth would be allowed. People of the future may value such a "living museum" (providing anything can still be kept alive within it) as an example of how not to develop a human community.

THE TECHNOCRATIC SOCIETY

Critics of the present organization of the biosphere cultures have spent considerable time in analyzing and defining its faults and problems. It is difficult to find anyone who is not a critic of society, although some confine their criticism to a few aspects of modern life, whereas others spend time looking for scapegoats to whom the blame can be attached. It is difficult, however, to affix blame in modern industrial society. In earlier kingdoms and empires, one could always blame the monarch, since he presumably had complete power and control. In the America of the 1980s, however, one can force out of office a president, vice-president, and most of the other higher officials of administration—and yet everything remains about the same. The more closely one examines the total system, the more it becomes apparent nobody is really in charge.

Lewis Mumford (1966, 1970) has examined the development of technics and technology in a two-volume work that reviews the history of mankind from this perspective. He defines the present technological organization as a megamachine. In his view this originated with the first civilizations—the builders of pyramids and towers of Babel. In these earlier empires the megamachine was powered by human components rather than by mechanical engines. Civilization thus was the first form of human organization that reduced the individual to being a cog or component of a machine rather than an equal partner in a human enterprise.

If We Surrender, We Die

Our ideas will overcome your ideas. We are going to cut the country's whole value system to shreds. It isn't important that there are only 500,000 of us Indians.... What is important is that we have a superior way of life. We Indians have a more human philosophy of life. We Indians will show this country how to act human. Someday this country will revise its constitution, its laws, in terms of human beings, instead of property. If Red Power is to be a power in this country it is because it is ideological.... What is the ultimate value of a man's life? That is the question.

Vine Deloria, Jr. (1971). Cited in T. C. McLuhan, *Touch the Earth* (1972)

Characteristic of the megamachine was the institution of slavery, of armies, of separate priesthoods removed from the people who alone could talk to the gods, of organized warfare and mass murder, and of the organization of working masses to build structures for the glory of those who held power.

In its original form, the megamachine broke down with the fall of the ancient empires. In Europe, at least during the long period following the fall of Rome, society came to be organized on a more human scale. The tradition of the megamachine lived, however, on and was to be reborn with the Industrial Revolution and the rise of the modern nation-state.

The industrial revolution grew from a highly organized and efficient medieval technology. This operated on a small, human scale with emphasis on individual skill and excellence. The machines that were organized in the factories of the Industrial Revolution were themselves turned out by individual craftsmen who were drawing from a long tradition. Mumford (1970) believes that if this original craftmanship and small technology *had not been condemned to death by starvation wages and meager profits, if it had, in fact, been protected and subsidized as so many of the new mechanical industries were in fact extravagantly subsidized, right down to jet planes and rockets today, our technology as a whole, even that of "fine technics" would have been immensely richer—and more efficient.*

The Industrial Revolution, with its creation of a new megamachine and its reduction of people to components and parts of an industrial process, depended on the rise of a new form of nation-state and its professional armies. In the old empires the emperor might be deified, but the state was not. The new nation-states, however, were endowed with godlike qualities. One was supposed to live and die for a strange spiritual entity known as "la belle France," "Mother Russia," or "Uncle Sam." Loyalty to this spirit was supposed to take precedence over one's love of family, friends, community, or the hills of home. Such idolatry could occur only in a world from which God has been effectively banished—through the increasing dualism of institutional Christianity or the abandonment of any meaningful spiritual beliefs. "My country right or wrong" is not a statement compatible with the teachings of Christ, but is one expected of followers of the goddess Columbia.

Mumford (1970) defined modern technology as follows: *The last century, we all realize, has witnessed a radical transformation of the entire human environment, largely as a result of the impact of the mathematical and physical sciences upon technology. This shift from an empirical, tradition-bound technics to an experimental mode has opened up such realms as those of nuclear energy, supersonic transportation, cybernetic intelligence and instantaneous distant communication.*

The growth of this technology, based on the application of science and mathematics to industrial processes, has resulted in its encompassing the world. With its massive size and rate of growth it is the dominant force in the biosphere, compared to which nation-states and international

a

b

THE TECHNOLOGICAL SOCIETY

(a) Conflict in ways of life. Must the technological society always prevail? (b) Destruction in Vietnam— where the "megamachine" broke down.

organizations appear as mere adjuncts. It exists in the Communist and capitalist world and dominates all who are caught up in its network.

Jacques Ellul (1964) has called the existing state of affairs the "Technological Society," and points out that one of its characteristics is that technology must prevail over the human being—everyone must play his role to keep the system turning over.

Theodore Roszak (1970) has used the term *technocracy* and defines it as *that society in which those who govern justify themselves by appeal to technical experts, who, in turn, justify themselves by appeal to scientific forms of knowledge. And beyond the authority of science there is no appeal. . . . Technocracy easily eludes all traditional political categories. Indeed it is characteristic of the technocracy to render itself ideologically invisible.*

No matter what is called or how it is defined, it is now obvious to anyone who thinks about it that we in America no longer live—if, indeed, we ever lived—in a society where "private enterprise" produces goods for the benefit of the people and is watched over by a benign government that has always the long-term interest of the people at heart. Yet not very long ago many Americans believed just that. Maybe some still do.

In the technocratic society, built along capitalist lines, the separation of government and private industry scarcely exists in practice. Private industry performs public work—the building of highways, dams, war machinery, and schools. Much of the action at the government level is directed toward subsidization, regulation, or development of the private sector. The Atomic Energy Commission existed to promote the development of nuclear power by private industry. The fact that it was also supposed to regulate itself and industry created a contradiction that led to its split in 1974 into two agencies. The whole complex, however, is geared toward continuing economic growth along directions that are difficult to modify. Decisions are made collectively and cannot easily be reversed by the person who may be the current general manager, chairman of the board, or even president of the United States. Planning for growth in a particular direction involves consultations among representatives of many industries and branches of government. Once a decision is made, contracts and subcontracts are let. People are employed and go to work. If it should be discovered after a few years that the original decisions were mistaken and the direction is wrong, the discoverer will hesitate to announce this, even if he occupies a high position. Once turned on, the technocracy rolls on, and he who would stop it will throw people out of work, disrupt the economy, and probably be fired himself.

A principal activity of the world technocracy, through most of its national branches, has always been preparation for war. War is the biggest growth industry, but it is not to be called by its own name. Instead it is referred to as national defense. Appropriations for war-related activities are expected to exceed a trillion dollars during the middle and late 1980s. This guarantees that a high percentage of the American population will be employed in research, development, or construction related to the various components of the war machine. During the peak years of the American involvement in Indochina, we were spending $20 billion a year for the destruction of that region and its peoples. For many years it was recognized by some that the war was morally wrong and by others that it was not being won—but it was easier to go on accelerating the destruction than to turn off or reverse the megamachine.

Productivity in the mechanical rather than the biological sense is a principal activity of a technocracy. It is measured in terms of gross national product or GNP. Anything produced, whether useful or not, enhances the GNP. Anything destroyed, if its destruction involves payrolls and machines, enhances the GNP. War always boosts the GNP. Production for waste particularly characterizes American technocracy. Quality and durability of products would lead to decreased consumption and therefore to decreased production and thus a decline in the GNP. Production for profit need not be an incentive in a technocracy. In the socialist model represented by the USSR, the same processes take place as in the United States. There, however, prestige, position in the hierarchy, and other rewards at least partly take the place of the profit motive.

All of the activities of the technocratic society are oriented toward the goal of "progress," which is defined in terms of continuing economic growth. Yet the system is wasteful, destructive of the environment, and unresponsive to human needs except for those that can be satisfied with material goods. Furthermore, it is almost beyond human control. The technocratic society could continue to operate so long as energy supplies and raw materials were abundant. Now that they are no longer cheap or abundant, changes must be made. The technocracy must be modified or it will grind to a halt.

The technocratic society, depending as it does on resources from throughout the biosphere, must endeavor to extend its influence globally. Thus assistance to Third World countries, during the period since the old colonial empires broke down, has consisted for the most part of investment in major developments: industries, big dams, massive irrigation schemes, or developments for tourism. All of these tend to strengthen the local technocracy and to tie it into the global technocracy. Considering that billions of dollars are spent on such "aid," it is remarkable how little of it seems to trickle through and actually improve the lot of the average person in the recipient countries. Instead the contrast between rich and poor becomes greater. Often, however, there is a comforting growth in the GNP that disguises the fact that the poor people remain as poor as before.

Jimoh Omo-Fadaka (1974) has described how industrialization and a high rate of growth in the GNP have disguised the realities of life in Jamaica. Between 1950 and 1965, the GNP grew at an annual rate of 7.2 percent. However, the per capita income of the Jamaican people declined. Unemployment climbed to 19 percent in urban areas and 10 percent in rural areas. Although 140 factories were built, which created 9000 new jobs, some 10,000 jobs were lost in the sugar industry alone through mechanization. Thus economic development, poured in from the top, brought increased poverty and misery. After examining the situation in other developing countries Omo-Fadaka recommends building from the bottom, starting with small-scale decentralized communities. These communities must relate to agricultural lands farmed by methods that are labor intensive and require small inputs of imported energy. Low-cost local energy production, on a small scale, using wind, water, and solar power needs be encouraged. Aid should be concentrated in providing and developing low-cost building materials and in establishing village industries and workshops that encourage local crafts.

There is more than a little danger that people will vote for a greater concentration of power in the name of greater efficiency and in protest against the chaos that is growing throughout technocratic society. This was the route taken in Italy, Germany, and Japan before World War II. It is being taken in many erstwhile democracies in the Third World, where military dictatorships have replaced the former governments. Although it is not inconceivable that a greater centralization of power could lead to more effective environmental protection and even to greater economic well-being for the people in the short run, it is impossible that any society geared to continued economic growth and expansion along the lines that have been followed to date can protect the human environment. Without such environmental protection, the society must eventually collapse. The other direction is toward decentralization of power, both in the political sense and in terms of energy production and distribution. This is the one that appears to hold greater hope for the future of the human environment, and for individual freedom. It needs careful exploration.

Howard Odum (1973) has warned of the dangers, and states the terrible possibility that economic advisers who do not understand ecological processes will insist on continued growth with our last energies. There would then be "no reserves with which to make a change, to hold order, and to cushion a period when population must drop." The end result could be that "At some point the great gaunt towers of nuclear installations, oil drilling, and urban cluster will stand empty in the wind for lack of enough fuel technology to keep them running."

> *The coming ideological debate is not over how the pie is to be divided; nor is it the old contest between efficiency and equity, property and state-enforced charity. It has deeper roots, and the stakes are higher. As the economies of America and all other nations slow down, and some begin to decline absolutely, many people are tempted to maintain their standard of living by expropriating a portion of the declining share of everyone else. But these beggar-thy-neighbor strategies, already apparent in Reagan's America, will undermine civic virtue and ultimately reduce the prosperity and security of everyone.*
>
> Robert B. Reich, Ideologies of survival. *New Republic* (1982)

SOURCES

Bakir, F., et al., 1973. Methyl mercury poisoning in Iraq. *Science* 181:230–241.

Bookchin, Murray, 1982. *The ecology of freedom.* Cheshire Books, Palo Alto, Calif.

Carson, Rachel, 1962. *Silent spring.* Houghton Mifflin, Boston.

Conway, R. C., 1965. Crop pest control and resource conservation in tropical Southeast Asia. *Proceedings of the Conference on nature and natural resources in tropical Southeast Asia.* IUCN, Gland, Switzerland.

Council on Environmental Quality, 1970. *Environmental Quality.* Government Printing Office, Washington, D.C.

Ellul, Jacques, 1964. *The technological society.* Vintage Books, New York.

Gilyarov, M., 1968. Soil fertility and zoology. *Nature and Resources.* UNESCO.

Goldsmith, Edward, 1982. The retreat from Stockholm. *The Ecologist* 12:98.

Henderson, Hazel, 1981. *The politics of the solar age.* Anchor Press, New York.

Hickey, J. and D. Anderson, 1968. Chlorinated hydrocarbons and egg shell changes in raptorial and fish-eating birds. *Science* 162:271–272.

Lave, L. B. and E. P. Seskin, 1970. Air pollution and human health. *Science* 169:723–733.

McLuhan, T. C., 1972. *Touch the earth.* Pocket Books, New York.

Meadows, Donella, et al., 1972. *The limits to growth.* Signet, New York.

Mumford, Lewis, 1961. *The city in history.* Harcourt, Brace, and World, New York.

———1966. *The myth of the machine: technics and human development.* Harcourt, Brace, and World, New York.

———1970. *The myth of the machine: the pentagon of power.* Harcourt, Brace, Jovanovich, New York.

Odum, Howard T., 1973. Energy, ecology and economics. *Ambio* 11:220–227.

Omo-Fadaka, Jimoh, 1974. Industrialisation and poverty in the Third World. *The Ecologist* 4:61–63.

Ratcliffe, Derek, 1967. Decrease in eggshell weight in certain birds of prey. *Nature* 215:208–210.

Reich, Robert B., 1982. Ideologies of survival (the return of social Darwinism). *New Republic,* September 20, 27, pp. 32–37.

Risebrough, Robert W., 1978. Pesticides and other toxicants. *Wildlife and America,* H. Brokaw, editor.

Roszak, Theodore, 1970. *The making of a counter-culture.* Faber & Faber, London.

Rudd, Robert, 1964. *Pesticides and the living landscape.* University of Wisconsin Press, Madison.

Shea, Kevin P., 1969a. Unwanted harvest. *Environment* 11:12–16, 28–31.

———1969b. Name your poison. *Environment* 11:30.

———1973. PCB. *Environment* 15:25–28.

Swan, Christopher C., 1981. *Transformation of transportation.* Office of Appropriate Technology, Sacramento, Calif.

United Nations, 1969. *Problems of the human environment.* Report of the Secretary-General. United Nations, New York.

Van den Bosch, Robert, 1980. *The pesticide conspiracy.* Anchor Brooks, New York.

Woodwell, George M., 1967. Toxic substances and ecological cycles. *Scientific American* 216:24–31.

Wurster, C. F., 1968. DDT reduces photosynthesis in marine phytoplankton. *Science* 159:1474–1475.

ECODEVELOPMENT—
A
DIFFERENT
WAY
TO
GO

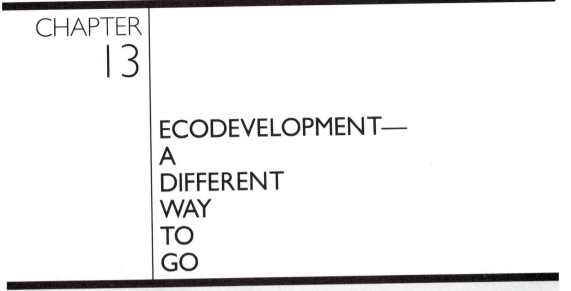

That's Revolution

Mother earth has been abused, the powers have been abused and this cannot go on forever. No theory can alter that simple fact. Mother Earth will retaliate, the whole environment will retaliate, and the abusers will be eliminated. Things come full circle, back to where they started. That's revolution. And that's a prophecy of my people, of the Hopi people and of other correct peoples.

American Indians have been trying to explain this to Europeans for centuries. But, as I said earlier, Europeans have proven themselves unable to hear. The natural order will win out, and the offenders will die out, the way deer die when they offend the harmony by overpopulating a given region. It's only a matter of time until what Europeans call "a major catastrophe of global proportions" will occur. It is the role of American Indian peoples, the role of natural beings, to survive. A part of our survival is to resist. We resist not to overthrow a government or to take political power, but because it is natural to resist extermination, to survive. We don't want power over white institutions; we want white institutions to disappear. That's revolution.

American Indians are still in touch with these realities—the prophecies, the traditions of our ancestors. We learn from the elders, from nature, from the powers. And when the catastrophe is over, we American Indian peoples will still be here to inhabit the hemisphere. I don't care if it's only a handful living high in the Andes. American Indian people will survive; harmony will be reestablished. That's revolution.

Russell Means, Oglala Sioux. For the world to live Europe must die.
Mother Jones

WHAT IS IT?

During the course of preparations for the United Nations environment conference that was held in Stockholm in 1972, it became apparent that many of the representatives of the Third World did not want to talk about environment at all, unless they also talked about economic development. This was reasonable enough. Many of them came from countries that were desperately poor. The question of survival today appeared more urgent than the question of quality of life tomorrow. Nevertheless, all recognized the importance of environmental issues, but could not see their way clear to doing much about them without assistance in their efforts to provide for their people. One of the preparatory meetings for the conference was held at Founex, Switzerland, and made clear the view that environment and development were inevitablly linked together (UNEP, 1981). The meeting, however, extended the concept of development far beyond its usual economic boundaries, stating: *In the past, there has been a tendency to equate the development goal with the more narrowly conceived objective of economic growth as measured by the rise in gross national product. It is usually recognized today that high rates of economic growth do not guarantee the easing of urgent social problems. Indeed, in many countries high growth rates have been accompanied by increasing unemployment, rising disparities in income—both between groups and between regions—and the deterioration of social and cultural conditions. A new emphasis is thus being placed on the attainment of social and cultural goals as part of the development process.*

Following the Stockholm Conference another meeting held in Cocoyoc, Mexico, in 1973 spelled out the problem in a different way (see Appendix): *The world today is not only faced with the anomaly of underdevelopment. We may also talk about overconsumptive types of development that violate the inner limits of men and the outer limits of Nature. . . . Even though the first priority goes to assuring the minima, we shall be looking for those development strategies that also may help the affluent countries, in their enlightened self-interest, in finding more human patterns of life, less exploitive of Nature, of others, of oneself* [Henderson, 1981].

Thus development is not just for the poor countries of the Third World, but must also be extended to the rich world in the form of a redevelopment toward a more ecologically sound and socially satisfying way of life.

Maurice Strong provided a name for this new pathway to development—*ecodevelopment*. This occurred at the first meeting of the General Council of the new United Nations Environment Programme, held in Nairobi in 1973 (UNEP, 1973). Strong was not particularly clear in providing a definition of ecodevelopment, and it was necessary to bring a number of people from various parts of the world together in Geneva in 1974 to begin to flesh out the skeleton of this new development concept. One of these was Ignacy Sachs, of Paris, who was to become the most lucid spokesman for the ecodevelopment idea. Writing in *African Environment* in 1974, he spelled out the characteristics of the new program:

1. In each ecoregion, an effort is made to develop specific resources for the satisfaction of the *fundamental needs* of the population as regards food, housing, health and education, these needs being defined . . . to avoid the harmful effects of the consumption style of rich countries.

2. Ecodevelopment should contribute primarily to human self-realization—taking into account employment, security, quality of human relationships and respect for cultural diversity.

3. Management and use of natural resources must be undertaken with a view to future generations, avoiding waste of nonrenewables, and emphasizing reliance on the proper management of renewable resources.

4. Recycling of industrial wastes offer a means for avoiding negative effects of human activities on the environment.

5. Reliance on photosynthesis as a source of energy, using local energy sources, seeking energy efficient means of transportation.

6. A new technological style based on ecotechniques (appropriate technology), associated with new modes of social organization and new systems of education.

7. Establishment of a new "horizontal authority" in place of the usual vertical government heirarchy, to bring together the potential of the poverty-stricken masses, and to supply capital equipment and production techniques suitable to the economic and ecological conditions of the local people. In particular, the participation of local people is essential to define and harmonize needs, identify productive potentials, and organize collective efforts, while avoiding exploitation by others.

8. Education to sensitize people to the environmental dimensions and ecological aspects of development so that this information is internalized and the value system based on domination over nature is replaced by one based on respect for nature.

In summary, *ecodevelopment is a style of development which, in each ecoregion, stresses the specific solutions for its particular problems, bearing in mind the ecological but also the cultural data, the immediate needs, but also the long-term needs. . . . it attempts to react against the prevailing fashion for so-called universalist solutions and general-purpose formulas. Instead of relying too much on foreign aid, it shows confidence in the ability of human societies to identify their problems and provide original solutions for them, drawing inspiration nevertheless from the experiences of others. . . . it gives priority to self-reliance.*

Sachs' approach to ecodevelopment was further spelled out and simplified in the *Comprehensive Environmental Management Plan* for the South Pacific region, prepared by the South Pacific Commission and the South Pacific Bureau for Economic Cooperation in 1980. In this ecodevelopment is defined as ''a new approach to development which from the beginning would consider not only economic development as strictly defined, but also the broad social and environmental context into which that development must fit if it is to be successful in benefitting the whole population. Such as approach does not question the kind of development *per se* only its appropriateness to a particular place and culture, an appropriateness that must be decided by the people themselves." The Plan goes on to spell out three postulates or goals for ecodevelopment:

1. The first of these is economic in emphasis: "The focus of all societal efforts must be first and foremost on meeting the basic real needs of people, especially the poorest of them, everywhere." This must always take precedence over efforts to increase the well-being of the already well-to-do.

2. The second is primarily cultural and social, but with important political and economic consequences. It states: *Self-reliance is a fundamental collective capability which must be sought by communities and groups, as well as whole countries. It refers to the need of people to search for and find solutions to their own problems, using their own knowledge, values and experiences in their own surroundings and circumstances. . . . Self-reliance is really to be seen as an alternative to the kind of development strategies which lead to even greater dependencies on external groups or organizations. Achieving self-sufficiency in food production is one important objective. In other areas the degree of self-reliance or autonomy preferred is for each group or community to choose. They should remain free to decide what kind of cooperation they would like to develop with others as well as the conditions under which they can accept it. Outsiders, whether governments or other communities, must respect this and strive toward helping other people develop their own capabilities for self-reliance.* This essentially calls for the use of *appropriate technologies* to achieve grass-root, home-grown, localized development leading to decentralization of economic and political power.

3. The third is ecological: "A working symbiosis between people and environments must be sought, leading to close inter-relationships and modifications beneficial to both. This relationship must be based on an ethical commitment to future generations. This at a minimum means striving to keep options open for the future and maintaining viable life-support and resource systems for other generations to use. Preservation of biological and cultural diversity is a prerequisite."

These three postulates represent the three sides of the "ecodevelopment triangle." The ecological side must be the base, since on it depends the sustainability of development. Development that is not, or cannot be made, sustainable must in the long term worsen conditions for everyone.

To contrast the development options, consider agricultural development in Central America. Conventional development led to conversion of large areas of tropical forest into banana plantations, often controlled by foreign investors—United Fruit, Standard Brands. Local people were put to work clearing forests, planting, caring for, and harvesting bananas, and for this they were paid some minimum wages. The government benefits from taxes, duties, or a share of the profits. Profits from the sale of the bananas goes to landowners and investors. It could be argued that all benefit: investor, landowner, worker, and the people in general. Why then is poverty endemic in what were once called "banana republics"? The food grown is luxury food for export to well-fed people in richer lands. The plantations growing this food occupy the best soils with the most favorable growing conditions. The workers on the plantation must either buy imported food at high cost or attempt to grow their own. But the space available for local food production contains the poorest soils or is on steep slopes where erosion eats away productivity.

An ecodevelopment approach would first question the need for clearing the forest and examine whether the same objectives could be met by redistribution of existing cleared land and more intensive care for lands already in food production. Run by the local people it would concentrate first on meeting their basic needs and developing their self-reliance. Only when basic needs were met would any surplus be devoted to exports—and these would go first to local towns and cities, to meet the needs of those people. People would be encouraged to remain on the land, or return to the land, thus decreasing the degree of urban poverty. Reliance would be placed on locally available energy resources and materials, and there would be minimum use of imported fuels, machinery, or chemicals. With intensive care one would expect yields to be higher and more people to be supported directly by the land. Those who would not benefit, however, are those who just happen to control the political power in most of these countries—the large landowners and the companies who wish to invest for a financial profit. Moves toward ecodevelopment are squelched and more people join the guerrilla forces.

CENTRALIZATION AND DECENTRALIZATION

Technologies shape societies and determine the impact of those societies on the environments that support them. This is as true of simpler technologies as of the most advanced. The bow and arrow changed the relationship between people and wildlife, the gun even more so. Modern industrial technologies have a centralizing effect on the societies that adopt them, as Galtung (1978) has pointed out. Industrialization requires concentrations of capital, expertise, and initially at least, labor, and these lead to centralization of such elements in industrial cities. A nuclear power plant, requiring as it does enormous amounts of capital and a high concentration of managerial and technical expertise, along with skilled labor, is one of the most centralizing technologies. By contrast energy technologies based on solar and renewable biological resources not only are inherently less centralizing, but are easily kept subject to local organization and control. The self-reliance called for in ecodevelopment is not compatible with all technologies.

A self-reliant community must have a high degree of energy independence. It cannot rely on a distant nuclear plant for the energy needed to boil an egg or cultivate a garden. A Pacific Islander owning a gasoline-powered pump to pump water for household use and irrigation is dependent on an energy source he can in no way control and is located at the end of a long and fragile supply line. One who uses a homemade windmill for the same purpose can be self-reliant. Ecodevelopment is thus dependent on the development and use of appropriate technologies. These can be highly sophisticated, but they must be related to local ecological realities and cultural traditions. They must increase self-reliance, not create new dependencies. Regrettably much of the so-called appropriate technology machinery sold to Third World nations can neither be manufactured nor repaired within those countries, and the new owner finds a new dependency on Chicago or Stuttgart perhaps, while being freed from a dependency on Saudi Arabia.

There is nothing particularly new about ecodevelopment in that its various elements have received attention for a long time. What is new is the bringing together of the economic, cultural, and ecological aspects of development into one total system. The idea of basic needs and self-reliance was taught by Mahatma Gandhi in India during the 1930s under the doctrine of *swaraj,* which is quoted separately in this chapter. India turned its back on *swaraj* to pursue European-style industrialization. Only now is it turning back to the village level and efforts to achieve rural self-sufficiency—although the ecological aspects of its development programs are not evident.

Some still consider that "development" refers to things and can be reduced to capital accumulation, economic growth and economic restructuring.... Development fundamentally refers to human beings ... to the whole man and the whole woman. It is a human experience synonymous with the fulfillment of individual mental, emotional, and physical potentialities.... the society, its economy and polity, ought to be organized in such a manner as to maximize, for the individual and the whole, the opportunities for self-fulfillment.... there is development when people and their communities.... act as subjects and are not acted upon as objects; assert their autonomy, self-reliance, and self-confidence; when they set out and carry out projects. To develop is to be, or to become. Not to have.

International Foundation For Development Alternatives (IFDA), 1980

> ### Swaraj
>
> *My idea of village swaraj is that it is a complete republic, independent of its neighbours for its own vital wants and yet interdependent for many others. . . . Thus every village's first concern will be to grow its own food crops and cotton for its cloth. It should have a reserve for its cattle, recreation and playground for adults and children. Then if there is more land available it will grow useful money crops. . . . The village will maintain a village theatre, school and public hall. It will have its own waterworks ensuring clean water supply. . . . As far as possible every activity will be conducted on the cooperative basis. . . . Any village can become such a republic today without much interference, even from the present Government whose sole effective connection with the villages is the exaction of the village revenue. . . . Here there is perfect democracy based upon individual freedom. The individual is the architect of his own government. . . . He and his village are able to defy the might of the world.*
>
> Mahatma Gandhi

THE APPROPRIATE TECHNOLOGY MOVEMENT

I don't know how long the idea of "appropriate technology" has been around—probably ever since people rejected the idea of massing great numbers of human bodies to build the pyramids. However, in the late 1960s and on into the 1980s, a movement toward appropriate technology has taken hold in America and Europe, with its greatest activity probably in the New England states and California, and in Great Britain. Great numbers of journals are now dedicated to it, in whole or part: *Resurgence, Undercurrents* and *The Ecologist* in Great Britain; *Rain, Tranet, Alternative Energy and Technology, CoEvolution Quarterly,* and *The Whole Earth Catalogue,* the *Journal of the New Alchemists,* and on and on, in the United States. The movement seems to divide into those who like to tinker, to work with materials, to invent and build—a long-lived strain of activity in the European tradition—but not necessarily get involved with social movements or politics on the one hand, and the political-social-ecological group, on the other hand, who are more concerned about how a technic will be used, by whom, for what purpose, than they are with the technic itself. Both sides need each other. Appropriate technology can be used to strengthen heirarchy and increase dependency, or it can be used to free people and attain self-sufficiency. Admittedly, since technologies are not neutral, this movement is more on the side of the latter.

Perhaps the strongest and most articulate spokesman for the appropriate technology movement has been E. F. Schumacher, whose book *Small Is Beautiful* has reached more people than all of the journals added together. Schumacher, a founder of the intermediate technology movement in England, lists four requirements for real development:

1. *Workplaces have to be created in areas where people live now, and not in metropolitan areas into which they tend to migrate.*
2. *Workplaces must be, on average, cheap enough, so that they can be created in large numbers without this calling for an unattainable level of capital formation and imports.*
3. *Production methods must be relatively simple, so that the demands for high skills are minimised, not only in the production process itself but also in matters or organization, raw material supply, financing, marketing, and so forth.*
4. *Production should be mainly from local materials and mainly for local use.*

These four requirements can be met only if there is a "regional" approach to development, and second, if there is a conscious effort to develop and apply what might be called an "intermediate technology."

Obviously, Schumacher's intermediate technology, and the appropriate technology (AT) movement in general, are aiming in the same direction and using the same means as ecodevelopment; yet because they have grown and operated in different institutional frameworks, they have been to a large degree unaware of one another. *The Appropriate Technology Sourcebook* (Darrow and Pam, 1976) shows the same convergence of ideas between AT and ecodevelopment: *Nicholas Jequier (1976) has described the soaring popularity of the appropriate technology approach as evidence of a "cultural revolution" in development thinking. The elements of self-reliance, local initiative, and local control that are essentially parts of this approach have far-reaching implications when they are logically applied to the development structure as it now exists. As with any cultural revolution, this one threatens to turn the whole organizational structure upside-down, and shake up the old ways of doing things.*

AN ECOLOGICAL SOCIETY

Coming originally from a much different point of view than the people who put together the concept of ecodevelopment, or from Schumacher's "intermediate technology," Murrary Bookchin (1982) sees the present and future as a conflict between the authoritarian and the libertarian ways of organizing society. The authoritarian approach has dominated civilization from its beginnings and depends on heirarchy and domination. The libertarian tendency has always been present, sometime underground, sometimes flowering for a time—emphasizing freedom, the absence of heirarchy, the rejection of authority. Some would see this in terms of the patriarchal and the feminist. If we wish to avoid the collapse of civilization, Bookchin sees no way but the libertarian path—creating small communities based on conscious cultural affinities rather than ancestry, networking them into confederations through ecosystems, bioregions, and biomes—communities that would "aspire to live with, nourish, and feed upon the life-forms that indigenously belong to the ecosystems in which they are integrated." He sees the organic farm and garden, recycling, the use of renewable energy, avoidance of waste, the restoration of labor to its one-time role of being scarcely distinguishable from play. *What humanity can never afford to lose is its sense of ecological direction and the ethical meaning it gives to its projects. As I have already observed, our alternative technologies will have very little social meaning or direction if they are designed with strictly technocratic goals in mind. By the same token, our efforts at cooperation will be actively demoralizing if we come together merely to "survive" the hazards of living in our prevailing social system. Our technics can be either catalysts for our integration with the natural world, or the chasms separating us from it. They are never ethically neutral.*

Thus Bookchin reaches the pathway to ecodevelopment coming from a totally different part of the forest, and being largely unaware of it as a movement. His "ecological society" is the goal of ecodevelopment.

> *In our time we have seen domination spread over the social landscape to a point where it is beyond all human control. The trillions of dollars that the nations of the world have spent since the Second World War on means of subjugation and destruction—its "defense budgets" for an utterly terrifying weaponry—are only the most recent evidence of a centuries-long craze for domination that has now reached manic proportions. Compared to this stupendous mobilization of materials, of wealth, of human intellect, and of human labor for the single goal of domination, all other recent human achievements pale to almost trivial insignificance. Our art, science, medicine, literature, music, and "charitable" acts seem like mere droppings from a table on which gory feasts on the spoils of conquest have engaged the attention of a system whose appetite for rule is utterly unrestrained. We justly mistrust its acts of generosity today, for behind its seemingly worthy projects—its medical technology, cybernetic revolutions, space programs, agricultural projects, and energy innovations—seem to lie the most malignant motives for achieving the subjugation of humanity by means of violence, fear, and surveillance.*
>
> Murray Bookchin, *The Ecology of Freedom* (1982), p. 349

ECOCULTURAL REGIONS

The idea of biotic or biogeographic provinces, which has been discussed earlier (Chapter 5), is a means for describing the distribution of animal and plant species on the planet. A biotic province is a relatively unified area, having in common a particular grouping of species or subspecies, which differ from those found over the mountain, or across the river, or beyond whatever barrier separates the two provinces. Sometimes there is no distinct barrier, only a gradual change in climate, in available water, or in the nature of the terrain. Species then change gradually from one area to the other along a *continuum,* a gradient of modification of living conditions. Within the province there are generally similar conditions of climate, vegetation, soils, plant species, and animal species—meaning that an identifiable ecosystem can be described.

To some extent the distribution of people in past times has followed natural boundaries. People get used to living in a particular area, with recognizable animals and plants, with reasonably predictable climate, with known sources of water, food, and other requirements. They feel less at ease in areas outside the known boundaries, where conditions are less predictable. This has not prevented people from picking up their belongings and moving on if conditions become unsuitable, ecologically or socially. But it does result in most people living long enough in a particular environment to develop a culture related to and suited to that environment.

In New Guinea there are hundreds of different tribal groups each speaking a different language from their neighbors, each occupying a relatively small area and maintaining a cultural identity. Amazonia was inhabited by a similar diversity of human groups. California was occupied by Indians belonging to six major language groups, divided into 50 little nations and 250 tribelets, each speaking a somewhat different dialect. But the homeland of each tribelet had a distinct ecological identity to which the inhabitants related.

It is not just traditional people who identify so clearly with a particular ecological region. As Leopold Kohr, and others, have pointed out, the map of Europe, before the rise of the great powers and nation-states of today, reflected a similar tribal grouping and regional identity. What we call France today was once known to its inhabitants as the separate nations of Brittany, Normandy, Burgundy, Aquitaine, Languedoc, Le Midi, Savoy, Alsace, Lorraine. There was a France also, but it was a smaller area around Paris—the Ile de France. Great Britain consisted of at least Cornwall, Wales, Scotland, and England—but these broad divisions blur the differences between Lancashire and Sussex, Devon and Northumbria. Despite all the melting and mixing of peoples and the efforts of the governments in power to convince people that they are English or French or German, the original ethnicity remains, and today there are stirrings toward independence or at least autonomy in each of these regions. Some are more determined than others to achieve autonomy. The Basques of Asturia have never accepted the right of Castille to rule over them. There are strong movements in Brittany and Corsica, strong also in Scotland and Wales.

> ...if we make a list of all the most prosperous countries in the world, we find that most of them are very small; whereas a list of all the biggest countries in the world shows most of them to be very poor indeed. Here again, there is food for thought.
>
> E. F. Schumacher, *Small Is Beautiful* (1973), p. 60

TABLE 13.1   Comparing the Three Wealthiest Countries in Terms of per Capita GNP with the Three Largest Countries in Terms of Population

COUNTRY	POPULATION IN MILLIONS	PER CAPITA GNP IN $
Africa		
Reunion	0.5	3,830
Gabon	0.7	3,680
Libya	3.2	8,640
Ethiopia	30.5	140
Egypt	44.8	580
Nigeria	82.3	1,010
Asia		
Brunei	0.2	11,890
Qatar	0.3	26,080
United Arab Emirates	1.2	30,070
Indonesia	151.3	420
India	713.8	240
China	1000.0	290
Europe		
Switzerland	6.3	16,440
Luxembourg	0.4	14,510
Sweden	8.3	13,520
Italy	57.4	6,480
West Germany	61.7	13,590
USSR	270.0	4,550

Source: Population Reference Bureau (1982).

Because of the persistence of regional identities in Europe, it is possible to envision a future Europe in which the old nations will reemerge, and the present highly centralized governments will be replaced by something like the Swiss Confederacy where the real power rests in the 22 cantons and not in the central government.

In the United States, however, it is not possible to reconstruct the old tribal boundaries of the American Indians, nor would it be useful even to the Indians to divide the nation up into its pre-European territories. Many of the tribes no longer exist, others have merged, and the ways of life that fitted the old boundaries are not likely to be restored. The existing boundaries of the 50 states, on the other hand, for the most part make no ecological sense, cultural sense, or any sense except in terms of "dog-in-the-manger" politics. Drawing straight lines on a map may have kept land surveyors happy by making their work easy, and was an easy way for government officials to slice up the pie into pieces of various sizes, but it is difficult to find any justification otherwise for boundaries that run across mountains or rivers and totally ignore the natural world.

In some earlier publications various people have tried to define bio-regions, meaning areas of ecological and cultural unity within North America. It is easy enough to start with biotic provinces, but these de-scribe the distribution of the original life of the land and do not take into account human perceptions, nor the ways in which the land has been changed by human action. It is possible to describe, for example, a Californian biotic province, which includes the foothills of the Sierra Nevada, the Central Valley, and south and central coastal California. There are marked differences, however, between northern and southern California that are not reflected in differences in climates, plants, or animals. The area south of the Tehachapi Mountains is definitely south-ern California and centers on the cities of Los Angeles and San Diego. The area north relates to the cities of the San Francisco Bay area and Sacramento. Peter Berg and I attempted to define a northern California bioregion (1976), which would have the Tehachapi Mountains as its southern border. The area east of the Sierra would be turned over to Nevadans, and negotiations with Oregonians would settle a northern boundary that took into account watersheds and mountain barriers. There are persistent arguments on the policital front in favor of making this area a separate state, and both Callenbach (1975) in his semi-fictional writings and Garreau (1981) have placed northern California, Oregon, and Wash-ington together in a separate nation-to-be known as Ecotopia.

The concept of bioregion, or ecocultural region, is primarily worth considering as a means for developing ecological sensibility and a feeling of regional identity to which people can subscribe. As such, both north-ern California and certainly the fictional nation of Ecotopia are much too large. More meaningful ecocultural regions would be smaller—perhaps as shown in Fig. 13.1 and Table 13.2.

To shift to another part of the country, the Florida Keys have a regional identify separate from the rest of the state. Tropical Florida, from Lake Okeechobee south, has little in common with northern Florida, whereas the Florida panhandle has more in common with parts of neigh-boring Alabama than with the area around St. Augustine or Orlando. Ecocultural regions should not be defined by people who live elsewhere, however, but by the people who live within them. Without the close feeling of belonging and identification they run the risk of becoming as meaningless to their inhabitants as the present counties and states.

Perhaps the greatest contribution that the ecocultural concept can make to creating an ecologically sane and sustainable future is through relating people once more to the lands and waters that they occupy and share with neighbors. To regard *your* landscape as the place where you *live,* and not just as the place where you *make a living* involves a change in consciousness that is fundamentally important for the human future. It would mean that people would cease to be invaders or conquerors, draining the riches from an area in order to take them somewhere else, and would become natives, responsible for and caring for their home territories.

There seems to be no verb to convey the concept of "becoming a native" since a native, by definition is born that way and does not become. The process of becoming like a native in attitude and responsiveness to one's home area does need some better term than "naturalize," which conveys the wrong meaning, or "reinhabit," to use Berg's terminology, which becomes awkward. Someone has suggested "indigenization," which is as difficult a word as you can construct. All we are talking about is coming home.

Bioregions, or in Sachs' terminology, ecoregions, or to use Schulze-Westrum's term, ecocultural regions, are a basis for developing a regional identify or for the existing feeling of regional identity. They are also a basis for the application of ecodevelopment, since they have relatively uniform ecological conditions that can be fully comprehended and either an existing or a developing cultural identity. The self-reliance that would come with ecodevelopment is not likely, however, to be enthusiastically received by those who presently gain wealth from exploiting other bioregions.

Galtung (1978) has explored what he calls "center–periphery" relationships in his discussion of the centralizing tendency of industrialization. The industrial, urban center tends initially to exploit the rural fringe—drawing from it labor and raw materials to which it applies capital and expertise to achieve financial gain. In time, however, the people of the peripheral area being exploited develop sufficient knowledge and sophistication to resist excessive exploitation. In a sense they become part of the center, which exploits the labor and raw materials of areas farther afield—the colonies, which become the new periphery. With independence and ability to resist exploitation, these areas become increasingly untractable, and it is desirable for the original imperial capital to develop secondary centers in the capitals of the Third World countries, involving the governing groups in these countries. These in turn begin to exploit their periphery—the Fourth World peoples who lack political power or real representation in the government, usually people of different ethnic groups. There is no Fifth World for them to exploit, however, and at some point, like now, it is necessary for the whole exploitation process to cease. That is where the ecodevelopment concept comes in. By building self-reliance and self-sufficiency in basic needs, the former peripheral bioregion becomes resistant to further exploitation. Naturally, the multinational corporation, headquartered in the original "cen-

TABLE 13.2   Bioregions: How Would the Birds Divide the State?

The map (Fig. 13.1) shows the faunal districts and areas occupied by the Boreal and Sonoran avifaunas of California. With some modification—suggested here—they seem to fall out into subdivisions of bioregions that relate to how humans see their home areas.
Shastan Bioregion.
 1. North coast forest province
 2. Central coast forest province
 3. Trinity province
 4. Cascade province
 5. Sierran province
 6. San Bernardino-Diegan province (to be included with 15).
11. Central Valley province
12. Clear Lake province
13. San Francisco province
14. San Benito province
Chumash Bioregion
15. Angeles province
16. Catalinan province
Sonoran Bioregion
 9. Mojave province
10. Coloradan province
Nevadan Bioregion
 7. Modoc province
 8. Inyo province
     As noted, the San Bernardino-Diegan province, subdivided into two faunal districts by Miller, are essentially part of the Angeles province as forming an ecocultural region. Certain areas designated by Miller: Shasta Valley (included with Trinity); Upper Kern (included with Sierran), Warner Mountains (included with Modoc), and Great Basin Mountains (included with Inyo) are lumped because of human, not avian, affinities.

Source: Miller (1951).

FIG 13.1

ter," is going to be resistant to such self-determination. The cheap labor and cheap raw materials that attract these corporations to locate their manufacturing and assembly plants in the Third World or to use Fourth World labor are no longer to be available when the people involved can supply their own needs through their own efforts.

PROTECTING THE FOURTH WORLD

The culture that appears superior under one set of circumstances will not always continue to look that way when circumstances change. Many civilizations have vanished, whereas those who seemed backward and inferior to the city dwellers have persisted in their cultural ways. In time some of these gave rise to a new advanced cultures. Protection of cultural variety on earth is one way of ensuring that the human race will continue to survive, as well as a way for providing a more interesting world for all who live today. It has the further advantage of offering alternatives to those who may not wish to follow the life styles offered by their own society.

During the nineteenth century when the worse impact of European expansion was being felt by other peoples, Europeans had reached a high level of chauvinism and self-conceit. It was almost inconceivable to a nineteenth-century American or European that anyone could prefer ways of living different from their own. The so-called blessings of industrial civilization were forced on other people. The "saving grace" of Christianity was imposed upon them, like it or not. Still, today, the advocates of technocratic society cannot believe that other people might have insights regarding living with the earth, or their relationship to the universe, that the technocratic world has lost. Today it is said that all people must be "developed." Earlier the word was "Christianized" or "civilized." The convential economic development, which is still dominant, is by its nature destructive to other cultures and favors homogenization of people so that they can fit into standard development patterns. Ecodevelopment is the opposite.

> On the tree of evolution, last season's flowers die,
> and often the most beautiful are sterile.
> While Triceratops sported his triple horns,
> while Diplodocus waved his graceful tail,
> something without a name
> was stealing their tomorrow.
>
> John Brunner, *The Shockwave Rider* (1975)

All over the world those of separate cultures are still being destroyed. It is not that this destruction represents a firm policy on the part of governments—although it often does. Brazil has been in the past, although apparently no longer, deliberately destructive of its Indian cultures. Indonesia today is crushing the indigenous cultures of Irian Jaya and simply brushing aside the culture of the Mentawai islanders. But more often there is a lack of any rational government policy and a hope that the problem will solve itself. Regrettably, the problem does solve itself. The peoples concerned die, or their cultures are destroyed.

ECOSYSTEM PEOPLE
TODAY

Throughout the world in various remote areas people who are sometimes called primitive continue to hold out. The ecosystems they occupy have nothing in common except that they represent the extremes—they are too hot, too dry, too wet or cold or mountainous to be of interest to the biosphere cultures—or they were until recently. One pervasive quality these people have in common is that they lack political influence. They belong to the Fourth World and are not represented by the governments of the other three worlds. Were the world arranged in a more rational manner, they would be autonomous. They were autonomous in the past, and many behave today as though they still are.

A second quality these ecosystem people have in common is that most of them have learned to live in a sustainable balance with their environment. Without overexploitation of its resources, and without need of outside sources of energy and materials, they live quite well and have done so for centuries.

The Indian anthropologist L. P. Vidyarthi has pointed out that the ecosystem people in India, where there are some 38 million people who live outside of the dominant biosphere cultures, have developed a style of the life that he characterizes as a nature-man-spirit complex. Figure 13.2 diagrams this idea as a triangle of which the two sides—human society and the natural world—are held in balance by the third side, the

FIG. 13.2
The balance in those "primitive" cultures where "God is alive. Magic is afoot."

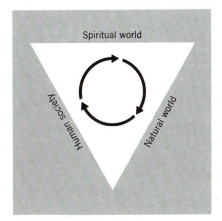

Spiritual world

Human society

Natural world

a

THE FOURTH WORLD

(a) Here and there, traditional hunter-gatherers survive. The Kalahari. **(b)** The impact of the global economic system has mostly destroyed the old self-sufficient ways of the Inuit (Eskimo) people. **(c)** Despite a century of attack and neglect, American Indians retain their old identity and **(d)** are beginning to hit back, as in this peaceful takeover of the Federal Bureau of Indian Affairs office.
(e) Still isolated, some Amazonian Indians retain their old ways. **(f)** In Papua New Guinea, the government seeks ways to maintain its cultural diversity.

b

c

d

e

f

445

spiritual world. It is the relationship of people through their spiritual beliefs with the natural world that permits them to maintain the necessary rhythms of planting and harvesting, hunting, fishing, and gathering. The religions are the old nature religions and have nothing to do with formal churches, but much to do with personal transcendence. Destroy the religion, as the missionaries from the biosphere cultures seek to do, and the balance between humans and nature falls apart. Destroy their environment and people and their beliefs will collapse—and this is happening in many areas.

There is little doubt that the hunter-gatherers of the world are in the most desperate straits. This is because they require a relatively large area for their subsistence—they cannot survive when crowded from the outside. Not much better off are those who practice a shifting agriculture, but depend basically on hunting and gathering to maintain a nutritionally adequate diet. The Indians of the American tropics are mostly in that category. They have been and are more and more being subjected to brutal treatment that is in the process of destroying them.

The gradient of cultures moves from pure hunting and gathering to various combinations with shifting agriculture, then on to a less shifting, but more rotational agriculture, and finally to a more or less permanent, peasant agriculture such as is represented by the Ifugao of the Philippines. Along another track it moves from pure nomadic herding to varying degrees of combination of herding with agriculture or with other forms of sedentary culture. All of these groups are under pressure and many have been totally shattered by the biosphere cultures. Few people around the world are much worried about them, since most who are caught up in the biosphere network have difficulty enough keeping themselves alive. Yet these peoples have lessons to teach the world that we have yet to consider seriously. They offer a hope for the future, if for no other reasons than that they have learned to live happily and in balance with their environment without drawing heavily on any of the earth's resources.

CONSERVATION OF CULTURES

It is today considered morally reprehensible that one dominant group of humans should exterminate another group who differ from them racially, genetically, or culturally. Nevertheless, the practice continues in one way or another. To halt it, the first step would be to recognize what is ethically or morally a law, even if it has not been enacted in any binding legal form: that these people have the right to the lands or resources on which they have always lived or on which they have always depended. This means suspending the "right of conquest" once and for all. It means forbidding those who have more power or greater numbers from invading, stealing, destroying, or bargaining away the lands and resources that have traditionally and rightfully belonged to these people. It means, at most, recognizing them as the autonomous nations they always have been, *in fact,* and giving that recognition status *in law.* At least, it means recognizing their property rights within a particular nation, again by law, and agreeing not to interfere with these rights. In the United States, insofar as the Indians are concerned, it means recognizing and adhering to the treaties that were once signed, and then providing adequate compensation for the damages the people have suffered since the treaties were broken. For those tribes who were crushed and set aside without treaties, it means negotiation to restore their fair share of land and property.

For those more fragile people, who have not been much exposed to biosphere culture and would be damaged by such exposure (the Amazonian Indians are mostly in this category), a further policy of "hands off" must be enforced in respect to their lands and resources. This means that within their territories these people would have a right to exclude all visitors. It means that the prevailing dominant culture on the outside would forbid its agents from entering these territories. This would apply to those agents of spiritual destruction, the missionaries, and the agents

There is not enough awareness among Westerners that they are losing the battle for the mind of the South, that one day they may find many people have turned away from the West—and then it will be difficult to have a reasonable dialogue. Governments should foster a change in attitude. Africa holds the world's largest reserve of natural resources, including many strategic minerals that will become important in the future—when the African people may be hostile.

Peter Enahoro, *Africa Now. World Press Review* (1982), p. 25

A Return to the Bush: Aborigines Abandoning "White" Australia

The exodus from white settlements started in 1973 when the new Labor Government decided to support decentralization of Aboriginal communities. A large number of Aborigines on reserves and stations began to receive social service payments in cash, becoming able to pool their financial resources and use them to establish new communities.

The Aborigines have established outstations that now house some 6,000 people throughout the Northern Territory and other parts of the Australian bush country. Communities average thirty residents who usually speak a single Aboriginal language. Residents frequently travel to the nearest mission or settlement and, at times, the entire family will leave after a death at the outstation.

Government officials say the movement has greatly improved the health and diet of the Aboriginal people and reduced psychological stress, social tension, and fighting. Families again are using traditional treatments for minor ailments, often just as effective as European medicine.

Lindsay Murdoch, *The Age*, Melbourne. *World Press Review* (1982), p. 56

100 Monkeys

In 1952, on the island of Koshima scientists were providing monkeys with sweet potatoes dropped in the sand. The monkeys like the taste of the raw sweet potatoes, but they found the dirt unpleasant.

An 18-month-old female named Imo found she could solve the problem by washing the potatoes in a nearby stream. She taught this trick to her mother. Her playmates also learned this new way and they taught their mothers, too.

This cultural innovation was gradually picked up by various monkeys before the eyes of the scientists. Between 1952 and 1958, all the young monkeys learned to wash the sandy sweet potatoes to make them more palatable.

Only the adults who imitated their children learned this social improvement. Other adults kept eating the dirty sweet potatoes.

Then something startling took place. In the autumn of 1958, a certain number of Koshima monkeys were washing sweet potatoes—the exact number is not known. Let us suppose that when the sun rose one morning there were 99 monkeys on Koshima Island who had learned to wash their sweet potatoes. Let's further suppose that later that morning, the hundredth monkey learned to wash potatoes. THEN IT HAPPENED;

By that evening almost everyone in the tribe was washing sweet potatoes before eating them. The added energy of this hundredth monkey somehow created an ideological breakthrough.

But notice. The most surprising thing observed by these scientists was that the habit of washing sweet potatoes then spontaneously jumped over the sea.

Colonies of monkeys on other islands and the mainland troop of monkeys at Takasakiyama began washing their sweet potatoes!

Ken Keyes, Jr., *The Hundredth Monkey* (1982)

of nature destruction from industry and business. This does not mean that the ecosystem people would be in any way prevented from leaving their territory, from joining the dominant culture or from changing their ways as they see fit. It does mean that they would have a breathing space and would be granted once and for all the right to determine their own future.

There are other steps which should be taken, in view of the past abuse many of these people have suffered, but these need to be determined on an individual basis. If these two requirements can be accepted by governments, a beginning at least will have been made. During 1974 the government of Australia at long last recognized fully the rights of its aboriginal peoples to the lands that had much earlier been set up as aboriginal reserves. These rights include mineral rights, with the result

a

ECODEVELOPMENT

Old systems must be examined to find ways to improve yields without losing long-established balances, as in these (a) rice paddies of Vietnam or (b) tea plantations in Japan. The goal—self-reliance in partnership with nature.

b

that great wealth is now available to the aborigines to use as they see fit. The aborigines, with some isolated exceptions, have been so knocked around and battered by their contact with the technocratic world that they can no longer be considered ecosystem people, but their rights remain, and the step taken by Australia is an enlightened one. One hopes that other countries would follow the example. For some countries, however, it seems that only the unrelenting pressure of international public opinion can result in a change.

HOW DO YOU GET THERE FROM HERE?

Obviously, if I could answer the question this section heading asks, I would have put the answer into a small pamphlet and saved the paper and eyesight involved in writing a long book explaining where "here" really is and why we must seek a "there."

Nevertheless, the ecodevelopment movement does outline a different way to go, and the appropriate technology movement provides the means of getting there. But the world is still dominated by governments and armies with the means to destory all life forever and who continually threaten to do so. You can't drop out; since they really have the means to make life impossible anywhere, there is no *out*. Furthermore, the economy of the world is dominated by large corporations, the "Fortune 500" and their like, who have more money and power than most nations. Still, wandering around on the same planet there is that "something without a name" that does appear to be gaining ground at the expense of the national and multinational dinosaurs. Some say it took dinosaurs a long time to die, because it took so long for their bodies to get the message that their brains were dead. We may have the same problem with our dominant institutions.

The hundreds of thousands of people who are demonstrating around the world in opposition to nuclear weapons and nuclear power may finally get their message across. A nuclear freeze came close to being passed by Congress in 1982, and was passed by the House in 1983. But the freeze is step one. Then must come the rollback—the cutting back on "defense budgets" and monstrous weaponry. That this can be done without the slightest risk to any real "national security" is obvious to anyone capable of shedding the blinders of single-vision, reductionist thinking.

Some take comfort in the "hundredth monkey" syndrome, described separately in this chapter. The story comes from Lyall Watson in his book *Lifetide* (1980). I don't know whether it would hold up under serious investigation by ethologists, let alone sociobiologists, but it makes a good story. Maybe we need those 100 monkeys because we have lost faith in human messiahs. We need all the friends we can get if we are going to break out of our urban-industrial-technological trap. Perhaps all of those movements for liberation and ecological sanity are reaching a break-through point, and tomorrow we will all wash the nuclear and techno-logical crud off our ecological sweet potatoes. I wish I knew.

> *... whatever political views we may hold on other matters, we are driven almost inescapably to take action to rid the world of nuclear arms. Just as we have chosen to make nuclear weapons, we can choose to unmake them. Just as we have chosen to live in the system of sovereign states, we can choose to live in some other system. To do so would, of course, be unprec-edented, and in many ways frightening, even truly perilous, but it is by no means impossible. Our present system and the institutions that make it up are the debris of history. They have become inimical to life, and must be swept away. They constitute a noose around the neck of mankind, threatening to choke off the human future, but we can cut the noose and break free. To suppose otherwise would be to set up a false, fictitious fate, molded out of our own weaknesses and our own alterable decisions. We are indeed fated by our acquisition of the basic knowledge of physics to live for the rest of time with the knowledge of how to destroy ourselves. But we are not for that reason fated to destroy ourselves. We can choose to live.*
>
> Jonathan Schell, *The Fate of the Earth* (1982) p. 219

SOURCES

Berg, Peter and R. Dasmann, 1976. Reinhabiting California. *The Ecologist.*

Bookchin, Murray, 1982. *The ecology of freedom.* Cheshire Books, Palo Alto, Calif.

Brunner, John, 1975. *The shockwave rider.* Ballantine, New York.

Callenbach, Ernest, 1975. *Ecotopia.* Banyan Tree, Berkeley, Calif. Bantam, New York.

Darrow, Ken and Rick Pam, 1976. *Appropriate technology sourcebook.* Vol-unteers in Asis, Stanford, Calif.

Enaharo, Peter, 1982. *Africa Now. World Press Review.* August, p. 25.

Galtung, Johan, 1978. Towards a new international technological order. *Alter-natives* 4:277–300.

Garreau, Joel, 1981. *The nine nations of North America.* Houghton Mifflin, Boston.

Henderson, Hazel, 1981. *The politics of the solar age.* Anchor Press/Doubleday, New York.

International Foundation for Development Alternatives, 1980. *IFDA Dossier.* Nyon, Switzerland.

Jequier, Nicholas, 1976. *Appropriate technology: problems and promises.* OECD, Paris.

Keyes, Ken, Jr., 1982. *The hundredth monkey.* Vision Books, St. Mary, Ky.

Kohr, Leopold, 1978. *The breakdown of nations.* E. P. Dutton, New York.

Means, Russell, 1980. For the world to live Europe must die. *Mother Jones,* December pp. 30–31.

Miller, Alden, 1951. An analysis of the distribution of the birds of California. *Zoology* 50:531–644. University of California. Press Berkeley.

Murdoch, Lindsay, 1982. *The Age,* Melbourne. *World Press Review,* August, p. 56.

Population Reference Bureau, 1982. *1982 World Population Data Sheet.* PRB, Washington, D.C.

Sachs, Ignacy, 1974. Environment and styles of development. *African Environment* 1:9–33.

Schell, Jonathan, 1982. *The fate of the earth.* Knopf, New York.

Schulze-Westrum, Thomas, 1981. *Ecoculture.* IUCN, Gland, Switzerland. Mimeo.

Schumacher, E. F., 1973. *Small is beautiful.* Harper and Row, New York.

South Pacific Commission, 1980. *Comprehensive environmental management plan.* SPC, Noumea, New Caledonia.

United Nations Environment Programme, 1973. *Proceedings.* UNEP Governing Council, Geneva.

———1981. *In defence of the earth.* UNEP, Nairobi.

Watson, Lyall, 1980. *Lifetide.* Bantam Books, New York.

THE COCOYOC DECLARATION

Statement of a joint symposium sponsored by the United Nations Environment Programme and the United Nations Commission on Trade and Development at Cocoyoc, Mexico in October 1974.

(From *In Defence of the Earth,* UNEP, Nairobi, 1981.)

Thirty years have passed since the signing of the United Nations Charter launched the effort to establish a new international order. Today, that order has reached a critical turning point. Its hopes of creating a better life for the whole human family have been largely frustrated. It has proved impossible to meet the "inner limit" of satisfying fundamental human needs. On the contrary, more people are hungry, sick, shelterless and illiterate today than when the United Nations was first set up.

At the same time, new and unforeseen concerns have begun to darken the international prospects. Environmental degradation and the rising pressure on resources raise the question whether the "outer limits" of the planet's physical integrity may not be at risk.

And to these preoccupations must be added the realization that the next 30 years will bring a doubling of world population. Another world on top of this, equal in numbers, demands and hopes.

But these critical pressures give no reason to despair of the human enterprise, provided we undertake the necessary changes. The first point to be underlined is that the failure of world society to provide "a safe and happy life" for all is not caused by any present lack of physical resources. The problem today is not primarily one of absolute physical shortage but of economic and social maldistribution and misuse; mankind's predicament is rooted primarily in economic and social structures and behaviour within and between countries.

Much of the world has not yet emerged from the historical consequences of almost five centuries of colonial control which concentrated economic power so overwhelmingly in the hands of a small group of nations. To this day, at least three quarters of the world's income, investment, services and almost all of the world's research are in the hands of one quarter of its people.

The solution of these problems cannot be left to the automatic operation of market mechanisms. The traditional market makes resources available to those who can buy them rather than those who need them, it stimulates artifical demands and builds waste into the production process, and even under-utilizes resources. In the international system the powerful nations have secured the poor countries' raw materials at low prices— for example, the price of petroleum fell decisively between 1950 and 1970—have engrossed all the value-added from processing the materials and sold the manufactures back, often at monopoly prices.

At the same time, the very cheapness of the materials was one element in encouraging the industrialized nations to indulge in careless and extravagant use of the imported materials. Once again, energy is the best example. Oil at just over a dollar a barrel stimulated a growth in energy use of between 6 and 11 per cent a year. In Europe, the annual increase in car registrations reached 20 per cent.

Indeed, pre-emption by the rich of a disproportionate share of key resources conflicts directly with the longer-term interests of the poor by impairing their ultimate access to resources necessary to their development and by increasing their cost. All the more reason for creating a new system of evaluating resources which takes into account the benefits and the burdens for the developing countries.

The over-all effect of such biased economic relationships can best be seen in the contrast in consumption. A North American or a European child, on average, consumes outrageously more than his Indian or African counterpart—a fact which makes it specious to attribute pressure on world resources entirely to the growth of third world population.

Population growth is, of course, one element in the growing pressures on world supplies. The planet is finite and an indefinite multiplication of both numbers and claims cannot be endlessly sustained. Moreover, shortages can occur locally long before there is any prospect of a general exhaustion of particular resources. A policy for sane resource conservation and for some forms of management of ultimately scarce resources within the framework of new economic order must soon replace today's careless rapacity. But the point in the existing world situation is that the huge contrasts in *per capita* consumption between the rich minority and the poor majority have far more effect than their relative numbers on resource use and depletion. We can go further.

Since a lack of resources for full human development is, as the Bucharest Conference on Population clearly recognized, one of the continuing causes of explosive population growth, to deprive nations of the means of development directly exacerbates their demographic problems.

These unequal economic relationships contribute directly to environmental pressures. The cheapness of materials has been one factor in increasing pollution and encouraging waste and throwaway economy among the rich. And continued poverty in many developing lands has often compelled the people to cultivate marginal lands at great risk of soil erosion or to migrate to the physically degraded and overcrowded cities.

Nor are the evils which flow from excessive reliance on the market system confined to international relationships. The experience of the last 30 years is that the exclusive pursuit of economic growth, guided by the market and undertaken by and for the powerful elites, has the same destructive effects inside developing countries. The richest 5 per cent engross all the gain while the poorest 20 per cent can actually grow poorer still. And at the local as at the international level the evils of material poverty are compounded by the people's lack of participation and human dignity, by their lack of any power to determine their own fate.

Nothing more clearly illustrates both the need to reform the present economic order and the possibility of doing so than the crisis that has arisen in world markets during the last two years. The trebling of the price of food, fertilizers and manufactures in the wake of world inflation has most severely hit the world's poorest peoples. Indeed, this winter the risk of a complete shortfall in supplies threatens the lives of millions in the third world. But it cannot be called absolute shortage. The grain exists, but it is being eaten elsewhere by very well-fed people. Grain consumption in North America has grown *per capita* by 350 pounds, largely in meat products, since 1965—to reach 1,900 pounds today. Yet this extra 350 pounds is almost equal to an Indian's total annual consumption. North Americans were hardly starving in 1965. The increase since then has contributed to super-consumption which even threatens health. Thus, in physical terms, there need be no shortage this winter. It requires only a small release from the "surplus" of the rich to meet the entire Asian shortfall. There could hardly be a more vivid example of what one might call the overconsumption of the wealthy nations contributing directly to the underconsumption of the world's poor.

The quadrupling of oil prices through the combined action of the oil producers sharply alters the balance of power in world markets and redistributes resources massively to some third world countries. Its effect has been to reverse decisively the balance of advantage in the oil trade and to place close to 100 billions a year at the disposal of some third world nations. Moreover, in an area critical to the economies of industrialized States, a profound reversal of power exposes them to the condition long familiar in the third world—a lack of control over vital economic decisions.

Nothing could illustrate more clearly the degree to which the world market system which has continuously operated to increase the power and wealth of the rich and maintain the relative deprivation of the poor is rooted not in unchangeable physical circumstance but in political relationships which can, of their very nature, undergo profound reversals and transformations. In a sense, a new economic order is already struggling to be born. The crisis of the old system can also be the opportunity of the new.

It is true that, at present, the outlook seems to hold little but confrontation, misunderstanding, threats and angry dispute. But again, we repeat, there is no reason to despair. The crisis can also be a moment of truth from which the nations learn to acknowledge the bankruptcy of the old system and to seek the framework of a new economic order.

The task of a statemanship is thus to attempt to guide the nations, with all their differences in interest, power and fortune, toward a new system more capable of meeting the "inner limits" of basic human needs for all the world's people and of doing so without violating the "outer limits" of the planet's resources and environment. It is because we believe this enterprise to be both vital and possible that we set down a number of changes, in the conduct of economic policy, in the direction of development and in planetary conservation, which appear to us to be essential components of the new system.

THE PURPOSE OF DEVELOPMENT

Our first concern is to redefine the whole purpose of development. This should not be to develop things but to develop man. Human beings have basic needs: food, shelter, clothing, health, education. Any process of growth that does not lead to their fulfillment—or, even worse, disrupts them—is a travesty of the idea of development. We are still in a stage where the most important concern of development is the level of satisfaction of basic needs for the poorest sections in each society which can be as high as 40 per cent of the population. The primary purpose of economic growth should be to ensure the improvement of conditions for these groups. A growth process that benefits only the wealthiest minority and maintains or even increases the disparities between and within countries is not development. It is exploitation. And the time for starting the type of true economic growth that leads to better distribution and to the satisfaction of the basic needs for all is today. We believe that 30 years of experience with the hope that rapid economic growth benefiting the few will "trickle down" to the mass of the people has proved to be illusory. We therefore reject the idea of "growth first, justice in the distribution of benefits later."

Development should not be limited to the satisfaction of basic needs. There are other needs, other goals, and other values. Development includes freedom of expression and impression, the right to give and to receive ideas and stimulus. There is a deep social need to participate in shaping the basis of one's own existence, and to make some contribution to the fashioning of the world's future. Above all, development includes the right to work, by which we mean not simply having a job but finding self-realization in work, the right not to be alienated through production processes that use human beings simply as tools.

THE DIVERSITY OF DEVELOPMENT

Many of these more than material needs, goals and values, depend on the satisfaction of the basic needs which are our primary concern. There is no consensus today what strategies to pursue in order to arrive at the satisfaction of basic needs. But there are some good examples even among poor countries. They make clear that the point of departure for the development process varies considerably from one country to another, for historical, cultural and other reasons. Consequently, we emphasize the need for pursuing many different roads of development. We reject the unilinear view which sees development essentially and inevitably as the effort to imitate the historical model of the countries that for various reasons happen to be rich today. For this reason, we reject the concept of "gaps" in development. The goal is not to "catch up," but to ensure the quality of life for all with a productive base compatible with the needs of future generations.

We have spoken of the minimum satisfaction of basic needs. But there is also a maximum level, there are ceilings as well as floors. Man must eat to live. But he can also overeat. It does not help us much to produce and consume more and more if the result is an ever-increasing need for tranquilizers and mental hospitals. And just as man has a limited capacity to absorb material goods, we know that the biosphere has a finite carrying capacity. Some countries tax it in a way that is far out of proportion with their share in world population. Thus they create environment problems for others as well as for themselves.

Consequently, the world is today not only faced with the anomaly of underdevelopment. We may also talk about overconsumptive types of development that violate the inner limits of man and the outer limits of nature. Seen in this perspective, we are all in need of a redefinition of our goals, of new development strategies, of new life styles, including more modest patterns of consumption among the rich. Even though the first priority goes to securing the minima we shall be looking for those development strategies that also may help the affluent countries, in their enlightened self-interest, in finding more human patterns of life, less exploitative of nature, of others, of oneself.

SELF-RELIANCE

We believe that one basic strategy of development will have to be increased national self-reliance. It does not mean autarky. It implies mutual benefits from trade and co-operation and a fairer redistribution of resources satisfying the basic needs. It does mean self-confidence, reliance primarily on one's own resources, human and natural, and the capacity for autonomous goal-setting and decision-making. In excludes dependence on outside influences and power that can be converted into political pressure. It excludes exploitative trade patterns depriving countries of their natural resources for their own development. There is obviously a scope for transfer of technology, but the thrust should be on adaptation and the generation of local technology. It implies decentralization of the world economy, and sometimes also of the national economy to enhance the sense of personal participation. But it also implies increased international co-operation for collective self-reliance. Above all, it means trust in people and nations, reliance on the capacity of people themselves to invent and generate new resources and techniques to increase their capacity to absorb them, to put them to socially beneficial use, to take a measure of command over the economy, and to generate their own way of life.

In this process education for full social awareness and participation will play a fundamental role and the extent to which this is compatible with present patterns of schooling will have to be explored.

To arrive at this condition of self-reliance, fundamental, economic, social and political changes of the structure of society will often be necessary. Equally necessary is the development of an international system compatible with and capable of supporting moves towards self-reliance.

Self-reliance at national levels may also imply a temporary detachment from the present economic system; it is impossible to develop self-reliance through full participation in a system that perpetuates economic dependence. Large parts of the world of today consist of a centre exploiting a vast periphery and also our common heritage, the biosphere. The ideal we need is a harmonized co-operative world in which each part is a centre, living at the expense of nobody else, in partnership with nature and in solidarity with future generations.

There is an international power structure that will resist moves in this direction. Its methods are well known: the purposive maintenance of the built-in bias of the existing international market mechanisms, other forms of economic manipulation, withdrawing or withholding credits, embargoes, economic sanctions, subversive use of intelligence agencies, repression including torture, counter-insurgency operations, even full-scale intervention. To those contemplating the use of such methods we say: "Hands-off. Leave countries to find their own road to a fuller life for their citizens." To those who are the—sometimes unwilling—tools of such designs—scholars, businessmen, police, soldiers and many others—we would say: "Refuse to be used for purposes of denying another nation the right to develop itself." To the natural and social scientists, who help design the instruments of oppression we would say: "The world needs your talents for constructive purposes, to develop new technologies that benefit man and do not harm the environment."

SUGGESTIONS FOR ACTION

We call on political leaders, Governments, international organizations and the scientific community to use their imagination and resources to elaborate and start implementing, as soon as possible, programmes aimed at satisfying the basic needs of the poorest peoples all over the world, including, wherever appropriate, the distribution of goods in kind. These programmes should be designed in such a way as to ensure adequate conservation of resources and protection of the environment.

We consider that the above task could be made easier by instituting a new more co-operative and equitable international economic order.

We are aware that the world system and the national policies cannot be changed overnight. The major changes which are required to answer the critical challenges facing mankind at this turning point of history need some time to mature. But they have to be started immediately, and acquire a growing impetus. The Special Session of the General Assembly of the United Nations on a New Economic Order has given the process a right start and we fully endorse it. This, however, is a very preliminary step which should develop into a great tide of international activities.

The Charter of Economic Rights and Duties of States, proposed by the President of Mexico, Lic. Luis Echevarria, and now under discussion at the United Nations, would be a further important step in the right direction. We urge that it be adopted as early as possible.

In a framework of national sovereignty over natural resources, governments and international institutions should further the management of resources and environment on a global scale. The first aim would be to benefit those who need these resources most and to do so in accordance with the principle of solidarity with future generations.

We support the setting up of strong international regimes for the exploitation of common property resources that do not fall under any national jurisdiction. We especially emphasize the importance of the ocean floor and its subsoil, possibly also the water column above it. An oceans regime has to be established with all countries of the world represented, favouring none and discriminating against none, with jurisdiction over a maximum area of the oceans. Such a regime would gradually develop the type of resource-conserving and environmentally sound technology required to explore, develop, process and distribute ocean resources for the benefit of those who need them most.

The uses of international commons should be taxed for the benefit of the poorest strata of the poor countries. This would be a first step towards the establishment of an international taxation system aimed at providing automatic transfers of resources to development assistance. Together with the release of funds through disarmanent, international taxation should eventually replace traditional assistance programmes. Pending the establishment of these new merchanisms, we strongly recommend that the flow of international resources to third world countries should be greatly increased and rigorously dedicated to basic needs for the poorest strata of society.

Science and technology must be responsive to the goals we are pursuing. Present research and development patterns do not effectively contribute to them. We call on universities, other institutions of higher learning, research organizations and scientific associations all over the world to reconsider their priorities. Mindful of the benefits deriving from free and basic research, we underline the fact that there is a reservoir of under-utilized creative energy in the whole scientific community of the world, and that it should be more focused on research for the satisfaction of fundamental needs. This research should be done as far as possible in the poor countries and thus help to reverse the brain-drain.

A rejuvenated United Nations system should be used to strengthen the local capabilities for research and technology assessment in the developing countries, to promote co-operation between them in these areas and to support research in a better and more imaginative utilization of potentially abundant resources for the satisfaction of the fundamental needs of mankind.

At the same time, new approaches to development styles ought to be introduced at the national level. They call for imaginative research into alternative consumption patterns, technological styles, land-use strategies as well as the institutional framework and the educational requirements to sustain them. Resource-absorbing and waste-creating overconsumption should be restrained while production of essentials for the poorest sections of the population is stepped up. Low waste and clean technologies should replace the environmentally disruptive ones. More harmonious networks of human settlements could be evolved to avoid further congestion of metropolitan areas and marginalization of the countryside.

In many developing countries the new development styles would imply a much more rational use of the available labour force to implement programmes aimed at the conservation of natural resources, enhancement of environment, creation of the necessary infrastructure and services to grow more food as well as the strengthening of domestic industrial capacity to turn out commodities satisfying basic needs.

On the assumption of a more equitable international economic order, some of the problems of resource maldistribution and space use could be taken care of by changing the industrial geography of the world. Energy, resource and environmental considerations add new strength to the legitimate aspirations of the poor countries to see their share in world industrial production considerably increased.

Concrete experiments in the field are also necessary. We consider that the present efforts of the United Nations Environment Programme to design strategies and assist projects for ecologically sound socio-economic development (eco-development) at the local and regional level constitute an important contribution to this task. Conditions should be created for people to learn by themselves through practice how to make the best possible use of the specific resources of the ecosystem in which they live, how to design appropriate technologies, how to organize and educate themselves to this end.

We call on leaders of public opinion, on educators, on all interested bodies to contribute to an increased public awareness of both the origins and the severity of the critical situation facing mankind today. Each person has the right to understand fully the nature of the system of which he is a part, as a producer, as a consumer, as one among the billions populating the earth. He has a right to know who benefits from the fruits of his work, who benefits from what he buys and sells, and the degree to which he enhances or degrades his planetary inheritance.

We call on Governments to prepare themselves for action at the 1975 Special Session of the United Nations General Assembly so that the dimension and concepts of development are expanded, that the goals of development be given their rightful place in the United Nations system and the necessary structural changes initiated. We affirm our belief that since the issues of development, environment and resource use are essentially global and concern the well-being of all mankind, Governments should fully use the mechanisms of the United Nations for their resolution and that the United Nations system should be renewed and strengthened to be capable of its new responsibilities.

EPILOGUE

We recognize the threats to both the "inner limits" of basic human needs and the "outer limits" of the planet's physical resources. But we also believe that a new sense of respect for fundamental human rights and for the preservation of our planet is growing up behind the angry divisions and confrontations of our day.

We have faith in the future of mankind on this planet. We believe that ways of life and social systems can be evolved that are more just, less arrogant in their material demands, more respecful of the whole planetary environment. The road forward does not lie through the despair of doom-watching or through the easy optimism of successive technological fixes. It lies through a careful and dispassionate assessment of the "outer limits," through co-operative search for ways to achieve the "inner limits" of fundamental human rights, through the building of social structures to express those rights, and through all the patient work of devising techniques and styles of development which enhance and preserve our planetary inheritance.

PHOTO CREDITS

Society-Photo Researchers. Pages 260 and 261: (a) and (b) Alan Pitcairn/ Grant Heilman; (c) Ron Church/ Photo Researchers. Pages 266 and 267: (a) Grant Heilman; (b) and (c) Robert Perron. Pages 274 and 275: (a), (b), (c), (d), and (e) U.S. Forest Service; (f) Georg Gerster/ Rapho-Photo Researchers. Pages 284 and 285: (a) Grant Heilman; (b) and (c) Georg Gerster/ Rapho-Photo Researchers; (d) Grant Heilman.

CHAPTER 10   Opener: Bernard Pierre Wolff/ Photo Researchers. Pages 300 and 301: (a) and (b) Georg Gerster/ Rapho-Photo Researchers; (c) Carl Frank/ Photo Researchers. Pages 312 and 313: (a) and (b) U.S. Forest Service; (c) Herbert Lanks/ Black Star; (d) and (e) U.S. Forest Service; (f) American Forest Institute; (g) K. W. Gullers/ Rapho-Photo Researchers. Pages 324 and 325: (a) Grant Heilman; (b) U.S. Department of Agriculture-Soil Conservation Service; (c) U.S. Forest Service; (d) Grant Heilman. Pages 332 and 333: (a) U.S. Forest Service; (b) U.S. Department of Agriculture; (c) Grant Heilman; (d) U.S. Forest Service. Pages 336 and 337: (a) H. W. Silvester/ Rapho-Photo Researchers; (b) Paolo Koch/ Rapho-Photo Researchers; (c) George Holton/ Photo Researchers; (d) Georg Gerster/ Rapho-Photo Researchers.

CHAPTER 11   Opener: Bradford Washburn/ Rapho-Photo Researchers. Pages 350 and 351: (a) Camerapix/ Rapho-Photo Researchers; (b) George Bellrose/ Stock, Boston; (c) Michael Gordon/ Picture Group; (d) Grant Heilman; (e) Leonard Lee Rue III/ National Audubon Society-Photo Researchers. Pages 374 and 375: (a) Tom Willock/ National Audubon Society-Photo Researchers; (b) Harry Engels/ National Audubon Society-Photo Researchers; (c) Leonard Lee Rue III/ National Audubon Society-Photo Researchers; (d) John H. Gerard/ National Audubon Society-Photo Researchers. Pages 378 and 379: (a) Phoenix Zoo Photo; (b) John Borneman/ National Audubon Society-Photo Researchers; (c) George Holton/ Photo Researchers; (d) George Rodger/ Magnum; (e) Marc and Evelyne Bernheim/ Woodfin Camp; (f) Russ Kinne/ Photo Researchers. Pages 380 and 381: (a) Paolo Koch/ Rapho-Photo Researchers; (b) George Holton/ Photo Researchers; (c) Ira Kirschenbaum/ Stock, Boston; (d) Harvey Barad/ Photo Researchers.

CHAPTER 12   Opener: Grant Heilman. Pages 396 and 397: (a) Paul E. Sequeria/ Rapho-Photo Researchers; (b) Max and Kit Hunn/ National Audubon Society-Photo Researchers; (c) Grant Heilman; (d) Bob Harrington, Michigan Department of Natural Resources; (e) Chester Higgins, Jr./ EPA-Documerica; (f) Michael O'Brien/ Archive Pictures. Pages 404 and 405: (a) Barbara Alper/ Stock, Boston; (b) State of Tennessee Department of Conservation; (c) Cornelius Keys/ EPA-Documerica; (d) Gerry Cranham/ Rapho-Photo Researchers; (e) Alan Carey/ The Image Works. Pages 410 and 411: Georg Gerster/ Rapho-Photo Researchers; (b) Owen Franken/ Stock, Boston; (c) Elliott Erwitt/ Magnum; (d) Mark Godfrey/ Archive Pictures; (e) Mark Antman/ The Image Works; (f) Pete Loud/ deWys. Page 421: (a) Henri-Cartier Bresson/ Magnum; (b) Philip Jones Griffiths/ Magnum.

CHAPTER 13   Opener: Bernard Pierre Wolff/ Rapho-Photo Researchers. Pages 444 and 445: (a) Constance Stuart; (b) Karl W. Kenyon/ National Audubon Society-Photo Researchers; (c) Hiroji Kubota/ Magnum; (d) Wide World; (e) James R. Holland/ Stock, Boston; (f) Malcolm S. Kirk/ Peter Arnold. Page 449: (a) John Spragens, Jr./ Picture Group; (b) Georg Gerster/ Photo Researchers.

INDEX